The Construction Industry

The Construction Industry
Processes, Players, and Practices

RALPH LIEBING

Registered Architect

Prentice Hall
Upper Saddle River, New Jersey   Columbus, Ohio

Library of Congress Cataloging-in-Publication Data
Liebing, Ralph W.
The construction industry : processes, players, and practices / Ralph Liebing
   p.   cm.
Includes bibliographic references and index.
ISBN 0-13-863853-5
1. Building. I. Title.

TH146.L54 2000
624—dc21

00-028565

Vice President and Publisher: Dave Garza
Editor in Chief: Stephen Helba
Executive Editor: Ed Francis
Production Editor: Christine M. Buckendahl
Design Coordinator: Robin Chukes
Cover Designer: Jeff Vanik
Cover art: FPG
Production Manager: Pat Tonneman
Marketing Manager: Jamie Van Voorhis

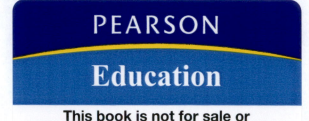

This book was set in Times Roman by Carlisle Communications, Ltd., and was printed and bound by The Banta Company. The cover was printed by Phoenix Color Corp.

Prentice
Hall

10 9 8 7
ISBN 0-13-863853-5

To my wife Arlene, my son Allen,
and my daughter Alissa

Notice to the Reader

The author and publisher make no representation or warranties of any kind, including but not limited to the warranties of fitness for particular purpose or merchantability, nor are any such representations implied with respect to the material set forth herein, and do not take responsibility with respect to such material. Neither the author nor the publisher shall be liable for any special, consequential, or exemplary damages resulting in whole or in part from the reader's use of or reliance upon this material.

The author and publisher do not warrant or guarantee any of the products described herein or perform any independent analysis in connection with any of the product information contained herein. The author and publisher do not assume and expressly disclaim any obligations to obtain and include information other than that provided to it by the manufacturers.

The reader is expressly warned to consider and adopt all safety precautions that might be indicated by the activities described herein and to avoid all potential hazards. By following the instructions contained herein, the reader willingly assumes all risks in connection with such information.

In addition, nothing herein is presented or intended as, nor shall it be construed as, legal advice. The inclusion of legal (case law) citations, contract information, and other legal information in this book is not intended as, and should not be used or construed as legal advice. The legal material herein is for general illustrative purposes and as a method of showing legal directions and decision in some professional matters. However, each set of circumstances is different and should be discussed with legal counsel to ascertain local legal parameters and liability. The author and publisher make no warranties or representations and assume no responsibility for any act or consequence resulting from the use or application of the data contained in this book. The book is meant to reflect some of the conditions that exist today, and in no way excludes other contractual configurations or lines of responsibility. It is important to recognize that every conceivable situation cannot be portrayed. This is general background information and material, not directed or mandatory technical advice.

This book uses established, standard construction vocabulary, which is replete with words of masculine gender (*manhole, journeyman, manpower,* for example). This reflects a traditional use of the words. As far as practicable, the use of gender-specific words has been avoided throughout this book, or both genders have been used. Since the English language does not include neuter personal pronouns, where masculine pronouns are used, it is the author's intention that they apply equally to women. Also, female readers are advised that many construction associations now address and facilitate the interests of women in this industry. In many cases, inquiries can be made to local chapters of national/regional organizations.

Preface

Construction is a fascinating activity, but trying to grasp the whole of the construction industry boggles the mind.

The breadth, depth, cost, skill/talent, types, and sizes of projects run the extremes. Everyone from a child to an elder is captivated by construction, no matter the size of the project—by the machinery, the odd chores being performed, the shapes and sizes of the structures, and the sheer power it takes to build something new! Construction work is everywhere, but everywhere a little different.

The aim of this book is to try to relate in short introductory form the overall aspect of the construction industry as a whole, in its worldwide activity. The task of trying to describe something as commonplace and well known as construction is complicated by the multitude of small pieces that make up the whole of the activity. Trying to capture in a few thousand words the true essence of the industry is quite a challenge.

Since there are innumerable publications describing various aspects, formats, techniques, programs, and activities of the industry, in whole or in part, we will attempt only an overview. Our effort, here, takes the form of a supplemental text with little detail, as compared to other publications. The text attempts to pique the interest of the reader to seek more information, to "whet the appetite." As students enter this complex industry, they need information, which provides some overall perspective. In addition, they need basic information and definitions, and an overall view of the industry, its people, and the process of construction projects.

This, then, is a beginning, a basis on which readers can build and customize their expertise. It is a supplement to other instruction about specific topics, so that through both the educational process and their increased experience in construction, project development, and project documentation, readers will come by a well-rounded and deeper understanding of the entire industry.

As facets of construction become clearer, the myriad details associated with each become almost mountainous. There is always something new to learn. New technologies, new equipment, new designs, and tremendous new innovation and design concepts constantly challenge every player in the industry. I have had the good fortune to practice in an urbanized area, in a general practice context, with a relatively constant level of construction activity involving various types and sorts of projects. Different functions, motifs, sizes, costs, complexities, and owners were associated with each project. Each project had its good points, but each had its glitches. However, a whole different culture thrived beyond my busy but narrow outlook. "Heavy construction," for example, goes far beyond the building of homes and other small structures. The construction of massive dams, cavernous but intricate navigational locks, sprawling airports, delicate but long-spanned bridges, on- and off-shore oil drilling rigs, military works from barracks to weapons facilities, space exploration launching facilities, and underwater tunnels is constantly underway in every part of the world. Between these projects and my own was another level of construction altogether: the erection of both slick, sophisticated high-rise office buildings and heavy industrial complexes, where piping and equipment are taken to a new level. The truth of all this is that a person can immerse himself for a lifetime in construction and never really grasp the extent of the industry as a whole.

I have attempted to capture a little of the basic essence of construction for the student, trying to provide some focus on the industry as a whole, its impact on society, and the magnificent works it produces. To say something is "global" in this day and age seems trite. But add to this the fact that worldwide construction makes a major contribution to human survival, to the financial success of people and countries, and even to added growth and stability. All this heightens the prestige, viability, and worldwide impact of the industry.

No other country comes close to matching the United States in new construction placed each year. No other nation has a gross national product (GNP) that attributes one of every eight dollars to construction. Yet, in its own way, each country garners major contributions, both tangible and intangible, from construction.

Introduction

Every student of architecture and the various engineering disciplines connected with project design and construction, as well as all others in ancillary businesses, needs to understand the construction process.

The construction industry today is a vast and imposing enterprise combining complex skills and procedures. Its magnitude is overwhelming when viewed in a general, global context. Individual projects run the gamut from small, detached residential buildings to massive and overwhelming structures of various types. While the scope, complexity, and cost of these vary, there is a fundamental flow of necessary events throughout each project, each in its proper context to the project; that is, every procedure is only as complex as necessary for the project.

The number of people involved in a construction project and their specific tasks vary over a wide range also. However, a strain of commonality runs through the array of projects: fundamental understanding of the many interrelationships and the contractual network is necessary for proper functioning in any project. While certainly there is not any type of caste system, there is a distinct configuration of personnel on every project, set out via the several contracts that are required. One's tasks vary, as do the obligations spelled out in the contracts. Therefore, it is incumbent that each party understand his or her exact "fit" into the overall scheme of each project; the building of good project teams requires this knowledge. Teamwork is the key to well-coordinated, timely, cost-abiding, and satisfactory construction.

To assist in the understanding of all this basic information, this book will address three specific aspects of the industry: the "players," the "processes," that is, the sequence of a project from inception to occupancy, and "practices," spelled out in a glosssary of terms to aid understanding. The intent is to devote approximately one-third of the text to each of these areas. In addition, numerous charts, photographs, and excerpts from documents will support the text itself.

This effort is designed as a textbook that can be used to supplement others by providing narrow-scope, specific information, in detail, regarding the construction process.

Brief Contents

Contents

The Construction Industry at Large

This chapter provides an overview of the meaning of construction and its impact on individuals and on society as a whole. Past and present systems of building are illustrated, with emphasis on the present and on newer systems of delivery. Construction management is critiqued. We look ahead to the future of construction to try to see what it holds for educational trends and for national and world needs.

Exactly what is construction and the construction industry?

DEFINITION

Construction is the massive, worldwide effort to build various types of structures and facilities. This is accomplished by assembling materials, parts, and systems into the major subsections of the structure; the finished structure itself then becomes part of the building stock necessary for the conduct of business and life.

The construction industry is the overall maze of large organizations and smaller companies that facilitate building. The industry is a combine of innumerable persons, firms, organizations and corporations, which perform a group of intricately related, but very different activities, in building. The industry is responsible for the construction of all fixed (immobile) facilities, including, among other facilities, factories, ship piers, tunnels, pipelines, canals, power and sewage treatment plants, railroads, and highways (Figure 1–1). Construction includes the building of everything from simple, light-frame sheds to massive dams. It includes such projects as intricate high-rise buildings, the complex launch facilities at Cape Canaveral, and the cavernous voids of dry docks in shipbuilding yards. This includes the majority of the work which has been and is still being done to develop the surface of the earth to meet civilization's needs. See Figure 1–2 for varieties of construction.

The size, influence and impact of the construction industry cannot be completely described in just a few words, but in making the effort the more prominent words would be:

- *Vast* working worldwide, in every country and climate
- *Enormous,* in the amount of money that projects can cost—the worldwide total is virtually uncountable
- *Extensive,* in that the industry builds everything from the smallest shelter to magnificent structures using the latest high-technology products and construction methods
- *Influential,* in that construction is a major factor in the economy of every locale; it contributes to the growth of the areas and employs great numbers of people
- *Inclusive,* utilizing a tremendous number of people of various talents and abilities, all operating in a highly skilled professional manner, in teams.
- *Professional and intelligent,* in that it uses the latest technologies, equipment, and techniques, the brightest of innovative designs, and the skills of dedicated professional workers
- *Versatile,* since it adapts rapidly to any climate, condition, circumstance, or need
- *Dynamic,* due to its constant movement toward better quality, higher/newer technology, safer structures, and better service
- *Wide-ranging,* providing whatever expertise or service is required to satisfy the needs at hand (Figure 1–3)
- *Creative,* by exercising continual imagination, innovation, and design skill (Figure 1–4)
- *Organized,* to cover every aspect of projects, from financing, to management, to regulatory controls, to the actual construction design and execution

THE PEOPLE

The construction industry involves a tremendous number of skilled trades. It includes an array of highly trained workers

Figure 1–1 Concrete being placed for the deck of a roadway bridge—an extensive, complex, and intricate construction project. Photo courtesy of Concrete Reinforcing Steel Institute (CRSI).

Residential: Housing	**Nonresidential Buildings**	**Engineering Facilities**	**Industrial Facilities**
Single-family housing	Institutional structures	Water treatment plant	Refineries
Multi-family housing	Educational: day care facilities, schools, universities	Sewage treatment and drainage facilities and systems	Heavy industrial plants, mills
Apartments	Light manufacturing plants	Utility structures and pipe lines	Chemical plants
Condominiums	Commercial establishments	Canals	Smelters
Elder care and retirement facilities	Hotels, motels, resorts	Levees, dams, navigational facilities	Power generation plants and transmission lines
High-rises	Religious structures	Reclamation projects	
Townhouses, row houses	Agricultural buildings	Marine structures	Warehouses
	Recreational facilities	Tunnels and bridges	Oil wells/rigs
	Medical buildings	Highways and streets	
	Offices	Transportation facilities	

Figure 1–2 Categories of construction.

who apply their training, knowledge and ability through hands-on activities in constructing the projects. Examples of the trades are bricklayers, concrete finishers, ironworkers, painters, carpenters, welders, to name but a few. Within each of these categories are numerous tasks and functions that the workers perform. In addition, unskilled workers such as laborers, carpenter helpers, hod carriers, and the like provide direct aid and support to those in the skilled trades.

Behind and supporting the actual construction work is a massive collaboration of people of many talents. They range from design professionals to management and administrative personnel. All of these people are professionals within their area of expertise. Their efforts are necessary for any construction to proceed. The design professionals establish what is to be constructed, and what materials, systems, types of construction, and ancillary features are to be used or incorporated into the project. This is done through their designs, drawings, and specifications. These documents show the workers what work is required, where it is to be done, and what materials are involved. They set the parameters for the work. The other engi-

Figure 1–3 A small corner of a guardhouse being built at an industrial plant. Note the number of materials involved in this small structure and the amount of detail that has been designed into the building. Photo by Phil Joehnk.

Figure 1–4 A small commercial project. Even small projects can be detailed attractively and can involve very precise construction. Photo courtesy of Concrete Reinforcing Steel Institute (CRSI).

neering professionals apply calculated solutions for structural problems, and establish systems capacities such as electrical, plumbing, piping, heating and cooling. These must be added to and incorporated into the basic design for the entire facility.

In one aspect the military is a good point of comparison to construction. For every member of the armed forces "on the front line" there are perhaps 12–15 support personnel. Construction is much the same. Numerous people are required to oversee, administer, pay, order materials for, process, manage, and so on for every actual constructor on a project. There are many different perspectives, attitudes, and directions to be dealt with on a single project. Each problem requires a subteam to work out the various aspects of a solution for the overall good of the project.

The design instructions/directions from the design professional must be broken down into minute items, so they can be coordinated and incorporated through proper and timely ordering and shipping, so as to be on-site at the correct time and ready for installation. Overall, each project must be managed to control cost, to provide adequate staff, to schedule, to control and oversee, and to coordinate in a manner profitable to all parties.

Behind the actual construction projects stands an elaborate system of manufacturers who produce the systems, materials, modules, devices, clothing, tools, equipment, and countless other items required by the construction industry. Builders must be able to purchase everything from the smallest item (a special tack or fastener, for example) to the largest, most sophisticated, and often most expensive item or system that each project requires. Each year more than 5,000 new products and materials come on the market and are made available for use in projects. These are newly invented or developed, have undergone extensive testing, and are the products of a thorough manufacturing process. Others are improvements or modifications of existing materials. A constant process of research and development serves the construction industry. This process endeavors to make things better, faster, cheaper, more convenient, safer, more numerous, more widely available, and of more colors and finishes. All this allows the industry to do its work in a more diverse and timely manner.

THE IMPRESSION

The word *construction* means different things to different people. Politicians, for example, see construction as a "gift" they give their constituents—new projects *and* employment! Some see this process as almost a bothersome fact of life that just has to be put up with. In most cases, construction activities will cause some inconvenience to the neighboring area—dirt on roads, noise, production of dust, odors, delays and detours, and other undesirable conditions. These are necessary, however, for the construction to be completed properly. Nothing good can be done in construction without some digging, changing, noise, and dust, despite the problems that may be created. However, while most people understand progress and the filling of new needs, many very quickly adopt an attitude called NIMBY (Not In My Back Yard). Progress and the construction that brings it about, they feel, is vital so long as it is in someone else's neighborhood.

Some people cannot see beyond the rather rough-cut appearance of construction workers; they may be often dirty, new to the area, transients, and so on. This appearance belies the talent and skill that is carried by the workers, and the capacity they have to produce the most utilitarian or most sensitive of structures. Others, however, see construction as a field that provides new and widening opportunity for women, as they train for, enter, and work in the skilled trades, manage projects, and operate construction firms.

Some people consider construction as "union" (organized labor) territory: highly organized, closely held, and often controversial. Most trades are unionized, but membership is not what it was several decades ago. Currently, there are a great many companies who operate with a nonunion work force. Other people think of construction work as a life constantly on the move—workers moving as necessary to "follow-the-work." Unless a worker lives in a large metropolitan area, travel to find work is necessary. Even in large cities, hours of travel each day may be necessary to reach dispersed jobs.

Many family members of construction workers see the industry as an unpredictable life, with great rewards (usually high wages), but also with deep and often long-lasting downsides (unemployment for lack of work or bad weather, for example). Such families must be very careful with their lifestyle, conserving money when it is available, so there is some available when work is limited. Even very talented and conscientious craftworkers go through periods of limited job opportunities.

Despite the great safety efforts within the industry lately, the work remains dangerous, even deadly, since it proceeds at great depths underground or even undersea as well as in high, open, precarious perches on top of high buildings or bridges. Companies have come to realize that they must actively create safe workplaces, not only to meet government regulations, but also to retain their work force, and hence their ability to produce projects quickly and safely, without costly downtime or lost time due to injuries, and profitably.

PERSPECTIVE

Much of construction is lost to the perception of the average person, since we do not have the luxury of being on a site from the start of the project to the end. Barricades, leaving just "peep holes" for the general public to catch a fleeting glimpse of the work, often surround projects. Suddenly, the structure emerges from the ground ("out of the hole") and rises far above the barricade. Still the public is at a loss to understand the totality, depth, and complexity of the project work being carried on. Perhaps several hundred workers, acting like busy ants, "infest" the project, each with a distinct task to accomplish, relying on their skill, knowledge, and experience. Construction is so complex that the average person has a difficult time absorbing it.

Construction has long been part of human life, and has increased in importance with the added sophistication of civilization. As life became more communal, and social complexes evolved, there was an increased need for construction. Housing, storage, the crafting of items, all required some enclosure to guard against wild animals, the elements, and, unfortunately, other humans who sought to take what belonged to others. Also, as life became less nomadic, there came a need to maintain and improve the structures to meet new needs and to ward off deterioration.

Construction has become so important to every society that it is one of the primary economic factors in every nation. Manufacturing, of course, is also important, but much of the manufacturing could not be done without adequately constructed facilities. This dependency comes close to the "chicken-and-the-egg" syndrome, but in most cases, the manufacturing process will seek some sort of shelter and then add specific equipment and capabilities to support its needs. This can only come about through construction. In fact, in recent years in the United States construction has accounted for some 16 percent of the gross national product (GNP). This is an economic factor representing the sum total of everything produced in one year. Simply put, out of every dollar spent in this country, 16 cents of that dollar involves construction of some sort.

Obviously the first crude structures of humans were not so financially important, nor so complex. They were satisfactory to primitive people who knew no better. However, later development came about due to strong and deep needs, and innovative thinking to satisfy them. This process continues today, but at a level of complexity that is mind-boggling. Future construction and what it may bring is almost unfathomable. Visionaries are now saying that in the next century we will build structures to equal the capacity of all of the structures ever produced in history, to support the increasing demands and needs of a burgeoning world population. Added to this is the outlook for not only space travel, but also space living, that is, the construction of various facilities in outer space itself to support human existence.

Construction, like many other "hands-on" occupations, often is open to the scorn of the general public. Mostly this shows a lack of understanding for the need of the work, first off, and secondly, for the skill required to do much of the work. The do-it-yourself fad that has taken hold in the world (particularly in the United States) has further dulled the impact of construction as a viable and important job. The mere fact that people can do some of the work to their own satisfaction in their homes does not lend credence to the low status often attributed to far more demanding construction work.

One has only to look around on any given day to see the results of the construction effort. Further, if one can understand how that effort has produced the structures now used for every function of life, then the hope is that construction can be respected for what it is—a major contribution to our way of life.

Not everyone can lay brick; not many can negotiate a walk on narrow steel beams high above the ground; most cannot endure the severe discomfort of heat and cold that construction workers often encounter; relatively few can foresee and plan the logical, correct application of activities leading to the proper construction of a project.

The world's population thrives on, and needs construction constantly. Often the loss of electric power for only a short time due to a storm seems like a major inconvenience. But what if there were no generating stations to house the generators, because construction was not available to build them? What if there were not enough hospitals, schools, churches, houses, stores, offices, public service facilities, not to mention bridges, utility lines, and power facilities? Also, consider how much flood control, navigational facilities, airports, highways, offshore drilling rigs, and other construction wonders all contribute to "normal" everyday life.

Construction and the need for correct application of construction technology are universal. Every country in the world, and every city, town, village, or community needs construction, in one form or another (Figure 1–5). All a nation's buildings are served by larger systems called *infrastructure*. These are the road, sewer, and water systems, for example, that governments build for their people, and for even further development of new cities and villages. Although the needs are the same worldwide, the methods of applying the technology, and the actual construction methods, materials, techniques, skill levels, and so on vary widely.

Both the types of projects under way and their locations cause the construction industry to be extremely versatile and flexible. The factors, natural and man-made, causing this

Figure 1–5 A new university building. Note the detail in the design, which was used to blend with other campus buildings.

diversity are numerous and varied. For example, if exactly the same building were to be built, but in different climates, the industry would have to adapt the design and construction to meet the necessities imposed by each region's weather. Obviously, a cold area necessitates different construction from a warm, tropic area. With companies working world-wide, there must be flexibility within the companies themselves. This applies in their work force, the products they use, the methods of construction, and the application of the entire technology program and its adaptation to local conditions. This is a major factor in construction today, since there is no limit or bounds to the location of projects. Facilities

Figure 1–6 Not all construction need be square and angular. Sometimes for eye-appeal and for interior function a rounded wall adds to the building, as well as meeting the approval of the client. Note that even hard, square material can be installed on a radius.

Figure 1–7 An unusual building and design. This type of project challenges the builders to use new methods and to adapt materials and systems to fit new needs, forms, and shapes. Photo courtesy of Concrete Reinforcing Steel Institute.

may look different and be constructed differently, but they are still functioning parts of the construction industry.

The construction industry is inherently flexible, and can adapt to almost any situation (Figure 1–6). This flexibility should not be minimized or overlooked; it is essential to construction. It is, in fact, one of the strengths of the industry. With the exception of prototypical and repetitive construction, where the same buildings are built over and over, as, for example, franchised fast-food restaurants, every project has a unique set of demands. This reaches beyond mere budgeting and project size. Every client is seeking a project that fits his or her needs "perfectly." This entails everything from the overall appearance and function to the minute details of the operations within the project and output from the project. It touches appearance, function, maintenance, production, everything, in short.

It is necessary for construction to supply whatever pleases the client. Satisfying this need requires a special relationship with the client from inception of the project to finale. And within this arrangement is the requisite need to find and provide in proper form whatever design innovations, materials, systems, equipment, forms of construction, and technology necessary to produce the project as desired (see Figure 1–7). This is a strenuous, far-reaching, and quite demanding process, with a tremendous number of nuances and encumbrances that forestall straightforward solutions. The industry truly must be the epitome of resourcefulness as well as a hotbed of flexibility, discovering and providing as necessary.

Flexibility also addresses the need to work and build under differing regulatory and climatic conditions (see Figure 1–8). Shelters of one sort or another are needed in the most frigid areas of the world, in the most arid, and in the most humid and overgrown tropical areas. This requires the industry as a whole to be nimble enough to adjust its design function to the needs of each location. Additionally, the selection and availability of materials to be used, monetary and financing differences, and the transportation of workers, equipment, and material to the job sites must all take into account local conditions. Each of these considerations is a tremendous challenge in itself. This has led to a key attitude in the industry—to meet every condition that arises on a project, in a fully successful manner. Those results that we can evaluate today indicate that the industry does extremely well in meeting this demand.

THE PAST

Construction can provide a great sense of pride, worth, and self-esteem in the workers, if they look for that. A worker's pride in today's work can be based on what the construction industry has done in the past. The achievements of the industry are many, marvelous, and apparent. The industry has risen to every need and occasion. The sheer magnitude in size and complexity of some projects shows the ability of the

Climate and Weather-Related Considerations in Construction	
Cold climate	added insulation
	difficulty in excavating
	adverse conditions for workers
	difficulty in transporting materials, etc.
Hot climate	added insulation
	adverse conditions for workers
	infestation
	humidity adverse to materials
	transport difficult in isolated areas
Regional climates	conditions specific to one area different from other areas
	new regulations
	matching construction to hazard/risk
Seismic (earthquake)	issue in many areas (Japan, U.S., SE Europe, India, S. America)
	severity and frequency
	availability of technology to minimize damage
Coastal areas	typhoon, hurricane, El Nino
	wave action/tidal erosion
	winds and storms
	unstable soil for construction
Prevailing underburden	bearing soil for foundations
	rock/sand/hardpan/lake mud
	depth of adverse conditions
	cost to meet conditions
Other Areas of Consideration (Some Affected by Climate)	
Urbanized areas	close-in construction
	spread of fire (building to building)
	high-rise construction
	presence of hazardous materials
	environmental issues (all types)
Regulatory issues	matching construction to identified public hazard or risk (mitigation)
	zoning (by right/appeal/conditional/suit)
	building codes
	fire prevention codes
	plumbing/electrical codes
	wetlands/floodplain
	reserved/dedicated lands
	endangered species act
	Americans with Disabilities Act (ADA)
	architectural review boards
	private (deed) restrictions

Figure 1–8 Some building considerations must be flexibly addressed under differing climatic and regulatory conditions.

industry to stretch our minds and resources, so as to accomplish what a few years earlier may have been unthinkable. It is innovative in solutions, adaptive to both needs and conditions, and equal to every challenge it takes. It is a shining example of what can be accomplished through the right combination of talent, skill, training, education, and ability.

In 1999, *Engineering News Record* magazine, a weekly publication covering the construction industry, celebrated its 125th anniversary. Two issues were published which should prove of interest to all construction-oriented people. One listed the top 125 projects, the other the top 125 people in the construction world during the 1874–1999 time period. The issues provide great insight into the progression of work and the type of people involved, their ingenuity and their contributions.

In many aspects, the industry still carries ties to the ancient "Master Builder" system, and later the guilds, trade unions, apprenticeship, and lifelong careers. Gothic cathedrals in Europe, such as Notre Dame in Paris, took hundreds of years to complete; whole families worked on nothing but these projects through many generations. With no stock, or mass produced materials, the ancients relied on the expertise of the Master Builder (as in the building of the biblical Solomon's temple), who in reality was a combination architect/engineer/contractor. Using methods as primitive as drawing portions of the structure on a nonreproducible trestle board, and then watching close at hand as the actual work was pursued, the Master Builder still brought forth amazing results. Also, materials were fashioned, on-site, to meet conditions that were created as the building was going up. All of this effort stemmed from the minds of the Master Builders, who, having nothing near the education of today's professionals, nonetheless were fully attuned to the needs and capabilities of their times.

Civilization was built through construction efforts. In 2000 BC King Hammurabi of the Babylonian empire issued the first building code. Along with penalties for faulty construction, the code in Section 228 provided that, "If a builder build a house for a man and complete it, that man shall pay him two shekels of silver per *sar* [approx. 12 square feet] of house as his wage."

Even further back in history, in 5000 BC, construction was under way. Archaeological excavations have revealed structures from that early time. During this period the factors influencing construction can easily be seen; slavery provided adequate manpower; priesthoods offered money and zeal; absolute rulers supplied riches, growing populations demanded shelter and so forth. Evidence of historic pyramids, ziggurats, canals, aqueducts, stadiums, and so forth, built thousands of years ago survive today. Even without all of the knowledge, methods, equipment, materials, and money at our disposal today, the ancients constructed large, complex, and lasting structures. Each civilization had a construction industry that provided for its needs and contributed to its way of life. During the Golden Age of Pericles in Greece, builders used new math and engineering skills. These made a massive impact on Greek and Roman life. Miraculous "engineering" calculations, principles of design, a sense of innovation and experimentation, imagination and inspiration, and the courage to try almost anything made the projects done in those times appear, even today, to be beyond the scope of the human mind. The very same daring and innovation that was present in olden times still exists in the construction industry today; it has only been enhanced by all of the technology that has developed through the centuries. This gives construction a status, a pride, and a motivation for those who like to work with their hands and for those who find satisfaction in creating, managing, and building.

Progress is a prized by-product of construction. The pyramids in Egypt were built by thousands of slaves who pushed the huge chunks of stone, by hand, up long ramps, to get them to the right level. In the early twentieth century, the Panama Canal was dug with horse and wagon, and steam-driven power shovels. Today, we have massive earth-moving equipment, and fully computerized cranes that are many times more efficient, with far greater capacity and ease of operations. Much of what we have today in technique and operations is the result of the construction needs met and solutions developed during World War II. Construction forces during that war had to build airfields almost overnight; they had to quickly erect housing and other buildings for the fighting forces and their support. Even bad weather was not allowed to stop that construction, because without the construction the war effort was crippled. The Quonset hut for example (a half-circle, corrugated metal building, formed in sections) came into being as a quick shelter, in which other construction could proceed in foul weather. In turn, this fostered the development of prefabrication of building sections. Made in the shelters, they were then moved to the site and erected during good weather. This very same principle is still in effect today in regular housing and in factory-built manufactured housing.

Construction techniques have evolved over the centuries, out of both necessity and the increase in the knowledge, awareness, and skill of the people involved. Early man was a builder, providing shelter for their families. Some of this self-styled construction survives; many farmers still build their own structures, including their homes. Of course, the do-it-yourself methods, brought to fruition in the 1960s and 1970s, have continued to flourish and expand. Much can be and is done by individual homeowners laboring on their own behalf; hands-on, step-by-step instruction books enjoy a large market. Homeowners may have limited skills, but they overcome that shortcoming through advice from others, books, and modest expectations for the projects.

However, from times past, society as a whole has needed to develop solutions to new problems. Forming communities brought a major new need, the need for community facilities. With the increase in commerce came the need for shops, stores, and a whole variety of new and different structures where wares could be stored and sold. Housing has been a constant need as new families were formed, moved to new locations, or increased in size. Groups have always needed support facilities, as well, to sustain both in-place housing and new development.

Developing societies were forced by necessity to learn new skills of construction to provide a rapidly expanding array of structures. Industrialization brought about the building of artisans' shops, factories, plants, and complexes of buildings housing differing functions and operations. Not all businesses, of course, needed large facilities (Figure 1–9). Smaller shops were popular, just as today the small boutique shop is back in vogue, providing often unique and unusual services and goods that many times are not available in larger shops and stores. But, for the most part, construction and safety requirements for these shops are the same as for the larger stores, although perhaps reduced in scale. The construction skills required are virtually the same with suitable adjustment for the size and complexity of the project.

An interesting example of this is seen on the East Coast of the United States today. Under European influence in the days of the first colonies, masonry construction was considered as the "state of the art"; the new settlers brought that expertise with them. This building technique followed that of the earlier settlers who foraged shelter from fallen trees, building lean-tos and eventually log cabins, relying totally on what materials were available to them—since there were no factories for making building materials. Then as society progressed, construction took on a more sedate and lasting appearance. It took on the look of stability and permanence. But the frontier maintained the "what-the-land-gives-us" demeanor of building structures with materials that were at hand. Often shelters were exact copies of native American structures, which showed a well-developed use of natural material and innovative skills.

Construction, then, from a historic perspective is a process influenced by:

- Materials available
- Knowledge/innovation of the builder
- Skills available in the labor force
- Needs and functions of proposed structure
- Desires of building owners
- Climate
- Continual research and development of new technology

NEW VIEW

Although all the influences listed above make their impact today, our perspective has expanded through the years. A major, relatively new factor came into the construction industry's operations: money available! Bartering, or the exchange of services, was the method used for construction payment in the past. As civilization moved forward, and a banking system came to be more prevalent, construction work was paid for in cash. Money at any time in the past surely was as closely held as today. Everyone is seeking value for the cost. The increasing importance of financing brings yet another challenge to construction, and another need which the industry must address.

Every owner today, no matter how small or large the project, faces the dilemma of balancing three elements: *cost, scope,* and *quality.* The ideal project for the owner would be one that produces "the largest building, of the highest quality, at the lowest cost."

Some authorities would add time as a fourth element. Every owner has the desire to have the project completed on time, in fact, as quickly as possible, as the need for providing for temporary locations and workplaces are major inconveniences. Also, the contractors often are using borrowed

Figure 1–9 A commercial retail store under construction. A distinct set of requirements provides for the functions to be carried on inside. Of course, it must also be attractive.

money to fund their operations. The cost of money (the interest due on loans) is expensive and it too is a factor of time; the shorter the time the money is owed, the less the interest required.

But time is not a factor like cost, scope, and quality, which lie totally in the hands of the owner and constructors. Too many other people, conditions, and ancillary factors contribute to scheduling, production, transport, installation, and prompt completion. Many of them are items that neither the owner nor the contractor can influence as they may desire; they must merely factor in adequate time as experience dictates.

The industry continues to deliver the optimum combination of these elements for each client. However, the basic situation remains a dilemma. The owner can only control two of the choices. Most of the time, the choices selected will be cost and scope (size of the project)—basically, seeking the largest project for the money available. It is the design professional who then must find the "proper" level of quality to produce a project that satisfies the other two elements. There is a wonderful though perhaps naive saying that holds that "You can build anything, so long as you have enough money." In the big picture this is true, but reality shows that other considerations will influence every project.

Quality, though like beauty, "resides in the eye of the beholder." Thus, quality is to:

The owner

- on time, and on budget
- reasonable life cycle costs
- operating and maintenance efficiency

The design professional

- well defined scope
- acceptance of design concept
- funding for fieldwork, design, documentation, and profit
- adequate time in each work phase
- prompt decisions by owner
- an array of products and materials which fit the budget while both enhancing and properly serving the project over time

The contractor

- good documents
- timely decisions
- impartial contract interpretation
- profitability
- adequate time to execute

Notice the common and predominate position of "time" and "money" considerations in so many of the items, under each of the participants.

IMPLEMENTATION

In the broadest sense, actual construction is the application of the construction technology available to the needs of the owner (private or public) and, in turn, those of the general population. Construction technology is one aspect of every nation's industrial technology; the other part is manufacturing technology. The latter, of course, is the technology required to produce, make, or manufacture our various gadgets and commodities; this sector will not be addressed in this text.

Construction technology deals with the function of building some type of facility, on the site (as opposed to in the factory—modular components, utilized portions, modular/manufactured housing are some exceptions). Simply, it is the knowledge of the use of tools and techniques to erect a structure on a given piece of land. In the design of each project, full and proper consideration must be given to how the project will be built, and with what materials and systems. It is inappropriate to try to utilize systems, techniques, and the like that simply do not adapt to the project conditions, be they part of the structure or of the land surface and substrate. Additionally, consideration must be given to the equipment required to perform the work, and the accessibility the site offers for positioning such equipment for the work. The construction technology for any project covers a tremendous range of circumstances and considerations, and often requires the combined expertise of many persons, each of whom has the ability for in-depth, full, and correct assertions and directions, both in problem identification and solution.

At its very best, construction is still an imperfect science. A popular put-down would say, "It isn't brain surgery." But then, what is? Construction is an amalgamation of thousands of diverse parts, combined and blended together into a new entity, which is intended to provide a shelter or a function far different from its individual parts. There is a level of precision in every construction operation, but in dealing with nature and natural conditions, including the limits of human skill, many times things must be varied or may not be as precise as the tight tolerances of machined parts—or precise as brain surgery. In the end, though, quite often construction challenges nature and the human mind by seeking to go deeper or higher; by being evermore complex; or by being splendidly simple.

Construction is the manifestation of the human imagination—it builds what the mind dreams. It brings to life—to reality—sketches, lines, intentions, desires, concepts, and philosophies. Yet in many aspects it can be crude, rough, heavy, and overbearing. In the end, it is simply what others want it to be. Given enough money, construction can build whatever the mind can envision. Although never built, renowned architect Frank Lloyd Wright envisioned, and several decades ago designed, a high-rise building *one mile high!* Absurd? No. Continuous cables on the floor of the Atlantic Ocean run from the United States to Europe. So why not build a building a mile high, which can be constructed of "pieces", and require "only a few miles" of continuous elevator cable. But this venture would certainly challenge the great minds of construction to their limits. Remember though, the United States is currently working with other nations on the construction of a space station, not a mile high in itself, but located miles above the earth. Our design and construction "minds" are working at the outer limits!

Such considerations give rise to the need for the vast body of knowledge encompassed in construction technology. In simple terms, we have long since lost the simple easy project. More and more often the application of the correct technology has become a major and intricate undertaking. The requirements on projects today are unrivaled in history. No longer can complex projects, like a Gothic cathedral, take centuries to complete. There is an absolute need for careful and purposeful direction of the entire project sequence, from inception to occupancy. A greater depth of skill training and construction-oriented education is needed. Projects and their circumstances are now so complex that they simply cannot be "run" without careful and knowledgable guidance from inception to completion. This complexity calls into being the great number of people in the industry, and the multitude of operations and tasks they perform.

The Three Major Elements

Every construction project is comprised of three major elements: management, engineering, and construction (Figures 1–10 and 1–11). This can be viewed as a pie chart with these elements present, but never in equal proportions. While each is vital to the overall success of the project, their influences vary, drastically, depending on what project work is being done. Even though the influence of an element may be relatively small in any given phase of the project, that input and influence is or at least should be present.

Each element has a contribution to make in each phase of the work. This leads directly to the overall success of the project. To totally close out that input, in any phase, would shortchange both the project and the owner, and lead to a project which is out of balance and hence faulty in concept or execution.

Figures 1–12 through 1–14 illustrate these principles. During the project initiation phase, there is a reduced but more than minimal need for engineering and construction information—hence management is the largest exercise, as noted in Figure 1–12. During design, engineering, and documentation, however, engineering is the predominant activity, as shown in Figure 1–13. Of course, when the project is being built (Figure 1–14), it is construction which is the major activity.

However, in all of these note that the other, smaller elements still exist and service the project scheme in their proper proportion. Engineering input during initiation and

programming can often change or add valuable insight into how the project from the very beginning can be made better, simpler, or less costly. Construction information in the engineering phase can assist design making and aid in formulating a better design and documentation scheme. Moreover, there is a continuing need during construction for input and guidance from both management and engineering to resolve changed conditions, added requirements, and the like which come to the project work.

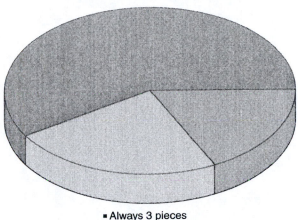

■ Always 3 pieces
■ Almost never of equal size

Figure 1–10 The project pie.

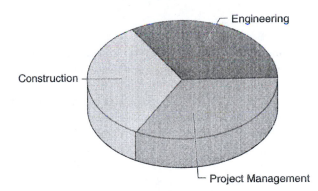

Figure 1–11 Successful project components.

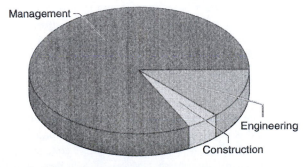

Figure 1–12 Project programming.

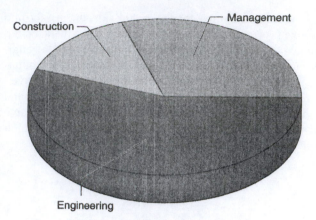

Figure 1–13 Project design.

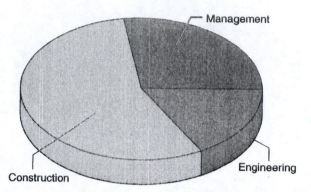

Figure 1–14 Project execution construction.

Due to the circumstances of the project, and the new array of personnel assembled, almost every project needs to come to a scenario where the various parties are brought into close alignment and a highly cooperative atmosphere is developed. This is a concept that is beyond reasonable and advisable—it is flat-out necessary. In far too many cases, though, the three elements have been made contentious and competitive instead of complementary and cooperative. The reasoning for this almost certainly lies in the human personalities involved. Perhaps it is to win some sort of advantage, mere power, or the favor of the owner. But without a careful, continual, and strong leadership presence, these individualized efforts tend to cause the focus and direction of the team to be lost fast. The project then is open to rifts, irritations, vying for position, and politicizing of the process. Quite often, too, a dismantling of defined responsibilities occurs, a perception that "if we can get them to do it, then we won't have to" overtakes the tasks, leaving gaps, and further aggravating what more than likely is an irritable situation already. Most of this is seated in two causes (1) lack of understanding of the work of the others, the time it consumes, the responsibilities/liability involved, and the end result sought, and (2) too little courtesy and respect for what the other fellow is to do that impacts your work.

One can easily suspect that a sort of misplaced ethical commitment to one's roles and duties to the project owner is also a factor. It is easy to observe, in too many cases, in the construction/engineering, as well as the owning/operating/developing camps, the same adjuration of personal responsibility for results that has characterized society as a whole. This suggests that there needs to be a balance, and that no one issue, aspect, or person should be or seek to be so extreme, dominant, or imposing that others are frustrated or ill-at-ease, or made to feel unnecessary or without due respect and status.

Often, however, much of the contention arises as the result of how the project was managed. This naturally has increased since the inception and development of construction management as a separate system. As new firms, new professionals, new educational directions, new perspectives, and new work programs (with new objectives) have evolved, more traditional work considerations and direction are changed. An ancient Greek adage holds, "Seek moderation in all things." A moderate demeanor tends to foster calm and cooperative spirits between persons who work together toward a common goal. Unfortunately, in all too many situations, there has been development of a high-profile enthusiasm, an aggressive methodology, and a new work effort. This has fostered a move to establish who is King of the Project Hill. This is a needless and wasteful effort.

Truly, though, the most successful projects have no "king". Rather they have a "leader" (lower-case), who facilitates the project team, fosters cooperation, forces recognition of each team member's *unique* and *valuable* contribution to the whole, drives for resolution of conflicts (many times in creative, nonconfrontational ways), and builds toward consensus. And this all is pursued in a quiet, studious, and professional manner, where personality is a key tool.

Perhaps a basic question is this: if a project is designed to meet budget, documented in short order, vigorously bid (and shopped), and vehemently driven in execution, is a quality project the result produced? On the other hand, if everything runs like clockwork, everything is coordinated, deliveries are made on time, productivity is better than average, and weather cooperates, do not these elements automatically produce or aid in the production of a quality project?

Is not the perspective of "quality project," then, fully in the eye of the beholder?

With several "beholders" on each project, the vying for the King position begins to dismantle the concept of "team" and "team effort." When one seeks to be ultimately dominant, the project atmosphere will shift, and the work, *which should be among equals,* will become some working for one, with other divisive profiles emerging. The overbearing zeal of one team member, who may not even be part of the actual construction work, is a direct inhibitor of good progress, quality, and other desirable aspects of a project. When minutely detailed, statistic-producing "bean-counting" becomes a self-perpetuating exercise, the actual skilled work will suffer—of that there is no doubt. Professional and skilled effort made subservient to the management and accounting functions bodes ill for the project. Where cooperation and mutual respect break down, the project will start down the path of tedious, confrontational, and misdirected efforts.

Extremely strong dynamics are at play in the construction industry, constantly. Everything cannot be bent to a singular, unilateral effort. The call, rather, is for a new sense of "team," new relationships that produce better and stronger teams, and far deeper understanding that no individual person, firm, or effort be dominant. Equality of status among team members has and continues to be vitally important.

Of course, the owner has a preeminence since the cost of the project is borne on those shoulders. However, in the scheme of producing the project the owner has another task, and that is being an equal partner in the project team—one who contributes in very positive ways to assist and move the project through its many phases. The owner cannot (and neither can any other team member) stand apart and watch. If this is done there will be a drag on the project—a void that no other member can fill, and hence the project will suffer and be less than it should be. An errant, vacillating, or semi-reclusive client contributing in a minimal or secretive manner will have a direct, negative, and often long-term influence on the project.

Traditional Roles

It is helpful to understand that traditionally the architect has been the leader of the design team. In the past, the first step an owner took when needing a new building was the hiring of an architect. The architect hired consultant engineers for the structural, electrical, plumbing, and heating and air conditioning design work, as well as for other specialty engineering designs. These persons were not under contract to the owner as the architect was, but rather they worked, literally, for the architect. The overall combined effort started the building process by determining the owner's needs and requests, and setting about design of the facility. Combining design and engineering skills, the architect made decisions about such things as the structural system, appropriate materials, finishes, and other portions or elements of the new building. The architect's task was to combine all these, with artistic talent, into a building design. This effort produced the design and documentation of the project, as desired by the owner, and as described in the project programming.

When a preliminary design concept was completed, it was presented to the owner, with an explanation of the concept and features. If the owner accepted the design concept, the architect furnished an estimate of the construction cost. Upon approval of the cost by the owner, the design team went about the task of documenting the project, i.e., creating the necessary drawings and specifications so the project could be put out for competitive bidding.

The bids were received by the architect and analyzed, and a recommendation was made to the owner as to the contractor(s) who presented the lowest and best bids; this process reviewed both price and reputation of the contractors. The project would then be placed under contract by virtue of a formal contract agreement between the owner and the contractor(s).

The architect, during the actual construction work, would visit the site periodically. These visits were to observe the work in progress, instruct the contractors of any necessary changes, and receive and approve the contractors requests for payment (this involved matching money requested with amount of work done, usually within the preceding month). Recommendations for payment would then be forwarded to the owner. In addition, the architect served in large part as the owner's agent (acting on behalf of the absent owner) throughout the entire progression of the work, up until the building was completed and turned over to the owner.

Changing Roles

The design/bid/build project delivery system, just described, is still utilized for a great deal of construction work. In the 1970s, however, as building and projects became more complex, and costs increased, this delivery system began to fall into disfavor with clients. Faced with surprise cost overruns, owners sought outside help with cost estimating. The architects usually did not have the latest and best cost information when making their estimates. More and more they began to rely on contractor input. Still bids would be at odds with estimates, much to the chagrin of the owners, who often needed their facilities quickly and within their budgeted costs. The owners often brought in outside cost-estimating resources to assist in the process—sometimes even to assist in the architect's design process.

With increased complexity in the projects, the on-site contractors began to need more management assistance to keep track of costs and schedules. As the contractors started to input more and more information about both costs and schedules, they also offered advice on construction systems and even design concepts. From this juncture it was but a short jump to formal, or professional (full-time), construction management services.

The contractor (usually in the form of a general contractor) came to the project either through the competitive bidding process, or through a negotiated contract with the owner. Here the various specialty- or subcontractors also came to the project, but usually under contract to the general contractor.

Management was conducted within the purview and offices of the various "players" on the project. There had always been a construction management team, comprised of the owner, architect, and contractor. When the formal construction manager (CM) was added, the owner in many instances continued to provide oversight of the project but with the aid of the CM, in a more managerial form, assisting the process and providing a direct link to the owner. Over the last few decades, however, this format has changed.

First, and importantly, there was a decline in the status of the architect, as many aspects of projects became more imposing or more far-flung than the design of the building. Planners came to the team for overall site analysis and for forecasting how the property could be developed in the future to meet the needs of the owner. At times, the planner was easily made to be the leader of the team, with the architect acting more in a consulting or ancillary role.

As money became more of a premium, owners demanded better and closer control and better value for each dollar spent. The cost of borrowing money established a basis for tighter control of project schedules—more rapid work, overlapping functions (fast-tracking, for example), and shorter overall project time frames. Several different approaches were taken by various owners to meet their demands. First, an unsophisticated version of construction management was developed as a new process, which removed the management of the project from the design professional and the contractor to a third entity. This provided a positive, on-going process wherein the manager was not also working actively on the actual construction work, and more construction-related perspectives could be applied to the handling of the project, overall. This separation allowed for closer and more in-depth analysis of the project. In fact, with this construction-oriented expertise on the project, there was even oversight or insight into the design process, so better construction information was available to the design professionals. This early analysis was able to bring more value to the project and better selection of constructible details and systems, and was able to interject a new orientation focused more on construction than design.

Gradually, construction management developed into an expanded activity, using different formats depending on the demands of the owner. The design firms, too, established more project control over their personnel and procedures. With an expansion of firms capable of both design and construction (but short of being full-fledged design/build firms), construction management techniques were utilized. These tend to track time and money, and involve forecasting, trending, effort hours expended and needed for completion, and so forth. In reality this trend brought much more of an accounting approach to the design process. When the breadth and depth of computer software programs are utilized, the combination is impressive, although a bit oppressive. The continual caution is that the "accounting" process does not overwhelm or shortchange the design process. While they can aid each other, their separate foci are entirely different— one watching process, procedure and money; the other immersed in the highly technical considerations, resolutions, and production of the project documentation. Here the fundamental "rub" or irritation comes into play.

Rivalries at Their Worst

In fact, there now in all too many instances is a literal tug of war between the factions. Management has the ear of the owner, and often is persistent and invasive in respect to the

technical effort. Roughshod budget cutting (without review or analysis of future implications, or the input of the professionals), requiring meticulous adherence to time budgets, unilaterally producing production schedules, and inappropriate procedures can impose on and adversely affect unwitting professional and technical personnel. The results can be substandard solutions, ineffective solutions which ill-serve the project—and the owner! Certainly, here is the opportunity, again, for "moderation in all things." There is a need for mutual respect, full cooperation, and a directed effort to blend all aspects into a coherent and efficient project team effort.

If the team is divided so a rivalry is created between management and technical direction, effort, procedures, and personnel, the project will suffer. Such a configuration is inappropriate and unacceptable for any project, no matter the size and no matter the money involved. Construction projects, by definition, are structures and buildings created for occupancy or usage for an established fundamental end. They are not pursued to prove management prowess or ingenuity, nor for bonus awards to those who save the most project money, or finish on time. Surely, inventive, timely, and correct technical design and documentation work is also capable of producing savings for the project; such work just never seems to see the "light of day" in the project sequence.

A certain level of competitiveness and good-natured puffery has always been evident between design professionals—particularly architects and engineers. In reality they are a team, each needing the expertise of the other to design and document projects that ultimately will be successful. Currently, the work of the professions in designing and documenting has found new challenges. Unfortunately not all of these changes are directly related to those items of the work itself, but rather to the overall handling of the project. With the addition of two managers (construction management and project management) as distinctive entities, a change in the team concept is needed. Architects are usually placed under contract as direct agents of the owner; they act for and on behalf of the owner. The various engineers usually are contracted by the architects, as their consultants; they are not contractually tied to the client/owner directly. The managers, though, can be in a variety of configurations. Project managers can be employees of the design firms. In addition, the owner may also assign a project manager. Construction managers usually are under separate contract to the owner, on a parallel track to the architect. In some cases they become the owner's agents, separately or in addition to the architect the owner assigns. However, in far too many cases, the concept of "team" has broken down. Irritation, competitiveness at a high level, and other forms of pique up to and including utter disdain appear periodically. The fact that the project and construction managers have overall responsibility for the cost of the project gives them a greater impact with the owner/client. In this, they gained the status and position of being the "prime movers" on the project. This impression tends to relegate the design professionals' effort to a minor and inconsequential status; or so it appears, and so it is often considered.

This is grossly unfortunate in several ways. First, all these "players" should have the same goal and perspective—pleasing the client, and producing a successful project. Second, while work, direction, and philosophies may vary, they are all basically equals. Third, each really needs the other, to perform their specific tasks as part of the overall production of a successful project. Fourth, a healthy team atmosphere allows room for strong disagreement between members as to direction, solution, methodology, and the like. However, the final decision is reached with civility and mutual and respectful professionalism. Fifth, the great interest of the client, the project, and the individual members of the "team" is best served by at least mutual understanding of, and respect for the role, work product, ability and expertise of the others.

Everyone on the team must forego the thought that their work is preeminent, of the highest value, and worthy of reducing the work of others to ancillary, minor, or inconsequential status, of limited (if any) value to the project. Yet, often this is exactly the case. Crass puffery and self-promotion become so invasive that the team concept is shattered; anger arises within the team, and the consequences that develop are "assigned" by everyone standing around pointing in both directions to other players. It is most unfortunate that in an effort to make projects better, the methods we employ are often counterproductive. Frequently, now, the team effort is overturned by the preemptive impression given by some team members who hold that their work is of such importance that all others must acquiesce to them—that their needs must be addressed immediately by all others. Even well-intentioned efforts, at times, are the cause of problems in or between projects and their various personnel. Egotism and the selfish attitude wittingly or even unwittingly cause far too much animosity, disruption, and irritation in today's project delivery, and for no good reason.

This discussion is not intended to alarm or scare off new professionals. However, we feel that knowledge of the "real world" within the profession will allow new professionals to assimilate more quickly, knowing more of what they may encounter. Obviously, every situation is different, ranging from exceptionally good to very bad. One can only try to ascertain what lies ahead before becoming firmly entrenched in a disagreeable circumstance. Becoming as expert in your field as possible, fully adaptable to changing conditions and to differing project circumstances best achieves this. Coupling this flexibility and learning with respect for and understanding of the other parties eases the entire atmosphere of the project.

Time Crunches

Budgeting the project's design and documentation efforts (effort and time in various work phases) has been done in differing formats for a long time, but not in the high-profile, almost obsessive manner seen in many offices today. The vast amounts of money it takes to produce and build projects have caused the need for such close and continual oversight, but not necessarily the manner in which this activity is often done currently. Management professionals, trained in those processes and procedures, carry a much different perspective and orientation toward projects. Quite often this is an unfortunately myopic view of the project, and can become so narrow as to lose sight of and become intolerant of any other project work or needs. Additionally, it can encumber the design professionals' work with added and often burdensome procedures, administrative documentation, and the siphoning off of productive time by requiring added management activities. This is not noted here to cause controversy, but rather to note that newer aspects of the projects now are becoming so imposing as to imperil the design professional's effort.

Professional work in design and documentation is now constantly being required to meet tighter deadlines and restrictive if not inadequate budgets, while still producing "better" projects. The demands are rather divergent and almost unresolvable, not that projects should ever be accomplished solely on the professional's terms—that is to say, "forget the cost" and "take as long as you wish." But by trimming the budget for design and documentation, we now are being forced into adding more and more procedures. Many try to impose set methodology on every project (a process usually doomed to fail). Others divert time to documenting "what happened," and "how did we get here," rather than producing needed project work. Checks and backchecks and yet more checking are used at several levels to try to catch the missing technical input and errors made during a production process that is truncated to meet its budget—a rather vicious circle. In addition are all of the management documents, processes, and procedures that are superimposed on the technical process; sometimes to the point of disrupting it and demanding too much time, which is then not available for production.

The new emphasis on project management (which has taken, in some instances, more than 50 percent of the project's overall allocations) coupled with the fascination with computerization, has caused a loss of perspective and purpose on the project effort, overall. *The project is the building or other structure.* In addition, the true success of the project lies well beyond the initial cost, finishing on time, and using the latest computer software programs and techniques. The lasting quality of the project lies in the quality built into it via the professional's efforts. Through proper design (meeting the client's needs and wishes) and appropriate documentation (that facilitates the correct and efficient construction of the project) the project will find its true and lasting success. Those aspects are the technology of the project. To dampen, abbreviate, or manipulate the proper conduct of that work runs counter to accomplishing that success. Project claims for faulty work are all too numerous, showing distinctly that forcing abnormally rapid production leads directly to more errors and construction problems. These add to the initial cost and often elongate construction time. Neither situation is ever seen as the fault of the management or CAD, but in the final analysis, one or both may well be the root problems. There is a need to understand that the total project cost is the sum of management, design/documentation, and construction costs.

Legal Concerns

Construction management often is begun during the early design stages. Valid input of a technical nature is offered so documentation (if not design) can be fashioned in a better, more constructable manner. This input can be valuable, if the owner does not assign it inordinate status, where it can tend to overshadow or outweigh the design/documentation functions. Also, there will be continued input during documentation, and certainly through the entire construction phase, where the prime function is expediting and facilitating the progress of the work.

Oddly enough but most importantly, it is in these two technical aspects of projects where the heavy onus of professional liability lies, and *not in either of the management functions or the computer operations.* In this, it is the design professionals who are, by law, held responsible for the project's design, level of safety, code compliance, and other aspects of public health, safety, and welfare. This provision is contained in the professional registration laws of every state. The professional, in each project, puts her or his personal, professional status on the line, legally, when responsibility is indicated by application of the professional seal and the signature on the documents. If problems arise, due to an improper design process, attributable perhaps to inadequate time, there can be a direct and very lasting impact on the professionals' private life, ability to work, good name, and reputation. Even when the professional acts on behalf of a corporation, the corporation no doubt will survive the situation; more than likely the professional will not survive, professionally. There is a deep, lingering, new need for complete understanding of, and respect for, this situation by all of the major participants in every project. Too often this is either unknown, put off, or ignored in projects today. This factor is almost totally lost because *those engaged in management and CAD operations have no such liability,* do not understand it, and see no need to respond to, meet, aid, or address levels of care, and efforts directed toward reducing such imposing legal exposure.

The risk we point out here is that too many projects are being squeezed from the wrong angles, for the wrong reasons, and are adding risk to the projects. By establishing competitive project fees which are too low, and setting firm project parameters too soon, the managers are continually urging or demanding compromise and cost cutting to meet the parameters they were party to, and which may well be set unrealistically low. Due diligence, meeting a professional standard of care, and pursuit of correctness are necessary ac-

> Contractors are not licensed under the same premise of health, safety and welfare of the public that architects are.
>
> J. Ronald Williams
> Registered Architect

tivities of the design professional; they all take time. Pressuring for cuts or summarily cutting production budgets is most unwise unless one understands what constraints are also being imposed on the staff, and how liability is being elevated. So, too, is the downplaying of the professionals' work and its value for the sake of trying to achieve an attractive services package.

Staff expertise must be part of this consideration. CAD operations are too often in the hands of machine operators with minimal if any substantive technical know-how, and not in the hands of those who can contribute new, correct technical data, information, and expertise to the project. The operators too often have no idea what a drawing is about (its content), what it is intended to do, how it directs what is to be built, and how it contributes to the project overall. Many extremely competent and astute CAD operators cannot perform well outside the understanding and manipulations of their machines, or beyond the level of replicating the hand sketch or data given them, or the adjustment of a previous iteration of the work. This, despite the speed of CAD operations, has a direct budgetary impact. Can, for example, slowed creation of technical designs and details caused by limited availability of proper staff be completely overcome simply by speedy CAD production? And, if you reduce the budget, which of these functions must be sacrificed?

The design professions are still in the business of producing construction projects (not management projects or CAD projects) as a means of providing comprehensive architectural and engineering services to the clients. To accomplish a successful project, there must be the proper range of technical information, properly employed. Great care must be taken to allow this to take place without intrusive, overwhelming, obsessive, or burdensome employment of management and computerized service. There is need for professional staffs that are understanding, fully coordinated, carefully styled, mutually respectful of the program of these services which, at their best, complement and assist each other. Overzealous, misdirected, and blind self-indulgence are not attributes that aid good project production and produce satisfied clients. Beyond this, too, is the survival of the professional office. Hopefully more projects will come. This is no place for a staff that is uncoordinated, at odds with each other, and so self-centered that every project becomes another battleground, with only the players changing. This is not a "turf battle." It is a matter of how best to serve the client, in a balanced and comprehensive manner, where all entities are satisfied, and, in some way, profit. Another old adage holds that "The bitter taste of poor quality lasts long after the sweetness of low cost." Some have realized this; some still have not caught the true and needed balance in the process.

A Model for Rivalries

For a long time, there has been a spirit of competitive rivalry between the various trades. This was almost always carried on in a friendly atmosphere, since all of the workers knew that the work of the other trades was vital to a satisfactory project. No one really was the "main, or primary" trade. The work of each trade brought a unique but necessary aspect to the project. Masonry exterior walls required bricklayers; interior walls, drywall hangers and finishers (or plasterers, more prevalent in the past). Obviously all the functions of equipment and use of the building required electrical service. Water service, as well as drainage and sanitary facilities were required for occupancy. None of this has really changed. Project to project, it was simply a matter of some projects requiring more work from one trade, and less from others.

In some instances, primarily between unionized trades, there were jurisdictional disputes on some projects. These arose to establish who had basic responsibility for and who had the necessary skills to perform or execute some work. Usually the disputes revolved around new work, or new materials or systems. For example, when storefront construction (a grid of aluminum tubing, infilled with glass) initially became more popular, both the glaziers (glass installers) and the carpenters claimed the work. The latter claim was based on the theory that this involved the building of the wall system. Of course, the glaziers' claim was based on the installation of glass that was required. At that time, the jurisdiction was split—carpenters installed the grid, glaziers installed the glass.

While this situation has changed through the intervening years, and still may vary in some jurisdictions, there has been a blending of the work, whereby the glass companies hired carpenters for their staff to perform the grid work. This shows the type of cooperative spirit and problem solving that, for the most part, is prevalent through the working trades in the construction industry.

Wider Trends

For a good many years, there has been an effort in many industries to increase productivity, and to reduce costs of labor. Often, owners would hire efficiency experts, and/or time-and-motion engineers to evaluate the processes of production and the work of the production workers. Classic movies of the early Ford Motor Company show production line workers performing some part of auto assembly sitting on stools with casters and moving along the line as the cars progressed toward completion. Even today, auto assembly optimizes time and motion, where work assigned to a worker is based on what can be accomplished at a single workstation, even though the work is on different portions of the auto.

Unfortunately, often the efficiency experts would report that more work could be done, per worker, if certain "adjustments" were made. Quotas were set in place requiring workers to produce so much work in a given work period. Of course, the workers would not be pleased with all of this, and some would rebel. In some measure this continues today, in an effort to reduce costs. Even in the construction industry, today, we are experiencing similar efforts. Not so much quotas, but tighter control on costs are seen, which in turn bring about pressure to work faster, better, and "cheaper." Those three attributes seem to be at eternal odds with each other, however, despite the fact that one large construction firm has even adopted that phrase as its motto.

The imposing of such pressures has lead to a more contentious atmosphere in many instances. Often this new pressure is imposed through activities of persons who are not thoroughly familiar with the technical aspects of the work, and are more business and management oriented. Here the basic understanding of design, documentation, and construction is not present, which leads to arbitrary and unrealistic expectations. (This can even occur with design professionals who are more active in planning, marketing, and other nontechnical aspects of their professions.) Also, the imposition is done without due regard for changing conditions (construction work in a single trade can vary a good deal), and with a singular perspective toward a lower bottom line cost. Inherent in this methodology is the belief that every technical problem (particularly those appearing very similar) can be resolved in the same manner and in the same period of time; this is simply and fundamentally untrue.

Every project requires a careful analysis of the interface and activities between the three project elements, management, engineering, and construction. This is a crucial element in formulating the project team. All parties, including the owner, need to understand the inner workings of the project's process and what will happen in each phase of the project.

Where a project is unique, for example, more effort—that is, more time and money—will be required to resolve the technical issues that arise. Even common and mundane functions can require added time because of added complications or other nuances specific to the project. This needs to be understood and respected by the management, and no assumptions should be made as to the engineering time required. Without due consideration, the technical effort can be grossly underestimated and literally relegated to a substandard result, merely because no one took due notice and understood the encumbrances.

Much the same can be said about the construction effort. Miscalculation or the lack of understanding of the problems involved can again lead to poor judgments as to effort, time, and costs. In both cases, the best management determination is one derived through mutual understanding and consideration, with further understanding by all that estimates developed in the initial stages of a project need to be adjusted as work progresses. Adjustments involving the technical effort and personnel also must be factored into the whole equation.

Moreover, a pervasive need is to review management efforts and documentation to ascertain what exactly is required at a minimum. Too many iterations of the same information, programs developed to "save money," and innovative statistical maneuvers often are more costly than the savings or results derived. "What," should be the question, "is this information used for, why, and by whom?"

Two factors tend to disrupt smooth project progress. First is the depth of each of the three elements, and the extent to which they are involved in the project at any one time. Second is the lack of adequate cross-training and full understanding of the other parties on the team. Due to educational patterns, more than anything else, most construction project personnel are steeped in knowledge of their own expertise or profession, but have relatively little meaningful knowledge of the others. Education without experience cannot fully meet the real need on the site: a cooperative and mutually aiding context for all the parties. Simply put, too many are too busy to bother about learning the nuances of the others—thus, the vying, contention, and competitive nature of relationships. The prevailing need is for setting and reaching mutually derived goals, and giving up of individualism for the sake of a project. This ideal has been approached in recent years through a scheme called "partnering." Partnering is really a formal coming-together to move in concert toward the goals set. Yet even in this effort success has been spotty, and some involved in it have even brought legal action, which is the very thing partnering was created to avoid.

It is helpful to see the breakdown of any construction program into three primary parts: management, personnel, and production technologies. As shown in Figure 1–15, every facet of the project work is given attention, in proper sequence, and to the extent of the information or activity required. The chart hints at the complexity of even small, simple projects today. Although this entire program is adapted to each project as specifically needed, without due regard to the program in every area, the project can and will suffer in one way or another. Additionally, this program calls upon each participant to be an honest, contributing partner in the project work. Self-centered renegades without perspective for the total project would wreak havok. The three areas, management, personnel, and production technology, have distinct directions and goals.

Management Once Again

Management is the process of controlling the project from start to finish. The success of any project lies in two factors—how well the work required to produce the design concept is executed, and how well every phase of the project is managed. Management oversees every level of the project and every operation, from the smallest portion of the work to the project overall. It supervises each area, including planning, design, execution, business, and administration. Controls facilitate the work, no matter what type of project it may be.

Of the three aspects, management is by far the "hot button" over the last decade, and is still increasing in importance. This is manifest in the popularity of the design/build and construction manager systems. Again, there is no denying that some projects require such activities, but it is a contentious situation on some projects. Primarily a "people-oriented" activity and one tied heavily to money, too often managers become somewhat overzealous in their approach to a project.

This is particularly true where the manager has little training or background in design and documentation, and really does not understand the work, direction, orientation, responsibilities, and liability of the design professional. At the same time, the manager may well attempt to "push" the contractor(s) to new configurations, methods of operation, and staffing practices, and disrupt the technical aspect of the construction work. Here again, where the manager is not familiar with the work required, and chooses not to address those issues, contention will increase. Of course, division in the project "team" bodes ill for the project.

Even many educational programs neglect to fully inform the student of the ancillary aspects of their work, beyond the manager of the project work. Having a myopic view of a project, it is often unfortunate that what should be a directed and combined effort becomes one of vying for position, with added costs for no reason beyond micromanaging, and parties at odds over the progress and direction of the project. Obviously the owner is highly attuned to the manager because of the cost implications, but often conditions imposed on or by the project are such that the technical work (design and construction) is confounded or more difficult than at first sight. The management penchant to produce projects "better and faster" is more of an oxymoron than a construction project truism.

No part of the work can be allowed to operate "at full throttle" without regard for other operations, schedules, costs, or deadlines. In a sense, management is the framework within which the project work is contained. In a sense, management could be defined as "getting work done through other people." In this, three separate aspects need to be considered and addressed: planning, organizing, and controlling. All three aspects appear in the work of each party to the project, owner, contractor, designer, suppliers, and so on. Successful projects directly reflect collectively proper approaches and activities in all these areas, so the project is well executed. Lack of good managerial work, even by a single party, shows up in unprofitable work, untimely completion, unsatisfactory projects, disputes, and even increased litigation.

Project management as practiced in the past has now taken on a new orientation, a stronger direction, and exerts a greater and more incisive influence over projects, particularly in the

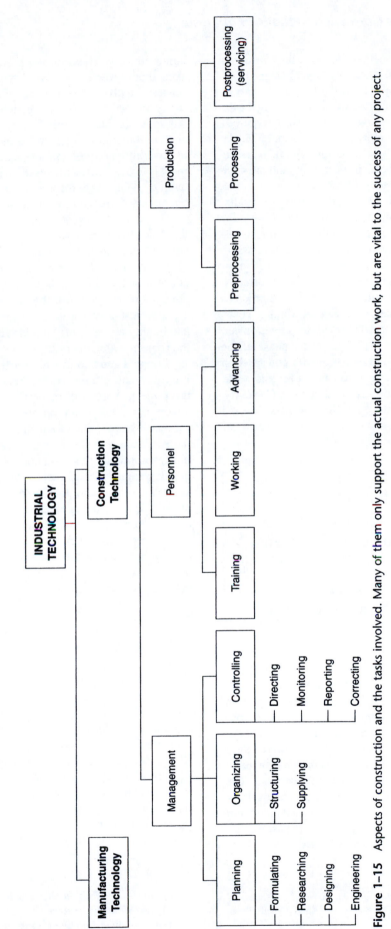

Figure 1–15 Aspects of construction and the tasks involved. Many of them only support the actual construction work, but are vital to the success of any project.

design and documentation functions. This, in turn, results in sending projects into the field which are better designed, better documented, more appropriate to the task, and more attuned to the desires and needs of the owner (including the desire for minimal cost commensurate with the work required).

The new process can be compared to a truck making a delivery. The project delivery system is the type of truck required; the load in the truck is the project itself; and the management of the project is the proper selection, loading, stabilizing, protection, routing, transport, unloading, installation, and payment for the project. The process facilitates the work. Managers with differing perspectives coordinate, order, ensure shipment and receipt in a timely fashion, assign crews, and otherwise see that the atmosphere around the project is such that the work can progress smoothly and correctly.

Managing is also the administrative process that keeps control over the project functions regarding timing, costs, changes, workforce matters, interface with the client/owner, and other ancillary activities. It touches every phase of the design professional's effort and every on-site construction effort. Managers generally receive little credit for this work, but it is vital to the eminent success of the project. Currently, the primary direction of management is toward a directed quality assurance assessment and effort in the entire array of programs, processes, and procedures of the work.

> Quality, like anything else worth doing, doesn't just happen. It's not like tomorrow; you can't just wait and it will come to you.
>
> H. James Harrington, Ph.D.
> President, Academy for Quality

Quality,[1] as noted previously, is a consideration in every construction project, no matter size, type of project, or complexity. It appears in two primary aspects of the project: in the value, serviceability, and appropriateness of all components, and in the processes that design and install them. If the processes can be made uniform, efficient, repetitive, foreshortened, and, in short, better, through quality management efforts, the cost of the total project will be decreased. The construction industry faces the effects of deficient construction on a daily basis. These ill effects are not intended, but are attributable to mindset, slavishly following past experience, the need for rapid decision-making, bias, and ordinary

human foibles. They are the products of "having done the same thing several times over," without real evaluation of the process involved. No one sets out to design or construct a faulty project. All too many of them come into being, though, due to happenstance; minor irregularities come to interface and combine into larger problems, and consequently lower the overall quality of the project. The function of management is to oversee the processes in place and to even improve them by being more responsive and quicker where possible, but always correct and well studied in their final resolve.

The cost of a project, in the minds of many, includes only the cost of construction. However, cost also covers the design and documentation of the project: the entire production of documents and information that directs and permits the construction. Usually in discussing project costs this factor is not even mentioned. But the fact remains that both of these areas of cost are open to review, upgrading, foreshortening, and quality assessment; both are the direct responsibility of the project owner, operating with the sound advice of the designer and a good contractor. Each area is fertile ground for improvement, and in so doing, reducing the real total cost of the project. A good decision that reduces the cost of construction, but takes an inordinate period of time for identification, research, development, and decision making, is faulty. "Lean and mean" is a modern catch phrase, but it is most apropos to this situation. With active, professional, quality-minded management as the impetus, better processes are a viable means to project cost reduction. No sacrifice of professional standards need result, nor of safety considerations, correct analysis and investigation, or adequate design. Better processes can even be an aid in all these areas. Cost reduction, which at the same time maintains quality in the built project, is attainable both in the construction work and in the design/documentation process.

Personnel

Personnel is the function that refers to having "the right number of the right people in the right place at the right time." This is no small task in any phase of the work. Expertise must be matched to work required. Essentials include the desire, dedication, and ability to cooperate, sometimes to research and upgrade skills, adjust, and move while performing project work. The best people available need to be sought out. "Best" does not always mean the highest-priced people. Rather it is the people with the expertise and professionalism to produce the project work. Attracting such people often involves numerous perks and benefits beyond wage rates and working conditions.

William Dudley Hunt, Jr., FAIA, in his *Encyclopedia of American Architecture* (McGraw-Hill, 1980) perceptively called this group

> . . . the loosely knit, diverse group of individuals and organizations that performs the many functions necessary to bring buildings into being. Often thought of as only

---

[1]See *Quality Handbook for the Architectural, Engineering, and Construction Community,* by Roger D. Hart (Milwaukee, WI: ASQC Quality Press, 1994).

consisting of those who design buildings and those who construct them, the building [construction] industry is actually much more complex. . . . All [elements] are essential in transforming a need for a building from any idea to a completed structure.

The elements to which Hunt referred are shown in Figure 1–16. His observation in reality applies to any type of project undertaken by the construction industry, be it an occupiable building or some other utilitarian structure. Starting with the owner (at the star burst), the owner's idea or need usually will require the assistance of a real estate agent, among other players shown.

A tremendous number of personnel can be required on some projects. Their skills and talents must be fully adequate to the work at hand, as there is no time for training or slow production due to lack of knowledge. The team that is formed must contain the correct combination of people, who can bring the proper orientation to their work and to the project. Personnel needs change frequently as the project progresses, so managers need to exercise foresight in planning staff needs well into the future. It is ill-advised to try to find the correct person at the very time when work must be done.

Production

The third construction activity, production, is the process of making new things from old, or from raw materials. It is the creation of something that did not exist, by a progression of steps. It is the progress that can be seen on a construction site day by day as more of the project work is accomplished. In construction there are two types of production: that which characterizes the progress of the project, and that which supports the progress. The latter includes the manufacturing of standard or raw materials that can then be incorporated, adjusted, or otherwise placed permanently or temporarily in the project work. The work is really assisted in many ways by the production of materials and devices which are used just once or repeatedly to hold, support, or form new work. Concrete, for example, relies on formwork which is temporary but which is required to hold and form the concrete as necessary.

On the job site, too, each individual worker "produces" a portion of the work, as part of her or his daily work effort. Some days a worker appears to produce little, but at the same time that small increment may allow greater progress or production on the part of other workers. Production is simply to add to or to supply that which is required.

In turn, each of the three main activities of construction technology contains several aspects of work, all of them vital to the success of any project. No longer is construction usually the activity of one person working on a simple project to satisfy his or her own limited needs. The construction industry is a direct reflection of massive needs in society today. The entire three-part program is applicable to all of the major parties on any construction site. Often, several people will approach quite different tasks at the same time, addressing the several aspects of technology. For example, planning can be done concurrently by bricklayers, architects, drafters, carpenters, plumbers, and contractors. While each of these parties plan in their particular areas and from their specific perspective, they also plan overall for the correct relationship of their work to that of the other parties involved, and to the construction project overall.

No matter the size of the construction project, a proper blend of project management, engineering/documentation, and actual construction work is needed. Where there is an imbalance between these aspects, the project will suffer. For example, to micro-manage (to tightly oversee and control even the smallest part of the work) a project may be needless when the documents are well executed and construction work follows the documentation. If the management gets so intrusive that it takes time and effort away from the other work, the project will become misdirected and could be delayed or unsatisfactory in the end.

In the words of Raymond A. DiPasquale, Syracuse University School of Architecture:

> Success of a project is the ultimate goal. It is one thing to be proud of your work, to do a good job, and to be decisive about your actions; you don't have to be arrogant in the process. Humility is a wonderful personality trait that makes you a valuable member of a team putting a complicated building together. Leadership goes to those who lead, not to those who intimidate.

This is not to say that management can be dispensed with, just that if that aspect becomes overwhelming, it will impact the other efforts adversely.

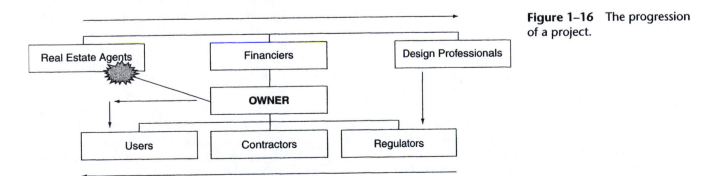

Figure 1–16 The progression of a project.

Without doubt there is a need to facilitate the actual construction work. Be it through scheduling crews or shipments, ordering material, tracking costs, or innumerable other such administrative tasks, management is the key. Management at its best assists and fosters the construction work; at times, it may even be a prod. It should be considered a partner in the process of completing the project. In the "running" of a project, management often has to exert pressures to achieve the proper result at the proper time. However, as to the actual work of the project, be it in engineering or construction, management has a distinct path to follow, and should not be allowed to intrude in the process. Rather, management should be the catalyst and the facilitator of all work, helping it to be better coordinated, and helping to eliminate problems that inhibit the other aspects of the project work. Obviously the management of a project is vital to its correctness, progress, cost control, and timing, but the process should act as an aid and catalyst, not be the prime effort. Producing paper is not the end goal for a construction project. Keeping tab of every minute item of the project more than likely is overkill, which really is nonproductive.

Engineering, of course, must be kept in its proper perspective too. There is no blank-check freedom to "do as you please" without any consideration of cost, timing, and overall project impact. The course that is best advised is to produce the project that follows the owner's choices of cost, scope, and quality; the owner will normally gravitate toward specifics of cost and scope. Engineering then must address its full effort toward those ends, establishing the level of quality along the way to match the other considerations as best it can. Where there is a problem (e.g., quality is needed but is not in keeping with cost), the owner must be asked to decide which course is to be followed. Obviously, this is part of the project management. But that management task, like others, should not impinge on the engineering effort, but facilitate and enhance it.

It follows then that the construction effort must be in full accord with the documentation effort. No doubt the various constructors could build a project simply with the knowledge they have gained through experience. This is similar to a homebuilder building a house with little instruction or direction—say, a case in which a new owner gives little direction except to want the house to match a certain appearance or configuration. Often, though, homebuilder and owner get into severe disputes due to the lack of directions and a common meeting of the minds about what the project should entail. Such disputes are not too common in other types of construction, where design professionals are hired, who set project parameters and directions. It is obvious, however, that without good, specific direction by someone, what the constructors produce may be far from what was desired by the client. Therefore, the actual on-site work should be executed in absolute agreement with the contract documents that the owner has approved. These are, after all, the explanations, directions, instructions, and the legal obligations of the project, as the owner desires it. Of course, various diversions can occur, such as poor site conditions (adverse to the foundation design, for example). These can be modified as needed along the way, through the proper procedures set out for the project. As much of the documentation as humanly possible, though, needs to be researched, designed, and configured to meet every possible consideration and condition required for the project.

As Figure 1–10 showed, many, many facets are comprised in the construction project. Each is complicated in itself; their interrelationships are even more complex. The process is not meant to be competitive, with the parties working for advantage, one over the others. Rather, it is a direct and obvious demonstration that cooperation and teamwork are vital to the success of the project—and to each party on the job site—and to the satisfaction of the owner!

IMPACT

Construction is the largest industry worldwide. Its total combined activities (including all types of construction) surely must run into several trillions of dollars annually. However, it is virtually impossible to capture a total world value, since there is no worldwide collection of such data.

The November 30-December 7, 1998 issue of *Engineering News Record* includes an exhaustive study of the worldwide construction market. By utilizing data from many and varied reliable sources in virtually every country in the world, the article pegs the value of the world's construction market at $3.22 trillion. The associated analysis reviews each major region/continent and each country individually. It provides an interesting and incisive look into construction as it now exists throughout the world community. Major variations are seen in expenditures, types of work, and number of projects from country to country, but it is vividly shown that construction "covers the globe." The industry is truly international, in that not every country has the complete array of expertise available for every project. This provides a wider market for other countries and their construction firms to find work overseas. A cycle becomes obvious—need generates work, work draws firms/personnel with proper expertise, these draw wages and profits, which are spent in numerous ways, which in turn develops activity in other markets and types of activities (as well as paying dividends back to investors). It is a lesson in economic viability, strength, success, and fulfillment of needs in the various venues.

Normal fluctuations in the level of construction activity and the value of the market will occur. Good economic times do end for various reasons, but this does not necessarily mean the complete shutdown of construction work. With a continual growth in the world's population, the needs of society will also continue to increase. New products and technology also will require new and upgraded facilities, all of which can be achieved through construction work. One of the major indicators of economic status is the construction index, since it contributes so much back to the economy after a major investment is made in it. Basically, this also is a circle—new needs require investment in new buildings and other structures; these are paid for by successful investors in the form of government agencies, and various businesses; that payment is returned to other manufacturers, and all the other people involved with the projects; who in turn spend the money in other economic ventures, including normal living and use of the facilities which are available.

In the United States, in 1998 it was projected that newly constructed projects would be valued at $635.1 billion, a 3 percent increase over 1997. The value of the year's new construction was broken down into $495.8 billion for private construction, and $139.3 billion for public construction. This was an all-time record for a one-year put-in-place construction value. Another $193.6 billion in contract awards was committed (which did not even include the numerous contracts under $50,000), according to figures compiled by the U.S. Department of Commerce and the F. W. Dodge Division of McGraw-Hill.

In the first six months of 1998, $294.6 billion of construction was put in place; $59.8 billion in June alone. Contract awards in 1998 were $19.2 billion in June, and $100.4 billion through 6 months (again, all figures not including contracts under $50,000 in value). These figures appear to support the forecasts from various construction information sources that 1999 will produce a level of activity that may well set yet another record. However, some variations are anticipated in the different categories of work (educational, industrial, single-family housing, multi-unit housing, highways, military, and so on) that are combined to produce these overall figures. It is common for American design firms to specify in a typical month something in the order of $3.5 billion worth of construction projects for domestic work and approximately $1.5 billion in international work, of all types. (See Figure 1–17.)

Money is an intriguing aspect of construction. Overall, as noted, the amount of money is well beyond one's imagination. Even the total cost of an individual project is difficult to imagine, much less establish, without knowing all information about the size, shape, and construction involved. A better

indication can be ascertained if one reviews smaller areas of projects; this is best illustrated by how much of a project's total cost is assigned to specific areas or types of work. An organization called The Construction Specifications Institute (CSI) has developed a standard format (index) for construction specifications. This is a book, known as a Project Manual, written for each type of project, which describes the various materials and systems. The CSI format breaks project work down into 16 Divisions, which are constant even though every project does not necessarily have work in each Division. In turn, the Divisions are subdivided into numerous Sections. Each Section contains a description and explanation of various construction systems, materials, or devices—for example, Metal Doors and Frames. The information gives extensive detail about the items, their raw material, how they are made or fabricated, what they are made of, how they should be installed, and how they must be finished.

Figure 1–18 lists the 16 Divisions currently in the CSI specifications format. (Some design organizations have added other Divisions for such work as Security Systems, Communications, and the like; CSI has not, and does not plan to make such additions.) The chart also gives the title and a short description of the work contained in each. Column 3 of the chart gives a very general indication of the percentage of the total project work that is represented by the work in the Division. It is virtually impossible to give a specific percentage applicable to every project because of the innumerable variations between projects. For example, in general terms, the complete mechanical trade work (plumbing, HVAC, and electrical) equals about one-tenth of all work on the project.

A similar analysis can be done to ascertain some very generalized indications about the cost of any specific project, and the work within each Division of the specifications. Again, though, the information is very general, and it must be pointed out that there is, truly, no such thing as a "typical" project; each has its own set of requirements, parameters, and conditions, which impact the amount of work in each Division and the associated cost. Figure 1–19 provides an indication of the percentage of the complete project cost that can be ascribed to the work within the Division.

A moderate sized project (e.g., a two-story office building, or an elementary school with about 12 classrooms) can

	Institutional	Commercial	Industrial	Other
Architectural	42	53	4	1
Engineering	27	21	27	31
A/E	54	33	11	2
E/A	25	14	27	34
CM	39	24	13	24
Gen Contr	24	42	21	14
Speciality	28	35	33	4

Figure 1–17 The percent of work done, by type, by different types of professional construction companies: "A/E" denotes architectural/ engineering; "E/A" denotes engineering and architectural; "CM" denotes construction management; "Specialty" denotes a subcontracting firm that performs limited portions of a project.

Percent of Project Work by CSI Division

Percentages shown are for a "typical" project. While the total project work will always equal 100%, variations in project requirements will cause the percentages to change; in some cases, for example, there may be little or no work in an entire Division, which causes adjustments in the percentages in the other Divisions.

CSI Div.	Division Title	% of Total Project	Type of Work
1	General Requirements	3%	Job procedures, regulations
2	Site Improvements	4%	Roads, walks, curbs, landscape, excavation/grading
3	Concrete (Cast-in-Place/Pre-cast)	8%	Foundations, columns, slabs, structural framing
4	Masonry	9%	Brick, CMU, stone, accessories, reinforcing, grouting
5	Metals (incl. Structural)	12%	Structural framing, light-gauge framing, fabrications, stairs, miscell.
6	Wood & Plastics	4%	Rough/finish carpentry, wood framing, laminates, cabinetry
7	Thermal/Moisture Protection	11%	Roof covering, insulation, caulking, water/dampproofing
8	Doors & Windows	9%	Interior/exterior; all types; all materials; glass/glazing
9	Finishes	9%	Paint, coatings, floor covering, ceilings, tile, wallcoverings
10	Specialties	4%	Miscell. items; flagpoles, signs, toilet accessories
11	Equipment	5%	Kitchen equip./appliances, dock equip., lab casework, special use equip.
12	Furnishings	4%	Furniture, office partition systems, artwork
13	Special Construction	3%	"Clean rooms," computer rooms
14	Conveying Systems	4%	Elevators, escalators, moving walkways, conveyors
15	Mechanical Systems	7%	Plumbing (complete), HVAC (complete), fire protection systems
16	Electrical	4%	Power, service, lighting, wire, alarms, low voltage, telephone and other communications
	Project Total	**100%**	

Figure 1–18   Percent of project work.

require the design professionals to be aware of, to evaluate, to understand, to use and incorporate, and to specify some 500,000 different items of construction materials or devices. This includes different types of nails and screws, various wall materials, doors and windows, paint, light fixtures, shingles, modified concrete, ceilings, glass, wood, man-made materials, plumbing fixtures, and on and on.

Other projects require the use of even more devices and materials due to their complexity, or size, or the need to use varied construction methods and systems. Some projects require great amounts of items, but not a great number of different types. Figure 1–20, for example, describes the amount of various items or work involved in the construction of one new church in central Kentucky in 1997 (note in particular the seating capacity of the church).

While the CSI listings show where the number of major products used in projects is listed in the specifications, it does not show the costs involved. Figure 1–21 shows a slightly dif-

ferent cost breakdown for residential building. In many cases there will be fewer major components, but a tremendous difference in cost. It is impossible to give an accurate cost estimate from the indexes due to the large number of things that can vary in any one project (function, size, construction, level of finish, amount of equipment, etc.). Changes depend on what is required by the project. For example:

- A prison may see 15% as the cost for equipment (Div. 11-12-13)
- Plumbing in a hospital may rise to 12.5% (Div. 15a)
- Site work for a warehouse may go to 14% (Div. 2), but an equipment cost may be less than 1% (Div. 11-12-13)
- Masonry costs (Div. 4) will rise for complex or multi-story work

The fact remains that the construction industry has a great effect on the basic economy of every country in the world.

General Comparative Building Costs* by Work in CSI Divisions			
CSI Div.	**Title**	**Residential****	**Commercial*****
1	General Requirements	18.50%	6–8%
2	Site Improvements	1%	4–6%
3	Concrete	6%	15–20%
4	Masonry	0.50%	8–12%
5	Metals (incl. Structural)	0	5–7%
6	Carpentry, Rough	17%	1–5%
	Carpentry, Finish	7.50%	combined
7	Thermal/Moisture Protection	8%	4–6%
8	Doors, Windows, Hardware	4%	5–7%
9	Finishes	19%	8–12%
10	Specialties	1.50%	NIC
11	Equipment	1.50%	NIC
12	Furnishings	0	6–10%
13	Special Construction	0	NIC
14	Conveying Equipment	0	NIC
15	Mechanical; Plumbing	8%	15–25%
	HVAC	3%	combined
16	Electrical	4.50%	8–12%
		100%	100%

*Cost of work shown as a percentage of the total project cost.

**For a 1600 sq.ft., 1-story, basementless wood frame house, with 2-car garage; average quality @ $67/sq.ft. in 1997.

***Very general costs due to great project variations; usually Div. 10, 11, 13, and 14 items are excluded from building cost budgets; NIC = Not In Contract.

Figure 1–19   General comparative building costs.

While the types of construction and the level of activity may vary widely, construction often drives the very viability, culture, economics, and survival of a country.

A better understanding of the size of the construction industry worldwide is provided by several special issues of the magazine, *Engineering News Record (ENR)*. These issues are in addition to the weekly cost information that *ENR* publishes, and are produced each year. They include listings of and information about the Top 500 Design Firms, the Top 500 Contractors, and other related information. The publications separate domestic from foreign work, and show the dollar value of different work categories, in various locations. The scope and dollar amounts are striking, almost overwhelming.

In addition, an extremely interesting analysis of the top 300 construction firms is available through an annual survey by *Building Design & Construction* magazine (Cahners). Similar surveys of the top 50 architectural firms, 60 architectural/engineering firms, 50 engineering/architectural firms, 40 engineering firms, 10 construction management organizations, 70 contracting companies, and 20 specialty (narrow scope sub-contracting) firms are also done. Besides ranking the firms, the survey also shows the number of employees, areas of activity, billings, and other pertinent information about each firm. This is an excellent resource for reviewing the major organizations in U.S. construction for commercial, institutional, and industrial work, along with multifamily residential projects. See also Figure 1–22 for an overview of types of construction firms.

CLOSER VIEW

While statistics reveal some of the breadth and enormity of the construction industry, it is interesting to review one small set of examples of how construction work can vary.

For example, a volume of one cubic yard is the common unit of measure for concrete. In an average single-family

A Monumental Project!

A group of subcontractors, in central Kentucky, encountered a project which was really a once-in-a-lifetime venture. The Southeast Christian Church project is the most monumental religious facility ever erected in the Commonwealth of Kentucky. To work on it had to be an amazing experience, yet the work was much the same as in smaller projects; there was just more of everything! It also serves to show that construction has many variations, in the most unlikely places and types of work.

- The entire project site is 103 acres.
- There are 50 acres of parking (approximately 4,800 parking spaces).
- Length of the Worship Center to Fellowship Hall (end to end) is approximately 2 city blocks.
- Total enclosed area for the project is 762,000 square feet.
- The Youth Center is 116,000 square feet; seats 1,024 persons in the Youth Auditorium; has 2 collegiate-sized basketball courts, 2 racquetball courts, a food court, a game room, a weight room, and a craft room.
- There are 14 miles of concrete curbing in the parking lot.
- There is enough paving material in the lot to pave a two-lane road, 15 miles.
- The metal roofing for the church covers 8 acres and would cover 175 houses.
- The Worship Center is as high as an 8-story building.
- The tip of the cross on the roof of the sanctuary is 150 feet high, or 12 stories.
- The cross also serves as a crucial steel member in the roof truss system.
- The Church rests upon "solid rock," as the weight of the building, including worshipers, is transferred to solid rock through concrete pillars (piles or caissons).
- The plumbing permit was the largest ever issued in the area; 400 water closets (¾ for women).
- The drywall surfacing covers 62 acres, and is fastened with 7.5 tons of screws.
- Metal studs for the drywall, if laid end-to-end, would reach 14 miles.
- Insulation in the building would cover 19 acres.
- The 7,000 tons of structural steel in the building would also build the 4,800 cars in the parking lot.
- There are 9,175 seats in the sanctuary; the chapel seats 450 persons.
- Each level of the Fellowship Hall seats 1,400 persons; 1,100 for dining purposes.
- There are 9 elevators, 8 escalators, and 1,200 doors in the facility.
- The Atrium Building houses the bookstore and library, in addition to the Chapel.

Taken from the newsletter
of the Kentuckiana ABC

Figure 1–20   A monumental project.

Residential Cost Information

Item	% of Total Cost
Excavation/site improvement	4.45
Foundation	7.28*
Structural frame (package)	9.52
Cement finish	5.44
Exterior masonry	6.58
Interior partitions	4.89
Carpentry/millwork	4.84
Windows/glazing	4.77
Roofing	2.47
Insulation	2.28
Dampproofing	0.12*
Interior wall covering	3.56
Hollow metal work	1.14
Misc./ornamental metal work	1.90
Tile (terrazzo, marble)	1.50
Floor covering	1.04
Painting	1.71
Finish hardware	1.55
Ceilings (incl. acoustic)	3.60
Plumbing	7.43
Heat, vent, A.C.	14.99
Electrical (incl. fixtures)	8.94
	100.00

Projected costs per square foot

Attics	$15
Second floor	$60
First floor	$75
Basement	$65
Basement room conversion	$20

*"Normal" conditions; may rise where bad conditions occur

Figure 1–21   Residential cost information.

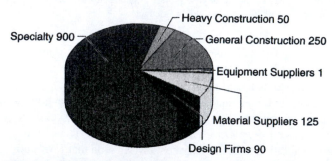

Figure 1–22   Types of construction firms by the type of work they perform, and the number of each type of firm. The chart distinctly shows that numerous subcontractors (specialty contractors) are available; this is reflected in the number required, normally, on each project to perform specific portions of the work.

house of approximately 2,000 sq. ft. there could be as few as 50–60 yards of concrete for the footings, foundation, and driveway, depending on the size and design. Usually, 3,000 psi (pounds per square inch—strength at 28 days) concrete will be used, and on average 4–6 people for a very short period will handle the installation (perhaps three 8-hour days

overall). How could these numbers vary for a larger project? Some indication comes from a magazine ad that describes a contract for just the equipment to place concrete on the Three Gorges Dam being built on China's Yangtze River. The contract value—*for just the equipment to place the concrete*—is

$30 million! But then there are to be some *30 million cubic meters* (approximately 39 million cubic yards) of concrete placed on this project!

Another example of both the enormity and the tremendous extension of construction can be cited. In June 1997, the Y-shaped foundation for a hotel in Las Vegas was placed. This was for just the first phase (3,000 rooms in the first of two towers, 36 floors in height, $1 billion overall project cost) of the development. The foundation was an 8 1/2 *foot* thick, monolithic (solid, one-piece) slab, that was placed continuously over a 24-hour period. This involved:

- placing 21,000 cubic yards of concrete—much more than the old U.S. record of 16,122 yards, but short of the 22,236-yard world record
- placing 1,000 yards per hour (17 yards a minute) using 360 mixers at the rate of one every 35 seconds
- using 300 workers, four 32-meter (m) truck-mounted telescoping conveyors, four 42-m concrete pumps, and one 52-m pump, among other pieces of equipment
- utilizing 5,000 psi concrete from two on-site and three off-site batching plants
- working in temperatures up to 97 degrees.

But all these efforts missed the goal set by the construction manager, to place the entire foundation—37,000 yards—all at once. The local concrete supply company simply could not get enough portland cement to make the additional concrete, nor the equipment and truck drivers to meet that goal.

Obviously, when a country has building needs of any sort (even luxury hotels), an organized construction effort must be present to provide the facilities. In these, then, are produced the other commodities the country and people need: from the tiniest and simplest, to the most complex and massive. The construction provides additional income, which, in turn, is spent by the workers in other ways—on food, shelter, clothing, tools, materials, education, taxes, and so on. This spending stimulates the flow of money and the economy itself, which leads to more construction (of homes for example), which adds jobs, and so on and so on. It makes for a wonderful cycle of development—almost perpetual motion.

Besides the mind-boggling amount of money involved, the industry just displays an amazing array of projects. These range from the very modest single-car detached garage for a residence to such prestigious projects as the World Trade Center, the Lincoln Tunnel, Hoover Dam, NASA's missile launching facilities, the recent Hong Kong and Denver airports, the Three Gorges Dam on the Yangtze River in China, and the Euro Tunnel, or Chunnel, under the English channel.

The industry seems to touch the clouds with its skyscrapers. In July, 1997, the Council on Tall Buildings and Urban Habitat changed its "leaders" in three new categories for tall buildings:

- Height to top of occupied floor—Sears Tower, Chicago
- Height to tip of antenna—World Trade Center, New York
- Height to structural top—Petronas Twin Towers, Kuala Lumpar, Malaysia

The construction industry, and the owners, are that stressed to build the biggest, best, most costly, you name it.

Construction projects reach the depths of the earth with freestanding offshore oil drilling platforms out in mid-ocean. Most people stand in awe when they first view a new structure or development. "How did they do that?" is the common response. Many times over the projects are beyond belief in sheer size, in complexity, in form, in eye-appeal, and in concept. Projects vary from cavernous aircraft hangers and bustling manufacturing plants, perhaps a thousand feet long, to the busy, beehive-like, hospital jammed full of small rooms. Other projects run the gamut from the grace and beauty of a new church or synagogue, to the new manufacturing plant soon to be marred by the grime and noise of production. Yet each project is the culmination of an intriguing human effort and the application of marvelous human expertise (Figure 1–23). Men and women apply their talents, skills, ideas, innovations, and flexibility to building projects of all kinds, piece by piece, work item by work item, until the project is finished. It is complete only because each small element is properly in its place and contributing to the success of its parent system or assembly and, in turn, of the project overall.

Almost every material or system is produced in a variety of quality levels. Sometimes this is done by varying thickness or finish; sometimes by utilizing different basic materials with differing costs as well as quality. There is a tremendous array of information on materials that the professionals must assess and then draw conclusions that best serve their client and project. This is no small task.

THE FUTURE

The construction industry is constantly challenged by the projects it is called upon to produce. The continual increase in the complexity and sophistication of not only projects themselves, but also the materials, systems, devices, and equipment involved causes the industry to upgrade its educational efforts. The basic need is to train new personnel to minimum levels and to increase the expertise of experienced personnel. But circumstances are changing so rapidly that the industry is hard pressed to maintain a level of training commensurate with the demands.

This is true not only in the trade work of the actual construction, but also in the design professions. Many people are able to achieve satisfactory levels of expertise in more than one area of their work, but not everyone can perform well in every aspect of their work. Our limitations, added to the range of specialization now present within the industry, have caused all construction industry personnel—professionals in all

Figure 1–23 In just this small portion of the project shown, note the numerous different materials that have been utilized. Designer and constructor properly combine these elements to function as intended.
Photo by Phil Joehnk.

phases and types of work—to become pigeonholed, or narrow in their range of expertise. Professional liability and the need to produce quality work demand that this "divisioning" be carefully employed, so gaps and errors are minimized.

Trade work has long been directed under this scenario. Because of more severe economic situations in recent years, however, a movement toward widening the expertise of workers has begun. While creditable as an effort to limit overall project cost, an inherent risk is incurred when the skills involved are not employed on a continual basis, causing some of the lesser-used skills to be degraded without use.

There is a danger in this for the industry. Mere numbers of workers do not necessarily produce quality work. To hire workers who are not skilled or otherwise adapted to the prevailing system only leads to added nonproductive training time, the need for more oversight, lower productivity, more rework of errant items, and a general lowering of work quality. The industry and individual firms cannot abide these maladies, particularly in a vigorous competitive market, and in the face of increasingly demanding clients.

EDUCATION

In general, three educational tracks in construction are in effect today: professional design and engineering schools, technical/professional education, and hands-on training. This section seeks to clarify the intent and the direction of these programs, and the eventual career goals of the participants.

Traditional professional schools offer a complete collegiate education leading to registration in one of the design professions. Over one hundred accredited schools of architecture are in existence, as well as 1,462 accredited engineering programs (in various disciplines) at 261 universities. They offer a complete education leading to bachelor's and master's degrees. In general, a good number of the graduates become active in some facet of the design of projects. Many, though, pursue careers in construction, material development and sales, and other ancillary branches of the construction industry.

Second, technical/professional education for technicians and construction professionals is offered at institutions which lead either to 4-year degrees (in construction management, for example) or 2-year associate degrees. Because of the growing size and complexity of projects, the need exists for those who understand design and engineering principles, but whose background lies in the control and management of the actual execution of the project work. These people are unique in that they understand the design process, but their chosen task is to facilitate, in full size, that which is drawn and described on the contract documents, plans and other drawings and the written specifications. They "design," schedule, evaluate, price, expedite, and facilitate the hands-on activities and processes that transform designs on paper to finished, usable, occupiable structures.

A significant cadre of such persons has come to the industry over the last few decades. These are people who have been trained in fully accredited construction education programs. They are construction specialists, in a sense, who bring new and different professional viewpoints and skills to projects. Since 1974, the American Council for Construction Education (ACCE) has been developing educational programs which train persons for professional management levels within the construction industry. Traditionally, persons out of the trades who have wide experience and perhaps, but not necessarily, added formal education have filled such positions. The formalized effort of ACCE currently has some forty 4-year, bachelor-degree programs, which are accredited by meeting ACCE standards; graduates number about 3,000 per year. The programs address education and training in construction management, construction science, construction, and construction technology. Construction industry organizations and contractors themselves heavily support these programs. The ACCE has met, and is further developing, one of the basic needs of the industry—for personnel who have the higher expertise to work within the industry to increase production, to establish better safety practices, and to manage individual projects in a smoother, more efficient manner. This concentration of added expertise and more highly trained personnel is to the benefit of all parties on the job site. In addition, the construction work is accomplished on the same level as the design work. This, in itself, has provided and will continue to provide a better, more team-oriented atmosphere between the very diverse groups within the industry and on each project.

Besides the programs noted above, there is a third educational effort—the hands-on training of construction workers. The primary effort has been in place for some time. Local Joint Apprenticeship Councils administer the program with oversight by state apprenticeship agencies and the United States Department of Labor. The Councils are formed with contractor, labor union, and nonunion members. These groups have all long participated in and augmented apprenticeship. Basically, the apprentice works on construction projects while also taking classroom instruction. Wages increase as the apprentice gains experience through time devoted to the program.

Other construction groups—usually combines of builders who then utilize the personnel they train—also carry out similar training. Some philosophical differences can be seen in the approaches these groups take, however. Apprenticeships and the labor unions subscribe to the development of skill in a single trade (not multiple or cross training advocated by other groups), which in years past has provided the basis for advancement within trades in the industry. The apprenticeship program is by far the strongest, due to its history, success, support, and government oversight and control.

It may seem that construction work is repetitive, mundane, common, and boring due to the monotonous nature of some operations. But if one can adopt a more flexible outlook, it can be seen that the circumstances and the work of each project has different aspects, and changed conditions. For example, setting concrete forms (work usually performed by carpenters) is a repetitive operation, i.e., the panelized form sections are set and connected together using the same process and devices no matter the project. True—but each project requires a different layout of sections and differing relationships of panels to form new shapes and new dimensions.

Simplistically, one can say that reading is boring since you see the same letters over and over. But the letters in each word, sentence, and story are in differing relationships, and form different units, i.e., words. The words themselves are set in differing relationships to form new information or story lines, each very different from others.

Of course, prevailing conditions of a particular job lead to circumstances beyond the control of the individual workers. Hot and cold weather greatly impact the workers, affecting their productivity and the quality and process of the project. High work locations bother some workers, as do those in very restricted or underground areas. The type of oversight, management, and control over the workers also impact what is done, how, and how well. Micromanaging (closely overseeing/watching virtually every move made by workers) in the end really only increases pressure, causes more errors, and adds an atmosphere counterproductive to good and prompt work. There are many other, more positive methods to better manage the work—education, teaching the reason for why and how things are done, sharing insight into the specific project and how the work at hand is necessary and contributory to the overall project.

Because of its wide-ranging activities and the various levels and types of expertise, the construction industry provides opportunity to a great variety of people and their interests. A review of all of the categories of people involved in construction gives some insight into what jobs are open to new employees. Many jobs, of course, are direct hands-on construction work of one trade or another. At the same time, professional slots are being filled, and overall a person interested in anything from a clerical/administrative role to the most stringent and demanding construction work can find satisfaction. Opportunities abound for those who dedicate themselves to the industry and who are willing to pursue their careers through the various paths open in the industry.

The tide of activity in construction changes mostly for economic reasons. However, there is always a need for construction, as the needs of the populace and the companies fulfilling them never really cease. Often it is a matter of location (are you where the work is?) and the happenstance of working in the most needed profession or trade. As with any employment situation, drawbacks and insecurity arise. But today, employment is no longer the "for life" situation of years past. Now one must be willing to move as the work demands, or move from company to company. This scenario has been constant in construction, since the work involved is never located in just one location, all the time.

In this scenario, it is clear that each project team member, no matter their work assignment, must be interested in what they do and be aware of the impact of their work. In a larger sense, they must be engrossed in their work. They need not take an obsessive, over-zealous, narrow-minded approach, where the person becomes convinced that their work is preeminent, overriding all other, and somehow becomes so key and necessary that all other team members must adhere to their mandates, their schedule, their needs. That is just as destructive, if not more so, than being passive and disinterested.

In truth, part of the "reward" in construction is to be involved in problem solving, and in detailing small portions of the work so they contribute properly to the project overall, and allow all trade work to be accomplished in an easier and faster manner. Delving into detail and solving problems is a continuous program, but it requires people who are dedicated to such work and find their sense of satisfaction in participating in that manner. Every project is a compilation of thousands of such situations, so there is much for the right people to do, *if* they are aware of the impact of their work and effort, and *if* they take the time and interest to participate.

THE WORKFORCE

Just as mental or creative work marks the professional in law, medicine, architecture, engineering, so skilled physical, hands-on work makes the trades worker a professional also. Many lives are dedicated to construction, whether in active hands-on work or in positions that aid, support, and facilitate construction. In fact, the reward of construction can be more open and obvious, as the products of construction are the buildings, structures, and facilities that everyone can see every day (see Figure 1–24). Pride can be taken in even the smallest contribution to any project; for without it, the project would be lessened. Still, in the United States there is an ominous growing shortage of skilled construction personnel. It appears that construction work does not provide the appeal it once did, and younger workers are finding their futures in other fields.

To a degree there are some groups of workers who are entering construction, finding an appeal in the work due primarily to their social and economic condition. These involve some minority groups, immigrants, and retrained or chronically unemployed persons. Here training is a problem as the workers move toward better wages and life styles. The problems, though, are lack of appropriate skills, unfamiliarity with methods and materials, language barriers, and educational backgrounds. A few small groups, though, come much

---

A Winning Essay: Our Solid Future

Congratulations to Mark Bockrath, Kalida, Ohio, the 1997 winner of the Norman J. Rex Scholarship, in the Ohio Ready Mixed Concrete Association's essay contest, Concrete, the industry with a solid future. Following is his essay, entitled, Our Solid Future.

Every day of my life I encounter many different uses of concrete. This amazingly versatile building product is found in almost every standing building in the world. From skyscrapers to barns, concrete plays a large role in the building process. Concrete can be used from foundation to roof top because of the many advancements made in both forming the concrete and the different types of concrete mixtures.

Many different types of tools and equipment have also made concrete both easier to place and finish. Power screeds and vibratory screeds quickly strike off the concrete and bring it to grade to provide a constant and level surface. Machines called slip-pavers allow contractors to easily pour curbing, short walls, and some flat work without using any forms. The use of forms is not needed because the machine takes very dry concrete from the truck and shakes it to form different types of products. This invention seems remarkable to me because it reduces both time and labor while creating a good quality product in the end.

As I look around the small village that I live in, I can easily see the importance of concrete to society. First of all, concrete roads and driveways allow me to travel easily and safely to where ever I want to go. When a river or stream approaches, a concrete bridge deck closes the gap between the two roadways. Concrete curbing and catch basins help to swiftly carry water to storm sewers, which lead into streams, and concrete dams control the flooding and drying out of the rivers. Concrete also greatly reduces erosion of our valuable sod. Waterways are formed and poured to handle the immense amounts of water that quickly runs off of developed areas. These manmade concrete waterways are very helpful in both conserving the land, and returning water to rivers. Concrete sidewalks and approaches provide a much easier way to get around. Concrete is also easy to form and shape to create smoother surfaces and to make approaches that are especially helpful to handicapped people.

With new technology, concrete is being used more widely through the world. Industry uses this technology by building buildings with concrete walls. One fairly new way that this is being done is by casting the wall panels on the site, and tilting them into place with large cranes. This type of concrete construction is known as tilt-up. This is an economical way to build and the structure will last a long time. Another fairly new concept of concrete building is that of forming walls with polystyrene blocks and filing them with concrete. I believe that this new way of building exterior walls for homes and residential buildings will be an advantage in the long run because a much stronger and waterproof wall will result in less repairs and a much more sound house. By creating a much stronger residential house with concrete walls, the house will be worth more and resist the forces of mother nature easier.

The importance of concrete is clearly evident in this constantly changing world. No matter where people go, anyone can see the large role that concrete plays in this modern time. Concrete is the most widely used building component known. It is said to be second to water as being the most consumed substance. The future of our country in a global economy depends on safe, economical and durable building materials such as concrete. This is why I intend to pursue a career in concrete technology.

Figure 1–24 A prize-winning essay showing the interest that can be generated in young people who have the desire and outlook to actively participate in the construction industry.

closer to filling the workforce needs. But, importantly, the largest group to come forward is American women.

Women, for many decades, have served construction projects in traditional clerical and administrative roles, either in the professional or company office, or in some cases as on-site clerical support. Since 1978, the roles of women have been increased. Now it is clearly apparent that women are the answer to current and future construction industry labor shortages. Over the last 10 years some 200,000 construction workers have left the industry; between 30,000 and 40,000 exited in 1997 and 1998, respectively. The average construction worker is now about 49 years of age. Major efforts have been mounted to overcome the negative image problem that construction has and to attract younger persons into the trades; even grade school students are being familiarized with the opportunities in the construction industry.

Women have been attracted to positions where manual dexterity is at a premium; this includes plumbing and electrical work. Changes in equipment and methods now negate the need for great upper body strength and allow women full access to more work positions. Still too much negativity surrounds women in the trades and on the job site; it is counterproductive. Under federal law, contractors with federal projects are required to employ a workforce that includes 6 percent women. Unfortunately, this law has seen little enforcement, as only two cases of noncompliance have been prosecuted although there are upwards of 200,000 firms with federal contracts.

Only very slight increases in the number of women in the trades have been made. Now just over 2 percent of the total hands-on production workforce in construction in the United States are women (96,800 women out of a total force of some 4.84 million workers, according to U.S. Department of Labor Women's Bureau, 1999). There are only 813,000 women in the entire industry, in all capacities. Major attractions for women in construction are the level of hourly wages and the benefits programs available. Both usually far exceed the pay and benefits open to women in other fields. With the increasing pressure to find additional construction personnel, more opportunities and training are open in the trades, and the workforce is in dire need of workers to match the current and projected levels of construction activity. In fact, the industry is counting on women to be the source of workers, over the long term, to ease future labor crunches. This is true in spite of the fact that construction is unfortunately at the bottom of the list of desired occupations. But as in the days of World War II, women have disregarded the all too apparent, distasteful aspect of the work and have fully met and overcome the challenges of the training, the working conditions, and the work itself. They have proven that they have deflected traditionalism and bias, and have moved forward so that they now occupy many different job positions, from trade work up to and including major management and ownership of construction companies. They can easily work side by side with men in nearly all the trades and effect similar results.

Another major breakthrough for women came with the institution of the Women in Construction (WIC) organization in the mid-1960s. This group, now organized in numerous groups nationwide, brought together women from all walks of construction life—from design professionals, administrative assistants, and secretaries to trade workers. Their common cause has elevated the status, skill, and utilization of women on the job site. In addition, they have contributed to the betterment of the industry in ancillary ways. For example, the Phoenix chapter of WIC made a major contribution to the industry in 1968 when the members compiled the first set of comprehensive, industry-wide construction definitions. This effort brought women together by combining their various work definitions into a single source—*The Construction Dictionary*. This book, now in its 17th edition, encompasses some 16,000 separate definitions and many tables and appendices, all construction oriented, and covering every trade and type of work the industry encounters. This volume is still a most important reference and training document, which adds to the well-being of the industry as a whole. It also stands as distinct evidence that women are interested in and are making major and valued contributions in the construction industry.

Think, though, of what drives, or causes, construction. Take a company like modern day Microsoft Corporation. In 25 years this organization, started in a modest building, has increased from three employees and $16,000 in income, to a staff of thousands and revenues in the billions of dollars. Their products have been translated into 30 languages worldwide and their products are sold and used in 50 countries. Now even someone who knows little of Microsoft can envision the great conglomerate, the diversified product line, and the worldwide influence. While not every company has had such expansion, still billions of dollars have been invested and spent in the construction of Microsoft's innumerable plant facilities around the world. Multiply this total by the number of major companies currently doing business. Then to this figure add the innumerable array of small businesses that have construction needs of varying size.

RELATIONSHIPS

Like other large enterprises, the construction industry can easily be considered as a separate and distinct entity—a world unto itself. Its far-ranging nature, though, can be seen in the offshoot areas of activity that are solely construction-oriented. Following is a listing of some of these areas, which have been created by the industry, and now directly serve and affect the industry. It is obvious that a whole new world has been created by the peculiar circumstances of the industry. For example, construction law adds many new angles and quirks to the law in general, and is quite complex.

You will find a series of short discussions on the following topics in *Encyclopedia of Architecture, Design, Engineering and Construction,* Vol. 2, by Joseph A. Wilkes (New York: John Wiley and Sons):

- Construction claims
- Construction contract administration
- Construction documents
- Construction equipment
- Construction funding
- Construction law
- Construction management
- Construction project reporting services
- Construction systems

While the construction industry is not self-sustaining (since it produces only completed projects, and not support activities), nor self-perpetuating (owners outside the industry hire "it" for their work), the industry in its comprehensive coverage touches a great many lives, businesses, and jobs.

The industry involves, directly or indirectly, about 15 percent of the total industrial workforce in the United States. Of this it employs directly something in the order of 5 percent of the total workforce, or roughly 3.5 to 4.5 million workers. The industry's indirect support involves development, research, manufacture, production, sales, distribution, servicing, and transportation of the materials and equipment required in the construction process. To this must be added over a million white-collar employees who work in the industry and add to its viability. In addition are the 1.5 million small construction companies (family firms and individuals), so small they don't even have a formal payroll.

Contractors for construction work come in a variety of sizes and configurations (Figure 1–25). A single person can be a sub/speciality contractor. Usually this involves a very narrow skill range, and one that is not widely practiced. For example, an individual could be a grainer (one who finishes mill-woodwork by applying distinctive grain patterns), or a refinisher of damaged or aged marble trim or statuary, useful in the restoration or fire repair of a church.

A family, a father, two sons, and a daughter, combines as a company that does nothing but pipe insulation. The father and one son do the estimating in the evenings after a full work day, work which includes the other son and the daughter, whose speciality is the tight spaces. The daughter along with her mother does the books for the entire organization. This is a skilled, highly regarded, and busy group that does exceptional work throughout their region.

Elsewhere, two brothers combine with one other person and do bricklaying. They hire one hod carrier. All of these persons use farming as their other source of income. At times, when the farming needs attention, they may leave a project for a short time, but then they may make up time on the weekends so they can meet the project's schedule. Bricklaying is one of several examples where families work together, with the father involving the sons and daughters early (carrying hod/mortar, cleaning up, etc., as youngsters) and training them up in the trade. Usually these are very skilled and conscientious workers, having been trained under close parental guidance and a strong work ethic.

In some circumstances, construction organizations are not that clearly defined. Often workers will perform different tasks on different days, as the project demands. For example, a worker may finish a concrete sidewalk one day, and the next apply a waterproof coating. Usually this is an experienced person, and not someone who is "learning by doing." In more remote areas (even in some areas of the United States) there simply is no compartmentalized workforce, wherein a person is restricted to performing only those tasks

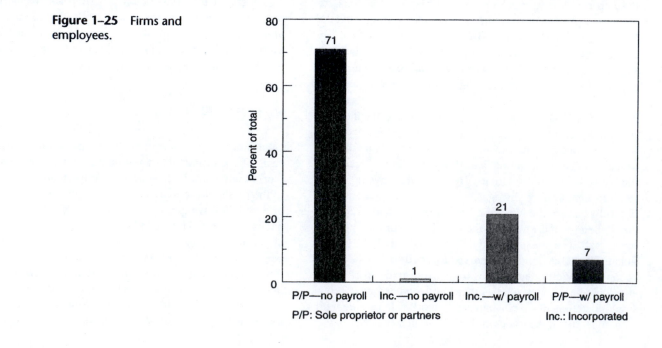

Figure 1–25   Firms and employees.

belonging to one type of work. Where the workforce has been organized under labor unions, a more confined assignment of personnel can be seen. This has changed drastically over the last couple of decades, where work on projects has changed from total union labor to a combined force of union and nonunion workers. Some labor organizations have created and implemented training programs which included at least cross-training, if not duplicate training, for new workers. Many observers feel that this adds versatility and cost-effectiveness to the construction process. Others claim it dilutes the skill level and produces inferior work.

Other construction firms vary in size and organization according to market demand. Over the last several years (5 years consecutively, and 10 of the last 11 years) a corporation called Fluor Daniel, a subsidiary of Fluor Corporation, has been ranked by *Engineering News Record* magazine as the leading engineering and construction firm in the United States. This firm has 50 offices worldwide, and had a staff of 57,711 people at the time data was collected. The corporation revenues exceeded $13.2 billion in 1997, from work in a wide variety of industrial, institutional, and commercial projects, throughout the world. A total of 61 percent of this revenue is from non-U.S. projects. These include building projects for petrochemicals, up- and downstream energy, mining, chemicals, and numerous other heavy industrial sectors. In 54 percent of the projects, the firm did both engineering and construction (design/build).

In each of the examples above, and the many other variations, the people involved earn their livelihood and at least part of their annual income through construction efforts. There is a fair wage for each hour worked no matter what the firm may look like, how it is organized, or how imposing or modest its work effort may be. The various trades and skills of the workers are needed to some extent in almost every project. How the workers are brought to the work is the variable.

Almost three-quarters (70 percent) of construction volume involves new construction, some 21 percent involves additions to or alterations of existing facilities; the remainder (9 percent) is repair and maintenance work. The industry is a conservative venture, whose expenditures are highest when the economy is strong. It is the largest single production activity in the economy of the United States. This is also true for many other countries, while in others it is gaining this position as the countries' economies flourish. Only the health care industry is anywhere near comparable to construction in terms of overall size (including all comparable factors).

NEW DIRECTIONS

Surprisingly, though, construction has long had a low level of productivity. It has been criticized for decades as being a haven for overpaid, underproductive workers. Some 20 years ago the chief executive officers (CEOs) of 200 of the largest U.S. companies combined to form The Business Roundtable

(BRT). Through its construction committee, this group set out to study cost effectiveness in the construction industry. As users of that industry, the CEOs were concerned about the declining value for their construction expenditures; the return was not high enough.

Their effort culminated in a 5-year study period involving an impressive and extensive array of experts. Some two dozen reports were produced, covering every aspect of the construction industry—management, technology, labor (supply, training, and effectiveness), and regulations and codes. These reports proved to be highly accurate and extremely helpful in making progress toward improving the industry.

Through implementation via 40 Local Users Councils nationwide, use of the BRT study information and techniques by the industry has consistently produced cost reductions in the range of 10 percent, and frequently topping 20 percent, or more. All told, over $10 billion per year has been saved. The overall program, Construction Industry Cost-Effectiveness (CICE), has created a new and growing determination within the industry to give America more construction for its dollars. History shows that this program is working quite well, and is achieving its goal—more construction for the money.

In their report in the mid-1980s, the Roundtable characterized the industry as follows:

> By common consensus and every available measure, the United States no longer gets its money's worth in construction—the nation's largest industry. . . . The creeping erosion of construction efficiency and productivity is bad news for the entire U.S. economy. Construction is a particularly seminal industry. The price of every factory, office building, hotel, or power plant that is built affects the prices that customers (the general public) must be charged for the goods or services produced in it, or by it. And that effect generally persists for decades. . . . Too much of the industry remains tethered to the past, partly by inertia, and partly by historic divisions.

In the years since that report was published, major efforts were put forth to change the face of the industry. Construction's finished projects remain constant in their variety and in their specific styles, composition, configurations, and functions. However, as new project delivery methods have been developed for quicker and higher quality projects, management has increased both its intensity and its quality. Owners now more fervently exercise their role as "project sponsor," sharing the pangs of making important decisions about a major capital investment—their acquisition of a new facility—and becoming much more active "partners" in the process, demanding enduring quality as well as dollar value in their projects. Still, a level of stigma hangs on.

This stems in part from the conservative nature of the industry and in part from the on-going low level of motivation, interest, and self-esteem on the part of many workers. No longer following the pride-filled efforts of the guild artisan, and removed from the high-powered union days, too many workers still find it difficult to visualize anything but "a pay check." They see a job with little or no redeeming value, devoid of any reward, enjoyment, sense of accomplishment, or egotism that serves to inspire them. Yet, strangely enough, the products of their work continue to amaze with their size, elegance, and complexity.

What is lost in all this is the fact that the success of any construction project depends directly on the effort and applied skill of *each* worker. Without a knowledgeable effort, the work assigned will not contribute to the success of the overall project. The old axiom applies here: "a chain is only as strong as its weakest link." This is eminently true in the relationship of individual work to overall project. Part of the solution to the dilemma is the concept of effective work teams. Each member must contribute to the overall effort, using his or her unique set of skills, else there is no success. Supervisors must recognize this truth and apply personalized staffing, using the best person and the best set of skills for the task at hand. This in turn provides the worker with higher self-esteem and quality of work produced.

An excellent example of the need for a proactive, interested, and cooperative spirit in the construction industry is the case for an informed, helpful CAD operator/designer. All too easily, these workers can become merely "operators" who process only the exact information given them. If they are not trained, or somehow directed in the proper techniques, the work they produce will be faulty and time-consuming, in that time will be required to redo, undo, or correct work.

An item as simple as a dimension change in one location can require "someone" to ensure that the change is made *in all other locations* where the change has impact. To make just the one change creates a "glitch," or error, in the documents. Similarly, a change in concept where a structural angle formerly was attached directly to a wall, but now is installed with space between the wall face and the angle, must be reflected in all pertinent details showing that work. To do less is to be incorrect, and the source of job-site questions, if not problems.

The spirit here, and in numerous other construction project situations, is that one cannot be a team member and merely sit back without interfacing with others. One cannot be passive and so disinterested that work is done without checking with others, without verifying with others, without simply finding out, without asking questions, without being aware of how one work item impacts others. It is easy to see that if a person has a negative or less than cooperative attitude, all of this work will slide to the detriment of the project. Multiply this in literally thousands of small instances and you have a project in disarray—misaligned information, slowdowns to make corrections, late completion dates, over-budget situations, not to say the source of much consternation on the part of all the major parties to the contract.

Another part of the productivity problem is the lack of an aggressive research and development (R&D) effort. While construction still manages to produce a fairly impressive number of new products each year, R&D is less than 0.5% of the in-place construction value. Other industries in the United States spend approximately 1.8% of annual revenues on R&D. Other countries spend in the order of 2.5% on construction research annually. In addition, the small amount spent is generated primarily (69%) from manufacturers, with 18% from government, and just 4% from contractors. Also, somewhat disheartening is the fact that almost all of the money is spent on new product development, not on improving productivity. Even the creation of several thousand new products does not add impetus to improving work production. It is then left to the individual tradeworker or firm to create innovation in work techniques and management programs.

It is extremely important to understand, though, that construction is quite different from other industries. Its primary product cannot be mass produced or standardized. Rather the industry is characterized by unique, custom-built projects. Each project has a distinct location, set of circumstances, and character to which the process of construction must adapt. Using standard materials, equipment, and devices, and some standardization of its own (prefabrication, prototype and modular units), the industry manipulates, changes, incorporates, fashions, and fits these standard items to the peculiar needs and conditions of the project. The result is a uniquely different project. This fact in itself should provide some inspiration for the workers by making them parties to new, different, and unique solutions. It is their flexibility and often their ingenuity that allows this whole process to succeed, time and time again.

Coupled with this concept is the fact that the project is best accomplished by a "combined crew" (Figure 1–26). This entails a number of subcontractors who are hired to perform specialized functions, such as masonry work and painting, for example (Figure 1–27). It is not unusual for the construction of a single project to require the work of 25 or more different trades. In fact, as much as 80 percent of the project work for a building will be done through subcontracting (Figure 1–28). Heavy construction projects use far fewer subcontractors (as little as 15 percent of the total work), since the basic contractor is organized and staffed for such projects, and is capable of performing most of the work. These complexities are major factors that contribute to inefficiencies at the workplace.

Further contributing to lower productivity and inefficiency is that a construction "team," gathered for one project, may never work together again. It is rare that successive projects will use the same array of contractors on the site. Many variables cause this—from the competitive bidding process, to the amount of work the contractors have back-logged, to location, to simple discontent between the contractors. This situation is one among several that are causing reevaluation and the use of alternate delivery systems for construction projects. Certainly, where the "team" survives and moves on to other projects, the work progresses in a far smoother and better coordinated fashion, to the benefit of all parties. Reality shows, though, that not many construction teams move intact from project to project. And now with al-

Figure 1–26 The work of several different trades, forming a "combined crew" is evident at this site. Note work of concrete foundation contractor, steel erectors, stair installers, drywall stud installer, and precast concrete panel contractor. The combined crew brings the highest expertise to the project by using persons who specialize in their portion of the work.

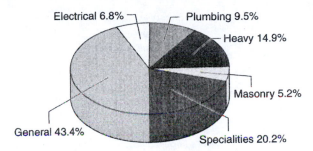

Figure 1–27 Work as a percentage of total cost.

ternative delivery systems (ADS), if they do move it is highly likely that they will encounter changed delivery procedures, methods, and conditions.

ALTERNATIVE DELIVERY SYSTEMS

Project delivery systems have become more than a buzzword among owners and construction professionals. These are the methods of formulating contracts for a project; they include both design/bid/build and design/build methods, along with many others (see Figure 1–29). Owners are now, more than ever, able to assemble their design and construction teams in a way that best serves their interest and needs.

In reality the project delivery system is important to the project overall, but has less impact on the sequence and performance of the actual work of the project.

The delivery system is a management tool, which has great importance to the owner and to those who are responsible for the actual delivery of the project. These include the design professionals, the construction manager, the de-

sign/build firm managers, and the project managers. The system is a definitive legal configuration, and a map directing the flow of information and authority across the project. In a sense it establishes the pecking order for authority, and sets out the pattern of that authority as it relates to communications, directions/instructions, changes in the work, and of course, the progressive payments due from the owner during the course of the project.

The sequence of the project can be changed for various reasons, mainly to adjust to the needs of the owner. However, even these adjustments have little impact on the work. There may be a realignment of what work is done and in what order, but still that work is done, eventually. Again, this falls upon the managers of the project to decide just how this is done, why, and in what fashion. With this it is virtually impossible to portray the "typical" project—variations, large and small, are too numerous.

To illustrate all of this, Figure 1–29 offers a brief discussion of some of the more widely used delivery systems. Of course, there are many other documents and resources which can greatly expand the amount and depth of information on these systems.

Over the last few decades, owners have been faced with several challenges, which have caused them to rethink how they approach their construction projects. Since most projects take some time to complete, and since money must be available for periodic payments, most projects are funded through some sort of borrowing or loan scenario. Of course, as with any loan, money borrowed must be repaid along with interest. This added cost of money has become a significant factor, to the point that owners have been seeking methods to shorten the length of loans, and thereby reducing the amount of interest due.

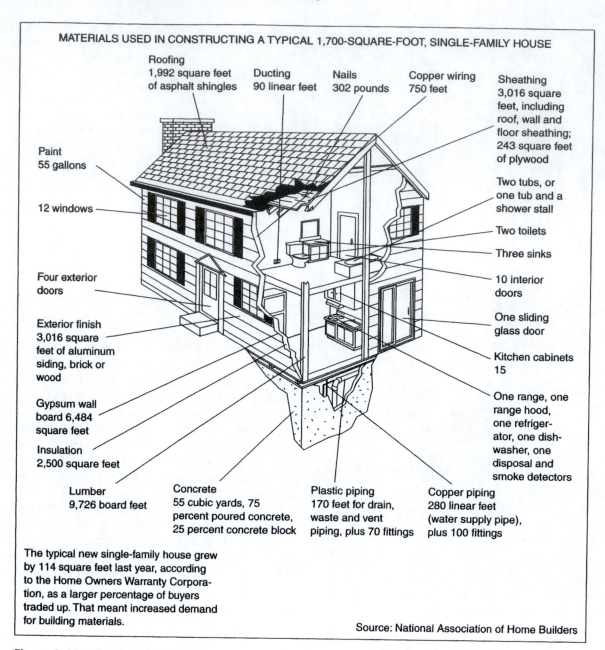

MATERIALS USED IN CONSTRUCTING A TYPICAL 1,700-SQUARE-FOOT, SINGLE-FAMILY HOUSE

Roofing
1,992 square feet
of asphalt shingles

Ducting
90 linear feet

Nails
302 pounds

Copper wiring
750 feet

Sheathing
3,016 square
feet, including
roof, wall and
floor sheathing;
243 square feet
of plywood

Paint
55 gallons

12 windows

Four exterior
doors

Exterior finish
3,016 square
feet of aluminum
siding, brick or
wood

Gypsum wall
board 6,484
square feet

Insulation
2,500 square feet

Two tubs, or
one tub and a
shower stall

Two toilets

Three sinks

10 interior
doors

One sliding
glass door

Kitchen cabinets
15

One range, one
range hood,
one refriger-
ator, one dish-
washer, one
disposal and
smoke detectors

Lumber
9,726 board feet

Concrete
55 cubic yards, 75
percent poured concrete,
25 percent concrete block

Plastic piping
170 feet for drain,
waste and vent
piping, plus 70 fittings

Copper piping
280 linear feet
(water supply pipe),
plus 100 fittings

The typical new single-family house grew
by 114 square feet last year, according
to the Home Owners Warranty Corporation, as a larger percentage of buyers
traded up. That meant increased demand
for building materials.

Source: National Association of Home Builders

Figure 1–28   The sum of all its parts.

For some time, owners have become increasingly concerned about getting full value for money spent on construction projects. Two factors play heavily in these concerns:

- How can the various contractors be placed under contract to produce the project as designed, on time, and at least at budget (if not below)

- How can any claims, problems, or defects be eliminated or resolved for the least cost and in the shortest amount of time.

Since these concerns are interrelated, a good deal of time and effort has been expended to create new ways in which owners can come closer to resolving both. The result is what is now called *alternative project delivery systems*. These, basically, are differing methods or configurations for the drawing of contracts, for better oversight of the project, for more reliable estimating and cost information, for better management of the project, and for perhaps the most important factor, the establishing of single-point responsibility for the entire project.

In any discussion of project delivery systems, it is important to note that many companies engage in projects which use a variety of systems. Some, of course, restrict their work to one delivery system or another. Most, however, establish their organization to meet the requirements of their client and

BD&C

PROJECT DELIVERY

A primer on project delivery

Handbook takes on controversy by evaluating pros and cons of delivery alternatives

By Christopher Olson, Editor in Chief

To summarize its comparative overview of delivery alternatives, the *Handbook on Project Delivery* contains a matrix of eight methods grouped under three categories: traditional, construction management (CM) and design/build.

The construction of the Tower of Babel was thwarted by a profusion of tongues; ever since, the construction of buildings has been thwarted by the lack of a common language for project delivery alternatives.

To help lessen the clamor, the American Institute of Architects, California Council (AIACC) has developed a kind of consumer guide to project delivery methods. The *Handbook on Project Delivery* is a 150-page primer that supplies some standard terms and definitions for project delivery. But its ultimate goal is much more ambitious: to outline the pros and cons of the various delivery methods.

This goal is especially pertinent today, when there is growing dissatisfaction among all team members with the more traditional design/bid/build process of designing and con-

Matrix of Project Delivery	Traditional methods		CM methods	
	Design/bid/build	NST	CM-Advisor	CM-Agent
—— Contracts - - - - Communication	ownr / dsgnr · bldr	ownr / dsgnr · bldr	ownr / cm-adv / dsgnr · bldr	ownr / cm-ag / dsgnr · bldr
Characteristics	Three linear phases: Design, bid, build	Three continuous phases: Design, negotiate, build	Three linear phases: Design, bid, build	Three linear phases: Design, bid, build
	Three prime players: Owner, Designer, Builder	Three prime players: Owner, Designer, Builder	Four prime players: Owner, CM-Advisor, Designer, Builder	Four prime players: Owner, CM-Agent, Designer, Builder
	Two separate contracts: Owner to Designer and Owner to Builder	Two separate contracts: Owner to Designer and Owner to Builder	Three separate contracts: Owner to CM-Advisor, Owner to Designer and Owner to Builder	Three separate contracts: Owner to CM-Agent, CM-Agent to Designer and CM-Agent to Builder
	Formal relationship	Informal relationship	Formal relationship	Formal relationship
Responsibilities Owner	Program, finance, mgmnt.	Program, finance, mgmnt.	Program, finance	Program, finance
Manager	n/a	n/a	Coord. Designer & Builder	Legal agent for owner
Designer	All normal services	All normal services	All normal services	All normal services
Builder	Prime and sub construction	Prime and sub construction	Prime and sub construction	Prime and sub construction
Selection process Owner	n/a	n/a	n/a	n/a
Manager	n/a	n/a	Qualifications	Qualifications
Designer	Qualifications	Qualifications/negotiations	Qualifications	Qualifications
Builder	Lowest responsible bid	Qualifications/negotiations	Lowest resp. bid or negot.	Lowest responsible bid

Figure 1–29   Project delivery system options.

structing buildings. Moreover, building owners are continually raising the bar for their building teams, demanding the delivery of better facilities in less time, at less cost and with less litigation.

The group assembled by AIACC to develop the handbook included architects, contractors, construction managers, attorneys, professional liability insurers and clients. Among their guiding principles was neutrality; they were not to advocate one delivery method or methods over others. Indeed, it was agreed that the appropriateness of any method will vary based on the size, scale and complexity of a project. Moreover, the role of the architect/engineer may be expanded, based on a firm's skills and capabilities.

To make an informed choice, building owners must appreciate the importance of evaluating delivery methods in terms of each particular project and building team. But too often, they don't.

"Owners 'channel surf' their delivery methods," says Gordon Chong, AIACC president in 1996 and chair of the handbook project, as well as managing principal of the architectural firm of Gordon H. Chong & Associates, San Francisco, a firm that has worked with all the major delivery alternatives. "They don't know what they want, but they know that they don't like what they have."

A new approach

Chong acknowledged that there are many other resources available that describe project delivery methods, but he believes that his

CM-Constructor	**Design/build methods**		
	Design/build	**DB-Developer**	**DB-Bridging**
Three linear phases: Design, bid, build	Two continuous phases: Design and build	Two continuous phases: Design and build	Four linear phases: Preliminary design, bid, design and build
Three prime players: Owner, Designer, CM-Constructor	Two prime players: Owner and Design-Build Entity	Two prime players: Owner and D-B Developer	Three prime players: Owner, Owner's Designer and D-B Entity
Two separate contracts: Owner to CM-Constructor and Owner to Designer	One contract: Owner to Design-Build Entity	One contract: Owner to D-B Developer	Two separate contracts: Owner to Owner's Designer and Owner to D-B Entity
Formal relationship	Formal relationship	Formal relationship	Formal relationship
Program, finance	Program, finance	Program	Program, finance, mgmnt.
Coord. Dsgnr. prior to const.	n/a	n/a	n/a
All normal services	Special services under DB	Special services under DB	Owner's Dsgnr. and DB Dsgnr.
CM is prime w/subcontr.	DB is prime w/subcontr.	Finance, prime w/subcontr.	Prime and sub construction
n/a	n/a	n/a	n/a
Qualifications	n/a	n/a	n/a
Qualifications	Qualifications/negotiations	Qualifications/negotiations	Qualifications/negotiations
Qualifications/negotiations	Lowest resp. bid or negot.	Lowest resp. bid or negot.	Lowest resp. bid or negot.

Figure 1–29 (continued)

"We have to be smarter about counseling our clients on how they should do their construction"

The handbook's matrix evaluates each alternative from the perspective of owner, designer, builder and manager for four primary criteria: quality, schedule, cost control and legal liability.

council's three-ring handbook is the first to compare and contrast them all in one place.

Although many building owners might want to ask simple questions like "Which delivery method ensures the highest quality?," the handbook is not designed to supply simple answers. Instead, it provides a comparative format to take the user through the process of evaluating delivery methods in terms of four primary criteria: quality, schedule, cost control and legal liability.

The handbook also evaluates each alternative from the perspective of owner, designer, builder and manager. A comparative matrix (reproduced below) provides a summary of all these criteria for each method covered.

Boiling down the alternatives

A critical step in the handbook's development was determining the number of delivery alternatives to be included. This was no small

step, because as the AIACC group began to survey how projects were being delivered around the country, they were "flabbergasted" at both the variety and the varying terminology. In particular, Chong said they found that architects in both small and large firms were expanding the little box of traditional design services in many ways.

Nevertheless, from all the potential delivery methods that could have been covered, the AIACC distilled a total of eight primary alternatives grouped under three major categories — traditional, construction management (CM) and design/build. The traditional category, which is the first to be covered in the handbook, is used as a baseline for the descriptions of other methods that follow. Included in this category are two methods: design/bid/build and negotiated select contract (NST). The CM category includes CM as advisor, CM as agent and CM as construc-

		Traditional methods								CM methods							
		Design/bid/build				NST				CM-Advisor				CM-Agent			
Perspectives of Owner, Manager, Designer, Builder		O	M	D	B	O	M	D	B	O	M	D	B	O	M	D	B
Quality	Highest / Higher / Standard / Lower																
Schedule	Fastest / Faster / Normal / Slower																
Cost control	Best / Better / Normal / Less																
Legal liability	Least (best) / Reduced / Average / Increased (worst)																

Figure 1–29 (continued)

tor. Under the design/build category there are also three methods: design/build, design/build by developer and bridging. Each method receives its own section in the handbook.

Chong fully recognizes that the ratings will be provocative to many, but therein lies their value, because those who disagree should discuss it with the owner and other team members. "We have to be smarter about counseling our clients on how they should do their construction," Chong says.

The handbook acknowledges some of these differences of opinion in a supplemental section entitled "Further Directions," where the comments of some industry professionals who reviewed the handbook — and some who disagreed with its evaluations — are reproduced. More than 150 reviewers commented on the handbook's draft versions.

To date, AIACC has distributed nearly 7,000 copies of the handbook, which may soon go into a second printing. AIACC sees the handbook as a document in transition, and it anticipates a need for updates, although none has yet been scheduled.

While many will argue with the contents of the AIACC handbook — particularly with the choice, description and comparative evaluation of individual delivery alternatives — all should agree that it's a step in the right direction. And by offering a common language, the handbook helps to avoid the kind of semantic confusion once described by comedian Steve Martin: "Boy, those French! They have a different word for everything." □

> The *Handbook on Project Delivery* is available from the AIA California Council, 1303 J St., Suite 200, Sacramento, CA 95814; (916) 448-9082.

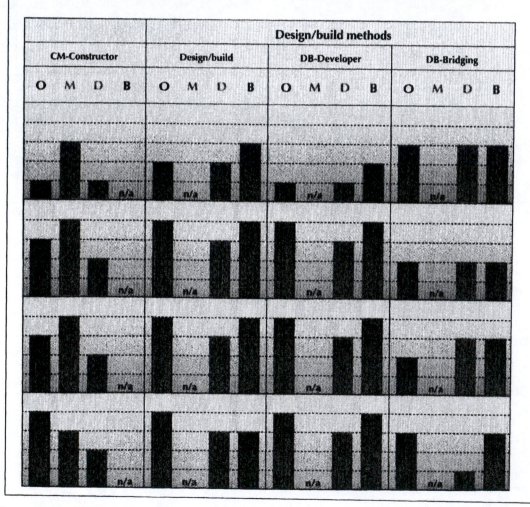

Figure 1–29 (continued)

customers, and to position themselves to address a wider range of work. By having the flexibility to use any delivery system, the organization offers any client a choice of systems from which the client can pick and choose; this is a marketing as well as a business direction.

Fundamentally the systems are quite similar in that the project work still must be accomplished in its proper scenario—it is only the contractual arrangement that really changes. By offering such a variety, a construction organization can maintain a larger workforce and retain a larger backlog of projects. This, in turn, can yield greater profits. Appendix G contains a listing of design, construction, and construction management firms (top ranked by *Engineering News Record* magazine). Note the number of firms listed in more than one category.

The owner has the ability and the right to hire the contractors in any way he or she pleases. The owner can assign work to one person or to a series of persons or firms, depending on what the owner feels will produce the best project for the money. Often owners have friends they wish to have perform a portion of the work. Others desire an open, free-wheeling competitive bidding process, seeking the lowest possible cost for the work. The methods that the owner can use are quite varied, and can be further adapted to the owner's specific needs. The system noting how the construction contracts are to be awarded is called the project delivery system. This is to say that using the stated system will "deliver" the finished project to the owner in the desired manner. As shown in Figure 1–29, numerous arrangements can be made for project delivery systems. No one set system is "right" for every owner and project. Many times, the choice is a matter of legal considerations, rather than technical or construction aspects.

Additionally, owners have found that the traditional system of construction, called design/bid/build, has proven unsatisfactory in several ways. While in 1999 it remains the predominant system used in projects, other systems are becoming more popular with owners. One system, called design/build, is growing rapidly and may well become the system of choice shortly in the new century.

For a long time, the perception has been that the best configuration of contracts for the owner is one in which there are four primary contracts: general construction, plumbing, heating-ventilating-air conditioning, and electrical. To set each of these up, there can be a period of vigorous competitive bidding. Contractors of similar expertise compete against each other to ascertain who is willing to execute the necessary work at the lowest cost to the owner.

It is obvious that the work could be further subdivided, with additional contracts. However, the easiest separation of work is as noted above, with the four primary trade divisions and their separate contracts. In some cases, owners have seen fit to have the general contractor (GC) oversee, administer, or completely incorporate the mechanical trades. However, usually a cost differential will result: the GC will require added payment for the added work. Also, there could be less than fully competitive pricing, whereby the owner is presented with a higher than necessary cost.

Some owners attribute similar concerns to the design/build (D/B) scenario. They are fearful of having their entire project in the hands of one firm without some other input. They feel the construction interests may unduly influence the design process to the detriment of the entire project, and add unseen cost to the owner and perhaps lesser quality. Of course, those engaged in D/B will challenge such accusations, but owners must balance the charm of single responsibility against the level of confidence in and acquiescence to the contractor's perspective that D/B entails. The D/B firm "packages" the project, fixing its price on the interpretations made about the owner's desires. Within the home building industry, this is exactly the scenario whereby new homeowners find that they do not always receive the house they thought they would be getting. Needless to say, professionalism and high ethics still exist in most instances, but a small minority of lesser-committed contractors are still at work, but not easily spotted.

Some would have you believe that the design/build project delivery system is taking the industry by storm, and in short order the other systems will be passé and falling into disuse. Their enthusiasm has a verve about it that is disquieting in that what is being said is not wholly true. But the talk is hard-sell, loud, and presumptuous to the point of overwhelming the listener.

A high level of intense discussion swirls about project delivery systems and the advantages and disadvantages of each. Design/build having found radically new life, and captured the eye of many owners, is widely discussed, being portrayed as the coming system for the majority of projects and the sole system that pleases certain clients. Still, this system services somewhat less than half of the total number of projects in the United States (Figure 1–30) and has been the topic of articles that have not been complimentary. Reason would say that it is appropriate when it best serves the client, and not when someone other than the client makes the choice. Many portray D/B as the new miracle system and solution to all construction ills. But it is not new, and surely is not a miracle. These speakers are high-profile, high-intensity activists out of the construction management contingent of the industry. Many would have all other systems eliminated, and blindly give D/B the hard sell, which is most unfortunate. The best results are achieved through a studious and appropriate matching of client, project, and system.

It is in the best interest of students and young professionals to become aware of, to seek out information about, and to fully understand how each system works, to know its attributes and limitations which impact the owner and the owner's desires for the project. With any system, an appropriate use exists, and there are places where a particular system is simply not what is needed. Therein lies the reason for the multitude of delivery systems we have available to us. The best

Figure 1–30 Delivery system: completed projects.

	Design/Bid/Build	Design/Build	Construction Management
Architects	72%	10%	14%
Architect/Engineers	70%	13%	13%
Construction Managers	26%	20%	27%
Contractors	19%	27%	36%
Engineers	63%	21%	9%
Engineer/Architects	80%	14%	4%
Specialty Contractors	37%	30%	6%

and most reliable information is set out by those who can stand back a little from the system and assess the program, based on their experiences. These are not partisans caught up in the zealous enthusiasm over one system. No other system currently has the open drive and organized direction that design/build does. At least one separate organization is dedicated full-time and solely to the promotion of this program, with the strong backing of many construction management firms, personnel, and instructors. The following articles provide good insight into different aspects of this subject:

"Architectural Decision Making in Design Build," *CSI Construction Specifier,* June, 1999

"The Heyday of Design-Build," *CSI Construction Specifier,* April, 1999

"Seven Steps to Project Success," *CSI Construction Specifier,* May, 1999

As discussed earlier, at least as far back as 2000 BC, a method of building projects has been in existence wherein a single person or firm was hired by the owner and made responsible for both the design of the project and its construction. It is fair to assume that much of the construction since that time must have been accomplished in a format now known formally as design/build. Obviously, in the past it was common for an owner to contact a contractor for the work. This entailed everything from ascertaining what to build to the actual erecting of the structure. Where the requirements of the project were reasonably limited, the contractor through past experience could produce the necessary drawings, to at least minimal specifications, could receive a permit, and so forth, and after this, the actual construction work would follow. For the most part this was a simple, direct method, wherein the owner dealt with just one person, who assumed responsibility for any failures or problems. Perhaps this process devolved from the simpler way of life, void of the nuances and changes that have come to bear down through history. Basically, other delivery systems have been developed to support the need for something additional to or different from design/build. This development, however, is not to the discredit of design/build; rather it reflects differing owner attitudes, and other circumstances.

Over the last 15 years or so, the design/build system of executing projects has been gaining in popularity and use. Primary among the reasons for this is the increased influence of construction managers and other construction-oriented personnel. This trend has emerged because many design professionals, working under traditional design/bid/build systems, have not, for various reasons, always followed through in a careful and diligent manner to ensure that the work was done correctly, on time, and within budget. These professionals were not responsible for highly developed cost estimates (as used in contracting), and also found themselves in a very chaotic situation regarding their legal liability. The construction phase of work elevates the professionals' liability to such a degree that many professionals simply stopped doing field observation of the work in progress, certification of pay requests, and other job site activities. This led directly to a loss of control over the project.

In addition, with restricted budgets and tight schedules, often project documentation was shortchanged to the point that documents were not complete, were left unchecked (for errors), and were bid without adequate time for proper assessment. All this, too, elevated professional liability. But doing these prudent things added to client irritation, when the project was not ready for construction promptly. Much then was left to on-site resolution and decision making. With the various consultants, contractors, suppliers, and subcontractors involved, problem solving often was confusing, irritating, and time consuming. Further, it was extremely difficult to pin down responsibility since so many "players" were involved. As budget has become an increasingly important factor in projects, owners desired a more expeditious process. Single-point responsibility, via design/build provides that, despite what some see as lingering negative aspects.

Among these is the status of the design professional, legally. Formerly an unbiased, interested third party, there now is no such party on the project. Also, it is still unclear how the responsibilities set out in professional registration laws impact professionals in a position of employment with a contractor; the loss is that the professional's word is not final, and may not be what the client truly desires. The lack of a third party in the entire construction process, who can assess and even resolve disputes and other situations evenhandedly, oftentimes set the D/B contractor and the client in direct conflict. Even the informed owner/client can have very difficult choices.

With the increase in the number of D/B projects, it may well become the delivery system of choice in the very near future. At this time, wide-ranging discussion and some controversy continues over the system. Some owners find it bothersome in one way or another; others find it the answer to all of their construction problems. In addition, there are still some lingering legal questions as to the role of a design professional who is really an employee of a contracting firm, dealing with how the professional liability and responsibility issues should be fashioned and resolved. One professional group is studying a new "value-based" delivery system, which focuses on the protection of the design professional's independence in the design/build scheme. In addition, some jurisdictions have enacted "seal laws." These require production of construction documents by registered design professionals in order for the building permit to be issued. This forestalls document production by nonregistered persons, who may be experienced and knowledgeable, but do not have the professional credentials.

Doubtless design/build has been resurgent and has increased in favor, mainly because it places the control and responsibility for both design and construction under one entity. With D/B, the owner now can feel more involved and in charge of the project, since there is but one place to look for resolution of any problem, and one place to exert pressure regarding cost and budget problems.

> One must never rest from one's obligation to see that the work is being carried out correctly.
>
> J. Ronald Williams
> Registered Architect

Construction management is another system that was formulated and has come to the fore over the last 25–30 years. The construction management delivery system has project responsibility split between the design professional and the construction manager (CM). Here the CM is placed under a separate contract with the owner to give added input to design (in some cases), construction, materials, systems, bidding, pricing, budgeting, and oversight of construction. This is in addition to much of the same work done by the design professional, who is under separate contract with the owner (usually there is no contractual relationship between design professional and the CM). As a contractual agent of the owner, the CM usually is strictly a manager who could motivate and interface with all parties, so the project was refined as it progressed through its various work phases. The CM was a "third-party" whose eyes and expertise could make the project better, from the owner's viewpoint. Additionally there is a semblance of neutrality, in that the CM quite often does none of the actual construction work, but rather acts exclusively in

an advisory, administrative, reviewing, coordinating, expediting, facilitating role. The bottom line is that the owner can feel more in control of the project and has another unbiased voice to address the project's various situations.

In summary, for the most part the owner is not overly interested in, and often is unaware of, the technical execution of the project, i.e., what materials are used, how they are incorporated into the work, who does what work, and so forth. Rather, the owner's interest is in the overall aspect of the project—that it was completed on the date expected; stayed within budget, had minimal problems, extras and claims; and met the desires and needs as ascertained in the first phase of the project. So construction projects today are highly managed on matters other than the technical design and execution. This is a drastic change from bygone days. Money is the key point now, and every construction professional is being challenged as to how costs can be reduced on jobs while still maintaining the quality, safety, and correctness of the construction. In the end, though, it is the owner who has the choice of delivery system, be it CM, D/B, design/bid/build, or one of the other related systems.

THE TEAM

One of the most crucial aspects of construction is creation of the team for the project. This creation is so vital that the methods used for doing this have been formalized and studied. To achieve a successful team, there must be a coming together of many divergent parties, each having a distinct set of qualities, skills, and knowledge required by the project. Also, each has a distinctive perspective on their work. Whether through the traditional general contractor (GC) or the more recently developed construction manager (CM) system, these parties must be aligned, motivated, and directed in a manner that faithfully executes the project in accord with the owner's requirements (see Figure 1–31).

While some team members may have worked together on previous projects, more frequently all parties are new, and really do not know what to expect from each other. This can be a very tenuous situation, but one that the GC or CM must control. Success here relates back, directly, to the application of the technology program that is established and should be properly used by all contractual parties for both their specific work and the project work overall. It is in this application that the team receives its major impetus, cohesiveness, direction, and focus.

Consider the differences between some of the design/construction team, other than the owner. Owners, of course, come in many sizes and configurations, and with quite diverse perspectives and needs, regarding their projects. Their ultimate goal is a successful project, no matter what its peculiarities may be.

Taking design professionals, construction managers, and contractors as a group, the differences between each subgroup

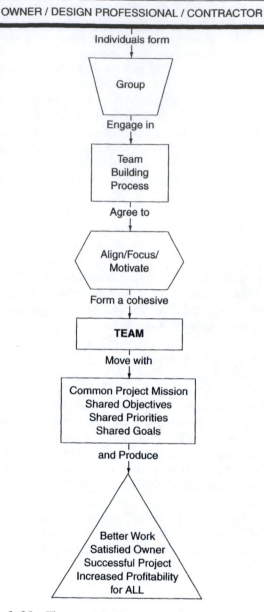

Figure 1–31   The construction team.

cost, and quality; techniques need to be employed within the framework of a knowledgeable background to best utilize the materials and systems that will work for this particular project, and best satisfy the needs of the owner. Overall, design is a process which transforms the ideas, needs, and desires of the owner and the mandated regulatory provisions from mental and written material into the reality of construction; the results are the "instruction" as to what to build, and how.

In addition the design professionals are tested and registered by the states, and carry the onus of liability for the design in a manner that protects public health, safety and welfare—no other party on the project carries this burden.

- *Contractors* bring the hands-on skills that are required to execute the "instructions" of the design professionals in the actual construction and building of the project. Usually this involves a series of subcontractors each dedicated to specific portions of the project, or to narrow-scope areas of work such as bricklaying or electrical. The contracting company oversees the entire construction process and is responsible for acquiring the correct personnel, as well as the required materials and systems, and bringing these together for the construction work. This involves not only work skills, but management, timing, staff resourcing, ordering, and traffic management of the products, and attention that ensures the work is done in a manner that meets the budget allocated to that area of the work.

  Whereas the work of the design professionals is more cerebral or mental, the contractor's work is physical, hands-on at the site, and managerial (personnel and accounting work) in the office. Even at the site there is a mental aspect in knowing what must be done and how.

- *Construction managers* usually have a background and experience in the field of the design professions or in the contracting business. Each background brings helpful and unique input to the process. In having been active in one area or the other, the CM can more easily assess what works and does not work, and can add this seasoned perspective to the current work of both the design professional and contractor. Design features that are risky, inadequate, or otherwise inappropriate can be exposed and resolved. Construction details, systems, and materials that will not well serve the project can be eliminated. Further, time-consuming work can be adjusted to produce more effective and less costly methods.

While each subgroup brings a slightly different "set of tools" to the project, they are vital to each other—complementary and supplementary, adding, supporting, informing and in general helping the others to do their work better and in tune with the project requirements. Just as the brain gets a message from the eye that there is a small foreign object in the eye, and then tells the finger to remove the object, so this

are marked, and often are the source of some of the nuances in the progress of the project. These differences, ideally, are respected and are utilized to bring out the expertise of each. No one subgroup should try to be just like the two others, but rather should contribute to the project the best resources and experience they have available.

For a moment let's look at what each subgroup brings to the project.

- *Design professionals* are educated and trained in programming projects, and in the various techniques for designing and documenting the project in a manner that brings the solution required by the owner. This, of course, is all done in the best possible sequence of scope, work is coordinated. Each part of the human body has special functions in itself, but the best work is done when the parts act in unison, contributing their unique function to the task. When this happens, there is an immediate effect of team and teamwork, which certainly should assist on a construction project. Differences in training, skill, capacity and inclination are irrelevant, individually; when combined, they can produce quality, beauty, and exceptionally good results.

One excellent way to aid the formation of the team is through a preconstruction conference, in which the inner workings, communications network, administrative matters, and the literal ground rules for the project are conveyed. In this way, everyone comes to understand the mutual needs of the team members and to follow established protocols. There is no room for any renegade performance, no matter how singular the talent, skill, or knowledge of that player may be. Attitude plays an important part in the creation of the team concept. It unifies or destroys. Only where understanding, cooperation, and mutual determination to create a quality project are present will the team function as it should.

Every participant must understand not only his or her position and relationship to the project effort, but also the contributions of the others. No one can claim knowledge of every part of the project; in concert, however, the combined knowledge produces a profitable project. Most important is the presence of mutual respect between worker and contractor, and between design professionals and constructors. There needs to be a clear understanding of who can and does do what, and who cannot. (See Figure 1–32.)

Design professionals serve a separate function. They are required to include certain information and restrictions in their documents. By doing so, they are not fostering an adversarial relationship with the construction personnel. Rather, they have a legal professional charge to set the parameters of the work and to fully and clearly explain what is to be done and how. Specifications and drawings establish the project scope and indicate the standards of performance that are required. This is no more threatening to the construction personnel than umpires discussing the ground rules at the ballpark. It merely sets out how the project will be executed.

These two differing attitudes and levels of understanding are fundamental to a successful construction project team. There is no competition; there is no attempt to undermine or create adversity for one another. Every participant, and indeed the project itself, will benefit from the harmonious atmosphere produced by the team concept. Productivity will increase, as will pride, self-esteem, quality of work, meeting schedules and budgets—and profitability.

Mutual respect is the key issue within the team. No one is better than anyone else. All are needed, bringing their particular skills and knowledge to be combined into an effective team fully capable of producing a successful project.

The owner is also a vital member of the team. Owner input is invaluable to the progress of the team and its project. By facilitating information, payment, and other administrative aspects of the project, owners can greatly influence and set a tone for the others to follow within their particular work.

Weekly job meetings facilitate the team effort. Here, all parties convene and openly discuss issues or problems that have developed. Here, too, the team can adapt and change its intention or schedule to meet the changing needs of the project. Many situations evolve through no fault of the team. They develop through actions or inaction of others, acts of God, strikes, delayed shipments, misroutings, ineffective communications, damaged products, and so on. Each team member needs to make an extra effort to alleviate, if not eliminate, as many of these situations as possible. When any party goes awry, there may be a need to "take that party to the wood shed," and get them back on the team as a fully productive partner.

The ultimate goal of the team is a successful project. That means on-time completion, that is on or under budget, profitable to all parties, and satisfactory to the client, in short, an effort that is rewarding and pleasurable to every member.

Figure 1–32 Understanding who does what.

	Architects	Contractors
Actions	Reasonable; prudent	Performance guaranteed
Status	Agent of owner	Primarily a vendor
Legal focus	Decision making process	Final results
Effort	"Endeavor to"	"Will achieve"
Others	Retain consultants	Hire subcontractors
Direction	Provide services	Do work
Evaluation	Performance based on meeting standard of care	Performance based on a no-fault standard; sole issue is comformance

All parties on a project need to fully understand the differing legal parameters within which design professionals and construction professionals act. The chart summarizes some of the fundamental differences. Each set of professionals must respond to the project's needs with variant solutions, while still ensuring that they fulfill their legal and contractual obligations required by the project. Often, without such an understanding, difficulties arise on the project. They are unnecessary if the professionals and others are familiar with and respect the circumstances surrounding the other parties.

Animosity, anger, pique, claims, litigation, or other such negatives have no place among the team. Every problem is solvable if the members cooperate and if management principles are correctly applied.

The owner is advised to create an atmosphere in which the team members will be willing to participate and give their best effort. The team's success will come much more promptly and satisfactorily when there is a feeling that all are giving their best. Even though the owner may not be fully acquainted with all of the technical aspects of the project, she or he can still encourage, and foster the team effort and individual contributions to it. More than ever now, the owner, in consultation with the design professionals, the construction manager, and the general contractor (if used), can directly influence the work of the team. Using alternative delivery systems (ADS) the owner can require contractual arrangements which function best for the project. (Chapter 3 will provide a fuller discussion and illustrations of ADS.) By creating a distinct configuration, team members can be obligated to perform their work in clear, unambiguous, and directed terms.

The construction team is not that much different from other teams. Divergent parties come together, bringing divergent attitudes, prejudices, and relationships. These all need to be molded into a single entity that works in harmony for the common good and success. The peculiar aspect of construction is that a team's success—the project—is then handed over to another. However, "a job well done," at a profit to everyone, is the lifeblood of all the businesses concerned.

RESOURCES—THE FUTURE

The outlook for the industry, the level of productivity, the proper utilization of the team concept, and other aspects have improved with both private industry and the federal government. The National Institute of Standards and Technology (an agency of the U.S. Department of Commerce) has produced a number of reports that attempt to set a series of goals for the construction industry in this country. The federal strategy aimed at supporting the construction industry touches on research, development, and deployment. This is all contained in the report, *Construction and Building: Federal Research and Development in Support of the U.S. Construction Industry,* published by the Institute. From this and additional subcommittee work has come a set of goals which the industry has embraced (see article and comments in Figure 1–33).

Another effort mentioned in the report notes the work and achievements of the Construction Industry Institute (CII). This is a 15-year-old organization made up of contractors and owners, who strive to develop a more cost-effective construction industry and process. CII is heavily involved in research directed toward a more competitive global construction industry through cost reduction, foreshortened delivery times, and improvement in project quality and safety of personnel. An extensive array of written and taped products reflect the research and provide direction for those seeking to participate in the betterment effort, mainly for heavy and industrial construction efforts. For information, contact

Construction Industry Institute
The University of Texas at Austin
3208 Red River Street—Suite 300
Austin, TX 78705-2650
Phone (512) 471-4319; Fax (512) 499-8101

In another effort endorsed by The Business Roundtable, the National Center for Construction Education and Research (NCCER) is dedicated to improving the construction industry. The Center's concentration is on craft training, management and leadership, safety training, research for increased productivity, and how these impact and improve the image of the industry.

The NCCER effort in affiliation with the University of Florida is responding to federal government studies that have found that the industry is aging (the average worker's age is approaching 50). Studies indicate that nearly one-quarter million new workers must be attracted and trained each year. The Center has been tracking labor shortages, by craft, to ascertain where new personnel and training are required. Starting in 1991, NCCER combined the varied training programs of some 5 crafts into one standardized curriculum, to foster universality and flexibility/mobility for workers. In 1993 they expanded this effort to 16 craft programs.

Over 20 major associations in the industry and major construction firms and organizations are supporting this program. Its endowment is ahead of a programmed goal, enabling it to make significant headway in working with school districts and other outlets for its programs, curriculum, and direction. Contact

National Center for Construction Education and Research
P.O. Box 141104, Gainesville, FL 32614
Phone (352) 334-0911; Fax (352) 334-0932

The size of the construction industry is but one aspect that needs to be considered. To understand it better, one should consider not only the number, but also the types of people involved in a project, the subject of the next chapter. Their unique contributions are obvious to the progression of a project through various phases of work, from initial idea to finished structure, the subject of Chapter 3. Construction projects, no matter how massive or small, how elegant or plain, how complex or simple, are made by piecing together smaller elements—devices, materials, and systems. Multitudes of very talented and professional people must work together or nothing meaningful can result.

All of this effort is directed toward just one end—filling the needs of the local community. Construction has been and will continue to be fundamental to the progress of society. The basic task has always been the same—filling the needs of people. The industry today is much more far-reaching, far

Industry Comments on the NCG

At the American Institute of Architects headquarters in Washington, DC on July 16, 1996, the National Institute of Building Sciences (NIBS) held a day-long workshop on the federal government's announced national construction goals. The meeting was initiated by the Subcommittee on Construction and Building of the Committee on Civilian Industrial Technology of the National Science and Technology Council. The meeting resulted from requests for NIBS to convene a workshop involving representatives from industry and commercial sectors of the construction field to discuss specifically what actions need to be taken to achieve the goals and who should carry them out.

The participants, from both the industry and commercial sectors, considered what actions need to be taken to achieve the goals through research and development and technological innovation, as well as how government fits into the scenario. Eventually, the focus shifted to the goals evolved into the total building process.

The secretariat of the National Science and Technology Council's subcommittee on construction and building, Andrew J. Fowell, stated, "I do not see this effort resulting in a lot of new funding becoming available to the building industry. Rather, the findings of these discussions will help it better focus the research that is needed today."

Fowell then addressed the common attitudes toward the goals as overly ambitious: "Perhaps some of the national construction goals are too low." He punctuated his point by relaying the success of the Construction Industry Institute (CII). CII has actively attempted to reduce injuries on the job. It achieved its goal and CII has a record of one-seventh the national average. Fowell then stated that the goals can be achieved without an increase in cost to construction.

All of the goals were discussed and several comments were made for each goal and how to achieve them.

The National Construction Goals

by Steve Cardamone
BOCA Staff Writer

The National Institute of Standards and Technology (NIST), a U.S. Commerce Department agency, has issued a series of reports which attempt to establish a sense of direction regarding goals for the construction industry in the United States. Construction and Building: Federal Research and Development in Support of the U.S. Construction Industry outlines a federal strategy for research, development and deployment in support of the "industries of construction." This report was developed with industry by the Construction and Building Subcommittee of the National Science and Technology Council's Committee on Civilian Industrial Technology. The subcommittee envisions a competitive U.S. industry, producing high-quality, efficient, sustainable and hazard-resistant constructed facilities. Goals for better constructed facilities and improved health and safety of construction workers are proposed. These proposed goals have been endorsed by the industry as national construction goals. The strategy for reaching the goals requires the involvement of sectors of the construction industry.

Background

The National Science and Technology Council (NSTC) coordinates research and development strategies across a broad cross section of public and private interests. NSTC has established nine research and development committees, including the Committee on Civilian Industrial Technology (CCIT), to collaborate with the private sector in developing a comprehensive national technology policy. The purpose of CCIT is to enhance the international competitiveness of U.S. industry through federal technology policies and programs. The Subcommittee on Construction and Building (C&B) of CCIT coordinates and defines priorities for federal research, development and deployment related to the industries that produce, operate and maintain constructed facilities, including buildings and infrastructure. Coordination efforts involve 16 federal agencies.

National Construction Goals:

The C&B subcommittee has studied research priorities expressed by the construction industry in forums and in a variety of proposals for the Advanced Technology Program of the Department of Commerce. Two priority agendas — better constructed facilities and health and safety of the construction workforce — were defined for focus of research, development and deployment (RD&D) in the construction and building area. The C&B program plans to make technologies and practices capable of achieving these goals available for general use in the construction industry by the year 2003. The baseline for measuring progress against the goals will be today's business practices; however, measurement tools still need to be developed.

According to the report, long delivery times, waste and pollution, and illness and injury contribute substantially to unnecessary increases in the cost of construction. Achievement of the

Figure 1–33   Goals set for the construction industry, over the next few years. All of this is part of a concentrated effort to improve construction—not so much the actual work, as the workers' effort, productivity, better delivery systems, and projects finished on time and on budget, consistently. Copyright January 1997, Building Officials and Code Administrators International Incorporated, International Conference of Building Officials, and Southern Building Code Congress International. Reprinted with permission from *Codes Forum*, January/February 1997.

"national construction goals" is seen as a major factor in reducing construction cost and making housing more affordable. The goals for the C&B Program were defined as:

1. Better Constructed Facilities (by 2003)

50 percent reduction in delivery time.

50 percent reduction in operation, maintenance and energy costs.

30 percent increase in productivity and comfort.

50 percent fewer occupant-related illnesses and injuries.

50 percent less waste and pollution.

50 percent more durability and flexibility.

2. Health and Safety of Construction Workforce (by 2003)

50 Percent Reduction in Construction Work Illnesses and Injuries.

A second report entitled, White Papers Prepared For The White House — Construction Industry Workshop On National Construction Goals further describes the goals.

50-Percent Reduction in Delivery Time

For nonresidential construction, delivery times vary greatly, depending on the use, ownership, funding source, provider and location. The report alleges that the process can take many years and can be characterized by burdensome permits, legal wrangling, reviews and inspections.

The document Construction and Building: Federal Research and Development in Support of the U.S. Construction Industry elaborated, "Reduction in the time from the decision to construct a new facility to its readiness for service is vital to industrial competitiveness and project cost reduction. During the initial programming, design, procurement, construction and commissioning process, the need of the client for the facility is not being met; needs evolve over time so a facility long in delivery may be uncompetitive when it is finished; and the investments in producing the facili-

ty cannot be recouped until the facility is operational. The need for reduction in time to project completion is often stronger in the case of renovations and repairs of existing facilities because of interruption of ongoing business. Owners, users, designers and constructors are among the groups calling for technologies and practices reducing delivery time."

Residential construction, on the other hand, has a much shorter overall delivery time and has significantly less variability, although many constructors would point out that there are exceptions to this and that there is room for improvement. According to the study, a reduction in delivery cost at the contractor level has a high probability of being passed directly to the consumer, thereby, making housing more affordable.

Given the state of current technology, an ideal construction cycle-time goal for on-site builders is approximately 63 work days (88 calendar days) for a 2,000-square-foot house from foundation excavation through finishing work and presettlement. This goal is derived from a pilot NIST-cited study of best-practice construction cycle times of innovative, on-site home builders and modular housing manufacturers. A recommended ideal but realistic construction cycle-time goal for modular builders is 28 work days (42 calendar days), a 56-percent reduction in the number of work days required to site build the house under the most favorable conditions.

According to the study, innovative builders combined a variety of new process-oriented management techniques with innovative technology to overcome barriers to rapid construction. Best practice ranged from 58 to 88 work days, depending on the size of the house. For complex operations with multiple sites, innovative builders expedited operations by tracking operations, solving problems, and adjusting schedules daily instead of weekly. Expedited operations took advantage of computers and telephone and facsimile interconnection services, which automatically and instantaneously

50-Percent Reduction in Delivery Time

Nancy Wightman, representing the American Society of Interior Designers, commented that the amount of time clients take to make up their minds hinders the rest of the process, causing a domino effect. "Some clients think the other players in the building process can condense their work to meet virtually any deadline."

Jack Beck, representing the Enterprise Electric Company in Baltimore, commented, "What we really need is more 'common sense.' We know what to do, I can give you a long list of what we should do, but it just doesn't get done."

David L. Grumman of Grumman/Butkus Associates in Evanston, Illinois, held another view. "How often do you call a code official for help in interpreting a code and get one interpretation. Then, when you submit your application using that interpretation, you get another interpretation from another code official. And then again, later in the field, you get yet another interpretation? I'd like to see one interpretation and decision and the ability to make that decision stick."

50-Percent Reduction in Operation, Maintenance Costs and Energy Use

It was decided that the methods to accomplish this goal exist, but such methods have to be applied. A school system in Maryland instituted a program to accomplish this goal. As an incentive, half of the money saved was returned to the school to use at its own discretion.

30-Percent Increase in Comfort and Productivity

The participants agreed that over time the money saved due to increased productivity in a structure is significant. They also decided that this goal may be a tough sell to the public, so proper marketing of this concept is vital.

50-Percent Fewer Occupant-related Illness and Injuries

All agreed that a commitment should be made to achieve it and research is under way.

Figure 1–33 (continued)

50-Percent Less Waste and Pollution

Richard Eustis from the University of Maine stated, "We are still putting materials into buildings that we don't know how to dispose of, once it's time to take them out of the building."

Lloyd Siegel of the Office of Facilities Quality for the Department of Veterans Affairs added, "There should be some research into more economical packaging of construction materials."

50-Percent More Durability and Flexibility

Yale Stenzler, of the Maryland School Construction Program, stated, "I have a problem with the use of the word 'flexible.' We have people who want us to design and build school buildings today that can be converted into apartment buildings 25 or 30 years from now. I don't believe it's a good use of limited funds to include in today's new schools plumbing for bathrooms in potential future apartments which might never be built. Who knows what the needs for that school building will be in 25 to 30 years. And, even if the need was for apartments, the plumbing codes might be different 25 to 30 years from now."

50-Percent Reduction in Construction Workers' Illnesses and Injuries

As with goal number 4, participants agreed that a commitment should be made to achieve this goal and research is under way.

The information on the NIBS workshop came from the August 1996 issue of Building Sciences, *a publication of the National Institute of Building Sciences.*

updated project status. Other innovative practices included concurrent scheduling of activities; reduced "wasted time" or gaps between subcontractor activities; use of precoded purchase order systems and just-in-time procedures; and reliance on variance purchase orders to speed budgeting and purchase of materials for correcting variances.

Shorter cycle times were associated with improved quality and increased customer satisfaction which led to more customer referrals, an improved builder reputation and greater profitability. The elements which the C&B group says could make significant contributions in the near term toward this goal are: information systems, engineering software, construction methods, materials, construction equipment, project delivery system and standardization (including codes). The major barriers in accomplishing this goal are cited as institutional in nature — excessive regulations, complex risk management and lack of financial incentives for innovation.

According to the report, significant improvements can be made if the funding for research and development and the political will to address the regulatory and liability barriers appear soon. Otherwise the target date of 2003 is overly optimistic, the report says.

50-Percent Reduction in Operation, Maintenance Costs and Energy Use

This goal is equally applicable to residential and nonresidential construction. There are two observations regarding the elements of this goal. First, the costs for operation and maintenance and for energy vary significantly, even within regions. As such, goals should be geographically adjusted. Secondly, for existing facilities, significant reductions in energy consumption may come at the expense of increased life cycle and maintenance costs — because older, existing facilities need to be extensively refurbished to achieve significant energy savings and their useful life may not be long enough to recover this investment at a

reasonable rate of return.

The report further stated, "Operation and maintenance costs over the life of the facility usually exceed its first cost and may do so on an annualized cost basis. To the extent that prices for energy, water, sewage, waste, communications, taxes, insurance, fire safety, plant services, etc., represent costs to society in terms of resource consumption, operation and maintenance costs also reflect the environmental qualities of the constructed facility. Therefore, reductions in operation and maintenance and energy costs benefit the general public as well as the owners and users of the facility."

This goal is best divided into the two parts: for new construction, no change in goal; for existing facilities, 50-percent reduction in energy use. The report claims that both parts are achievable by the year 2003. Elements affecting this goal are: Information and real-time control systems; High-performance construction materials; Energy conservation technologies, e.g., solar, insulation, efficient appliances, lighting, etc.; Expert systems for maintenance; and condition assessment systems.

30-Percent Increase in Comfort and Productivity

The appropriateness of this goal will require more detailed analysis. Comfort is a characteristic that has many shades; measuring improvement will therefore be problematic. Also, it seems intuitively obvious that a person who is uncomfortable in his or her working environment will not be at peak productivity, but the corollary is not clear at all — i.e. an individual may be quite comfortable and quite nonproductive. There is no clear relationship between comfort and productivity in today's facilities, thereby making an incremental improvement a measurement challenge.

The report elaborated, "Industry and government studies have shown that the annual salary costs of the occupants of a commercial or institutional building are of the same order of magnitude as the capital cost of the build-

Figure 1-33 (continued)

ing. Indeed, the purpose of the building is to shelter and support the activities of its occupants. Improvement of the productivity of the occupants (or for an industrial facility, improvement of the productivity of the process housed by the facility) is the most important performance characteristic for most constructed facilities."

This goal is intended to address the productivity of the users or inhabitants of the constructed facility. The achievement of goal number one—a 50-percent reduction in delivery time—will require substantial improvement in construction productivity.

50-Percent Fewer Occupant-related Illnesses and Injuries

The report notes that, "Buildings are intended to shelter and support human activities, yet the environment and performance of buildings can contribute to illnesses and injuries for building users. Most of these occurrences are avoidable, suggesting that the goal is not sufficiently ambitious. Examples are avoidable injuries caused by fire or natural hazards, slips and falls, Legionnaires' disease from airborne bacteria, often associated with a workplace environment (sick building symptoms) and building damage or collapse from fire, earthquakes, or extreme winds. Sick building symptoms include irritation of eyes, nose and skin, headache and fatigue. If improvements in the quality of the indoor environment reduce days of productive work lost to sick days and impaired productivity, annual nationwide savings could reach billions of dollars." For example, the number of fire-related deaths in residential homes in 1993 comprised 80 percent of all such deaths in structures in the U.S.

Indoor air pollution is alleged to be a significant cause of occupational illnesses. Although causal relationships have not been articulated and accepted, the report points to what it sees as a direct relationship between complaints of indoor air pollution and occupant illness.

The elements which the C&B group says could make significant contributions in the near term toward this goal are developing technologies for heating, cooling, ventilation, humidity control, lighting, acoustics, etc., that provide a healthy and safe work, residential or recreational, environment.

50-Percent Less Waste and Pollution

Because they shelter and support most human activities, improved performance of constructed facilities would provide major opportunities to reduce waste and pollution at every step of the delivery process, from raw material extraction to final demolition and recycling of the shelter and its contents. Examples are reduced energy use and greenhouse gas emissions, and reduced water consumption and waste water production. The report claims that wastes and pollution also can be reduced in the construction process, and that construction wastes are currently estimated to require 20 to 30 percent of the volume of landfills.

There are several proposed elements that could aid in accomplishing this goal. First, provide information systems and decision support systems to provide real-time information on the waste and pollution implications of alternative materials, components, systems and practices for construction, operation, maintenance, renovation, demolition and waste recycling. Then dispense construction materials, components and systems that conserve resources over the life cycle, are adaptable to changes over time in users' needs and activities, and are suitable for recycling or re-use. Finally, provide technologies for heating, cooling, ventilation, humidity control, lighting, communication, water supply and waste handling and treatment, etc., that reduce production of wastes and pollutants.

50-Percent More Durability and Flexibility

Durability denotes the capability of the constructed facility to maintain (given appropriate maintenance) its

initial performance characteristics over the intended service life, and flexibility denotes the capability to adapt the constructed facilities to changes in use or users' needs. High durability and flexibility contribute strongly to the life cycle quality of constructed facilities since they usually must serve for many decades. However, they also contribute greatly to the first cost of the facility.

The report posits that two components that could aid in accomplishing more durability and flexibility: to provide automation in techniques for design, construction, operation and maintenance to improve durability, sense needs for maintenance or repair, and adapt the system for changed users' needs as well as supplying construction materials, components and systems that are durable and adaptable to changes over time in users' needs and activities.

50-Percent Reduction in Construction Workers' Illnesses and Injuries

According to the report, "A factor affecting international competitiveness is the cost of injuries and diseases among construction workers." Although the construction workforce represents about 10 percent of the nation's workforce, a NIST report estimates that the construction industry pays for about one-third of the nation's Workers' Compensation. Worker's Compensation insurance premiums range from 7 to 100 percent of payroll in the construction industry. Construction workers die as a result of work-related trauma at a rate that is three times the annual rate for workers in all other industry sectors (24.1 deaths per 100,000 construction workers, as compared to 7.9 deaths per 100,000 workers in all other industry sectors). Construction workers also experience a higher incidence of non-fatal injuries of varying severity than workers in other industries.

Figure 1–33 (continued)

To reduce construction workers' illnesses and injuries, the report suggested providing management practices, information systems and decision support systems characterizing workplace safety and health hazards and safe work practices. Also, utilizing automation to make equipment safer to operate and to reduce workforce exposure to hazardous environments and tasks as well as reducing vulnerability of incomplete and temporary structures to natural and manmade hazards such as wind, earthquake, fire and toxic substances. Finally, developing and implementing standards providing explicit attention to workforce safety performance for construction activities and equipment and for incomplete and temporary structures and equipment.

Current Goal Status

The National Construction Goals are just that—goals. Before they become prescribed rules of procedure for the construction industry at large, numerous questions remain. For example, how will the results be measured? Will they be enforceable? Can these goals be maintained indefinitely? If construction costs are reduced, will such savings actually be passed on to the consumer?

The success that the Construction Industry Institute achieved in reducing construction related industries is noteworthy, and a good start to meeting these objectives. However, it remains to be seen if all of the goals can be achieved on a national level.

Figure 1–33   (continued)

more complex and technical, but is still providing facilities for shelter, food, education, protection, transportation, and the manufacture of products for the betterment of humankind.

EXERCISES

The following activities can be used to enhance the text material and provide wider exposure to and understanding of construction.

Some portions of these items may be assigned as individual projects, but overall they are group projects that every class member can benefit from. *(No activity that requires going onto a construction site should be undertaken by a single individual, nor without prior notice and permission from the site manager; ensure full and proper safety measures in any event.)*

1. Tour a construction site to assess the work in place, the work processes being performed, the materials, and the overall layout and appearance of the site. Give an oral report to the class.

   It may be helpful to plan this for a lunch hour, or after work shuts down so as not to interfere with workers. (Do *not* trespass; an escort from the construction firm is recommended.)

   It would helpful to visit several sites to see projects of various sizes and at various stages of work (excavation, foundations, concreting, structural framing, exterior finishes, interior finishes, etc.).

2. Invite a person from a construction firm to attend and speak with the class. A helpful visual aid would be a sand table on which a construction project site could be laid out and various functions and arrangements reviewed.

3. Research construction projects close by, and in other cities. Solicit photos of the project, both after completion and in-progress. Use as illustrations for explanation and analysis in a group-authored report.

4. List cold-area and hot-area projects, high-area and low-area (undersea or underground) projects. List projects on solid ground/rock and those in the sea, or on isolation springs or launching pads (seismic and missile launchers). Collect articles and photos from various construction sources such as magazines, contractors, associations, and design professionals. Keep on file for the class.

The "Players" in Construction

The intent of the construction industry mirrors that of an individual project: production of a facility that meets the needs and wishes of the owner. Without the needs of owners, there is little impetus for construction—and hence no industry. Each individual and each community has a continuum of needs that in one way or another must be fulfilled or met by constructed projects. Not every family builds their own unique home, but each family does avail itself of community facilities that require planning, design, and construction. These structures range from schools and churches to stores, utility plants, fire stations, elderly housing, medical facilities, and so on. The need for construction—even in the worst of economic times—remains simply to allow the continued functioning of the community and each person therein.

Before exploring the process of constructing a project, it can be helpful to identify and discuss most of the people who could be involved in the project, their functions, and most importantly, their interrelationships.

The primary fact behind a construction project is simply that the owner has determined (using personal criteria) that a new structure is required. It might be a small residential room addition or remodeling or it could be a massive industrial, utility, or perhaps governmental facility. The owner needs help to bring the personal vision to reality. In that venture the owner needs designers of various skills and disciplines who can provide information about working relationships, placement of equipment and functions, and exactly how and with what the new project will be built. These professionals include architects, engineers of varied interests and abilities (electrical, mechanical, piping, structural, civil, etc.). In some states it is necessary that a registered design professional be engaged for the design of the facility. Through such "seal laws" the states endeavor to protect public health, safety, and welfare through quality design in construction.

The resulting design team, which is a combine formed by all the design personnel, then proceeds to work with the owner to ascertain exactly what the owner needs and wants, that is, what type of structure is involved and what it might look like. Once an overall design scheme is reached and is acceptable to all (primarily to the owner, who pays all the bills), the project must be documented. This entails converting design information and general schemes into a form that the various builders, contractors, workers, and suppliers can understand and directly apply to their portion of the project. This is a time of detail, exactness, specifics, and coordination; it is a direct bridge between a concept (the approved design "idea") and the actual construction.

For the actual construction work, the owner looks to a contractor or, more specifically, to a team of contractors, trained in particular tasks and work. This includes the necessary administrative and managerial personnel who will organize the project and see that it is run in a smooth, coherent manner. These people are brought together through a costing or pricing process: in some cases, the various contractors submit bids offering to do their portion of the work (including the management of it) for a certain price. The team is then put together, formed of the contractors whose bids are the lowest ones submitted.

Here again, some states have licensing programs for contractors. These require contractors to verify their fitness for the work through expertise, financial stability, and other criteria. Again, this is public protection; it ensures better quality and less controversy in the construction process.

In other cases, the overall project cost is negotiated. This is a process of discussing, explaining, and coming to an understanding of all of the work to be done, and ascertaining what the real cost should be. When all parties can agree on a figure, the contract can be written. Within this process, established or verifiable cost figures are used so that the process uses realistic and not phantom cost figures. This is important so the owner and contractors are not misled and find out later that the project cannot in fact be built for the price agreed upon.

In simple terms, the key entities in the construction project are the owner, design professional, construction manager

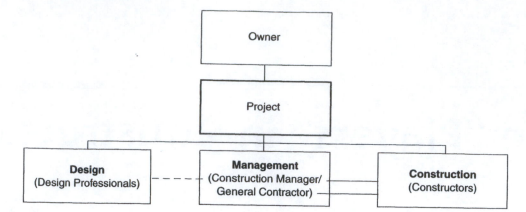

Figure 2–1 The primary participants in any construction can become four, depending on the owner's choice of delivery systems. Note in the chart that if the owner hires a construction manager, this person/firm will be active in both the design and the construction phase.

(if retained by the owner), and the constructor. Figure 2–1 charts the people who can be involved in a project. Figure 2–2, then, is a listing of those more directly involved on all projects, although this list is not all-inclusive. Each project attracts its own particular set of "players," who are appropriate to the type and size of the project, to the project delivery system being used, and to the overall composition of the project, from inception to completion.

This list is written in roughly chronological order, as the various players make their appearance on the scene of the project. However, again, each project has not only its cast of players, but also its contractual and schedule variations that can change how and when the players' appearances are made.

THE OWNER AND RELATED RESOURCES

The **Owner** is the individual or organization (of any business or contractual configuration) who is the instigator/initiator and ultimate buyer and possessor of the project. By virtue of these roles, the owner is totally responsible for the financing of the project, prior to, during, and subsequent to construction. It is also the person or firm who has identified the need(s) which could be resolved by a construction project (whether a new building, addition, and/or renovation of an existing facility). Usually the project owner is also the landowner who has direct and proper control of the site on which the project is to be located. In some cases the building owner merely leases the land, but has the legal authority, from the landowner, to build the project. In any event the "owner" (or jointly, owners) is the entity who holds bottom-line responsibility for compliance of the project with all applicable codes and regulations. This onus comes as part of ownership, and is often an aspect not apparent to the owner. It is a legal responsibility that the owner needs to know about

and, thus, should be told about. The local government in issuing a building permit will place the issue of compliance on the owner, since this is the person who will own, maintain, use, pay taxes on, and be in total responsible charge of the facility. This is, after all, the person or representative of the organization who will have a major impact on the concept and execution of the project, in every aspect, from start to finish. That includes the impact of the project on the community, initially and on-going. Ownership involves dedication of time over the term of the project, although not necessarily daily involvement. Often project decisions will rest with this person or organization, who must assess project decisions against the owner's concept or intention.

The owner is referred to as a **Client** when involved in the hiring of and relationship with legal, design, construction management, constructor, and other professionals. The words *owner* and *client* are often used interchangeably. Usually *client* is also applicable to the actual user of the project, such as the lessee or tenant of a single space in a shopping mall, or the owner/user/occupant of an isolated building or complex.

The **(Land) Developer,** in the main, is a speculator who purchases a tract of vacant land, installs (usually) the infrastructure and utilities, creates lots or sites (as owner or separate entity), and then offers such sites, or portions thereof, for further development through building construction. For example, a developer will purchase a tract of land, clear and grade it as necessary, install streets and utilities, and create a subdivision or commercial park. The individual lots/sites that are created are considered to be "undeveloped sites" which can then be sold to others for construction of their facilities. In many cases, the developer will offer an expanded service package by offering the sites on a "build to suit" basis, in which the developer will hire the professionals required to design and build a facility for the purchaser. The completed building and the land is either sold and turned over to the buyer or is leased out by the developer.

1. Concept Initiation	2. Design and Documentation	3. Bidding and Award	4. Construction and Contract Administration	5. Finale and Occupancy
building products mfr.; research and develop.; ad copy writers; sales reps; dealers and applicators	owner and staff; planners; architects; engineers; project mgrs.; schedulers; systems analyst; estimators; program developers; using agencies	clerks; news media; builders exchanges; bid depositories	project mgr.; contractors; building depts.; public relations; sign painters	owner/using agency reps; building mgr.; operating engineers
industry assoc.; code writers; building/zoning	consultants; architectural planners; designers; landscape; interior; artists; sculptors; civil; structural; HVAC; electrical; electronics; acoustical; millwork; hardware; roofing; waterproofing; painting; food service; elevator spec; drafters; spec writers; clerks, typists; computer support, editors	prime contractors; subcontractors; manufacturers; suppliers/vendors; installers; estimators; const. superintendent; boards; financiers; insurance writers; sureties; attorneys; notaries	subcontractors; purchasers; accountants; suppliers/vendors; shop supervisor; shop drafters; shop checkers	attorneys; witnesses; judge/jury; arbitration board; mediator; contractors; subcontractors; manufacturers; sureties
owner, owner staff; A/E staff; using agencies; legal counsel; boards; commissions; financiers; feasibility and budget; analysts; realtors; insurance underwriters	contractors; subcontractors; trade reps; manufacturers reps; technical support	owner staff; A/E staff; addenda writers; clerical support; clerks	job superintendent; trade leads; trade workers; shop drawing checkers; contract analyst; contract administrator; estimators; change order writers; inspectors (code/OSHA); testing labs; consultants; building mgr./operators	
private donors; grants; govt. agencies; general public; environmentalists; special interests; minority groups; procurement consultant		project mgrs.; bid analysts; boards/commission; attorneys; signatories; sureties; notary publics		

Figure 2–2   A listing of the many classification of persons who are active on or connected with a construction project.

User is a term with multiple meanings in the construction industry. It usually refers to the person or organization legally defined as lessee or tenant, who uses at least a portion of a project, but is not the owner of the entire complex. It also connotes the individual occupants or employees of the facility, who live or work within the building, and it can be made to include the public in general, who may visit or do business there.

Occupants are nontransient users. The term most frequently is applied to those who live or work in a facility. This contrasts with those who occasionally visit, or conduct business for relatively short periods of time. Often *occupant* is expanded to include guests in hotels or motels, and similar types of usage. The term is applied by many building and other codes to denote those who can be expected to be in or around buildings which the regulations control and safeguard.

A **Lessee** is a person or organization who gains the right of access to and use of a property/facility through a relatively long-term agreement, i.e., a lease, usually set forth in terms of years of use, and usually outlining parameters for use and maintenance, including periodic fee payments. Although now used for apartment and condominium units, the lease was primarily a commercial instrument for many years, because of the complexity of language, the rights conveyed, and other legal parameters. This instrument conveys no aspects of ownership, and hence places less responsibility for property development, maintenance, compliance, and so on.

Lessor, of course, is the person or organization (or agent for either) who is usually the owner of the property/facility offered for use to others, the lessees, on a long-term basis. The lessor would be the entity that receives the fee payments required by the lease, and provides those services and utilities provided in the lease agreement. Legally responsible for the property, the person is also the owner.

A **Renter** is one who gains access and use of property, through payment of a rental fee. Although similar in concept to a lease, a rental agreement (if written) is on a less formal basis than a lease. Mainly it involves a shorter-term process (rent a tool on a daily or weekly basis, rent a motel room for a weekend) than a lease. Oddly enough, such a person is often considered differently in some regulations, since their presence in a facility involves far less familiarity, and hence they could be placed in greater peril in an emergency situation.

Lender/Banker/Financier/Financial Institution/Mortgage Company/Insurance Company: This is an array of individuals and organizations that specialize in supplying money for the construction of projects. These may be banks, savings and loan institutions, mortgage companies, insurance companies, or private investors. Such financing can be done through interim financing (commonly called a "construction loan"), where payments are made at specific points throughout the progress of the construction, and then converted to and paid off as a mortgage. A straightforward mortgage could also be used, that makes one payment when the project is complete (common in home building). Money for project work as it progresses is supplied in advance by the builder or contractor who can borrow it for that purpose, or uses available funds for which the new owner makes repayment. In some cases contracts for supplies and subcontract work are written so payment will be made when the owner pays the contractor. Courts frequently frown on this practice. However, the flow of money for the project is a constant consideration. Since no one participant wants to be forced into an untenable situation, there are constant efforts to transfer financing to others. It is not uncommon for financing to be a major cost in the construction process. No matter what the source may be, there will be added interest costs.

Owner's Representatives are persons on the staff of the owner or hired separately to act in the owner's absence and to offer the owner's perspective in all matters. Usually this is a person with a design and construction background, who easily understands the project work, and can contribute the owner's perspective in a meaningful manner. Depending on the desires of the owner, this person either does or does not control or direct design and/or construction. Usually direction is for this person to evaluate and participate in the process and assess compliance with the contract documents. The primary function, then, is one of liaison, and of being a direct, easily accessible communications link to the owner. The separately hired person may be called clerk-of-the-works (see below), and be on the design professional's payroll (with full cost reimbursed by owner). If the person is a staffer of the owner, there may be other duties assigned within that organization. Usually though, the owner seeks more of a clerk-of-the-works presence which is available daily, in lieu of the staffer who is on a part-time, prescribed schedule for meetings, observations, and so forth. Whatever

the format, the person acts in regard to owner, much as the project representative does to the design professional.

THE DESIGN TEAM

The term **Design Professional** is a collective title which refers to a person (or firm) who has the education, training, experience, and other qualifications to meet the prevailing state laws which offer "registration" (a form of licensing) of professionals; more specifically it refers to architects and engineers. It usually involves passing an extensive written examination after the receipt of a college degree; also, a period of experience is required in all states of the United States (other foreign jurisdictions have similar requirements), prior to final registration. This also can be used to indicate the person who can take responsible charge of a project by applying the required registration seal and personal signature to contract documents, as required by the law. Once registered, the design professional may be required to take continuing education for registration renewal. Generally, though, the term indicates persons who have all of the necessary legal credentials to engage in their profession.

An **Architect** is a design professional whose primary role is the compilation and analysis of information for, and the creation of, a detailed design for the project to meet the specific needs and desires of the client. Best hired very early in the project, the architect's services involve work on the project during each phase, including but not limited to initial programming, site feasibility/selection, development of the design concept, and overall control and administration of the documentation and construction of a project. To act as the client's agent involves collecting information regarding the owner's needs and desires for the project, and the conversion of that information into data and drawings that are usable by the contractors, who build the project.

The architect is often characterized as "part engineer/part artist," educated and skilled in good engineering (in a somewhat limited manner—but understanding the various engineering systems), with the added responsibility of artistic considerations (i.e., aesthetics—the talent to make the project look pleasing, in addition to being correctly and substantially constructed). Some architects are dually trained, and perform final engineering designs as well as the architectural work. Still others are trained as both attorney and architect. The registered architect can function in many capacities, including code official, educator, corporate project manager, construction manager, and so on. The architect usually does not practice in a specific narrow specialty, such as structural engineering.

(Professional) Engineers are persons who are registered, similar to architects, according to state law for work, participation, and practice in one or more of the many fields of engineering; numerous areas of engineering are not, of course, construction oriented. Engineering covers a wide range of activities, but this discussion focuses on those persons educated, trained, tested and experienced in one or more aspects of engineering related to construction and building design. Civil, geotechnical, structural, electrical, consulting/mechanical (plumbing and HVAC work), acoustical, and the like are engineering disciplines used in building design. The work can be extremely involved, quite complex, and high profile, from building foundation design so as to withstand seismic conditions, to process and production equipment design and installations. The work is highly mathematical in nature, wherein analysis and calculation lead to conclusion and selection of members, designs, equipment, and systems appropriate to the required task. In construction, the engineered systems are either incorporated into the overall building design, or the building is designed to specifically enclose their functions.

A **Principal** is an individual, usually a registered design professional who is one of the primary owners and functionaries in a firm of design professionals, that is the person or one of several persons who have the final responsible charge of the work produced by the firm. This person's expertise may be architectural or engineering, but it lies in an area closely allied to the main orientation of the firm; the firm could be architectural/engineering or engineering/architectural. Depending on how the organization is structured, a principal is concerned with both the technical aspect of the work produced and the running of the business operations of the firm. He or she may function in a narrower area—marketing, document production, or contract administration, for example. Other principals in the firm would function in other allied but different areas of the practice for a coordinated, overall program. In small firms, of course, the principal may by necessity function in many roles, as the work and business demand.

Partner is the term denoting a party to a business operation wherein fiscal and technical responsibilities are shared between persons legally combined as partners. In many instances there is full equity between partners; in others, there can be a differential based on capital investment of the party (and amount garnered from firm profits) and the level of responsibility assumed. "Junior partners" often are brought in (made members of the firm) as a means of rewarding and elevating competent, experienced employees and as a means to smoothly perpetuate the firm. Basically, a partnership is a formal arrangement wherein the parties share fiscal, technical, and administrative responsibilities; they exercise their own particular expertise to the mutual benefit of the other partners and the success of the organization overall.

Often a person is promoted "from the ranks" and is given added authority in the firm's operations, with or without a capital investment. Their title of **Associate** is a means of identifying (1) second-level responsible members of the firm, (2) those in a higher administrative position, who can speak on behalf of the firm, and (3) those who have added technical expertise, and are capable of leading a design team in one or more aspects of work. It is another form of promotion to retain employees and reward those experienced with the firm, of high skill and ability, and with potential for even higher advancement (to partner, or perhaps even principal, at a later date). Usually associates are supervised by a principal, partner, or other owner, but also, quite often, they supervise staff members in project production and other work phases, for example, in the role of project architect, or job captain.

Sole Proprietors are single registered professionals who own and operate a business or professional practice, with no partners or others having a financial interest in the business. They may have backers, investors, or stockholders (if incorporated), but none who have an active part in the technical operations. Quite often such firms are an outgrowth of the professional's acquiring work while in the employ of others—perhaps as a sideline or while "moonlighting" projects. With enough backlog of such work, the person feels secure in opening a new firm. In most instances such firms thrive on smaller projects; they might have a limited number of very active clients who produce a continuous stream of work. The firm may expand with added employees as the number of projects increases, larger projects are commissioned, or deadline demands become so imposing that additional staff is required. Also, some firms appear to be sole proprietorships (signature name architects, for example) when in fact there are unnamed or "silent" partners or associates.

The term **Designer** can be applied as a short title for the design professional who develops the basic overall project design concept. This involves assimilating the programming input from the owner, client, regulatory agencies, and the like into a preliminary or schematic design. Quite often the designer will be active only in the early stages of a project, and will function as the design input on many or every project entering the office.

In some states, certain buildings may be designed by "designers" who are not registered design professionals; this is most obvious in the home building industry. Nonregistered persons may do design in professional offices, so long as they are supervised by a registered design professional. The designer assembles, assimilates, and accommodates all of the diverse information into a properly working and related overall scheme of operations for the owner/user. Then the task is to create the enclosure in which this scheme will be housed, including selection of forms and shapes, materials, and to some degree construction systems. The final design is a direction to the production staff as to what, exactly, the client is expecting, but in a general, overall perspective, lacking the minute (but necessary) detail required for actual construction. Quite often the designer plays a relatively small part in the project after the design concept is finalized, approved by the owner/client, and translated into the production and construction sequences.

Contractibility Manager: An individual, or team leader, with strong construction background who can act in a formal program as a "third-party assessor" in a project; usually on the staff of the design or design/build firm. This function is to seek improved or more appropriate project design, production, methods, materials, procedures, procurement, and costs, which can then be employed to produce a better project overall. Such a person is best utilized throughout the project sequence to assess each phase of work for optimal results. The individual also can serve as an aid and support for the entire design/construct team by offering and utilizing high-level expertise not common to others.

Drafter/CAD Operator/Designer are terms currently used as names in lieu of the traditional "draftsman." They represent a more accurate designation noting a rather generic title, and the equipment utilized. The term pertains to those who work with, and convert information supplied by the professionals. In keeping with the overall design concept, their work is incorporated into a set of working documents, suitable for use during construction. This may be an entry-level or more experienced person (even a registered professional) trained in operation of various computer software programs which aid production of contract documents. It is necessary to assign them an appropriate level of responsibility based on experience, technical knowledge, expertise acquired, and depth of contribution the individual can make to the project. The operator may also be trained in and capable of properly applying a limited amount of technical knowledge training (see *Technician* below for the opposite training sequence). In any case, the operator requires oversight, direction, and guidance of a design professional (or perhaps even a technician) for correct application of technology, proper display of the information, and a direct meaningful contribution to project production process. Most firms select employees in this classification only when they have a level of technical know-how which permits them to make a direct, sound, and substantial contribution. This is preferred in lieu of just a mere "parroting" of sketches—making accurate, CAD-produced drawings based on hand sketches from the project architect or other persons on higher levels than the drafter, but without being able to add any significant information to the drawing.

Cooperative (Co-op) Student: These are staffers who are usually college students enrolled in an academic program designed so the student cycles between periods (6–12 weeks is normal) of work and school. The work often is arranged by the school, and is usually in the field of academic concentration or one closely allied (not merely "working while in school"). It is not unusual for academic credit to be given for this work; at least separate acknowledgment is made. This program allows a student to gain meaningful and valuable experience, closely related to the profession or work status sought, while still engaged in education. The programs are noted for their graduation of "experienced graduates" who will assimilate to new employment and will develop as full contributors much quicker. The program was pioneered at the University of Cincinnati in the mid-1920s, in the College of Engineering and Architecture.

The **Specifications Writer** is usually a senior person or at least a highly experienced person in a firm, who is fully dedicated to production of project manuals and specifications.

More often a full-time assignment, this work or assignment can be part-time in smaller firms, or can be done by the project architect, in times of low levels of work. More often than not this person also maintains the firm's technical library and is the primary "investigator and evaluator" of new products, information from manufacturers, salespersons, and manufacturers' representatives. This work requires an experienced eye and full understanding of the legal as well as the technical construction information contained in specifications. In this way materials and systems can be selected with confidence and not by whim. Without this type of person carefully handling such activity, the firm is susceptible to faulty construction through indiscriminate, unsubstantiated selection of inadequate or untested materials that may fail or prove inappropriate.

Project Representative/Contract Administrator: These titles (which are interchangeable) denote the professional firm's on-site (field) representative. These persons may be full-time or part-time as required by the project, the firm's work load, and the client's desires. This staffer acts as close liaison between contractor(s) and the professional firm and staff. They convey information both ways, resolving problems which have no drastic impact on the design concept, observing the work in progress for compliance with contract documents, and assisting the professional in certifying the monthly payments to the contractor(s). The representative/administrator has no authority to supervise, direct, change, or stop the work itself. The person embodies the design professional on the site to facilitate the work and do problem solving that depends on input from the professional. A registered or unregistered (but highly experienced) person, knowledgeable about construction materials, methods, procedures, operations, activities, and of course the project itself, may be given this assignment.

The **Project Architect (Engineer)** or **Job Captain** is the individual member of the design professional's staff who is in charge of and responsible for the technical development of the project, including contract documents and construction. Usually this is an experienced, registered person, who also may be an associate in the firm or even a principal (depending on the size of the firm and the type of project). The project architect is responsible for taking the final approved design concept and seeing to its conversion into a fully detailed, properly specified set of technical documents. This conversion must be both faithful to the design concept and usable by the contractors. It must be in keeping with good construction and budget controls. This person will assign, direct, and supervise a team of staffers (of varying skill levels) who produce the documents. She or he also develops details, selects materials, coordinates with design and the specifications writer, establishes procedures and standards for the project, and provides both general and specific supervision over the production staff.

(Land) Surveyor: This is a person trained, qualified, and registered in the art of surveying and establishing land boundaries, and establishing grade (height) elevations, variations, and profiles. Also, the surveyor calculates mathematical "closures" around land areas to verify or establish correct dimensions and ownership. From this, surveyors or their staffs can create plats (maps/drawings) which depict the field operations and show the various aspects of the land area and surface. (See Figure 2–3.) The surveyor will research and show various utility lines, easements, and all other legal considerations concerning the property/land. The land area may be one lot, a parcel, a tract, or numerous adjacent tracts—as for the right-of-way of a highway. The surveyor may also serve as the layout engineer who physically establishes the building lines and other theoretical project parameters on the project site. They set permanent monuments and other surveying markers to indicate property lines and other aspects of the land area which impact the project, and indicate ongoing ownership.

Consultant (various disciplines): Persons or firms who specialize in a narrow aspect of a project are called consultants. Really this is a broad range of experts who are highly skilled in a limited area of technology valuable to a project (listing of consultants, Figure 2–4). Usually the consultant is hired by the owner directly, as an added contract, or by the design professional with the cost included in the whole fee structure, or as an added expense. Their term of work is usually for a limited amount of time, a portion of the project, or to specifically deal with resolving problems within their area of expertise. In many cases they are registered design professionals who have chosen to specialize in the one narrow field; others come simply with ample and appropriate experience in

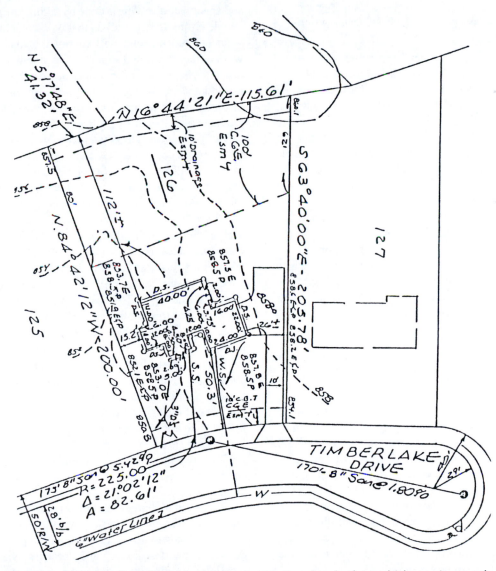

Figure 2–3 A survey plat for a typical residential lot. It is representative of such plats, which vary in complexity and size as necessitated by the actual land area and the features which serve the property. Note the number and locations of the legal encumbrances on the property—easements and the like.

Structural engineering	Behavioral science
Mechanical engineering	Life cycle analysis
Electrical engineering	Master planning
Civil engineering	Scheduling
Interior design	Development building
Landscape architecture	Energy conservation
Fire protection engineering	Food service
Construction manager	Fine arts
Value engineering	Graphics
Traffic engineering	Surveys
Acoustics	Codes and regulations
Lighting	Construction costs
Models/photos	Special equipment
Renderings	Computers
Process piping	Communication systems
Real estate	Audio/visual equipment
Facilities programming	Conveying systems
Geotechnical/soil investigation	Research/programming
Color	

Figure 2–4   An (incomplete) list of consultants that are available when necessary on a project. It is important to properly match expertise (via a consultant) with a project requirement, for optimum results.

their field. Good examples are structural/civil/mechanical (HVAC)/electrical engineering, acoustics, geotechnical/soils, traffic, food service, value engineering, color, A/V equipment, as well as signal and alarm systems.

More often than not, the efforts of the consultant are blended into the contract documents and made part of the overall design scheme—for example, the inclusion of prescribed, increased acoustical treatment as a part of the basic wall, floor, and ceiling construction. Some consultants may include their own specific drawings and specifications with the set of drawings and the project manual (plumbing, subsurface soil borings, HVAC, electrical, civil works, etc.).

THE CONTRACTING TEAM

Contractors are the persons or organizations that actually perform the construction work on the project. The term in its most common form is used to mean the traditional "General Contractor" who oversees the entire project work, may perform portions (called general construction work) of it, and hires and supervises the work of specialty subcontractors—see detailed definition below. The term can also be used to indicate huge corporations who both design and build. In a short form it can indicate any individual/person who is under contract to perform a portion of the work; in some cases, the term can include the design professionals.

A more current term, **Constructor,** means much the same as Contractor. It is thought to be a more accurate and descrip-

tive designation in that it refers to, and emphasizes "constructing" (building), and not so much to "contracting" (being party in a contract), which is an old generic term to describe the overall purview of the Contractor. No doubt the term is quite valid, but carries no meaningful change in responsibility, expertise, or legal status. The constructor has a different perspective of the project than that of the design professional, be it the professional architect or engineer. Both, of course, are seeking to make a profit through the work and services they provide to the owner through the project work. It is the route by which each proceeds wherein the difference lies.

By contract language and definition the constructor is responsible for the "methods and means of construction." The design professional is responsible for the overall concept, design, and documentation of the project. The constructor's effort must be in filling in the methodology used to execute the requirements of the contract documents, that is, the drawings and specifications. This is done by taking portions of the work and determining who will do that work, exactly how and with what equipment, who will supply the materials, when the work will be done, and so forth. The planning of the work site is just the beginning of this work and can be a tremendous aid or hindrance to the work. The placement of the tower crane, the location of contractors' storage areas, loading and unloading areas, location of office trailers, access roads (temporary or permanent) all play a part in this first function.

A general contractor (GC) must determine what portion of the work will be done by her or his own workforce and what other portions will be accomplished by subcontractors. During the initial bidding process (in a design/bid/build scenario) the GC will receive numerous bids from subcontractors who seek to do portions of the work. The GC must formulate the construction team of these contractors based on price, but also taking into account previous work done jointly and knowledge of the subs, including their financial status, work ethic, expertise, and so on. To ensure a maximum profit for all, the GC will seek to establish the team with compatible, skilled subs, who will work well together, coordinate their efforts, and meet all schedules and cost situations.

Often a single area of work will entail a number of subcontractors. The GC must ascertain the correct sequence of the work, while ensuring that no conflict is created between the work of the various trade subcontractors. For example, it is foolish to allow finish work to proceed before the building is covered, enclosed, and suitably heated. Many finishes are sensitive to damp and cold and will not perform as desired if conditions are not optimal, or as required by the product manufacturers.

Obviously the larger the project, the more critical the coordination of the work portions among the different contractors. This leads to added personnel on the GC staff to coordinate, expedite, order, and process various billings, schedules, product/material orders, and the like. Also, a larger size entails having the right array of subs on the project at the right time, working in the proper areas.

Within those areas of work, the GC, working with the appropriate subs, must determine what materials are required, what amount of each is necessary, if all of the material is required at one time, where excess can be stored until needed, and finally, just exactly how the work will be done. This is the key issue for all of the constructors. Despite complete and rather meticulous drawings and specifications, the design professional is not responsible for and does not show every minute item of the work. The documents show the overall concept for the work area, the configuration, and the materials required. They do not show, necessarily, all the detail of how connections are made, the sequence of installations, nor exactly how the work should be accomplished; this all being part of the "methods and means" of construction under the purview of the constructors.

The contractor generally is awarded the work after a successful competitive bid, and is then held responsible for executing the project in accord with the construction contract. In essence, this means to build the project as designed and depicted, for the amount of money agreed upon with the owner, and in the time frame established, to mutual satisfaction. How all this is done is the sole responsibility of the contractor.

The contractor's or subcontractor's **Project Manager** is an office staffer who coordinates all aspects of the work assigned or under contract. The person may handle more than one project at a time, depending on project size, complexity, and timing; doing so requires the ability to start a new project well before one in progress is complete. The manager schedules crews, adds/assigns staff, orders materials, and negotiates with suppliers and sub/subcontractors, to name just a few functions. The manager usually supervises the superintendent (or foreperson in the case of a subcontractor), and provides assistance by facilitating work process and flow. This also involves handling the "paper work" (general administration) aspect of the project work and in general supervising and running the project from the contractor's point of view. Also, this manager will attend monthly and other progress meetings and act for the contractor when necessary. They have authority to convene meetings with subcontractors when necessary for problem resolution or other coordination matters.

The contractor's primary on-site person, the **Superintendent,** has overall responsibility for the construction of the project. A small staff (1–3 persons) may assist with scheduling, cost control, and like duties where the project warrants. Ideally—and usually—the superintendent will not perform any actual construction (trade) work, but will oversee all work by all trades and coordinate the efforts of subcontractors. Basically the charge is to "run the job," and all that goes with that. Almost without exception this is a trade worker— primarily a highly experienced carpenter—who is trained to envision not only the project as a whole, but also the process that produces the project. She or he acts as the contractor's "eyes" on site (when the project has no construction manager), and will represent the contractor in meetings and communications; although somewhat limited in authority, the super can act and speak for the contractor to a large degree. This person works very closely with the contractor's project manager, to provide the full range of service required for administration of the project.

The **Foreperson** is an individual who is in direct charge of a work crew or of a subcontractor's entire workforce on the site. Usually an experienced worker in a single trade, this person can resolve problems with the work involved and assist workers in correct execution of tasks required by contract documents. The person has the know-how and expertise to adjust work as necessary to meet changed or unusual conditions encountered on the site, while still meeting the contract requirements. Also, the foreperson is responsible for coordination with other trades where their work interfaces, relies on, or supports work of the contractor. Through experience this person will fully understand all ramifications of the work assigned, everything about the materials being installed and how best to install them, and in general, how the work/installation fits into the overall project.

On the staff of the contractor, or more typically, the construction manager, may be a **Value Engineer.** This person seeks to identify unnecessary costs in both design and construction, and proposes alternative schemes or technology, without sacrificing project quality. Obviously this role requires a person who is well experienced with a broad knowledge of construction methods, materials, techniques, systems, equipment, capabilities, and other technology. The person could be considered as a major advocate for the contractor or manager, who is committed to providing the services outlined above. This person and work is best utilized prior to the start of the construction phase. As one of the preferred aspects of construction management, utilization of a value engineer early in the project's design sequence is becoming more common and is producing better project value and cost control.

The **Estimator** is one of the contractor's most trusted employees, whose task is to gather and maintain actual costs of work items, materials, and subcontractor bids and prices. Also, this person may track costs as they appear on each project. It is important for the contractor to have a reliable and wide-ranging set of actual prices and costs for various items of work. The estimator must know basic, individual prices for small "pieces" of work. These are called "unit prices" and include, for example, cost to excavate one cubic yard of rock material from a depth of 15 feet below grade. Other examples include not only the cost of a door, its frame, and its hardware, but the labor cost for the time it takes a carpenter to apply the hardware, and hang a single door. Changing wage rates, added benefits, or the normal upward rise of construction costs adjusts these prices, overall. Good estimating is necessary to properly establish both the reliable and anticipated cost of the door installation. The contractor relies on such information; the individual prices are then assembled with the many subbids, and formulated into the primary bid the contractor submits on a project. This pricing is most important to the contractor, so he or she can be confident that the work can be done as required, but also in a profitable manner. Consequently, the estimator must have a large number and wide range of resources and sources of materials, information, and cost data. All this must be tempered by an intelligent understanding of the construction work and process as it impacts cost, and vice versa.

In some cases contractors have separate staffers, **Expediters,** on the payroll who are specifically assigned to "make things happen." Such a person may absorb some duties performed by the project manager; this depends on the company and project size and type. The expeditor schedules crews, acts as traffic manager, schedules material deliveries, and coordinates operations with deliveries and crew availability. The fundamental goal is a formal and on-going program of bringing people and "things" together so work can be accomplished properly and quickly.

Construction Managers are part of a newer group of people in the construction industry. These are individuals or firms placed under separate contract with the owner to evaluate design approaches and contractibility and to provide value engineering and management on a project. This added oversight serves to bring better value to a project by identifying potential problem areas and offering alternative solutions. More and more this is seen to be a way to best utilize construction knowledge and information early in the project sequence, where work and recommendations can be incorporated at the proper stage of development, such as during the design phase. Primarily, it is aimed at injecting construction information to assist in creating more focused design, better cost efficiency, and documentation that is more appropriate to construction methods and procedures. Although construction management can take several forms (for fee, GPM, at risk, etc.), the firm usually will not perform any construction work, but will oversee all contractors—usually without contractual relationships, but other forms involve contracts. The CM may act as the owner's agent during construction, but also has an expeditor/coordinator role to facilitate every aspect of the project regarding cost, schedule, and prompt, successful completion.

The CM system has a wide and varied range of possibilities, and often is formulated in a manner specific to the needs or requirements of the owner. There is no single configuration for CM work; the owner can decide what set of contractual arrangements best suits his or her needs. However, the arrangement will set out the CM as the single point of responsibility.

As noted in Figure 2–5, the CM is active during the design and documentation processes and from the outset of the construction phase. The degree of involvement varies, as desired by the owner. For example, in the design sequence the CM can offer costs-comparison information, which helps to ease the decision making for systems and materials. Alternative construction methods can also be suggested. However, the CM is *not* the primary design professional, but acts as an

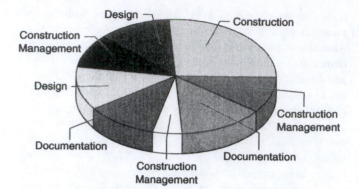

Figure 2–5 Construction management is used—and contributes heavily when utilized—within each phase of the project. Note, for example, that design work is conducted on both sides of management, to indicate that CM is an ongoing part of the design process. In the construction phase, CM work starts at the outset and continues throughout the project.

advisor who provides valuable insight into the design process. The hope is that design needs will be more easily ascertained, and design then will be truer to the budgetary needs and constraints, while still providing a satisfactory appearance and function to the owner. In late 1998, at least one state (Idaho) enacted a registration system for construction managers. Primarily aimed at publicly funded projects, this appears to be a trend. The criteria for such registration includes training, education, experience, and so forth. Further, the law sets out certain contract configurations and relationships that are required, so the public agencies have less discretion in how the CM will work on their projects.

Much the same interface occurs during documentation. Some cost impact data is helpful, and alternative construction methods, sequences, and details can enhance implementation of the basic and approved design. Here again, the CM is not the primary functionary, but rather serves in an advisory role, if that is what the client desires. Normally, this is not set out as a "policing" function or one that creates dissension among the professionals. Each has a role and an obligation to the owner. Their best effort is one that is fully coordinated, where professionals are respectful of each other. Differences will arise, but the final authority on the project's final conception is the owner.

Perhaps the most dramatic changes, in the scheme of construction management, occur during construction. There are several methods in which the CM can be established on the project, and variations of those methods. These were outlined in Figure 1–23 (along with other contract scenarios). The primary issue with CM in construction is whether or not the CM performs some of the construction work, has a contractual relationship with some or all of the contractors, or simply serves in an advisory, oversight, coordinating role with no contractual relationship to the various contractors. Again, the explicit form used depends on what the client desires and what the resulting contract obligations of the CM are.

It should be understood that this is another service that the owner has the option to utilize; construction management is *not* a replacement for the services of a design professional. The work of the design professional and the construction manager complement each other, interface for better coverage, and provide the owner with a different scenario for responsibility in the various phases of the project. There must be a full and continuous exchange of information between these parties to ensure that the project's direction is maintained and that progress is proper and consistent. In the main, owners will contract with both parties for complete overall project administration and improved project attributes.

Subcontractors are the individuals or organizations with expertise in one of the specific and narrow ranges of work required on the project (supplying and installing ceramic tile, for example). By concentrating their efforts in a narrow range of work and materials, these organizations become more expert and can perform with good speed and good quality work. In a sense, they "know a lot about a little bit". Usually a project team is an array of different subcontractors combined in their effort by being placed under contract by the general contractor (or construction manager), and not the owner. They are beholden to the general contractor for their work, payment, and a correct technical and administrative interface with others on the project. Their contract normally comes about through a competitive bidding process, wherein the subcontractor bids against others for the portion of the work. The contract is with the general contractor. The "sub" is under the administrative control of the GC as to schedule, direction, quality of work, interface with others, and so on. The general contractor makes periodic (usually monthly) payments for the subcontracted work done.

Worker is the general, all-inclusive term to describe those who have particular skills, education, training, and knowledge about specific types of construction work. This includes the employees of both the contractors and subcontractors. Although training and direction varies, trade unions prefer—and confine their effort and training to—single-task orientation. Other groups prefer cross-training in several tasks. Workers can usually function in many specific ways—for example, install framing for partitions, but not the drywall (which is installed by other workers), or (with cross-training) perform both functions with equal skill and success.

Tradesperson: Workers trained and skilled in a narrow-scope trade, usually involving a single or fairly limited range of materials or systems (glaziers for glass installations, carpenters for several building tasks, but not an extremely large range of work). These persons are well-versed and experienced in applying the best methods for installation of the material(s) or system(s) using the latest techniques and technology and their personal experience. They will usually have an in-depth understanding and working knowledge of all of the work they are to perform. In many instances the jurisdiction

of the trade has been established, primarily through a collective bargaining contract (bricklayers, electricians, carpenters, painters, tile setters, concrete finishers). Some in the industry advocate cross-training and multitasking, but in the large majority concentration is still on a single area of work.

The term **Journeyman,** as used by the unionized construction trades, indicates a worker (male or female) who has served a term of prescribed apprenticeship and has acquired requisite training, knowledge, skill, and a level of experience in the trade. This designation then is usually tied into the wage rate agreement and benefits package offered through the union contract with the construction industry. For the individual it is an indication of a level of expertise, which when coupled with years of experience denotes a well-skilled worker, as opposed to a novice.

Apprentice is the name and program which has been carried over from the historical system of a young person learning a trade in the shop, or working with a "guild" (early form of union) craftsman who was highly skilled and experienced in the work. Primarily a function of the construction trade unions, the program is the prime "feeder" into the trades of about 30,000 American apprentices in 1995; 75% were union. Of journeyman level workers in the unionized trades, between 75 and 99% are apprenticeship graduates; contrast this with 7–25% in non-union trades. It involves a progression of mentoring in physical work and a teaching/learning process of maintaining and carrying forth the quality work, skill, and reputation of the trade. This system remains today in a similar form in even non-union home building and professional situations (co-op students, for example). The major change is that the teaching/learning is a more formal and structured program; in many cases it is carried on in vocational, community college, or even full university programs. The apprentice now works during the day and attends classes in the evening or on weekends. Apprenticeship programs are usually regulated and controlled by the states. The period of time varies, but is usually in the range of 4 years. During that time the apprentice works, at a reduced rate, gaining insight and experience in the chosen trade.

Technicians appear in several different forms in the construction context. The designation involves two different groups of people. First, this is another name for worker in a specific area of work: that is, a mechanic or person doing repair or other work of adjusting, testing, or calibrating of an item of equipment (as opposed to the person who actually installs the piece). Secondly, in the design professions, the technician is a person trained perhaps to the associate degree level, who operates in a technical support role to a design professional. For example, a CAD designer who has a good level of technical knowledge as well as CAD skills, but who has not been educated or trained nor has the experience of a registered professional would be a technician. Oddly, the first group is usually trained to a higher and more technical level, to contend with all of the various systems that may be encountered in different equipment. The second group has been trained formally in an area that previously was confined to persons of high school education who trained through on-the-job training, rising in status as their skill level increased—for example, a young person hired as an entry-level drafter, who gradually gained expertise through on-the-job training (OJT).

Installer: This is a trained worker whose principal function is to locate, assemble as necessary, anchor, and adjust materials, equipment, or apparatus for full and proper functioning. The installer ensures through prescribed procedure and a trouble-shooting process that all items of equipment are complete and as specified, and ready for use by the owner/occupant/user.

Job Clerk: Depending on business philosophy, staffing level, and type of project, a contractor often will have a staffer whose purpose and efforts, on-site, are to track documents, monitor costs, and generally engage with the documentation involved in the progress of the work (but not the design/contract documents). The person may act in any of several ways from assisting the superintendent, to running necessary errands, filing for permits, and, to some degree, expediting; but in total, the clerk is more a technical clerical than anything else.

Site Secretary: On projects of some extent or complexity, a contractor or the construction manager may provide a secretary for on-site administration. This person would be heavily engaged in clerical pursuits—handling correspondence in and out, keeping current files, recording minutes of meetings, coordinating and publishing meeting notices, and proper distribution of documents and information, including various computer functions—but might also be assigned some of the functions of the job clerk. Also, on particularly active sites, this secretary will act as receptionist and executive secretary to the manager, superintendent, or even the clerk-of-the-works (where one is utilized). In general, he or she acts to assist with, and relieve the superintendent and others from, the day-to-day administrative duties.

Clerk-of-the-Works: In many aspects, this person is the predecessor to the construction manager. Mainly hired as a full-time, on-site representative of the owner, the clerk ensures compliance with contract documents through daily exposure to and inspection of the construction work and process. Quite often the clerk is hired by and placed on the staff (and payroll) of the design professional, with all salary and costs involved reimbursed by the owner; the clerk could also be hired directly by the owner. She or he aids the task of and works closely with the design professional and the project representative, but is not the professional's on-site presence or representative. With the clerk on-site daily, the professional may be able to utilize just a part-time project representative, relying otherwise on information and observations from the clerk. Usually this is a highly experienced construction person, who can aid problem identification and solving, with limited bounds somewhat similar to the project representative. While titled differently, a person in this position is a major player in the process of contract administration, acting as the CM's full-time site presence.

(Material) Supplier is a company that is in business to provide various building and construction materials, systems, devices, equipment, and so forth for use on the project work, or for incorporation into the actual construction. Also, a supplier may be a "rental agency" that provides pieces of equipment on a short-term rental basis, for use by the contractor(s)—for example, hoists, scaffolding, cranes, welding equipment, or portable toilets. Most often the supplier is a dealer, or perhaps a distributor (in some cases, an exclusive distributor) for a material manufacturer. The supplier acquires, or provides from a stock inventory, the products needed on projects throughout a specific assigned geographical area. For the most part, suppliers operate on informal sell/purchase arrangements, and have no contractual tie to the project. This is a very competitive business since most materials and devices are produced by and available from several manufacturers. Besides pricing, service is a key factor in the success of the supplier. Any delays or other problems can adversely affect the progress of a project, and can lead to the use of another supplier. See Figure 2–6.

The **Manufacturer's Representative** is basically a "contract salesperson" hired by a manufacturer to service a specific geographical territory. Usually the representative acts individually or through a small-company format that handles a number of different products from several manufacturers. This person or company may provide a number of items to a project from different sources. Primarily active as a face-to-face salesperson, the rep reacts to inquiries (for the manufacturer) and supplies technical information/literature to professionals. Such service is aimed at keeping items constantly in the view of professionals; the hope then is they will be specified outright for upcoming projects. In most cases, the representative's service acts strictly as a source of information; they "take no orders" per se. This is a strong PR element for a manufacturer within a given area.

REGULATORY AGENTS AND OTHERS

(Chief) Building Official: This is an employee of the local governmental jurisdiction, the primary person for enforcement of a building code within that jurisdiction. Basically a law enforcement officer, since the building code is locally adopted law, the official may or may not be a registered design professional (depending on job description requirements). Currently in many instances the official must carry a certification from a bona fide agency or group attesting to the ability and knowledge to perform the tasks of the position; this may be necessary in addition to professional registration. In many situations the official will also be the department head of the permit and inspection functions—in smaller jurisdictions the official may be the sole person for all such functions. The person may be titled in any number of ways, i.e., Building Commissioner, Code Official, (Chief) Building Inspector, and the like. No matter the title, the person is re-

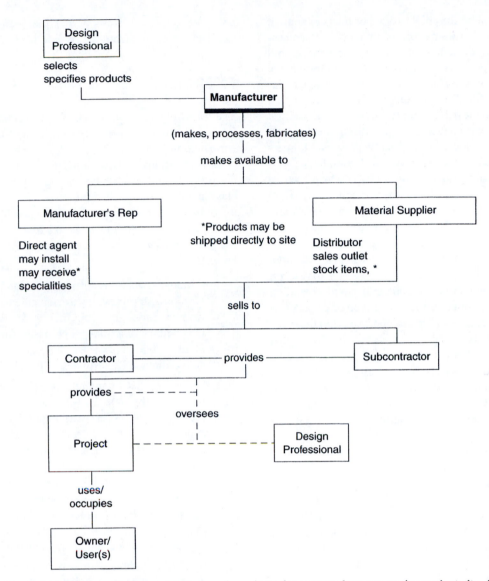

Figure 2–6 The flow of materials and other manufactured products from manufacturer to the project site. Note in particular the different routes and persons who may be involved.

sponsible for proper administration of the entire building permit and inspection functions, as required by the local jurisdiction. In addition, they usually share very close working relationships with other governmental regulatory agencies: public works, sewer department, water department, zoning, electrical, planning, road engineer, and so on.

Plans Examiner: This official reviews contract documents submitted for a project building permit. The review is to ascertain if proposed construction (shown and described on documents) complies with the code requirements. In many jurisdictions examiners must be a registered design professional; in others they must carry a certification from a code agency to attest to their competence to examine plans. The examiners also work with the permit applicant (owner, contractor, design professional) and resolve differences

(noncompliance), where necessary, before approving documents and allowing issuance of the building permit.

One or more persons who work in the same office as and for the chief building official are called **Building (Field) Inspectors.** Their duties are less inclusive than those of the building official. They perform in-progress construction inspections, on-site, to ascertain that the actual construction work complies with the approved drawings and specifications. (Approval is required to receive a building permit; approval results from an agency review of the documents.) The jurisdiction and official will develop a set list of inspections and criteria for uniformity in making inspections, as and when appropriate, on each project. The inspectors do *not* function as work supervisors, and have no authority to suggest or allow any deviations from approved documents—

except with approval by the chief official or plans examiner. The inspectors travel between projects, under permit, and assigned to them; react to calls for mandatory inspections; and follow progress of projects to ensure continued compliance throughout the construction sequence. After the project successfully passes a "final" inspection, the inspector grants a Certificate of Occupancy. This allows full use of the facility.

Inspectors (governmental agency/disciplines/trades): Most regulatory agencies have a corps of persons who perform various on-site inspections to ascertain compliance with agency regulations and who monitor in-progress work where complying elements will be hidden from sight in the final work. Examples include the federal Occupational Safety and Health Administration (OSHA), local Environmental Protection Agencies (EPA), water and sewer departments, zoning agencies, road engineering (road renovations/widening, openings for utility access, curb cuts, aprons for driveways, etc.). Such agencies are numerous and quite varied depending on the type of locale (urban or rural), the type of project (industrial versus residential or light commercial), and the operations that are regulated. These inspections are factors that must be accommodated in the project schedule.

Cost (Controller) Clerk/Project Controller: Another position that is available on the construction project, primarily a function of the contractor. The person(s) involved would be dedicated, both on-site and in the office, to monitoring the actual costs of the project functions, comparing them with budgets and anticipated expenditures, payrolls, effort hours, and other projections and trends. This effort is to ensure that money and project work "run out" at the same time, in synchronization. Of course, this is another expression of "the owner deriving full value for dollar paid."

Construction Scientist: This is a title that can be applied to a person with an academic orientation and in-depth knowledge and expertise in construction, or a portion thereof. Essentially a consultant, this title is a more academic term used to identify and define a person who acts in an advisory or oversight/review role. It is more one who studies and researches construction technology, materials, systems, and construction methods, as opposed to one who actively works in or participates in actual construction work. Usually this is a person with both wide-ranging and in-depth experience, exposure to quite varied situations and problems, familiarity with innovative solutions, and one who can aid others in understanding construction, its problem solving, processes, needs, operations, and direction. These services are accomplished through analysis, study, and applications of theory. This person should be perceived as one who serves at least a dual role, researcher/consultant and educator, and who is able to convey to various parties the results of studies and experiences gained from the research.

EXERCISES

The following activities can be used to enhance the text material and provide wider exposure to and understanding of construction.

Some portions of these items may be assigned as individual projects, but overall they are group projects that every class member can benefit from. (*No activity that requires going onto a construction site should be undertaken by a single individual, nor without prior notice and permission from the site manager; ensure full and proper safety measures in any event.*)

1. Arrange visits to the office of design professionals, of various disciplines. Try to visit at least an architectural firm and an engineering firm. Ask a staffer to explain the various functions, such as drafting, CAD equipment, technical library, specifications writing, and design critiques. Report back to the class.

2. Compile a list of manufacturers' representatives and material suppliers. Assign a team of students (3–4 at most) to each representative, and have them make an appointment for an interview, to talk about the work involved and the products represented. Find out how a rep works. Who does he or she regularly talk to or approach? What material lines are represented? (Ask for literature on these, for each student and for the class library.) Ask about problems or pet peeves that the rep may have about projects or documents; ask about design professionals and clients in general.

3. Invite the technical field representative from one or more of the trade associations (the Engineered Wood Association, formerly the American Plywood Association, for plywood manufacture and application, is a good example) to give a presentation on their products in the classroom. Most will also distribute literature for student use.

4. Contact one or more manufacturers of construction products, who usually have representatives available for meetings and presentations in which they explain their products and hand out literature for reference. This type of meeting can be of great help to students, by exposing them to new products and to the type of persons they could encounter in their careers.

3

The Sequence of a Project

Every project has a progression of activities that transform the initial ideas for the project into the reality of a structure that is usable to the client. Within each such progression is an array of activities, some of which recur at the same instance in almost every project. Other activities are peculiar to the nature of the project, specific needs of the owner and the work. Therefore, it is next to impossible to set out an absolute sequence to be followed in every project; this chapter sketches the broad, general categories of activities that are predictable and included in most projects.

The progression is well illustrated in the rationale of the Construction Specifications Institute (CSI) 16-division format for specifications. The format is relatively chronological. Each division contains information about work that may be required in various time frames within the project schedule, but in general Figure 3–1 shows the relationship of the Division's position (and number) in the overall project scheme, from beginning to end.

Figure 3–2 summarizes the complete project sequence from initiation to finale. It provides additional activities that occur during the project, but which are not listed in the CSI or other construction-related listings. This chart shows the general categories of activities covering the entire project work effort and the primary participants. There are others who play a part— the figure merely indicates the parties that have the greatest influence over the process at the juncture shown.

As the 21st century begins, the construction industry adapts to ever-changing conditions. This constant change marks both the technical aspects of construction projects and the administrative and legal aspects.

Owner concerns about the added cost of projects (interest on borrowed money) and identifying the point(s) of responsibility for the work have led to the development of various project delivery systems, as discussed in Chapter 1. These new systems give owners the opportunity to adapt the project work to their particular needs. In reality, though, while the project delivery system is important to the project over-all, it has less impact on the sequence and performance of the actual construction work.

The delivery system is a management tool which has great importance to the owner and to those who are responsible for the actual delivery of the system. These include the design professionals, the construction manager, the design/build firm managers, and the other project managers. Little of the scheme chosen, if anything, has a direct influence on the individual tradesworker installing a portion of the project work. The system is a definitive legal configuration, a roadmap directing the flow of information and authority across the project. In a sense it establishes the pecking order for authority and sets out the pattern of that authority as it relates to communications, directions/instructions, change in the work, and of course, the progressive payments due from the owner during the course of the project.

The sequence of the project is not an absolute, inflexible process. It can be changed for various reasons, mainly to adjust to the demands of the delivery system (if so required) and to the needs of the owner.

However, even these adjustments have little impact on the work. There may be a realignment of the order in which work is done, but still all the work is done, eventually. Again, it falls upon the managers of the project to decide just how the work is sequenced, why, and in what fashion. With these qualifications in mind, it is virtually impossible to portray the "typical" project—variations, large and small, are too numerous.

To illustrate all of this, a brief discussion of some of the more widely used delivery systems follows. Of course, many other texts and resources can greatly expand your understanding of these systems. (See Figure 3–3.)

Owners have found shortcomings in—and are becoming less satisfied with—the traditional system of construction, called design/bid/build (D/B/B). It has proven patently unsatisfactory in several ways. Primary bones of contention are the extended time it takes to produce a project and the lack of definitive responsibility, which elongates the disposition

Figure 3–1 General listing of work included in each division of CSI specifications format.

Division No.	Work Efforts Addressed
1	Specific project conditions, procedures, interrelationships, and requirements applicable throughout the project, and by all parties; overall project control, responsibilities, definitions, etc.
2	All activities dealing with earthwork operations and site improvements; overall site preparation, excavation, grading for walks, roads and curbs; landscaping, lawn sprinkler/irrigation system
3	All forms of concrete, which is the primary foundation material; concrete systems and materials; also appears as a finish material both exterior and interior
4	Masonry is one of the primary enclosure materials for the envelope of the building; also an interior finish and partition material and system; CMU, brick, stone, facings, pavers, etc.
5	Metals include structural steel, columns, beams, girders for main walls and supports, roof framing and decking; and light-weight, miscellaneous light-gauge framing for non-load bearing and drywall partitions; also appears in stairs, some decorative trims
6	Carpentry covers the full range of rough and finished wood work; includes plastics and other material with a carpentry connotation; from framing to highly decorative paneling
7	Thermal and moisture concerns are addressed in roofing, insulation, caulking, fire proofing, penetration sealing, siding/cladding
8	Elements of enclosure include doors, and windows of all kinds, glass and glazing, entrances, skylights, and other such features to augment and complement the basic material of masonry, roofing, etc.
9	Finishes including almost all exposed systems and features; paint/coatings/floor and wall coverings, ceiling, ceramic and other tile
10	Specialties is a potpourri of devices, small equipment and elements which convert a simple building into a usable and occupiable structure with proper functions; flag poles, mail boxes, rest room accessories and compartments, signage, bulletin boards, write-on boards, platforms/risers
11	Equipment includes unitized systems (usually considered "fixed") which are designed to function for a specific purpose; bank equipment, for example, includes counters, undercounter units, etc. for full outfitting and bank-type operations
12	Furnishings are everything from overstuffed furniture to office partition systems, and other movable items, which allow proper use of the building
13	Special construction deals with modules such as "clean rooms," and other segments of a project which can be built off-site, transported and installed in the building intact; usually special and high-tech requirements which are better achieved in a factory controlled atmosphere than on a construction site
14	Anything that moves people or material is part of conveying systems; escalators, conveyors, moving sidewalks, elevators, lifts, dumb waiters, and so forth
15	Called Mechanical, it is normally sub-divided into plumbing and heating, ventilating and air-conditioning (HVAC); contains every element of those systems including all necessary devices, controls, etc. as well as the basic equipment, supports, units
16	Electrical covers the full range of devices and equipment for the delivery of power and lighting to the building; again, from simple small devices to transformers, panels, cables, cable trays, and light fixtures; designed to provide the correct power to the various units regarding such anywhere in the building

of claims and full completion and resolution of projects. While in 1999 D/B/B remains as the system used in the majority of projects, other systems are becoming more and more popular with owners. One system in particular has become quite attractive to owners. This is called design/build (D/B). Its use is growing rapidly, and it may well become the system of choice for the new century.

Design/build is not a new concept. For many years one method of building projects has been to hold a single person or firm responsible for both the design of the project and its construction. It has long been an option for owners, perhaps even predating D/B/B, and has been used for all types and sizes of projects; probably it is more widely utilized for smaller projects. Simply, an owner has always had the right

	Categories of Tasks
Owner	Project Initiation
	Selection of Design Professional(s)
Design Professionals	Programming
	Site Selection and Feasibility
	Development of Preliminary Design
	Revisions, Changes, Additions
	Approval of Design Concept
	Design Refinement
	Final Approval of Design Concept
	Design Development
	Production of Contract Documents
	Regulatory Review and Permitting
Owner & Design Professionals	Contractor Selection
	Bidding
	Award of Contract/Notice to Proceed
	Pre-Construction Meeting
Contractors (Administration & Management)	Initial On-site Operations
	Mobilization
	On-site Mobilization and Staging
	Project Organization/Progress Meeting(s)
	Create/Review/Finalize Project Schedule
	Initial Purchase/Ordering of Materials/Systems
Contractors (Actual Construction Work Process)	Earthwork, Grading, Fillings, Excavation
	Install Foundation System (Substructure)
	Install Underground Utilities
	Erect Structural Frame System (Superstructure)
	Install Floor Framing System
	Extend Utility Lines/Systems
	Build/Install Envelope (Exterior Walls)
	Install Roofing System
	Install Mechanical Systems
	Install Interior Walls/Partitions & Accessories
	Connect Branch Systems to Mechanical Equipment
	Install/Apply Finishes
	Install Specialties/Equipment/Furnishings
	Energize Mechanical Systems; Troubleshoot/Adjust
Contractor Design Professional Owner	Substantial Completion; Final Inspection; Punch List
	Partial Use/Occupancy by Owner
	Resolve Punch List; Final Cleaning; Clear Project Area
	Certificate of Occupancy; Operating Manuals; Training
	Final Completion and Payment
All	Turnover to Owner/Occupancy/Use

Figure 3–2 Overview of the project sequence.

Figure 3–3 The numerous project delivery systems currently available to owners for use on their projects. Note that several functions have different leads (CM as advisor, for example) whereby the owner can choose who will head a given set of activities. See further explanation of these systems in Figures 1–23 and 3–22.

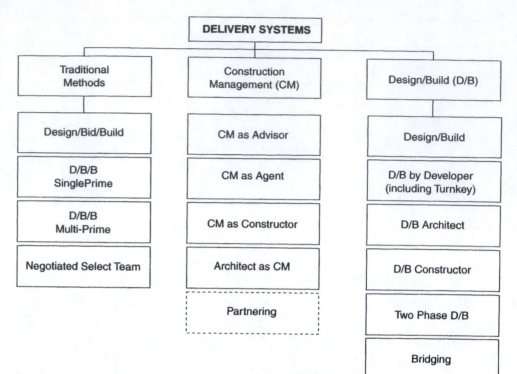

to contact a contractor to do both the design and the project work, as well as securing permits and so forth. Obviously this process is still used today; examples are quite abundant.

D/B is much in the same mold of other American efforts. We solve problems quickly by producing new systems and materials, but these in turn create other problems. We invent and produce wonderful new materials, even construction materials, which turn out to be fire or environmental hazards. It has not been too long ago that new foaming insulations were actually banned in some areas because of their adverse effect on human respiratory systems. Other materials prove in short order that they are flammable, and hence while solving a need or problem they create new, different, and often worse problems.

So too, with design/build. First there are no adverse problems, it is just that the program has inherent legal problems, and may in time prove harmful, financially to both the owner and the D/B contractor. Also, with D/B the chance exists for "stretching" on the part of the contractors; they feel they can do the project, only to find out that they are not up to it. That also occurs in other systems, but D/B tends to isolate the contractors, who then tend to overestimate their abilities. This is most apparent in smaller, residential contractors trying to move into larger, more complex projects in the field of commercial and institutional construction.

This tendency sometimes leads to a rather disturbing instability in the engineering efforts of D/B firms. Since relatively few firms do every project via D/B, their construction efforts often sustain them through slack times. As projects come to the firm without need for engineering by the D/B firm, the engineering arm is subject to rise and fall in staffing levels. This "revolving door" aspect of engineering staff

coming and going (through attrition, turnover, layoffs) causes that department to become more and more unstable and perhaps unreliable. Aspersions are then cast when there is a cost overrun or in cases of less than complete and proper design and documentation. Unfortunately, the firm then carries this negative baggage with the client(s); it is a problem the firm can resolve and manage in a creative and fairly permanent manner, but only if they so choose.

Summing up,

- Design/build is an old system with direct ties to the ancient Master Builder system
- Single-point responsibility is attractive to many owners
- D/B requires a more sophisticated owner, who participates more deeply in projects as a leader on the team
- D/B has long been widely used in Europe; it is still emerging in the United States, where it is not yet preeminent
- Continuing educational and training efforts are needed to attain full understanding of the system, the nuances inherent in it, and the many forms it can take
- It is still illegal in some areas of work in the United States—on publicly funded projects in particular
- It still needs to resolve itself with professional registration law requirements
- It must work on its team-building techniques, to be properly attuned to all parties
- It should not be undertaken simply to "do something different, or faddish"; to be successful it needs work by all parties, in concert and with a common goal

Design/build has increased in favor, primarily because it places the control and responsibility for both the design and construction of the project under one entity. In addition, it can produce projects in a shorter time frame, especially where "fast-track" (see Glossary) methods are used. Also contributing to its increased use is the fact that larger construction companies are moving to its use, as a means to be flexible in satisfying clients and to control projects more closely. The CM scenario had the same shortcoming as D/B/B: the responsibility split between design professional and CM. With D/B, the owner now has but one place to look for resolution of any problem, and one place to exert pressure to try to contain cost and budget problems.

It is not a perfect system; particularly worrisome is the question of hiring a design professional whose primary loyalty is to the contractor who signs his or her paycheck. Since the final decisions on every project, in this system, lie with the D/B contractor, there is the possibility that crucial design elements and decisions made by the design professional can be modified, obviated, or eliminated. This type of action would then place the professional in a severely adverse liability situation, since registration laws make the professional responsible for the work produced. If the documents contain the seal of the professional (which is required in many jurisdictions) and include contractor changes, the problem is further aggravated. This situation is not uncommon, since it is the contractors who now have the momentum and greater input to D/B and who most commonly have the resources to create the D/B firms. The design professional is then reduced to employee, or subcontractor, with little if any final say over decisions that may prove quite important. Since the contractor has quite different responsibilities and liabilities than the professional, this aspect is most worrisome, and as yet, is not fully resolved legally.

Construction management (CM) was one system that came to the fore. Here the CM is placed under a separate contract with the owner to give added input to design (in some cases), construction materials, systems, bidding, pricing, budgeting, and oversight of construction. The CM is an experienced manager, neutral in overseeing conflicts, skilled in motivating and expediting. See Chapter 1 for further details.

For the sake of clarity, and to aid understanding, we have chosen for this chapter's discussion the design-build project delivery system and sequence. In this, the project from inception to completion is a series of activities running consecutively, one after the other. Other delivery systems and project sequences combine or overlap some of the activities for the sake of reducing project time, and to allow the owner earlier use of the facility. For example, in the "fast-track" sequence portions of the construction are started while the finished drawings are still being prepared. Obviously, where the work has not yet been documented, it is not pursued in the field. Foundation work can be started prior to completion of the upper building design, provided that adequate information is available about weights and loading so reasonable conclusions can be made for the foundation design.

The period of time required by each portion of the sequence is directly dependent on the size and complexity of the project. Some portions are left out in some projects since they are not needed, for one reason or another. The traditional design/bid/build project delivery system involves separate time periods, running in tandem, for each of the three phases of the project: design, bidding, and construction. Currently, numerous other more innovative delivery systems can be chosen to better meet the owner's specific desires. Space prohibits full discussion of each; however, see Figures 3–3 and 3–23. Since each of these different contracts causes some variation in the sequence of a project, D/B/B was chosen for this discussion since it is the clearest and most straightforward.

For the following explanation it should be assumed that the owner plans to enter in a "multi-prime design/bid/build" contract configuration. Four separate construction contracts will be executed; one each for general construction, heating-ventilation-air conditioning (HVAC), plumbing, and electrical work. This will be done after the project has been properly designed, documented, and bid through the normal or standard competitive process.

(Numerous terms are used in the following narrative that are commonly used in the construction, but which the reader may not know. In lieu of stopping to define each where it is used in the text, we refer the reader to the Glossary at the end of the book that contains most of the terms. The reference documents listed in the appendices are also recommended as good resources for other terms and for further explanation.)

Project Initiation

The impetus for any project emanates from the inspirations, needs, or desires of the owner. This may come in the form of outside influences, such as increased business (or potential), new technology, request for added space from a tenant, opportunity to operate in a new area or reconstruction after an incident or disaster. Usually a period of evaluation and analysis precedes any definitive information about the actual construction. Consideration is given to what is needed, how much financing can be developed, and where and how repayment can be achieved and sustained, and other matters that impact on the current operation when (or if) some new construction is undertaken. Obviously, to build is not a decision made easily, quickly, or frivolously.

At the end of this process, the owner will have a good, but still general idea of what is required in the project: its size, image, function, perhaps the construction materials, capacity, maintenance needs and the like. More than likely, though, the owner will not be fully versed on current construction, unless she or he has been engaged in other projects recently. (It should be noted that owners of businesses are almost always completely involved in their business, not in the planning and construction business; they need clear, straightforward, pragmatic help, advice, guidance, options and alternatives, direction, understanding, education (in construction/planning), and simple good sense. Quite often the owner is actually aided in drawing conclusions or making decisions by the design professional. Unable to resolve a situation, the owner/client may need to hear a solution or a series of options/alternatives from the professional, in order to crystallize their thinking and direct it toward their desire or need. This process is one of the major and most positive aspects of project programming. Also, owners will seek (or should be advised to seek) legal counsel for the contractual and other legal matters.

Selection of Design Professional

Who comes first? Most business people will have an ongoing relationship with an attorney, for obvious reasons; even well-run, sound businesses need legal assistance on occasion. While an attorney can be helpful, we suggest that the attorney should not be the driving force behind selection of the design and construction teams. Rather, that person can best serve as an advisor to the process for selecting the professionals.

Usually the process of selection is based on:

- Previous experience with a professional (repeat business)
- Advice from a colleague or others whose opinion is valued by the owner (a recommendation)
- Advice from other persons in the business
- Knowledge of another similar project which is attractive to the owner and presents the image desired
- A list of possible candidates from a professional society and interviews of as many parties as necessary
- Results of a formal competition (expensive to do, but may produce better and more innovative designs—confined generally to large governmental and institutional projects)

Whatever method is used to form a list of potential professionals, a process of one-on-one interviewing will follow. This, in the main, is the best business-like process for an owner trying to ascertain the best person(s) to execute the project. Interpersonal interviewing gives the owner a "feel" for the professional both in a technical sense, and in personal qualities (compatibility with owner's thoughts, demeanor, attitude, personality). It is vital that the owner be fully comfortable with the professional(s) since their relationship will be lengthy, often quite close, and in need of harmonious consensus and understanding on many issues.

DESIGN PHASE

Programming

Client input and regulatory searches are the two primary elements of programming. This is a process of "problem-seeking," whereby the design professional attempts to ascertain, in depth, the needs and desires of the client. A number of meetings, use of formal questionnaires, and interviews with major operating managers within the organization of the owner are necessary. Much as the tailor or dressmaker takes extensive notes and measurements in order to produce a quality, custom-fit garment, so the design professional seeks all of the information that will allow the production of a quality, custom-fit building or complex. It is entirely possible to make or break a project in this early phase. Such problems as forgetting issues/concerns, miscalculation, misunderstanding, unwarranted assumptions, unilaterally filling in information, miscommunication, and lack of recording and addressing important details can lead to a faulty, unsatisfactory, errant project, disliked by the owner, and very possibly the source of a major dispute if not litigation. No owner wants to pay for a project that has not captured the desires or imagination of the owner, much less the proper operational and functional aspect of the owner's business. It is unrefutable that the better and more complete the programming, the better the project. This is so true (especially in an atmosphere of extreme financial pressure and high costs of projects) that professional curriculums in several colleges have programming as a specific, separate study—some even have a separate, added discipline or option for people to be specifically trained as architectural programmers.

It must also be said that clients often cannot list or articulate their needs and desires. This information must be literally drawn out of them through incisive questioning, in-depth analysis, probing, and correlating bits and pieces of diverse information. Programming is directly akin to the itinerary for a trip: it lists important issues, and directs one to distinct milestones. It is detailed, precise, and, hopefully, all-inclusive. The owner may have to be "sold" on this effort, but in the end the time spent in this venture will pay dividends in lower initial cost, smoother running projects, and a better "fit" of project to owner needs/desires. Long-term it provides a more efficient facility and lower operating costs. Contrasted to the other costs of a project, programming is but a very minor item, which belies its true value. (See Figure 3–4.)

Programming also involves the search into the regulations that apply to the specific project (Figure 3–5). These parameters are required as the regulations and codes are law and must be observed through compliant construction (Figure 3–6). In many cases formal permits are required, so it is better to uncover the requirements early and incorporate their solution into the basic design than to "run across" them later. In the latter case, frequently there is major disruption of the design concept to allow for proper addressing of the regulations. In reality, the codes and regulations are project requirements from the point of view of the general public. They exist because certain aspects of every project involve public access and/or occupancy, and therefore, governmental attention is required to provide a safe environment. Owners must be made to understand that meeting these provisions is part of their responsibility, under law, even though some compliance may add cost to the planned project.

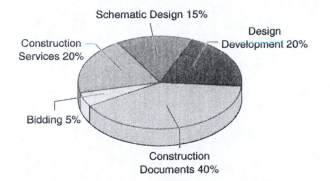

Figure 3–4   Normal percentage of a design professional's fee allotted to each phase of the professional's project work. Basically this is a method of budgeting time and expenses in each phase to provide a profitable project. New methods, such as CAD (in lieu of manual drafting) can reduce costs in one phase, so that the fee allotted can be used elsewhere in the sequence or converted to additional profit.

When programming is actively and correctly used, it acts as a powerful lens to focus a large amount of divergent information regarding the project in a logical manner and form that facilitates its use in developing the design concept, in the subsequent execution of project documentation, and, of course, in the actual construction work.

Site Selection and Feasibility (If Required)

Many owners require one or both of these services, and often involve the professional as at least one voice in the actual land purchase or use. One of the owner's contractual obligations is to provide a detailed survey of the property (including topography) to be used for the project. Quite often in searching for a site a land surveyor will be utilized. Since surveyors continually engage information about land—from the size and shape of the property to the available utilities with their sizes and locations, the topography, and the encumbrances—they prove

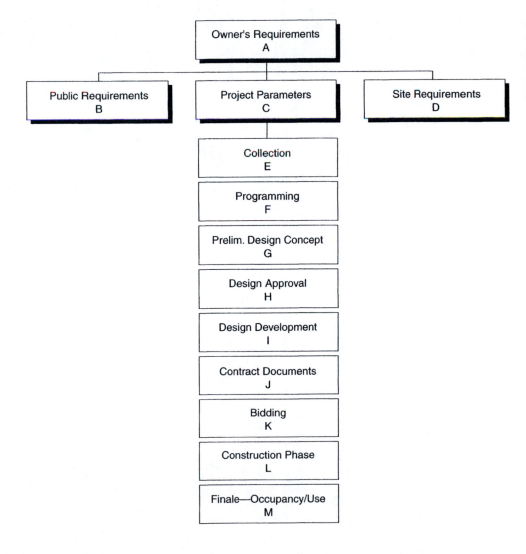

Figure 3–5   The initial collection of information (i.e., programming) and the sequence of the process that produces the project, using the traditional design/bid/build delivery system.

Code Provision	Material Selection	Assembly Selection	Documentation	Construction	Inspection and Approval
The text of the code will state a required rating, performance, or other criteria.	Of all of the available materials which meet the code's demands, the design professional must select what material(s) are to be used in accord with use, budget, design, and aesthetics.	Most materials function as parts of constructed assemblies; here, too, code compliance is necessary for the entire assembly; many assemblies are tested as a unit and can be reproduced but with no changes or substitutes.	It is necessary that the contract documents specifically show and/or describe exactly what is required by the design professional, in answer to the code's demands; upon approval this data becomes the criteria for the actual construction and basis for in-progress inspections.	Install the partition as detailed and specified, in the location(s) shown on the approved drawings; no deviations.	Both design and code professionals need to inspect the work; give approval for contract compliance, and code compliance, respectively. Compare actual work to requirements of approved documents.
One-hour fire resistant wall required.	Use Type X rated gypsum wallboard and metal studs.	Find UL design which uses these materials; ascertain all details required.	Show UL design, show location(s) and extent; properly specify all required components.	Documents approved by the regulatory agency become the criteria for the actual construction.	Follow up service by both professionals ensures that the requirements of both are met.
				This process brings together the code requirements and the design decisions of the professional.	This process provides assurance that the project is built as designed and as required by regulations.

The linkage between code provision and final construction is direct, pervasive, and collective. It becomes an accumulation of data, assimilation of parts into pieces/systems, and their incorporation into the whole. It is obvious, here, that code compliance is not a one-time, paper exercise, but rather a process that parallels the development of the project, from programming to final acceptance and occupancy.

Figure 3–6 The building code regulations need to be properly applied and accounted for in each phase of the work. The illustration shows how this is done and what the code requires in each work phase. By following procedures, the code requirements will be properly incorporated into the finished project.

valuable in quickly ascertaining the adaptability of the site for the project. When a suitable site is selected, all of their research information can be formally applied through their usual office and field procedures, and converted into a useable survey for the design team.

Of course, a real estate expert/agent would also be engaged, but for pure technical/building considerations, the various design professions are invaluable members of the site team. A warehousing or manufacturing operation may seek a location close to an interstate highway interchange, and preferably one that provides both east-west as well as north-south access. Perhaps railroad access is desired. These issues would fall under the purview of the realtor. It is the other factors impacting building layout and design that will involve the design professions (Figure 3–7). For example, adequate area for the planned facility as well as some increment for future expansion must be provided. Other concerns are encumbrances on the land (easements, wetlands, environmental issues, soil bearing capacity, drainage, infestation, possible flooding including "flash" floods, zoning issues that bear on "footprint area," setbacks, "give backs" such as road widening and reciprocal access, height limitations, etc.). Each owner and project has its own unique set of site considerations; no one wants a shopping center that is not easily accessible, nor a school in an industrial district. Within each discipline a feasibility report can be formulated with guidelines and options for the client to utilize with the realtor to find the exact and proper site. Some owners choose to do this search on their own; others already own the land to be used. In any event, the project can be inhibited or disrupted where a faculty site is selected and the design professionals are not used early to uncover the nuances. Any site can be used, but each has its own set of problems that impact any planned project. It is better to uncover and know about "worst case" conditions early than to proceed based on inadequate, faulty, or incorrect information and conclusions. Site selection can occur before or concurrently with programming, but usually is mistimed if done after the program is established; that would reduce the number of sites that could be considered, or could force the programmed project onto a site that could not fully or properly accommodate it.

Development of a Preliminary Design

Following, or perhaps even as part of programming analysis, the designer will begin to formulate an overall scheme for the project. This is crucial to the project since it must accurately reflect the relationships and locations of the various functions of the project, both within the planned structure and surrounding it. The process is one of building from a nucleus, and expanding the plan by incorporating more and more functions, areas, personal work stations, and activities. This work is based on and verifies the programming and will disclose where more information is necessary. This process is

---

Site Programming/Selection Considerations
(Establishing *actual* buildable area; impact on same)

ZONING
- The NIMBY syndrome
- Use "by right"; conditional; change/appeal
- "Planned" (contract) district project; give-backs
- Building setback lines
  - limited footprint
  - district restrictions; reasonable
- Interface to surrounding districts
  - buffering; berms; distances
  - barriers (sound or visual)
  - landscaping; nondecorative reasons
  - treatment of parking/vehicle areas
  - lighting: type, level, number, location
  - restricted hours of operation
- Beware(!) of aesthetics review/control/requirements

EASEMENTS
- Utilities: natural gas, oil, water, electric, sewers, pipelines, telephone, coaxial, high tension
- Drainage: private/public
- Access; reciprocal use; shared facilities
- Structures (towers, head walls, etc.)

DRAINAGE
- Storm; surface/water course/sewer/inlets/outflow
- Stormwater regulations; control (giving/receiving)
- Easement(s): public/private/reciprocal
- Dedicated facilities (retention/detention)
- Flood plain/fringe
- Wetlands
- Subsurface drainage; springs/sink holes/caverns

LAND FORMATION
- Soil bearing capacity; problem soils (muck/rocky)
- Topography/contouring; slopes/stability/formations/rolling/radical/outcroppings
- Environmentally sensitive; hillside regulations
- Earthwork regulations; required cut and fill
- Erosion/sedimentation control

OTHER CONSIDERATIONS
- "Fit" into other public master plans (development/roads)
- Other restrictions/covenants/reserves: public/private (deed)
- Natural cover (heavily wooded, etc.); scenic
- Existing man-made features/structures/facilities

Figure 3–7   Considerations for analyzing a site for location of a project. The site can influence not only what is built, but how, where, and how much.

---

roughly akin to fitting pieces of a jigsaw puzzle together: finding what piece fits where, and how exactly must they all fit to allow other "connections" and expansion of the picture. Considerations in a project are a little simpler in that the "pieces" may be fitted in any of several ways and still meet the need or function. There is no one set, firm, unchallengeable solution. Obviously, this is the time for presenting options to the owner; selection here could influence (even drastically) what happens or must happen in other aspects of the overall scheme.

Revisions, Changes and Additions

Since design is the seeking of solutions in differing ways, no project has but one finite design. The usual process for a construction project is akin to trial and error, whereby the design professionals formulate varied designs which meet the programming requirements. Configurations, orientations, and even some relationships may change, but without drastic impact on the overall function of the plan. It is for the owner to make the subjective decision of which design scheme or concept is preferable; the professionals usually aid the selection process by discussing various pros and cons of each plan with the owner. It is extremely rare that the first design is so satisfactory that no further preliminary work is required. In the main, several meetings and discussions are required as the professionals create, develop, and present options, take comments and instruction from the owner, and then revise, change, modify, add, or delete to adjust the scheme to the new criteria. Skilled programmers and designers can shorten this process by being very incisive and analytic, coming very close to a final preferred choice very quickly. Obviously this is to the credit of the professionals, and can be a source of added funding to the entire project sequence since the entire allocated fee (most firms budget each phase of their work) was not absorbed in the preliminary design phase.

Approval of Design Scheme

It is advisable that once the overall project scheme has been established and proven satisfactory, that this be formally approved and documented in writing. Some firms seek signed drawings as evidence of the approval. At this point, it is usually just the floor plan(s) that are developed, since these drawings control other aspects of the project, and provide a good deal of information for other drawings, documents, and concepts. Indeed, if the plan does not work, the project can be in jeopardy again of not achieving a good final result.

Revisions, Changes: Design Refinement

The design process continues with the addition of more information and development of other project documents. These include exterior elevations, wall sections, some critical details, identification of crucial specification items, and so on. As this development progresses, there will be a natural process of having to "tweak" other elements or aspects of the project that have gone before, perhaps even the overall scheme; no major revision, or disruption to the approved scheme, should result, though. In essence, since so many elements must be fitted together, and as new information continually comes to the project, the need is for minor adjustments and refinements to make everything work in harmony for a good final design.

Final Approval of Design Concept

This is the first major milestone of the project. This approval must be documented, formally and in writing, even including signed drawings. This is needed so there is no hesitation as to what exactly the project is to entail. Often guide specifications listing materials and systems are also included, to give further indication of just how the project will be constructed and how the contract will be fulfilled. The information at hand is still very preliminary, lacking minute detail, but it sets firmly the direction, requirements, and intent of the professionals in meeting the programming needs; this is truly the manifestation of the programming. Also, this marks the formal end of the Schematic Design portion of the project's Design Phase (as noted in the various documents of the AIA; see listing of work items contained in each project phase in Figure 3–8).

Design Development

This is the second portion of the Design Phase, and brings much of the detail required for the project to the documents. This involves selection of materials and systems, based on the detailing developed to meet the design concept. Simply put, this is the gathering and piecing together of data which shows, exactly, the construction to come. The documents developed during this process are usually done in a manner that allows them to be utilized as the actual contract (working drawings) for the project. This, of course, requires the incremental addition of the complete array of necessary construction information during the production phase (see again Figure 3–8 for listing of services provided in each portion of work).

Production of Construction (Contract) Documents

This portion of the Design Phase is a major staff effort to produce a complete set of well-executed and well-coordinated working drawings and associated technical specifications (with appropriate administrative provisions and forms) for the project. Usually an extensive amount of time is involved, sometimes requiring many months and even years, depending on the size and complexity of the project.

Construction, because of the complexity of projects, the high cost of building, and the need for safety of workers and later users, is heavily dependent on what is shown and what is written about the project. There is a need to graphically show what is required. However, to provide readable drawings, there is a further need to put a tremendous amount of project related information in written form. This has evolved into a pairing of documents—a *set* of drawings (graphic representations of the project), and a *set, book,* or *manual* of specifications (written material about products, systems, and procedures specific to the project). Figure 3–9 lists the categories of

Services Performed [X yes; P preliminary; — not done]	Schematic Design	Design Development	Construction Documents
Project Administration	X	X	X
Program/Coordinate Client Information	X	X	X
Agency Consulting/Review/Approval	X	X	X
Architectural Design and Documentation	X	X	X
Structural Design and Documentation	P	X	X
Civil Design and Documentation	P	X	X
Mechanical Systems Design and Documentation	P	X	X
Electrical Design and Documentation	P	X	X
Discipline Coordination/Document Checking	X	X	X
Landscape Design and Documentation	—	P	X
Interior Design and Documentation	—	P	X
Materials Research and Specification	—	X	X
Project Development Schedule	P	X	—
Statement of Probable Cost (Estimate)	P	X	X
Presentations	X	X	—

Figure 3–8 The architectural/engineering services that are usually provided in each phase of the work of designing and documenting a project. Services other than those considered "basic included" can be added as additional services (at added cost) should the client require them.

information that should be contained in each type of document. This is based on the theory that the information can best be shown in the location noted in the figure.

As outlined below, the contract documents consist of several items, be they drawings, legal instruments, or other documents. While all are important, the two most difficult to execute are (1) the construction or working drawings and (2) the specifications. Both are necessary to convey all of the information that the contractors require in building the project. Their extent and content is wide-ranging, in-depth, and very, very detailed.

For the most part it is necessary that these two sets of documents be supportive of each other—*complementary* and *supplementary* are the legal terms—since neither one can fully explain the project in itself. Figure 3–7 shows the breakdown of information for a typical project, illustrating how some information can be shown graphically (in drawings) while other information is so detailed and descriptive that it must be shown in written form (the specifications). An analysis of the chart easily shows why the items are listed as they are: it is obvious that some information is "normally" written, and some "normally" drawn. The essence of this decision is, really, what is the *best* way to convey the information?

The size of these documents can vary from a single page to sets or booklets of several hundreds of pages; some drawings are sized 42″ × 48″ each, with some bigger yet but the majority smaller. Figures 3–10, 3–11, and 3–12 show the types of drawings involved and their importance for the

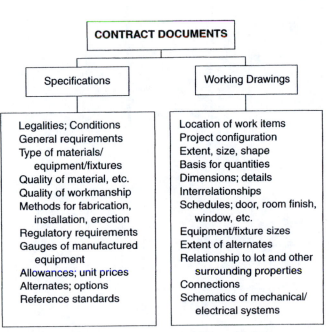

Figure 3–9 The best location for the various pieces of construction information. Sometimes graphics are proper, sometimes written descriptions—usually both means are utilized.

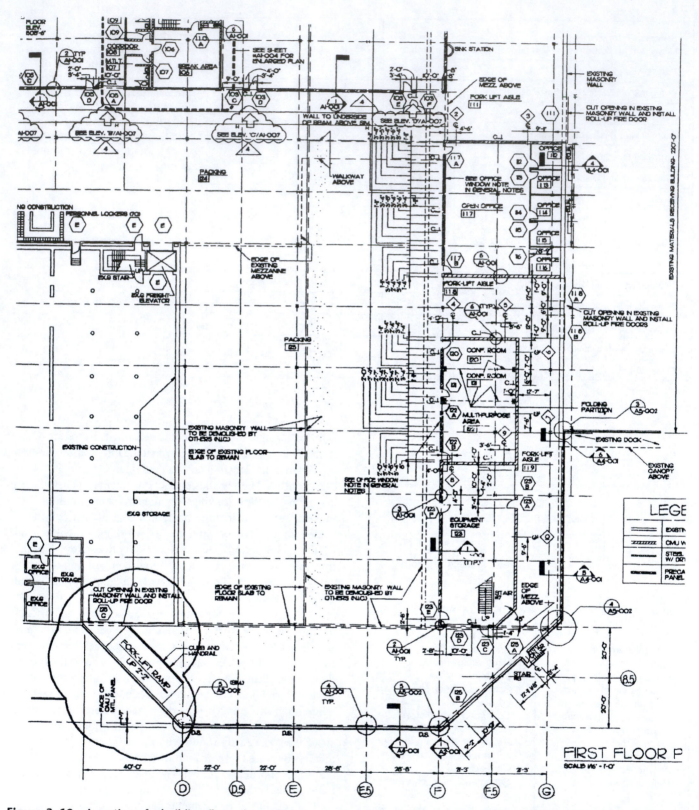

Figure 3–10 A portion of a building floor plan, which is a sectional view looking downward on the building (drawn as if the roof were removed so one could see inside).

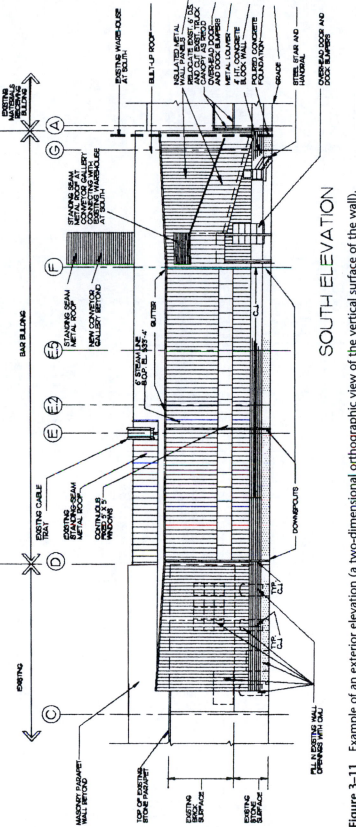

Figure 3–11 Example of an exterior elevation (a two-dimensional orthographic view of the vertical surface of the wall).

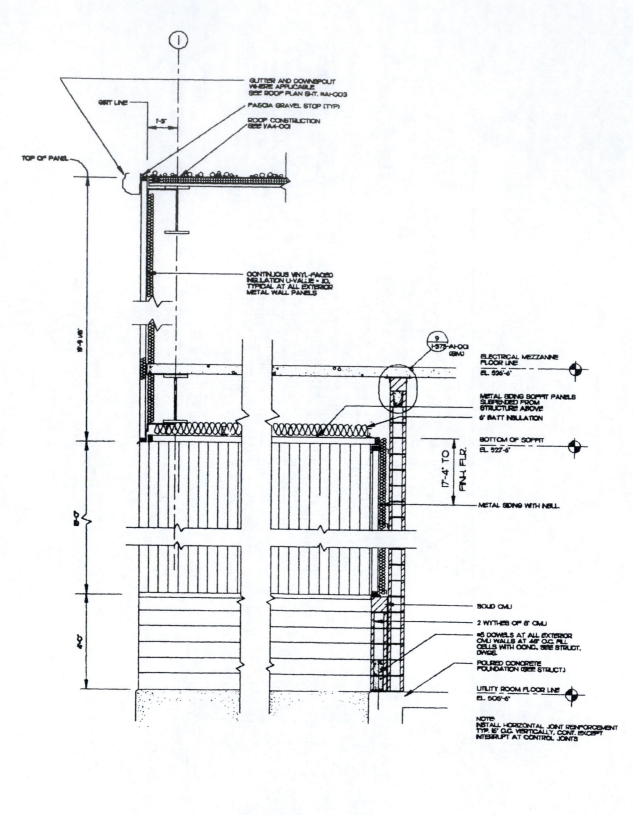

SECTION
SCALE 1/2" = 1'-0"

③ A1-001

Figure 3–12 This typical example of a wall section is a sectional view, as if the building wall were cut through, top to bottom, and one viewed the end of the cut portion; it shows the construction on the wall.

sharing of information or the showing of added detail or information to augment each other. The specifications then add a wealth of information that is physically impossible to show on the drawings. (Some very small, simple projects do utilize typewritten specifications right on the drawings, but this is much more the exception than the rule.)

Since every aspect, piece, system, detail, and nuance of the project *must* be shown or described, these documents not only take on a heavy responsibility, but they cannot leave gaps or create any confusion on the part of the constructors. They simply must explain, in the clearest, simplest terms possible, even the smallest part of the project; the use of a comprehensive checklist is advised. The cost of the project is directly dependent on how well these documents are executed. As complexity in the project escalates, so does the need for commensurate documentation—and the cost will reflect both. This is in no way an easy or off-handed exercise. It is the crux of a successful project.

Also, a staff team must be brought together entailing a variety of skill levels, experience, and expertise. Led by a project architect/engineer, an associate, or a principal, the team is best located in close proximity (if at all possible). Some firms physically relocate team members, and form "task force"–type configurations. However, this often proves disruptive to the members, as they are required to move their entire work stations elsewhere; disruption is increased if the term of the project is relatively short. In days past team members, more likely than not, were members of different firms and completely separated, in different buildings, and locations. No matter the physical layout, there is a prevailing pervasive need for on-going communication, checking, coordination, and simple conversation to ensure that information is available as needed, and is in the hands of all of the correct parties.

It is necessary that the team embrace as many disciplines as needed to produce the various aspects of the work. Where the firm is a single-discipline entity, an architectural firm, for example, there is a deeper need for very close, ongoing coordination with other offices that will provide the services of the other required disciplines. Considered by many as the "nitty-gritty" work of the project design sequence, documentation entails the research, development, analysis, and incorporation of the multitudinous details required for the construction. The work is wide-ranging, rigorous, complex, intensive, and in need of steady and dedicated persons. Shortcuts here could lead to eventual project failure—in function, longevity, weathering, soundness, or aesthetics. While constantly striving to maintain faithful execution of the design concept, this work must provide all that is needed for the design concept to become reality, and the structure to remain intact and pleasing to the eye over its entire life. Precision is required in the detailing so each nuance of the design concept is in its assigned place, proper, well-executed, and sound. "Attention to detail" is an understatement in describing this work effort.

For example, see Figure 3–13, and give answers to the questions. Draw conclusions where answers are not apparent or easily derived.

The final documentation of a project is contained in four groups of documents specifically designed for and directed exclusively to the project (Figure 3–14). In some cases the groups of documents contain sets that are used in other groupings.

The **Project Manual** contains:

Bidding Requirements
- Invitation to bid
- Instruction to bidders
- Information available
- Bid forms and attachments
- Bid security forms

Contract Forms
- Contract (agreement)
- Performance bond
- Payment bond
- Certificates

Contract Conditions
- General Conditions
- Supplementary Conditions

Technical Specifications
- CSI Divisions 1–16

Bidding Documents contain the:
- Project Manual (see above)
- Construction Drawings
- Addenda (information/drawings issued during the bidding period, which are added after the documents are complete)

Contract Documents contain the:
- Bidding Documents (see above, but *excluding* the Bidding Requirements)
- Contract Modifications (changes made after award of the contract for construction; may add, delete, or change work)

Construction Documents contain:
- All of the documents above, *including* the bidding requirements

The Contract Documents are the most crucial group, since the contract between Owner and Contractor is based on the proper execution of these documents. See Figures 3–15 through 3–18 for notes on the drawings and for a representation of their relationship with one another.

Within the design professions, various systems are used to form the set of drawings, setting out how they are formatted,

Figure 3–13 This is a good example of a detail, which is widely used on project drawings. They depict very small, restricted areas or items of work, at a scale (size) where the total work can be shown. This sample shows the attention paid to the very smallest items of work.

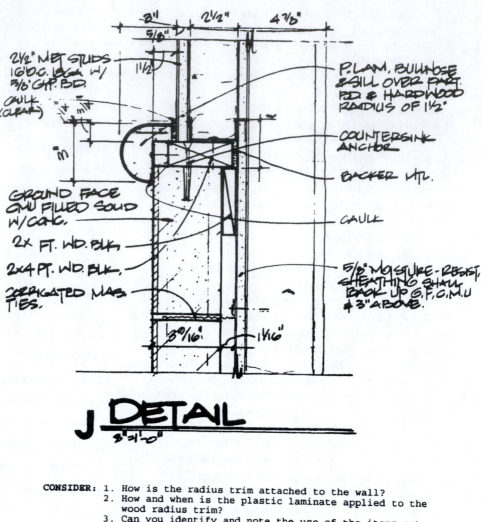

CONSIDER: 1. How is the radius trim attached to the wall?
2. How and when is the plastic laminate applied to the wood radius trim?
3. Can you identify and note the use of the items not described in this detail?
4. What alternative(s) can you offer for this detail to clarify any issues and to make a more workable detail?
5. Do you understand all of the notes on this detail?

how they are numbered, and how they are interrelated. Some clients, in addition, have their own particular requirements. For the most part, drawings concerning the site development work will be located first in the set. This is followed by foundation drawings, floor plans, structural layouts, building elevations (exterior views), sections (cross- and longitudinal), wall sections (showing wall construction), finishes, schedules, and then the engineering drawings for plumbing, mechanical (heating, ventilating, and air-conditioning), and electrical. Usually a cover sheet is used to list all of the drawings in the set, in the order of their appearance.

For many years, the specifications were not quite so simple as they might seem to be today. Each design office seemed to have its own system that only led to confusion among contractors. Information about the same product never seemed to appear in the same location in the specifications booklets for different projects. Finding information was both puzzling and frustrating, and confounded quick and easy retrieval. Profes-

sionals who were engaged in the production of specifications, many of them full-time, formed the Construction Specifications Institute. Over a period of years the group was able to develop a format of 16 numbered Divisions, each of which was assigned a material or trade designation. This format caught hold and is now very widely (but not yet universally) used. Specifications define the qualitative requirements for products, materials, and workmanship, upon which the contract is based. The more prevalent organization for specifications is the 16-Division format of the Construction Specifications Institute (CSI). This system has served well, and has brought a great deal of much needed uniformity to specification writing. Further, contractors depend on the system since it locates information in the same Division, on each project. Some design organizations have seen fit to expand the format into 17, 18, 19, or even more Divisions. This has led to some confusion, as this has not been done by nor is it approved by the CSI. The firms, though, use these additions for work/

CONSTRUCTION DOCUMENTS

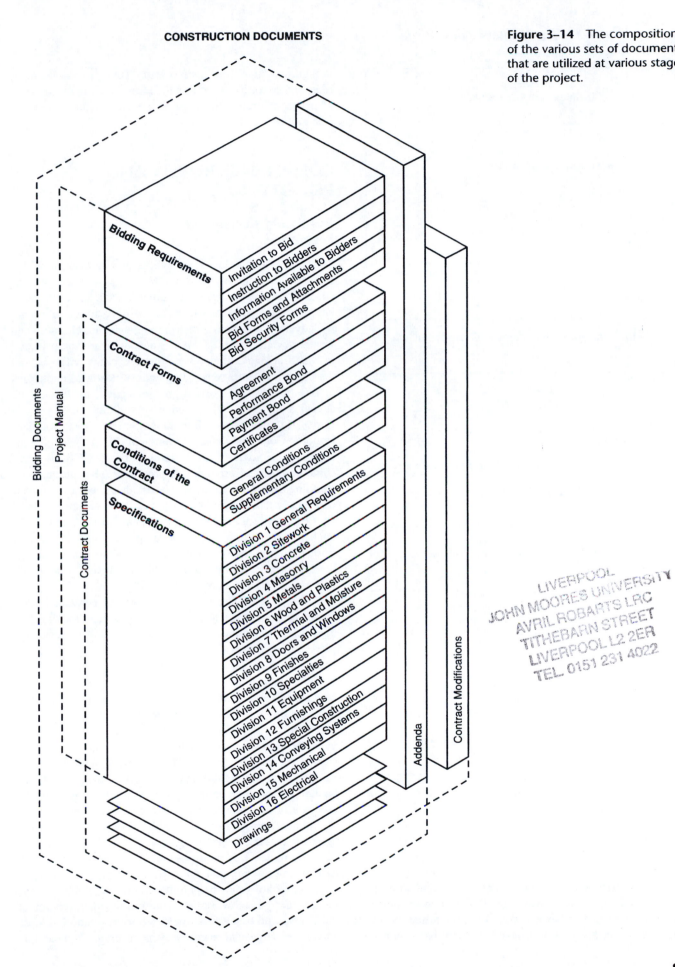

Figure 3–14 The composition of the various sets of documents that are utilized at various stages of the project.

Bidding Documents

Project Manual

Contract Documents

Bidding Requirements
- Invitation to Bid
- Instruction to Bidders
- Information Available to Bidders
- Bid Forms and Attachments
- Bid Security Forms

Contract Forms
- Agreement
- Performance Bond
- Payment Bond
- Certificates

Conditions of the Contract
- General Conditions
- Supplementary Conditions

Specifications
- Division 1 General Requirements
- Division 2 Sitework
- Division 3 Concrete
- Division 4 Masonry
- Division 5 Metals
- Division 6 Wood and Plastics
- Division 7 Thermal and Moisture
- Division 8 Doors and Windows
- Division 9 Finishes
- Division 10 Specialties
- Division 11 Equipment
- Division 12 Furnishings
- Division 13 Special Construction
- Division 14 Conveying Systems
- Division 15 Mechanical
- Division 16 Electrical

Drawings

Addenda

Contract Modifications

**Drawings:
Definition and Responsibility**

Purpose
Graphic representation of the work to be done.

Contents
* Relationship of materials to each other
* Sizes
* Locations
* Quantities
* Connections
* Schematic diagrams of mechanical and electrical systems
* Schedules of:
  * structural elements
  * equipment
  * finishes
  * other similar items

Figure 3–15   Drawings: Definitions and responsibility.

**Drawings:
Do's and Dont's**

Drawings should not:
* Use comprehensive notes
* Use too many notes
* Use notes that define work to be done by a specific contractor
* Use proprietary names
* Cross reference with specifications by indicating "See Spec"

Drawings should:
* Locate each material, assembly, component, and accessory
* Identify all components and pieces of equipment
* Give dimensions of components and sizes of field-assembled components
* Give details and diagrams of connection
* Give only generic names, shapes, and locations
* Identify, but not describe, a material or component
* Indicate extent of alternates
* Indicate areas of construction phasing
* Indicate limits of work
* Indicate specific areas of work by owner or others
* On multiple contract projects, designate work of separate contracts
* Identify drawing symbols used in a schedule of symbols
* Identify items of equipment by a short generic name or coded symbol that is defined in specifications
* Identify components with a bare minimum of information
* Indicate boundaries between materials of different capacities

Figure 3–16   Drawings: Do's and don'ts.

---

systems that they commonly encounter, for specific work of their clientele (usually used repetitively), and for systems not fully contained in a specific CSI Division. Figure 3–19 lists these Divisions, which remain constant for any and all projects; the Sections contained within the Division on any given spec sheet vary, in number and content, as required by the project work. The Sections, too, have a fixed format as shown

in Figure 3–20 of three distinct Parts. Text, provisions, materials, and so forth vary within the Parts as required to convey all pertinent information about the specific material or system (see Figure 3–21).

COMPLIANCE REVIEW AND PERMITTING

Regulatory Review and Permitting

The construction industry, as a whole, and its work are highly regulated. This involves, where the work is concerned, the enacting of laws (building and other codes), and other regulations with regard to fire resistance, safety, structural capacity, adverse conditions (for example, seismic, climatic, and weather events). In the United States there are some 19,000 jurisdictions including states, counties, cities, villages, and the like which enforce building codes; most are adaptations of one of the three current "model codes" available. The agencies that write these codes—Building Officials and Code Administrators, International (BOCA); Southern Building Code Congress, International (SBCCI); and the International Conference of Building Officials (ICBO)—have combined their efforts and are producing The International Building Code (IBC) and associated other codes for publication and enactment in 2000. Each of these groups has their codes adopted for use in several other countries, but it is still unclear what pattern of use and adoption worldwide will be forthcoming in response to this new array of codes. Ideally, there will be wide adoption worldwide of one code which will provide uniform control of construction.

As an aside it must also be noted that the construction industry, because of its inherent safety exposure, is regulated by the U.S. Occupational Safety and Health Administration (OSHA), as well as by state Workers' Compensation provisions, industrial relationship rules, and other occupational and workplace constraints. All of these, however, are aimed at the workers and their welfare and not at the project work itself.

Quite often, the completed contract documents are submitted to the regulatory agencies for their review of the methods used to comply with the regulations, and for issuance of required permits. The filing of the application may be done prior to the bidding period, since changes that may be required can then be incorporated into the project via the issuance of addenda. Good practice would note that there should be an on-going rapport with the regulatory agencies, to ensure that the project progresses in accord with the various requirements. It is not prudent to make a code search early on in programming, and then never approach the agencies again until time for permits. There are almost always items of design and work that require some interpretation of these laws, and best effort would call for resolution of these situations so they can be correctly incorporated into the final

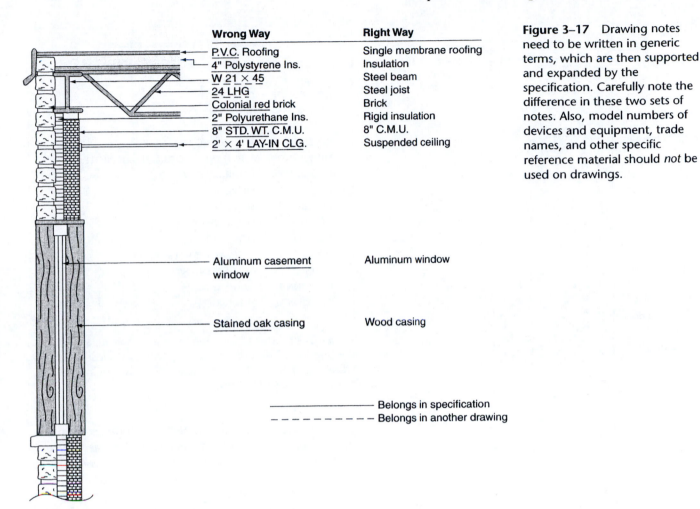

Wrong Way	Right Way
P.V.C. Roofing	Single membrane roofing
4" Polystyrene Ins.	Insulation
W 21 × 45	Steel beam
24 LHG	Steel joist
Colonial red brick	Brick
2" Polyurethane Ins.	Rigid insulation
8" STD. WT. C.M.U.	8" C.M.U.
2' × 4' LAY-IN CLG.	Suspended ceiling
Aluminum casement window	Aluminum window
Stained oak casing	Wood casing

———————— Belongs in specification

– – – – – – – – Belongs in another drawing

Figure 3–17 Drawing notes need to be written in generic terms, which are then supported and expanded by the specification. Carefully note the difference in these two sets of notes. Also, model numbers of devices and equipment, trade names, and other specific reference material should *not* be used on drawings.

documents. Additionally, the regulations are changed periodically, and new provisions may apply to the project; these may aid or inhibit the project as designed.

This application sequence is critical so that the time required for review of the documents does not forestall or inhibit project progress. This is even truer when there is a need for an appeal or variance from the regulations to meet the specific circumstances of the project. These procedures should be initiated as soon as it appears they are needed, since they can be time-consuming and could delay the anticipated start of work. Hence, the design professional oftentimes will file the permit(s) application early on and will "field" any questions coming back from the agencies. Usually the contractor is required to receive the permit, and pay for it (as part of the overall project cost); in fact, in some cases the permit fees are known and noted in the bidding documents.

CONTRACTOR SELECTION

The basic premise of any construction project lies in the relationship of three parties—owner, design professional, and contractor—in accomplishing a mutual goal. These parties can vary from a single person in each category, to large corporations represented by several persons. Nonetheless, the relationships are set out, legally, in two separate contracts; these also can vary widely reflecting the value, extent, or complexity of the project. One contract is the Owner–Design Professional Agreement, in which the owner retains the design professional for requisite professional services for the design and documentation of the planned project. This may include any of an array of other additional services, and is usually written to the requirements the owner chooses to impose. Nothing therein concerns actual construction work, although administration of the construction contract, including observation of the work by the professional, is normally included.

The other contract is the Owner-Contractor Agreement. This addresses the actual construction of the project, as set out in the contract documents (drawings and specifications) produced by the design professional. In essence, the owner is "buying" the services and expertise of the contractor for construction of the structure, as designed specifically for the owner's needs. A key point to note here (see Figure 3–22) is the absence of a legal/contractual relationship between design professional and contractor, although both are parties to a contract with the owner. In fact, the professional is positioned

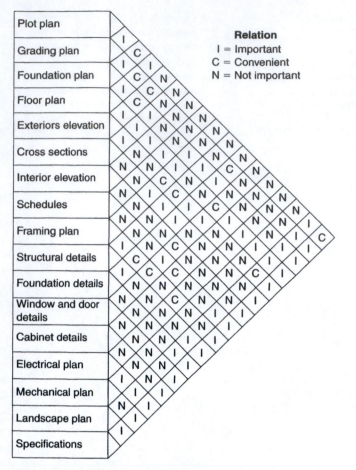

Relation

I = Important
C = Convenient
N = Not important

Plot plan
Grading plan
Foundation plan
Floor plan
Exteriors elevation
Cross sections
Interior elevation
Schedules
Framing plan
Structural details
Foundation details
Window and door details
Cabinet details
Electrical plan
Mechanical plan
Landscape plan
Specifications

Figure 3–18 The interrelationship and the relative importance of the drawings in a set. Note that nothing in this chart is frivolous or irrelevant—it is just that some drawings are more closely related than others.

Index to CSI 16 Division Format	
DIVISION 1	GENERAL REQUIREMENTS
DIVISION 2	SITEWORK
DIVISION 3	CONCRETE
DIVISION 4	MASONRY
DIVISION 5	METALS
DIVISION 6	WOOD AND PLASTICS
DIVISION 7	THERMAL AND MOISTURE PROTECTION
DIVISION 8	DOORS AND WINDOWS
DIVISION 9	FINISHES
DIVISION 10	SPECIALTIES
DIVISION 11	EQUIPMENT
DIVISION 12	FURNISHINGS
DIVISION 13	SPECIAL CONSTRUCTION
DIVISION 14	CONVEYING SYSTEMS
DIVISION 15	MECHANICAL
DIVISION 16	ELECTRICAL

Figure 3–19 The 16-Division format for specifications developed by The Construction Specifications Institute, now widely used. Properly used, there is no variation in numbering or titles of the Divisions.

as the "policeman" over the Owner-Contractor Agreement (through contract administration), to ensure that those two parties fulfill their respective responsibilities. This duty is set out in the Owner-Professional Agreement, as one of the responsibilities of the professional.

For a moment let us step back and review this arrangement in very basic terms. The owner, in some fashion, decides that a new building/facility is required for the continued success of the operation/business. Since the owner is not fully acquainted with the design and construction processes, a design professional is retained. Usually several professionals are interviewed, and the selection made from those resources. There, of course, can be a direct hire, where the owner knows personally, has reliable knowledge of, or has worked previously with the professional. In some cases, the professional is hired based on previous projects which the owner finds attractive and responsive to current needs. Many times this involves "signature architects," whose work is renowned, widely known, and published—and often is "cutting edge" distinctive or controversial. This person creates a program for the project by ascertaining the owner's needs

and desires regarding every aspect of the project: from aesthetics (appearance) to the functioning of the new facility. This information is then converted into usable construction information, which indicates not only what is to be built, but also how, and with what.

The contractor can be retained in any of several ways, again depending on the knowledge of the owner and that of the professional. The owner can hire the contractor directly; there can be a negotiated contract; there can be an invited, competitive bidding between several prospective contractors; or in the case of publicly funded projects, there can be a bidding process open to all interested contractors. Usually, in privately funded work, the list of contractors invited to bid is compiled jointly by the owner and professional. Here both parties can contribute information and names based on previous experience, knowledge of the contractors, or other levels of information which bring some understanding of and knowledge about the contractors—it tends to eliminate the semblance of a situation popularly known as "buying a pig in the poke" (i.e., purchasing something without really seeing it). The more that is known about the contractor, his or her work habits and philosophy, reputation, expertise, and so on, the better for all concerned.

The absolute need is to form a three-party combine that respects each other, has confidence in each other, and can work through the worst of problems that may occur in a reasonable, businesslike manner, reaching mutually acceptable conclusions. In most cases there will be a natural affinity whereby the parties will easily come together, get along well, and accomplish their mutual goal. Other than personality

Section Format
Outline

PART 1 GENERAL

SUMMARY
  Section Includes
  Products Supplied But Not Installed
    Under This Section
  Products Installed But Not Supplied
    Under This Section
  Related Sections
  Allowances
  Unit Prices
  Measurement Procedures
  Payment Procedures
  Alternates/Alternatives

REFERENCES

DEFINITIONS

SYSTEM DESCRIPTION
  Design Requirements
  Performance Requirements

SUBMITTALS
  Product Data
  Shop Drawings
  Samples
  Quality
  Assurance/Control Submittals
    Design Data
    Test Reports
    Certificates
    Manufacturer's Instructions
    Manufacturer's Field Reports
  Closeout Submittals

QUALITY ASSURANCE
  Qualifications
  Regulatory Requirements
  Certifications
  Field Samples
  Mockups
  Pre-Installation Meetings

DELIVERY, STORAGE, AND
HANDLING
  Packing, Shipping, Handling, and
    Unloading
  Acceptance at Site
  Storage and Protection

PROJECT CONDITIONS OR SITE
CONDITIONS
  Environmental Requirements
  Existing Conditions

SEQUENCING

SCHEDULING

WARRANTY
  Special Warranty

SYSTEM STARTUP

OWNER'S INSTRUCTIONS

COMMISSIONING

MAINTENANCE
  Extra Materials
  Maintenance Service

PART 2 PRODUCTS

MANUFACTURERS

EXISTING PRODUCTS

MATERIALS

MANUFACTURED UNITS

EQUIPMENT

COMPONENTS

ACCESSORIES

MIXES

FABRICATION
  Shop Assembly

FINISHES
  Shop Priming
  Shop Finishing

SOURCE QUALITY CONTROL
  Fabrication Tolerances
  Tests, Inspection
  Verification of Performance

PART 3 EXECUTION

ACCEPTABLE INSTALLERS

EXAMINATION
  Site Verification of Conditions

PREPARATION
  Protection
  Surface Preparation

ERECTION

INSTALLATION

APPLICATION

CONSTRUCTION
  Special Techniques
  Interface with Other Work
  Sequences of Operation
  Site Tolerances

REPAIR/RESTORATION

RE-INSTALLATION

FIELD QUALITY CONTROL
  Site Tests
  Inspection
  Manufacturer's Field Services

ADJUSTING

CLEANING

DEMONSTRATION

PROTECTION

SCHEDULES

Figure 3–20 The standardized, 3-Part format used for specifications Sections within the CSI format. The 3 Parts occur in every Section (even if only noted "not applicable"). However, not every listing is required in every Part of every Section; where used, though, they should appear in the order shown here.

Figure 3–21 Although this is a very narrow and limited Section, it serves to show the final layout and proper use of the CSI specifications format (both Divisions and Sections/Parts).

Client Name:
Project Name:
Project Name:

Project Specification 055.220.11166
21APR97
Page 1 of 1

DOCK BUMPERS

1.0   GENERAL

    1.1   Summary

        A.   Scope of Specification

        This specification includes but does not necessarily limit materials and labor to furnish, unload, store, and install dock bumpers for a complete, operational system.

        B.   Related Specification

        Work in this specification shall be coordinated with:

        • 000.220.01000: General Requirements
        • 055.220.08360: Overhead Doors
        • 055.220.11162: Dock Levelers—Hydraulic
        • 055.220.11165: Dock Seals

    1.2   References

    Referenced publications within this specification shall be the latest revision unless otherwise specified; and applicable parts of the referenced publications shall become a part of this specification as if fully included.

2.0   PRODUCTS

    2.1   Manufacturer

    Dock bumpers shall be Model VB420-11SF, as manufactured by Frommelt Industries, Inc., or an approved substitute.

    2.2   Materials

    Dock bumpers shall be 4″ × 20″ × 11″ with 3/8″ steel face plate equal to the rubber surface dimensions. Plate to be welded to two (2) steel support brackets which are to extend back to 3/4″ supporting rods. Brackets to be punched with elongated holes to allow steel face to "float" upon impact.

3.0   EXECUTION

    3.1   Installation

    Each dock area shall have 2 steel face dock bumpers installed as shown on the drawings and in accordance with approved shop drawings and the manufacturer's recommendations.

---

clashes (often difficult to prevent) three attributes prevail in successful relationships and projects—professionalism, communications, and trust. Failure in any of these, on the part of any party, will doom a project.

Trust is fundamental: each party must understand their limitations and respect the ability and intelligence of the others. It is a confidence that the others are up to their tasks, and their work will enhance the project. It is a form of respect and acknowledgment of the skill and ability of others to perform well

in their assigned tasks. Although the parties may never have worked together before, the level of trust must be that which would allow and encourage them to work together again.

The matter of trust relates back to the contractual configuration. The design professional, as overseer of the Owner-Contractor agreement, must chastise the owner when a monthly payment (certified by the professional as being reflective of work done) is late and not made in accord with the contract. Here the contractor "trusted" the owner to make

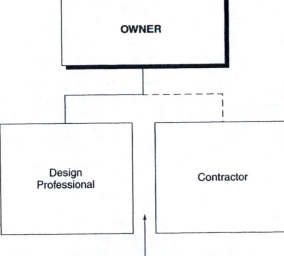

No contractual agreement; working
relationship required via contracts with Owner

Figure 3–22   The basic project.

such payments promptly as required in the contract to which they both agreed.

In the same manner, a claim by the contractor for additional time to complete the project, due to days lost to inclement weather, will find no support from the professional, who must certify the cause and value of the delay, when the contractor cannot produce proper records to show the days involved and the impact on the project. Here the owner trusts both of the other parties to properly uphold their parts in the project in a true, accurate, and "trustworthy" manner.

A contractor who has opened trenches for the installation of footings and is forced to clean out these trenches three times due to soil sliding back in because of rain also has a problem of trust. In this instance, the trust is a more complex contractual issue. If the design professional has not promptly reviewed the shop drawings for the reinforcing steel for the footings, that is the cause of the problem. Although not tied together by contract, the contractor trusted the professional to act promptly, on behalf of the project. This is basis for a complaint to the owner, via contract provisions, to request the owner to see that the professional performs more diligently.

These are but three fairly typical breeches of performance on a project, which involves just one of the primary operating attributes the project parties must exercise. This type of thing is not uncommon, and has an adverse impact on a project, to say nothing of the time/money expended to resolve needless problems.

From the above, it is abundantly clear that communications are the lifeblood of the project. Simply put, the parties must "share" information, in an open, voluntary, continual, meaningful, and helpful manner. Absolutely nothing should permit the shutdown of any segment or branch of communications, not only between the three primary parties, but between all project participants both on and off the site. The

system of communications does not need to be overwhelming; its greatest value is being pertinent, informative, inclusive, timely, appropriate, and an aid to all concerned.

In an age of ever-increasing technology in communications equipment and formats, there is no excuse for the lack of communication. It is people, though, who make communications "good." The cost of communications on even a moderately small project is minimal, but certainly should extend to telephone, fax, e-mail, express deliveries, and certainly face-to-face conversations and productive meetings.

The last attribute of a successful team, professionalism, is easy to spot but difficult to define. It means doing your job, helping others to do their job, with a respectful attitude and a dedication to task, with pride in work produced and in the finished product. It includes giving ground on some issues for the good of the project. It is appreciation and respect for the work and expertise of others, and doing your job in a manner that draws those same virtues to you. For example,

- The owner must give up any penchant to micro-manage the project
- The design professional must give up being stiff-necked and uncompromising
- The contractor must give up a renegade attitude to go off and do the project despite others' wishes
- All must give up absolute control in different ways and times for the good of the project

Currently there are numerous configurations for writing the contracts (Figure 3–23), and establishing the proper relationships. In this, the owner will naturally (by default, really) take the lead role, since the expenditure of money for the project comes from the owner, and the final reality of the project must meet the owner's needs and satisfaction. The professional and the contractor have the right, it goes without saying, to control and "defend" their status, expertise, and business success as it relates to the owner and the project. Should the owner try to impose unreasonable conditions, the professional and contractor have the right to "walk away from" the project. It is, of course, the wise owner who will fashion the project to meet her or his needs, but at the same time fully utilize the best efforts and expertise of the professional and contractor—all in a harmonious atmosphere.

Bidding

This is the process of determining the overall cost of the project's construction. The process is carried out in the manner desired by the owner; much of the actual estimating process, however, is standard operating procedure with each contractor, and not open to change. Often in private sector work, there is a list of bidders (developed with the design professional, and/or construction manager) who are invited to participate (none others "need apply"). Usually this list contains contractors for the four major trade contracts (general construction,

Figure 3–23 The various contract options used for the variety of delivery systems. There is no firm direction for an owner; the choice of what is proper or correct is a consideration for the owner to determine.

	A/E	Contr.	Contrs.	CM	
Traditional	P(D)	GC	Mechs.*	—	5 separate contracts
Tripartite	P(D)	P(GC)	**	—	2 separate contracts
Multiple Primes	P(D)	GC	Varies	—	Numerous contracts
Design/Build 1	P(D)	GC(S)	—	—	1 contract w/ A/E
2	JV	JV	—	—	1 contract; 3 parties
3	D(S)	P(GC)	—	—	1 contract; w/ GC
4	—	P(D/GC)	—	—	
Const Mgt. 1	P(D)	—	—	SC	Sep. A/E contract for CM
2	D(S)	P(GC)	—	SC	Sep. GC contract for CM
3	D(S)	—	—	P	
4	P(D)	—	—	P(CM)	2 separate contracts

P(D)—prime contract/design
GC—general construction
GC(S)—gen'l const./subcontract
JV—joint venture
D(S)—design/subcontract
*P, HVAC & E contracts

P(GC)—prime/gen'l const.
P(D/GC)—prime/design and gen'l const.
SC—separate contract
P(CM)—prime/const. mgt.
**Mech. contracts bid separately and assigned
    to GC, or are direct subcontracts

Number of Contracts
a. single prime contract
b. multiple prime contracts

Contract Types
a. construction management
b. design/build
c. owner/build
d. construction subcontracts

Tripartite; Owner/Arch.-Engr. contract; Owner/Contractor contract
Single const. contract; competitive bid; separate A/E contract
Multiple prime contract; competitive bid; several O/C contract; sep. A/E contract
Construction Management; O/A-E contract w/sep. Contr. and sep. CM contracts
Design-Build; O/A-E, or O/Contr. contract w/appropriate professional sub; also O/Admin. Professional
    contract
Owner-Build; O/A-E contract; numerous subcontracts w/Owner

plumbing, HVAC, and electrical) who are familiar to the professionals and who have performed well on other projects. There could be an open bidding whereby any interested general contractor can submit a bid for the work. Actual selection of the contractor is at the will of the owner and is usually unencumbered legally. In publicly funded projects the list must be open to all, which makes ascertaining the "best qualified" contractor a difficult task. Public work, most frequently, also requires the acceptance of the "lowest, and best bid" regardless of qualifications (lowest is the numerical lowest— best is much more difficult to ascertain, and often leads to many disputes including litigation). This process can lead to difficult (slow, disrupted, inadequate, improper) projects, as the contractor endeavors to recover costs on at least a "break-even" basis. Low bids most often are created by pure error on the part of the contractor in putting together the bid—leaving work out, transposing numbers, misplaced decimal points, forgetting taxes/wage rate changes, and the like, and/or cutting margins and subcontract funding too close. Also, some

contractors may bid simply to "get the work," even though the project is beyond their actual capabilities.

Fairness is the key word in the bidding process. The bid documents require that everyone base their bids on the same documents. While there may be variation in methods and procedures between bidders, projects must be bid in a manner that will provide full accord with those same documents. Addenda (noting changes in the documents) must be distributed, prior to the bid date, to all those with documents for estimating the work. Questions asked by one bidder must be answered to all. The bids must be sealed, and received prior to the appointed hour (late bids being excluded almost 100 percent of the time). There is little if any room for any kind of advantage to some bidders but not all: helps such as added time, answers which give added insight, explanations/interpretations of documents, or even correction of errors. For contractors, bidding is a high-risk exercise—extensive, expensive, meticulous, highly competitive, and frequently disappointing. No fee is paid for the bidding, it being done at the contractors' cost to search out new projects for their work-force and their own profit. There is a distinct and highly developed methodology, technique, and bank of knowledge used in bidding; prices for units of work (installing a door and its hardware, for example) must be known and must be reliable. These must then be applied to the correct number of items as taken from the drawings and specifications (called a "take-off"). Items missed, or miscounted are at the contractor's expense, be the error a shortage or an overage. It is high-stress, intensive work to ensure that *every* item, no matter how small, is accounted for (see Appendix E for further explanation). Additionally, the contractors seek to assess, visualize, completely understand, and envision how they would approach and execute the project. This entails understanding not only the construction but also the various nuances and encumbrances that will (or could) impact the project work. Estimators can make or break contracting firms; they are held in high repute and are a valuable asset to an active firm. They must know construction methods, materials, sources, equipment, techniques, "politics," and all of the nuances in order to convert contract documents into an appropriate, accurate bid, and hopefully into a new contract. In reality a good estimate is a "plan" for the project—a plan ready to execute.

Additionally, much of the work will be given over to subcontractors—specialty contractors who perform work of limited scope, usually in a specialized field, or material installation. The "sub-bids" must be received (usually from several firms of the same trade) and analyzed so the best and lowest sub-bid can be factored into the overall bid. Many times the general contractor will use a sub-bid that is a little higher from a certain sub who is known and has worked well previously. Not all subcontractors usually bid to every one of the general contractors who may be developing bids—here again competition is extremely high as the subs vie for more work.

In soliciting bids, the owner must provide documents for the bidders to use in their take-offs. Normally a deposit is required to ensure that the documents, in the hands of unsuccessful bidders, will be returned. These can then be reused by the various contractors who are selected to work on the project. Most of the bidding contractors, though, will have limited amounts of work, and will not seek full sets of documents for bidding. To allow them access, sets of contract documents are placed in public "plan rooms." These facilities are offered by local construction industries offices and by F. W. Dodge, Inc., which is a construction-reporting agency that provides the service as a courtesy to local contractors. Here a subcontractor or material supplier can make a take-off of the items with which they are concerned. They then can formulate their bid and call it in to the general contractors they choose to bid to. In this way the owner is not made to pay for an overabundance of documents that may never be needed. The documents are made available to the entire array of contractors on an equal basis, which leads to better and closer pricing—stiffer competition—which in the end benefits the owner through the lower cost of the project.

Award of Contract(s)/Notice to Proceed

The owner, in consultation with the design professionals, attorneys, and construction manager (if utilized), must review and understand all of the bids and how they could influence the project. If bound by law ("lowest and best" bid usually must be used for publicly funded projects), the owner needs to know the type of organizations which are represented by the low bid and their expertise. If an error is claimed (usually by the contractor very soon after the bidding) there needs to be a resolution as to the impact and severity of that error and whether or not the contractor can overcome the problem and execute the project. If not, proper action must be taken to void the bid and move to the next lower bid for the same consideration. Sometimes a bid is extremely low, and the contractor claims no error. Here, obviously something is wrong, and an attempt must be made to find out what it is. Construction is not the place to seek or take advantage of an apparent "bargain" by default—simple equity and correct pricing is the better route. In Europe, for instance, the "correct" cost of the project is sought. This is done by eliminating the highest and lowest bids received, and awarding the contract to the contractor whose bid is closest (higher or lower) to the median of the remaining bids. It is felt that this process awards the contract to the contractor whose bid most accurately reflects the probable actual cost of the project—certainly an issue of "fairness"!

Should the current American process continue, and the apparently errant bidder is awarded the contract, there could well be a very adverse situation sometime later in the project. Problems can arise when the contractor attempts to recover from the error or provides substandard work to cut costs, or a slower progression of work results, or shut-downs by unpaid subcontractors, or other financial problems detrimental to the project. In addition, the progress of still other contractors can be affected, who may well seek to recover for their unanticipated extra costs.

Awarding the contract should be a very thorough and careful process, so no unfounded assumptions are made, and so the contract can be formulated with all of the proper provisions. The client's attorney should come into the picture at this point to protect the client and to produce an equitable contract, but to the ultimate good of the client. Quite often, the attorney will simply use the standard contract forms from such organizations as the American Institute of Architects (AIA), or the Engineers Joint Contract Documents Committee (EJCDC) of the National Society of Professional Engineers (NSPE). It is not all that infrequent that the client will require a specific contract form, written to the needs of the client (such as a governmental agency), or the peculiarities of the project, or the contractual configuration. Such forms must be made available for review during the bidding period, so the contractor can assess what the project entails. If, however, the contract proves to be too extraordinary, the contractor may balk at signing it—particularly if it appears to place hardship or added risk on the contractor alone.

Many times the client will issue a Notice To Proceed (or Notice to Award) telling the contractor(s) of the client/owner's intention to enter into a contract based on the bid price (and any negotiations that may have taken place subsequent to bidding). With this legally binding notice, the contractor can start mobilizing his forces and begin to formulate the project team. Often this process starts with the subcontractors listed on the bid form (List of Materials and Subcontracts) being given similar Notices or their contracts. Fairly soon after the Notice, the formal signing of the contracts with the four major contractors will take place, and the contractual relationships will be established; also, the "project clock" starts running, ticking off the days until completion of the project (as required in the contract).

Pre-Construction Conference Meeting (Kick-off)

It has been found that a pre-construction conference or meeting of all concerned parties to the project is profitable, so that they can best be aligned and familiarized with each other, and project conditions and procedures can be made known. As part of the mobilization process, the contractor in conjunction with the design professionals calls for the conference. Usually at least a notice of intent (to issue a contract) is required to get the parties to react to the meeting and attend. Formal contract signing is not necessary, but is preferable. However, the meeting should occur before actual construction (and even on-site mobilization) is started.

If not done in preparation for the meeting, an accurate and current directory of all parties should be compiled and distributed; include company name, contact persons, addresses, phone numbers, facsimile (FAX) line numbers, and other such data. There should be a formal agenda for the meeting, which includes personal introductions of all parties and short presentations by the owner (or the designated representative) and the design professionals (including the construction manager and consultants). Topics specific to the project should be included and problems resolved—communications, distribution lists, site security, assigned storage areas, site operations, site office/trailer location, temporary services, and peculiar parameters regarding excessive noise, dust, traffic control, parking, safety issues, and so on. Additionally, there can be a distribution of documents and review of contractual obligations and the Conditions (both General and Supplemental) and Division 1 General Requirements of the specifications, and there should be an open discussion of how, exactly, the general contractor intends to run the site and the project. Figure 3–24 outlines the different responsibilities of the primary players.

While this is not a social meeting, neither should it be a dictatorial, fist-pounding display of demands; rather the tone of the entire project can be set by having an amicable, friendly interchange, whereby all parties can meet each other and recognize each other by sight (and first name). With this, and a sincere, firm, and fair explanation of the need for cooperation and combined effort, the project can be set on a good course. Also, it is helpful to create an open atmosphere where any question is welcome and will be resolved, promptly, fairly, and in keeping with the obligations of all contracts.

CONSTRUCTION PHASE

Initial On-site Operations

The very first operation is to physically lay out and establish the limits of the project work on the job site. This entails a survey and engineering crew who will traverse the property and set stakes and monuments on all property lines and corners. They also establish all bench marks, easements or other legal (but mostly invisible) encumbrances; establish clearing lines (the edge of an overgrown or wooded area which is to remain) and mark the plants and trees that are to be removed for the project; find and mark all utility lines, although this is better done by each utility company, who maintain their own, accurate records. It is important that this matrix is set out so no part of or party to the project will violate any of the parameters (which could have legal consequences).

Prior to moving on-site, the contractor will have determined how the temporary construction facilities—storage trailers and area, parking areas, office trailers, work sheds, toilets, water supply, electric service, and the like—are to be located. This must be done in a manner that allows adequate work area for the contractors in the construction area, while also allowing for maneuvering of equipment and receipt and storage of various materials. If done improperly, the site layout can be a direct impairment to satisfactory work progress and completion.

Next the building(s) is laid out, accurately according to the site plan, by establishing the building lines, turning required angles, and setting batter boards or other indicators for long-term use at each corner of the structure. These indicators are set outside the excavation or grading line of the project so they will not be disturbed by such operations. On both very open and very tight (inner-city) sites, and where appropriate for the type of building, column centerlines will also be established and indicators set. In essence, this is a full-scale site plan coming to life; it places the project structures physically on the land area.

Mobilization

This is the process the contractor uses to energize the project, with both physical and administrative activities (on- and off-site). Administratively, the process involves securing insurance and bond coverage, acquiring permits, preparing progress schedules, and so on. Additionally, the list includes a number of activities and work items that are performed or provided on the actual site. The next section covers these.

Work Item/Task	Responsibility		
	Owner	A/E	C/CM
Preparation/mobilization for construction	—	—	P
Insurance requirements; verify/monitor	P	S	S
Contracts for contractors; prepare/process	—	S	P
Provide full-time, on-site coordination	—	—	P
Prepare schedule for beneficial occupancy	—	—	P
Supervise or observe contractors' work	—	S	P
Assess for compliance with contract documents	—	P	S
Make interpretations of plans and/or specs	—	P	S
Update construction schedule to reflect progress	—	—	P
Process and control shop drawings and samples	—	S	P
Review, check, and approve shop drawings and samples	—	P	S
Certify payment requests from contractor(s)	—	P	S
Disperse payments to contractor(s)	—	—	P
Provide cost control for project	—	—	P
Convene job meetings	—	S	P
Bulletins for contractors; prepare/process	S	P	S
Approve quotations for bulletins	P	S	S
Issue change orders	—	P	P
Oversee and administer safety program for project	—	—	P
Oversee and administer security program	—	—	P
Oversee and administer quality control program	—	S	P
Maintain "as-built" drawings	—	P	P
Coordinate owner occupancy schedule	P	S	P
Prepare "punch list"	—	P	P
Oversee completion of punch list	—	—	P
Certify substantial completion	P	P	P
Secure regulatory agency(ies) approvals	—	P	—
Secure certificate of occupancy	—	—	P
Demonstrate operation of systems/equipment	P	S	S
Start-up and recommended maintenance	P	S	P
Submit operations manuals and warranties	—	P	P
Inspect for final compliance	S	P	P
Final accounting, determine final payment	P	P	P
Final review, approval and acceptance	P		

Key: P = primary   S = secondary   — = none

Figure 3–24 Responsibilities of owner, architect, engineer, contractor, and construction manager.

On-Site Mobilization and Staging

Some earthwork operations may be required on-site, to allow for setting of office trailers or opening storage areas. This may entail activities like clearing, grubbing, or scraping of top soil if these facilities occupy a portion of the project site, and there may be need for restoration of these areas at the completion of the project. The following (and perhaps other items) are required, and in some cases are listed in the project specifications:

- Move plant and equipment onto site
- Furnish/erect plants and temporary buildings
- Install temporary construction power, wiring, lighting
- Establish fire protection
- Install construction water supply
- Provide furnishings and utility services to offices
- Provide on-site communications
- Provide on-site sanitary facilities
- Establish contractor storage areas, furnish/install/maintain storage buildings/sheds
- Post all OSHA and other required labor/employment placards

- Establish site bulletin board

- Establish all safety programs, safeguards and signs/instructions/placards

- Have project superintendent on-site, full-time

- Plan, submit design, provide and erect project sign

- Install fencing, gates, parking areas, truck delivery locations, tower or other crane(s), hoists, debris and waste collection facilities, garbage facilities, eating/break/smoking areas, and traffic controls

Project Organization: Set Project Progress Meetings

Very soon after the first personnel from the contractors come on-site and work begins, it is necessary to hold a meeting to establish the organization of the project and the site. This should be the first of a series of periodically scheduled project progress meetings, and should be a detailed expansion of the information discussed at the pre-construction conference. The contractor should convene these meetings with a firm and appropriate agenda distributed prior to the meeting, so all participants can arrive fully prepared to discuss the project, answer and ask questions, and simply coordinate. (This is not to be a free-for-all, rap session, or social event.) The participants should be all contractors currently working on-site, those to arrive shortly, and those leaving shortly; the design professionals' representative(s) and the owner's representative should also attend. Others may be invited as required to discuss special situations or to give specific information to all present.

Often these meetings are set for a time just prior to the deadline for submitting monthly payment requests, so there can be review and discussion of the requests, the work completed to date, accuracy of information, completeness of information, and extenuating problems and circumstances. This speeds processing of the requests by the professionals and provides for prompter payment by the owner.

Create, Review, and Finalize Project Schedule

The general (prime) contractor is responsible for the execution of the project work and also responsible for the methods, techniques, and process of construction. With this comes the necessity and responsibility to organize and schedule the work and the interface of the various subcontractors. Obviously the contractor is concerned if some work is not done on time, or if other work that follows disrupts, removes, or mars the first work. Repair or replacement in such cases is at no cost to the owner, but can be a detriment to the project.

There are numerous different techniques for scheduling, and the choice will be made of the system that best serves the project. Some schedules are simple bar charts, noting start and completion of each subcontracted task or work item. These can be done by hand, but more than likely today will be computer generated. Several specific software programs, ranging from simple to highly complex, can produce the proper schedule for the project (of course, if given good data to work with). Mostly the schedule is predicated on good weather, but has flexibility built in to adjust the progress when the work is interrupted or delayed by weather conditions. Some projects in colder climates actually shut down completely during winter or during other adverse seasonal weather.

The project schedule is crucial to many aspects of the work, and to the successful completion of the work. It spells out "what gets done, when," in a basic form. It is necessary to schedule for the ordering and flow of material and the application of money to the work functions, to avoid confusion caused by having the wrong workers on the job at the wrong time, and to ascertain when other material, work, and personnel will be required. It is a road map about how the project will be run. In this it avoids having rough work done after some finish work—which is counterproductive to good job progress and completion. Also, it allows the various contractors to forecast when they must service the project (and when they can service others). The owners thereby know when the various aspects will be complete, when they can expect to see an increase in the level of payment requested (the more work activity, the more payment required) and when, finally, the project will be completed—which impacts final payment, as well as nonconstruction activities as owner move-in and occupancy.

Figure 3–25 is the project schedule for a small building. Many projects use a schedule similar to this; others use more detailed schedules, due to the added complexity of those projects. There are numbers of computer software programs that develop schedules in various layers of detail to show how the intricacies of the project will correlate. Also, there is a CPM (critical path method) format for scheduling, which relates the changes that occur and the concurrent progress of various project work efforts. This can be an extremely complex but valuable tool.

Start of the Construction Process

Usually the Notice to Proceed (and eventually the contract) will call for work to start within seven to fourteen days after the date of receipt of the notice. The schedule then must reflect that date and the end (completion) date as set out in the contract; most contracts now use a number of "calendar" days for the work period. This schedule is used as the basis for all discussion of project progress, and is usually the topic of some discussion at every project meeting. While the schedule is flexible, every contractor takes note of its provisions and works within the time frames outlined—all this being discussed and resolved prior to issuance of the final schedule.

Initiate Purchases of Materials and Systems

As soon as they have contracts signed, all of the contractors will start to order the necessary materials, supplies, and equipment

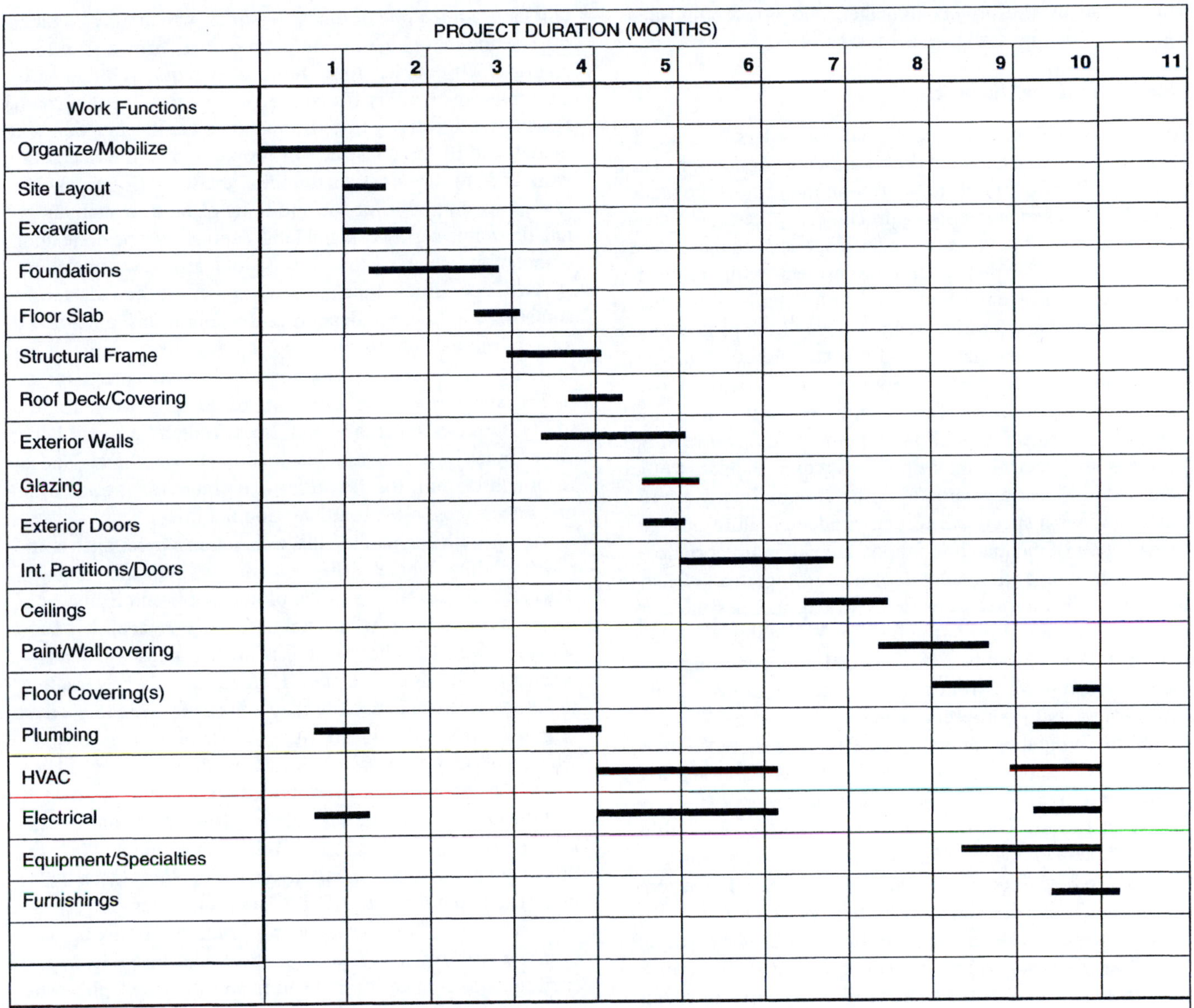

		PROJECT DURATION (MONTHS)									
Work Functions	1	2	3	4	5	6	7	8	9	10	11
Organize/Mobilize	▬▬										
Site Layout		▬									
Excavation		▬▬									
Foundations			▬▬▬								
Floor Slab			▬								
Structural Frame				▬▬							
Roof Deck/Covering				▬							
Exterior Walls				▬▬▬							
Glazing					▬▬						
Exterior Doors					▬						
Int. Partitions/Doors						▬▬▬					
Ceilings							▬▬				
Paint/Wallcovering								▬▬			
Floor Covering(s)									▬		▬
Plumbing	▬			▬						▬▬	
HVAC				▬▬▬▬▬						▬	
Electrical	▬			▬▬▬▬▬						▬	
Equipment/Specialties									▬▬▬		
Furnishings										▬▬	

NOTE: In some cases the bars on the schedule overlap. This indicates that the activity noted by the lower bar can begin while the latter stages of the upper bar work are still in progress and being completed. Also, some activity bars are not continuous. Here an activity has some work early in the project, and other activities later; the two, though, are not pursued in a continuous effort. (For example, Plumbing has a function early on in the underground piping that must be installed while the excavation is open. Later the plumber will install roof drains, and will set supports for fixtures. Still later, near the end of the project, the plumbing fixtures themselves will be set.)

Figure 3–25   Project schedule for a small building.

they will need to perform the work. Some of this procurement is driven by the schedule, that is, there is no need to order material which will not be needed until later in the project sequence. Paint would be a good example. However, it is necessary that all contractors monitor the project's progress and schedule so prompt ordering can be done to prevent any delays due to inadequate supplies of materials or excessive delivery time. Often material is ordered "for later release and delivery"; this is a method of reserving the needed materials, but receiving them promptly so as not to create a storage problem on the site.

Some materials will have delivery times in the range of 10–12 weeks from the date of order, so care, knowledge, and monitoring is an absolute necessity to the contractors. Also care must be taken, primarily by contractors who work with numerous items specified throughout the Project Manual, so all of the devices, equipment, and materials required by their work are ordered, and in a timely fashion. Occasionally, one item will be overlooked (or assumed to be part of another contractor's work) and not ordered in time to allow prompt and in-sequence installation. Almost all of this work is office work, done by the project manager, and is accomplished while other on-site activities are taking place.

Shop Drawings/Submittals

Yet another process is started as material orders are placed. This is the activity known as shop drawing production. The vast majority of the items to be used in the project are made through various manufacturing processes. Quite often "standard" materials or devices are specified, but even these must be made proper for their fit into the project—minor adjustments and spacing may be involved. Other items will be fabricated specifically for the circumstances of the project, and must be made in special ways. For example, a countertop must be made to fit, exactly, between two end walls. Obviously, its dimensions must be determined in the field, and then the shop must be told how to fabricate this work. Shop drawings are precisely that: drawings which indicate to the manufacturer's shop what is to be made, how many are required, and what special, different, or added features need to be made part of the material or apparatus. In many instances, the shop drawings will depict a specific arrangement of standard (stock) parts, pieces, or items which matches the configuration or conditions in the project. While the individual items are common and mass produced, their combinations and relationships vary from project to project, or even on the same project, but in different locations.

Before giving these drawings over to their shop, the manufacturer will submit them to the design professional and contractor for review, and to ascertain whether or not the proposed fabrication meets the intention and requirements of the contract documents. No manufacturer wishes to produce an item only to have it rejected or have it not fit the dimensions or purpose. These drawings, along with product data sheets (cuts, descriptions, and listing of product features) are part of the submittals required in various sections of the specifications. In some cases, actual samples of the material or device are also required, to show actual items for assessment of quality, or in some cases, for selection of color(s). All of these submittals are not required, and are not submitted, at the beginning of the project. They will be submitted throughout the progress of the work, but in a timely manner to allow for production and shipping time, so the actual material or devices are on the site, ready for installation at the right time.

Earthwork: Grading and Excavation (Utilities and Buildings)

Field operations continue in successive order concurrently with the office and administrative activities. Once the site is laid out, and the various limits, parameters, and locations set out, the operations turn to earthwork. This starts with a process called "grubbing and clearing", i.e., removing unnecessary brush, trees, undergrowth, existing features/structures, and the like from the job site. Often large project sites will have a huge pile of discarded trees, which may be taken off-site and dumped, or perhaps sold off as firewood to local residents. Of course, stump removal is required, and can be a troublesome activity if there are large units, deeply grown. Basically, the activity is to thoroughly clear the area that will be devoted to the construction proper and to the necessary work and storage areas surrounding the work (Figure 3–26). It is not uncommon for the site to be cleared to such an extent that some earthwork and landscaping must be done upon completion, just to restore the site to nearly new condition.

Two operations then follow, sometimes concurrently, sometimes in tandem, depending on conditions, extent, and areas of mutual activity and use. These are excavation for the building substructure (foundation system—see Figure 3–27), and the various trenching/excavating work for the utility lines (which entails both linear trench lines and fairly large "holes" where manholes, junction boxes, vaults, and so forth will be built for the utility equipment (e.g., transformers, sewer lines, retention/detention facilities).

Along with, or part of the excavation operations, is the rough grading, whereby the "cut and fill" sequence is put in place, that is, the cutting down of high spots and filling-in of low spots on the site. This is not necessarily to achieve an absolutely level, flat site, but to create flat areas—plateaus—where the building can be placed. There may still be variations in the site profile, but usually they will be more moderate than originally. Also, this is the base for the site drainage plan, which will carry storm water away from the buildings and into the various drainage facilities, both natural and man-made.

Where required, topsoil will be stripped off and stockpiled on the site for future use; this is an economical measure where good, deep topsoil layers are in place. Once this is done, the actual "moving of dirt" can occur—scraping, pushing, moving, filling, compacting, rolling, removing soil (where excessive, or of poor quality), and bringing in soil (new, good soil or additional soil from a "borrow" pit, either elsewhere on-site or from another source).

For larger buildings soil borings will have been taken earlier, for analysis and use during foundation design. The most common method of taking soil borings is to drive a two-piece (split) hollow steel tube into the ground, and then withdraw it. The soil that fills the void is then exposed, and shows, distinctly, the type, color, depth, relative positions, and composition of each soil layer. This data indicates not only the various types of soil present, but their bearing values based on composition and the thickness of their layers. The bearing value shows the structural and soils engineers where the foundations can be carried, safely, to provide stability for the building.

These are tasks which the earthwork must entail. No site remains intact without some earthwork involved, if only minor clearing and regrading for positive drainage. Only very light buildings, sheds or single-car garages, for example, rest *on* the ground; all other structures and buildings actually rest in and on the soil under and around them.

Figure 3–26 The upper portion of the photo shows a graded area that has been prepared for a new plant complex. The area of the new project is about one-half that of the existing building, and covers an area equal to approximately six football fields.

Part of this work is the actual excavation—the creation of a hole in which the building foundation will be set. This can range from a modest 8–12 foot deep opening for a house basement and foundation, to a depth of several stories where a high-rise building is to have several basement and subbasement levels (for parking, storage, mechanical equipment).

These operations may sound relatively simple and easy. But beyond them can be very extensive, expensive, and imposing operations. There is a need to carefully select the proper foundation system that best matches the imposed loads of the building to the capacity of the soil to bear. It is not uncommon that the building is so big or heavy, or the soil so poor or weak that the common excavation will not expose a level of soil capable of carrying the building weight. In such cases very unique, heavy, and/or deep foundation systems must be considered.

Installation of Foundation System (Substructure)

Numerous foundation systems can be considered before one is selected to best serve the building (see Figures 3–28, 3–29, and 3–30). In this process, though, it must be kept in mind that the foundation system likely will never be fully exposed again unless expensive changes or repairs are needed. Better, then, to select and prudently design a totally adequate system and have it installed correctly—a second chance is not probable.

Two basic categories of foundation are available: shallow and deep. These can be explored and explained in detail in other resources—suffice it here to list several of the variations:

Shallow	Deep
spread footings	piling
wall/strip footings	caissons
isolated footings (columns)	deep wall
combined (trapezoidal —2 cols.)	mats
cantilever	mats with piles
continuous (3+ cols.)	cofferdams
grade beams	vibra-flotation
mat or raft	piers
rigid	soldier beam/breast boards
thickened slab	
dropped (turned-down) slab	

For the most part, the shallow systems reflect light building loads, adequate soil bearing pressures, and modest excavation (perhaps 1–2 stories deep). Foundation walls and grade beams require a continual footing system, whereas columns stand alone or are closely located, and are carried by other types of footing combinations. Thicker or turned-down slabs indicate very light loads, like partitions or light wood frame "out buildings." Mat or raft foundations are extremely thick layers (10–12 feet is not uncommon) of a single homogenous concrete mass.

Figure 3–27 Foundation system substructure.

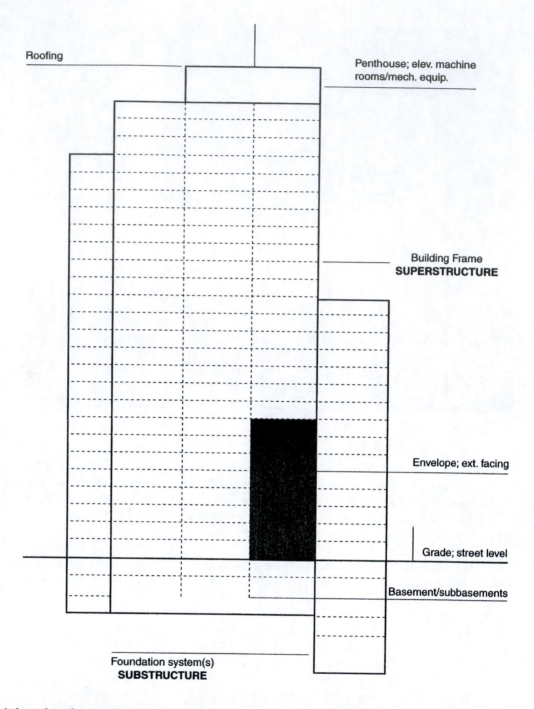

Roofing

Penthouse; elev. machine rooms/mech. equip.

Building Frame
SUPERSTRUCTURE

Envelope; ext. facing

Grade; street level

Basement/subbasements

Foundation system(s)
SUBSTRUCTURE

Where the soil bearing ability is low, there is a need to either excavate more deeply or select an alternative foundation system. Some systems create "legs" for the building by having piling, piers, or caissons built or driven into the soil below the excavated level. These are made of such length (sometimes hundreds of feet) as to reach a level of soil (mainly bedrock—the strongest "soil") capable of holding up the building. Fundamentally, the weight of the building itself, plus its furnishings, equipment, and people, is taken up in the upper structural system. That loading is transmitted to columns or walls, which transfer it downward. Eventually, the load must engage the earth's surface. Here there has to be

an equal upward strength to match the downward loading. The load can be spread over a large area (such as a column footing much larger than the column itself) or carried to stronger soil. It is for the structural designer to find just the right combination of systems to achieve a balance, so the building is adequately supported and stable.

Installation of Underground Utilities

Intertwined between the features of the foundation system are the utility lines which will serve the building systems. Com-

Figure 3–28 Footings for a new apartment building. These footings were formed in earth trenches, not in wooden form work.

Figure 3–29 Foundation for a small commercial building. The forms are still in place but will be removed when the concrete has gained sufficient strength.

monly called "the underground," this work can be done concurrently with the foundations (usual in smaller, lighter buildings), or may lag slightly behind foundation work, so as to avoid direct conflict or intrusion. It entails the sewer (sanitary and storm) systems, water, fire protection, natural gas, perhaps steam (where supplied/purchased from another building), and, of course, electrical, telephone and other communications systems, along with alarm and security lines. These all are the larger, primary sources being brought into the building area, from which they are distributed throughout ("run to") the various levels, rooms, and areas of the building.

Hidden away like the foundation system (hopefully never to be seen again), most of the lines and piping are laid in trenches on the surface of the excavation bottom. These must be routed around footing and foundation features; also, care must be taken so the required slopes in the piping do not cause interference or conflict with the foundation system. Some of these foundation features may be embedded in the excavation bottom, in isolated holes; others are installed on top of the excavation surface. Only rarely—and in true last-resort necessity—do pipes and other mechanical trade elements run through foundation features, usually with considerable added cost and effort. The lines are covered with fill material prior to the lower slab installation, or perhaps encased in concrete for durability. They vary in size depending directly on the size and number of features or fixtures they serve or drain

Figure 3–30   A digital photo, which can be processed through a computer, showing the forms for the tops of some piling.

throughout the entire building or complex; often they are quite formidable in size, to say nothing of their extent.

The lines and piping are then carried under or through the foundation outside the building area and connected to the mains or primary supply sources in the street that are owned by the utility companies. This is an extensive system; it also must be well designed to be all-inclusive and properly sized to provide an adequate supply of all services required by the people, operations, equipment, or work to be imposed on or connected to it.

Erection of Structural System (Superstructure)

Once the foundation system is brought up to approximately final (outdoor) grade level, the upper structural system is started. This may be merely an extension of the foundation system; for example, additional column lengths are sometimes installed on the foundation columns. In larger structures this stem is usually a skeletal "grid" of structural framing bays with a column at each intersection of the grid. Normally, these bays are in the area of 15 to 40 feet (center to center of columns) on a side, with the columns and horizontal members sized to carry the imposed load accumulated over the spacing (span) between supports. Of course, in many places, as well as in lighter building systems, a number of walls—load-bearing walls—can be installed. Most homes, for example, use light wood or masonry framed exterior walls as the primary bearing supports for floor and roof framing; these walls rest directly on top of the foundation system.

Choices of framing systems are varied but fall into three areas: concrete, wood, or steel (Figures 3–31 and 3–32). Within these areas numerous products and systems are available for selection, depending not only on loading but also on aesthetics, finishes, and adaptability to the functions and plan layout required within the area. While the structural system is, of course, necessary to support the structure, astute structural engineers and designers can manipulate their grid layouts, so there is no conflict with the operational functions. Structural bays (with the basic grid) can vary in size, columns can be offset or even eliminated, and different structural systems, for example, walls versus columns, can be used within the same overall structural layout. The expertise of the structural engineer allows adjustment, accommodation, and modification to meet the demands or requirements of the owner's operations. In addition, the structural designer has the ability to create entirely new shapes, such as concrete domes or arches that permit new uses. Stadiums, for example, show the flexibility to allow unrestricted sight lines, large/high open areas, retractable roofs, and the like. These would be "normal" requirements of the facility's owners.

Installation of Floor Framing System(s)

Within the primary framing bays, there will be a series of smaller (more closely spaced) grids, made up of girders, a beam, joists, and purlins—each grid perpendicular to the one below. These members will be progressively smaller as their spans and imposed loads become less. While there are a variety of ways to form these grids, the intent is to get supports

Figure 3–31a Some wood framing for stub-walls, and the floor of a new condominium project. The entire upper structure will be constructed with wood; this is the first installment.

Figure 3–31b View of an extensive wood frame project with plywood decking. Courtesy of APA—Engineered Wood Association.

about 16 to 24 inches apart, which can be easily spanned by some form of decking—such as metal, concrete, composite, precast concrete, or plywood. The decking becomes the overall membrane which can act as the structural floor or perhaps the subfloor on which other finishes can be applied.

Extension of Utility Lines and Systems

As the structural frame is extended upward, so too the utility lines follow. These are usually run in close proximity to the columns, since both must rise with the building. Keeping these lines close to the columns minimizes the space required

for these more utilitarian features of the building. Necessary as they are, the client/owner will want their existence and space requirements held down to maximize the usable space, so there is no intrusion or interruption of the work and service to be operational in the building spaces. It is normal and standard procedure that all vertical lines and elements be "bundled" together—also, they can share the same floor openings, further reducing intrusion into operations.

The lines (branches, or risers) at this point are reduced in size from the underground sources, but they will be increased in number so they can be run horizontally to provide service throughout the individual floors. They decrease in size incrementally since the amount of material carried is lower due

Figure 3–32   This view shows the structural steel framing for an office building. The columns and main beams are in place; note the groups of steel bar joists that will be spaced out across the tops of the beams, to form the floor structure.

to less demand and fewer outlets and people served. At their lower ends, they will be tied together and eventually connected back to the main underground system.

Building of the Envelope (Exterior Walls)

Once the superstructure framing is in place (or has progressed far enough) the outer skin, or building envelope, construction is started. From an amazing and quite varied array of materials, the design professionals will have created this enclosure. Simple wood siding can be used, not only in houses but also in such buildings as churches, stores, and the like, which may be larger than houses, but whose construction is quite similar. Masonry can be used, from unit masonry (CMU or brick) to quarried stone blocks or panels. Curtain and window walls may be used with a grid of mullions and crossbars into which translucent, transparent, or opaque panels can be fitted. These can be colored or tinted (to prevent the passage of unwanted heat and light into the building proper). The creation of this enclosure is a direct application of technology and aesthetics, in that this application will create and become the image of the project (see Figures 3–33, 3–34, and 3–35). The framing, of course, gives the project its shape and form, but the envelope gives it the texture, color, weather-resistance, wearing surface, water-tightness, energy efficiency, and, yes, its eye-appeal; it projects the wish of the owner(s) as to what they want their building and consequently their image to be. Obviously a building can be a direct reflection of the owner, the business philosophy, and the prestige or image that the company wishes to portray to the public and to its customers.

Within the construction of the envelope are features that provide for insulation, fire resistance, safety, ease of mainte-

nance, and translation of mechanical systems both vertically and horizontally to places of use. It can be a covering expressing closed, blank, tight feelings, or the image of openness, lightness, and sparkle; it can lend itself to viewing the surroundings, or creating a cloistered closed environment for protection of employees or product. Surprisingly, much of the basic impact and philosophy behind the project is manifest in this enclosure; it serves to create the environment desired for the operation of the facility, in the end.

The Roofing System

Closing off the top of the structure is the roofing system. This is as varied in materials as it is in shapes, textures, and colors. The simplest roof is a single-slope flat plane, tilted to drain in one direction. Starting from this basic type, the design professional can create a multitude of planes, shapes, and interesting forms to enhance the overall impact of the project and further the design concept. Much of the decision is seated in the current style or motif of the day; it varies in almost a faddish manner, based usually on what is seen as the "current state of the art" and what is both readily accepted and desired by the clients. Usually the roof formations will have some relationship to and kinship with the envelope system, and both together relate to the design concept—what exactly the client wishes.

Since the roof is largely forgotten, the need is to install a system as long-wearing as possible. New materials are usually directed at extended life, but the elements play havoc with roofing systems, much more than they wear out those in the envelope. The roof lies fully exposed to the sun (a most debilitating force) and receives untold amounts of water from rain and snow. Shifting of the building or parts thereof tends to open joints and cracks in it. All of this creates leakage and

Figure 3-33 An office building in the making. The precast concrete panels on the trucks were made off-site at a precast factory and then transported to the site. They will be attached to the steel framing of the building. This is a very cost effective and efficient way to construct a building in a short time.

Figure 3-34 A brick veneer being installed over a lightweight wood-framed wall of a new model. This is a traditional residential type of construction now being used for commercial and other types of buildings.

Figure 3-35 A retail store framed with metal studs. The sheathing in place backs up a masonry facing (started at grade line). Above this wainscot there will be an exterior insulation facing system (EIFS).

problems that the owner is not happy to accept. Perfection, of course, does not exist, but this system in particular comes in for a lot of scrutiny and criticism if not done as well as it can be, within budgetary constraints.

Installation of Mechanical Systems

Following (perhaps very closely behind) installation of the outer envelope, the various mechanical systems trades will start their work (see Figure 3–36). Taking advantage of the open areas on each floor that exist prior to installation of interior walls, these trades can run ductwork, conduits, cabling, water and soil lines, in short, all of the branches and amenities required for properly functioning systems. The need here is for close coordination so no competition is created between trades, i.e., the mentality that "whoever gets there first, gets the space." This tends to cause warm discussion, claims, anger, and disarray in the project. The drawings must themselves be fully coordinated, so as to present exact locations and routing for execution by the tradeworkers. Where the structure becomes more industrialized, and hence more utilitarian (almost totally dedicated to mechanical systems and functions) there is an increased need for this coordination, and for conflict/interference analysis. Simply put, things must be done smoothly, neatly, precisely, and completely.

Where numerous interior partitions and finishes are to be installed, added precaution must take place so all of the mechanical functions and devices are contained and confined, able to be easily concealed and covered by the finish work. Again, the need is clear for coordination with the documents displaying the finish work.

When space is made available, the mechanical equipment itself may be installed. Usually areas will be set aside for this work, and a very concentrated work effort is needed to install all of the machinery and the piping and instrumentation required for its proper operation. It should be remembered that in all but the most utilitarian buildings, these systems must be ready for use when the building is complete. Where the function of the building is more industrial or mechanical, some equipment may be long-delivery items, and could take added time (beyond building completion) for installation and start-up.

Interior Walls and Partitions

The layout and installation of the interior walls and partitions is usually a direct reflection of the complexity of the project—at least for the area involved (see Figure 3–37). Obviously a warehouse will have few such dividers, and those will be of more utilitarian materials (masonry, metal, etc). But in a hospital, for example, there is a myriad of areas, rooms, alcoves, niches, recesses, nooks, and so on. Each will be enclosed in whole or in part, and will require a good deal of attention to meet the requirements placed on the area, or to provide the services to the area. Some require numerous and complex mechanical systems for plumbing, electrical, and ventilation, along with other utilities such as oxygen, natural gas, suction, or monitoring, despite the relatively confined area involved.

All this impacts the installation of the enclosure. Stud framing can become involved, with much cutting and fitting of small pieces, or creation of numerous openings or extra support framing (for grab rails or fixtures, for example). The same holds true for masonry where units must be adjusted and fitted to confined areas, numerous unusual conditions, and, of course, the final finish and appearance.

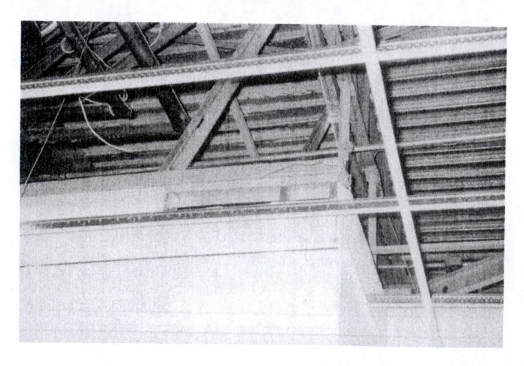

Figure 3–36 The space above the new ceiling (note the grid for the new ceiling). Several pipes and lines of electrical wiring can be seen in this view, as well as the roof deck and structural members. This serves to show how the mechanical systems must be adapted to the building construction, and still function as necessary at their point of use. Photo by Phil Joehnk.

Figure 3–37a   This series of photos shows the installation of various walls and partitions. Note the amount of work that is done, but never seen in the finished project. All of this is required to provide a base for the final (finished) material that is exposed in the completed project. Round balcony Project by A: Architecture (architects) Kling Bros. Builders. Photos reprinted with permission of the Gypsum Association, which does not constitute an endorsement by the Gypsum Association of this or any other specific product, system, or material.

Major or long elements, like corridors, will be laid out using a laser beam, so alignment is near perfect. This care ensures that misalignment will not lead to encroachment or unanticipated reduction of space and area sizes, which could impact use, equipment size, or other key concerns. Still, worker care is required to make necessary adjustments, to fit, attach, and fasten in a proper manner, and to meet the dimensions and configurations noted on the project drawings. Also, to fulfill the requirements of the specifications for the work involved, great care must be taken.

Part of the installation of the walls and partitions is the work of setting door frames and frames for other openings, the building of bulkheads, and the installation of blocking and anchorage for various devices and items of equipment. This work must be done in the sense of a negative, in that the installation will not be seen in the final project but is vital to the ultimate success of the project. At the appropriate time, doors will be hung and their proper hardware installed; still later they will be field-finished (if they are not ordered pre- or factory-finished).

A good deal of time will be allotted to surface preparation (prior to application of finish coverings or coatings), as well as to closing gaps and cracks, and creating an overall ap-

pearance of a smooth, complete series of surfaces and planes. Finish, here, alludes to a good looking, neat, carefully executed, complete, proper, and unmarred appearance of all surfaces, items, and devices. Everything should be plumb, level, and true to line; properly coated or covered; and neatly and carefully fitted.

This work, while no different in overall concept for all project work, does require skill and care since so much of the project is yet to be applied or installed. Certainly the mechanical systems need to be installed and connected, but their function is to supply air or water or electricity, not necessarily to present a proper and acceptable finished appearance. This is not to favor one trade work over another—it is simply that some trades contribute to final appearance, while others do not.

Connection of Branch Systems to Mechanical Equipment

In reality, much of the mechanical systems work is accomplished by working from both ends. Ductwork may be run at the extremes to be connected to the basic units later in the project. The same process works with electrical wiring that

Figure 3–37b Angular wall
openings project by S.F.A.
Architects, Inc. Photos reprinted
with permission of the Gypsum
Association, which does not
constitute an endorsement by
the Gypsum Association of this
or any other specific product,
system, or material.

is later connected to lighting and power panels and equipment, and with plumbing that connects later to the sewer taps, meters, and service supply lines.

The majority of the final connection work takes place within the areas dedicated to the equipment, machinery, and service entrances. Quite often, through poor planning and short-sightedness, these areas are very confined in area (no one wanting to allow too much space to be devoted to such functions), and hence will be extremely crowded, congested, and greatly in need of cooperation and coordination. Piping, tubing, switches, gauges, valves, fittings, and equipment will be everywhere; pads are required for many items to keep them up free from the floor. Good mechanics will be at their very best where their work is neatly planned, accurately and carefully executed (tight bends, well anchored, plumb/level except where slopes are necessary, fully identified, with fittings and connections of the best skilled work). While utilitarian in nature, these areas usually will come to finale in a very professional manner, fully functional, and well executed—this being a tremendous aid to maintenance, repair, replacement, addition, and adjustment. In reality the rooms reflect awareness and field experience on the part of the systems designer engineer(s), and a real credit to the care, skill, and expertise of the tradeworkers.

Finishes

In this area the array of available products is mind-boggling. The finishes involve the final, exposed decorative face or surface of walls, ceilings, floors, equipment/built-ins (see discussion below), doors, glazed areas, and other surfaces exposed to view (Figure 3–38). From the simplest of unpainted CMU to painting of exposed structural work, one can proceed at almost any level up to the massive, carved, solid wood paneling of the corporate president's office suite, or the gold-leaf covered trim in a cathedral. Variety takes on new meaning— materials, colors, textures, patterns, shapes, combinations, joinery, utility, surface finish, coatings, attachments, serviceability, maintenance included. The design professionals have a mighty task in ascertaining how the needs and wishes of the owner can be met. They must resolve how utility and function can be supported by attractiveness; undergirded by ease of maintenance, length of usefulness, ability to repair, replace, or refresh; and purchased at an acceptable budgetary level.

The finishes, of course, require the careful application of skilled workmanship so the final result is both appealing and functional. To achieve this, much of the other work of the project needs to be in place to support, and literally to allow, the application of the final finishes. These are the "interior skin," much as the facing of the exterior building envelope is akin to an outer skin (and often is called just that). Ceramic tile, for example, appears to the eye as the finished surface, but is applied to an under board of gypsum wallboard, which in turn is applied to stud work framing, which in turn is supported by the floor slab, and tied to the roof or floor structure above.

The process of applying the finishes must be carefully programmed and scheduled with the understanding that the finer, more sophisticated, and final materials cannot be placed where there still is peril of damage or even slight marring. Obviously, certain installations, even some finishes themselves, can threaten or harm other adjacent surfaces and their finishes. As an example, rolling out wall-to-wall carpeting can mar finished walls if particular care is not taken. Here, quite often, large rolls of carpet are merely unrolled even though they may be wider than the space available— hence mars and roll marks appear on the walls. If these walls are painted with the final coat, touch up work is required (and can lead to claims as to who pays for this, since the painting contractor has finished and met the contract obligations).

In some cases, care must be taken to ensure that the finishing process does not add other hazards to the structure or the remainder of the work. Moisture from plaster, drywall, or interior (decorative) masonry work can be a deterrent to other finishes which must follow, such as floor covering and adjacent surfaces, or to finishes already in place. Sanding or grinding operations in one area may well intrude on newly painted surfaces in other areas. Finishes in walkways used by workers and suppliers are open to great abuse, and are best reserved for later application after traffic is minimized or eliminated. Cases can be cited where unlike materials impact the finishes and cause blemishes or deterioration (e.g., incompatible backing behind a finished sealant joint).

Another caution, primarily for designers, is the selection of materials and finishes which simply cannot be made to match. Staining of wood items is a good example, where different wood species appear different even when finished in the same natural manner. This often leads to dissatisfaction on the part of the owner and can be the cause of remedial work very late in the project.

The task is one of trying to leave the job ready for owner occupancy, in a fresh, new, clean, unmarred, unblemished, bright, neat, sparkling, as-near-perfect-as-possible condition. This should be the culmination and mark of a fully successful project, from a technical viewpoint.

Installation of Specialties, Built-ins, and Furnishings

Throughout the final phases of the project, the contractors must provide for the timely, proper, and unobtrusive installation of quite a variety of items. Some are manufactured products (rest room accessories, basketball backstops) which are provided in a standard form and are accommodated to the project by installing required openings, framing, and support for attachment of the units. Some items are made in finished form and require only unpacking and installation; others require more extensive installation and may also require finishing of some parts of the assembly. Others are custom-made to fit the project specifically and exclusively (countertops, work tops, cabinets, casework). In the main, these are fabricated by contractors/suppliers close to the job site, and are fitted to the circumstances, dimensions, and other aspects of the project work. Much of this work is prefinished, or fabricated with finished materials; some items do require finishing on-site, mainly to match other features.

Still other items are "installed" or "movable" pieces, such as furniture, desks, file cabinets, chairs, tables, and the like. Supplied by manufacturers remote to the site, these usually arrive on the job complete, prefinished, and needing only to be unpacked and set in place. Some very minor adjustments may be required, or installation of small hardware items may be necessary.

These three different types of items will appear on the site. Where they require some accommodation, it is necessary that this be done "along the way" (in its proper time and place, when it is convenient), so there is no need to accommodate the work in the finished surfaces. This involves making or framing openings, not cutting them later; installing backing, blocking, or other anchorage, and not trying to provide this in or behind a finished surface. Although many items and materials in the project require the submittal, review, and use of shop drawings, no other instances show the value of such shop drawings clearer than the items noted above. It can be ruinous if the contractor(s) "misses" proper

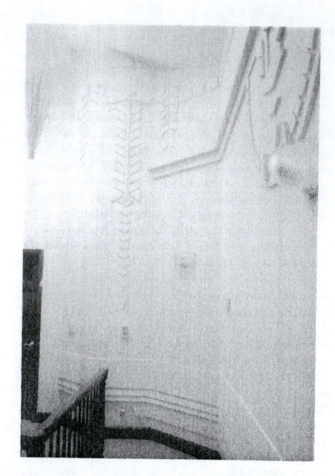

Figure 3–38 This group of photos shows the final appearance of the construction work (although some still need painting). Much work has gone before this, but it is this final appearance that the owner is most anxious to see. Drywall photos of Marshall residence (above), Richard Houston, architect; photo reprinted with permission of the Gypsum Association, which does not constitute an endorsement by the Gypsum Association of this or any other specific product, system, or material. Bridge pier photo (left) courtesy of Concrete Reinforcing Steel Institute.

installation features, and must remove newly finished work to allow these installations.

WRAP UP/CLOSE OUT

Energize all contractor supplied/installed systems; troubleshoot, and modify as required for proper performance:
As completion of the project approaches, there is a normal process of bringing all of the various systems into operation. After all the lines, branches, and accessories are installed and connected, there comes "the moment of truth" when the system is energized and made to run. At this juncture the contractors can check out their accumulated work to ascertain if (1) the work is complete; (2) the work is proper, operating as required, with no leakage, proper balance, and proper levels of performance or output, that is, basically doing what it was designed and expected to do; and (3) if, and what, remedial work must be done to achieve the expected result(s).

There may still be some other work in progress; usually this is work that is benign and has no real "operation" or operating parts (for example, paving, curbing, landscaping). Each trade has a distinct and specific "end point" at which the workers know that the work is finished, or ready for running. Other trades may have to run active tests to ascertain if their work is complete and proper—checking temperature and volume outputs, filling and seeing if the pool holds water or is leaking, and so on.

This also is the point where managers and superintendents should be checking the work against their records and the contract documents for completeness, accuracy, and full compliance with their contract obligations. This is a necessary function even in well-managed projects (and is best done on a continual basis throughout the project). It is more crucial toward the completion, as there are numerous items that tend to drop through the cracks, and are overlooked, dismissed too early, or put aside for execution by others. Such items as documentation and warranties may be overlooked. Yet these remain part of the obligations—part of the complete package the contractor is, by contract, to deliver to the owner. Obviously, where such items are "left undone" they become a source of real embarrassment to the contractors, require expensive reworking of finished work (even requiring work by other contractors), imperil operation of a system or facility, or may provide a source of severe noncompliance with some regulations or codes.

As the project work winds down, the contractors will demobilize the site, removing all office and storage trailers, excess materials, and temporary facilities. Most will do this as their individual work is completed, and they will handle any needed work (see below) without a full crew and without either the need or presence of the full array of equipment and plant. In most cases, some refurbishing of the site is required—from cutting uncut grass, to filling and minor grading and planting grass seed, to removing temporary roads and returning the unused portions of the site to its original condition.

Substantial Completion/Final Inspection/Development of "Punch List":   Often there is confusion, even among knowledgeable participants over what, specifically, constitutes "Substantial Completion," and what must occur next. Simply, Substantial Completion is *not* Final Completion—it does not signal the end of contractual obligations, or the walk-out-the-door finale of the work. Rather it occurs roughly 30 days *prior* to Final Completion, and no closer.

It represents that point where the vast majority of the work is complete (except for minor adjustments, etc.), and the project is in such condition that the owner could take partial occupancy; for example, users could begin to move in, but not occupy or put into operation the structure. It also is that point at which the contractors should have reviewed and inspected their own work for both properly executed work and for completeness. Only then are they ready to present it for final inspection, approval, and acceptance.

In a full-blown, scheduled event, the entire project is subject to "final inspection" by a party of all discipline design professionals, the general contractor, or construction manager, the owner, the various on-site representatives, and others who are pertinent to the task. The "tour" is a working activity in which every aspect of the work is inspected. Visual and physical checking of such matters as, do lights light, do receptacles deliver electricity, do doors swing smoothly and latch, are painted surfaces smooth and uniform, does equipment function properly, are joints neat, straight and clean (or invisible, if that is the criterion), is concrete finished, and so forth. Each discipline will have a complete list of specific items to check, as well as a general list and format/agenda to be followed to ascertain and ensure that the work is what and where it should be, and is in full accord with the contract documents.

Using pads and written notes, or tape recorders, a list is compiled—this is commonly known as "the punch list." Quite often this list will contain several hundreds of items (the number will vary with the size of the project, complexity of the work, and diligence of the contractors) which are not acceptable and are in need of repair, adjustment, tightening, redoing, recoating, removal and replacement, or perhaps initial installation. This process needs to be understood. It is not a "grade card" for the contractors, but rather is an assessment to ensure the owner that for every dollar paid, full and commensurate value is being received, as required by the contract documents.

No one is perfect, and perfection is not the goal of the list: every human misses, overlooks, or accepts conditions that are not as they should be. Perhaps one can cast this off as a "difference of opinion," but really it is a matter of the persons responsible for the project (design professionals) acting as the owner's agents, making sure that dollars and value match.

Partial Use by Owner (no occupancy); Owner-supplied equipment, finishes, systems installed by other than project contractors: Once the punch list has been compiled, the project is in such condition that the owner can begin the process of moving in. While this does not entail actual occupancy and use of the facility, it is a time when the owner can take over certain finished areas for use as storage areas for the arrival of new equipment and furnishings. Also, quite often owners will have some work done by contractors other than those involved with the construction directly. For example, the supplying and laying of carpeting is one work item that can be done in this manner. Problems, though, can arise, if the owner's contractors are not careful in their work, and damage or mar the work of the construction trades (who would still be active on the site, to a reduced degree). Correcting any such damage would have to be back-charged (billed separately) to the owner and/or their contractor, since the construction contract still prevails, and requires a proper level of completion and "like-new" condition of the work.

Care must also be taken in the instance of partial owner occupancy to ensure that insurance coverage is such that both owner and construction contractors are protected in case of any accident. Basically this is maintaining proper control over the job site, while both owner and contractors continue their work; it is to their mutual benefit, just as the coincident occupancy is.

In addition, coordination is needed between the efforts of the owner and their desired results, and the continuing efforts of the contractors to meet their deadlines and achieve the correct state of the project for final completion. Undoing work, changing work, or making new demands on the part of the owner is counterproductive. Stalling, causing delays or confusion, or requiring extraordinary owner effort on the part of the contractors is similarly discouraged. After all, it is the owner who is the sponsor and "bill-payer" and certainly has the right to use the building—it just should not be premature, nor in a manner that disrupts the final construction efforts.

Resolve all "punch list" items; final cleaning; removal of debris and excess materials: The work of the punch list should be pursued in a line-by-line sequence, doing each item as listed, once and for the last time. Often these items are quite involved, even to the point of having to remove some work (and involving other trades) to make the corrections. Also, late-arriving items must be installed, again involving other trade work where proper accommodation has not been built into the original work. Still other items may involve discussion as to responsibility, who injured the work, or the fact that the work is correct as done, and that the punch list is not in keeping with the contract (as the contractor interprets it).

In the main, though, this work usually proceeds quite well. The on-site personnel must understand, however, that there has to be a sequence for this work. Quite often all contractors are given the same identical completion date for their work. This leads to confusion as each then thinks he or she can be "last-out-the-door," working to the very end of the contract time. This can be the source of not only confusion, but also anger, disruption, and other reactions that could delay actual completion. Some finish trades (painting, for example) are required to provide a neat, finished, and unmarred set of surfaces. If other work is done behind them, and there is some marring, then the painter is not complete, even though the painting was complete and satisfactory just prior to the other work being performed. Obviously a time of dispute and frustration sets in as the painter must, again, refinish already "finished" work.

The professionals must anticipate this, even to the point of requesting the general contractor to issue specific instructions for the punch list work sequence, or giving each contractor a different completion date, which furthers the sequence. Also, this sequence must be coordinated with the owner, who may have other workers coming on-site to perform separate work, or where moving and occupancy is imminent. Legally, where every contractor has the same completion date, they can work until that date. But, everyone, by this time, is anxious to leave the project and move on to other ventures. Any added delay in completion is stressful and quite irritating. It is worth some extra effort to alleviate, if not eliminate, the situation.

During this period, too, more and more demobilization will occur, as the contractors remove their resources and facilities in preparation of totally leaving the site. One of the most contentious work items is final clean up and removal of debris and excess materials. Good materials will be salvaged and removed by the contractors, but contractual care must be taken to ensure that cleanup of the project and project site is done, and done well. Often this chore is laid at the door of the general contractor, much to his or her chagrin. Other contractors will avoid the issue and merely do what they absolutely must do in this regard. It can be a very elaborate, time-consuming, and costly issue. Tons and truck-loads of debris may have to be removed—though much depends on how vigorously and well this chore was accomplished continually during the progress of the work.

Certification for Occupancy; Turnover of Operating Manuals, Training of Owner Personnel; Final Completion and Final Payment: A series of final inspections is required on most projects, prior to final completion. Some of these occur prior to Substantial Completion; others during the punch list period. Several will be governmental inspections by agencies that have issued permits on work in the project—building/structural, electrical, plumbing, and so forth. In many jurisdictions there is a requirement for the issuance of a Certificate of Occupancy. This document will be issued after notice from the contractor(s) that their work is ready for inspection, the final inspection, and approval of the work as satisfactory (meeting the minimum standards of the regulations).

Also, during the period between Substantial and Final Completion, the contractors will turn over manuals of operating instructions to the owner, and will train the owner's personnel where required in the operation of the equipment and systems. This is a key interface, especially for very complex projects or where very sophisticated equipment or new technology has been used. Obviously the best of systems is useless to the owners if their personnel cannot make the system do what it is supposed to do. There may even be a flaw in the contractor's work. In addition, these manuals provide information regarding maintenance, spare parts, warranties, and the proper continued use of the units.

The most important of the inspections is the final inspection of the design professional/owner team. Here the project is once again "toured" so the remedial work on the punch list items can be assessed and hopefully found to be satisfactory and acceptable. Any discrepancies cycle back through the remedial work program until finally accepted. However, where the work is found to be contract abiding, the project is deemed "Complete" and all parties demobilize and move to the last function: certification of the project work, and its completeness, and the final payment to the contractor(s). Checklists are available so each required contract item is checked and made right, if necessary, so the project certification can be made. Within the terms of the contract, the owner is then obligated to make final payment, at which point the project is hers or his, and becomes part of what is called "standing building stock"—an existing building. Now the owner is free to move in en masse and to occupy, operate, and work the project as seen fit.

FINALE

Turn building over to Owner, complete as required by construction contract; also, security of building and site; operation of all systems and functions: When the last contractor has "walked out the door and turned off the light," the project belongs to the owner. From this point on, the owner will have to outfit, occupy, operate, and maintain the project, hopefully finding it in full accord with design concepts and programming, i.e., the building or facility is what the owner desired in the beginning.

Sometimes this is merely an anticlimatic event—a murmur—gone unnoticed by most. The owner shows up one day, uses the new key and finds no construction personnel on the site. The event and work of occupying is ready to start.

Other projects are much higher profile and culminate in formal ceremonies, turning over of the keys, flowery (and overlong) speeches, bands, parades, dedication, and blessing, followed by tours, and simple "showing off." It is a grand day and time! In some cases, the owner will sponsor an event for the contractors (and families at times), where the workers can see and show the work they performed in final form. Other times, the owner may sponsor a party—a buffet, luncheon, or a more informal "do" to salute the workers and to thank them (see Figure 3–39).

In any event, the long-anticipated project is now a reality, pristine (or as near that as possible), ready for the life and function it was built to support. With the exception of a few very minor glitches, the project is finished and ready for day-to-day operation.

EXERCISES

The following activities can be used to enhance the text material and provide wider exposure to and understanding of construction.

Some portions of these items may be assigned as individual projects, but overall they are group projects that every class member can benefit from. (*No activity that requires going onto a construction site should be undertaken by a single individual, nor without prior notice and permission from the site manager; ensure full and proper safety measures in any event.*)

1. Plan a visit to a large contractor's office and also a small, or subcontractor's office. Ask for a guided tour and explanation of the estimating room, the shop and yard functions, and other in-house functions; review the various resources and operations available in the office. Discuss operations with staffers. Report back to the class.

2. Create via student participation a class technical library and a sample display. Collect, with permission, and from various sources, samples, or small excess pieces of construction material. This aids hands-on, close-up viewing and analysis of these items. Combined with the literature library (see Chapter 2 Exercises), this can be an excellent resource and visual aid to instruction.

Figure 3–39 The true measure of a project.

Who Is Responsible for a Successful Project?

by Dennis Crawley, Project Manager

I was driving across town one day with a friend who was a bricklayer. Occasionally, he would point out a building and tell me that he had built it, and point out some detail that was particularly challenging.

It struck me as odd that this craftsman, whom I knew by reputation as being talented, took such ownership and pride in his accomplishments. Although he was not the designer, owner, or construction manager, it was clear that he felt responsible to a large degree for the success of the project—he had built those buildings.

I had worked for two design firms and was convinced that the Owner and the designer had invested enough of themselves or their money to say without reservation that they had built the project. After all, it was the Owner's idea and financial assets that gave the project its birth. The designers took the idea, enhanced it with their own creative talents, and developed the plans in detail. I also felt that the contractor, especially the general contractor, had a right to claim that they had built the building, because a general contractor had to select subcontractors who had talent for the work, take charge of purchasing major construction materials, and prepare and maintain a schedule while affording the lowest possible cost to the Owner. Certainly, without the general contractor and their industry contacts, it would be very difficult for the Owner and designers to get the project built.

It had not, until that time, occurred to me that a workman being paid by the hour could feel responsible for building the project. But, the more I thought about it, the more I came to understand the craftsman's investment. It was his talent, experience and hard physical labor that caused the final assembly of the project. He had to brave the elements and deal with aching muscles in order to please the general contractor, designer and the Owner.

From the mason's stories, I could sense that he took great pride when the Owner, designers or his supervisors asked him to help solve a problem. It was the greatest compliment and acknowledgment of his work he could receive.

This man's excitement and dedication are examples of how each of us are an important part of building a project. No matter how insignificant or important our part may seem, everyone involved with a project, from the Owner to the laborers, has an impact on the quality of the finished product.

Our work is a direct reflection of us. We should all strive to do the best possible job, and take pride in it.

4

Communications and Documentation

In addition to knowledgeable and skilled people, successful construction requires the accurate exchange of knowledge and information between all parties. Although this is just one among several major needs in the entire project sequence, few of them are more crucial to the success of the work than the real exchange of information—communications.

Every construction project is in need of continual, meaningful communication. It can be in the form of verbal, written, electronic, graphic, or video exchanges. The primary need is that the necessary information is shared—and then acted upon if necessary, and then, again if necessary, stored for ease of future retrieval.

Each instance of communication is characterized by (1) a sender who decides what is to be sent, creates the message, and determines the medium to be used to transfer it to others; (2) a message in the form of some information that is of value to more than one person on the project; (3) a receiver to whom the message is transmitted; and (4) some mutual understanding. The latter is required to ensure that the message means the same thing to both sender and receiver. The message must be clear, direct, complete, and instructive if some action is required on the part of the receiver. Without these attributes, "miscommunication" takes place, together with a high risk of misunderstanding, misdirection, incorrect interpretation, errant action, and sometimes even a harmful result.

In choosing among the methods the need is, first to establish the best media to use to transmit the data in the clearest and most timely method. To do this each person must anticipate the timing, the person who is receiving the message, and what format is best used by that person for analysis, further transmission, or response. Today, e-mail and other electronic programs have brought about a tremendous reduction of interpersonal (face-to-face) communication. That is not all for the good.

Of course, seeking out a person over a large, extended construction site can be time-consuming; another communications method might better be used. But far too often people use the nonpersonal electronic media simply to avoid personal contact, confrontation, rejection on the spot, or other ill effects. In essence, we now seek to "slide a message under the door, and then run" without fear of being discovered. We perceive that bad news is best transmitted in this manner.

On a construction site, however, all news and information must be properly and promptly transmitted, be it good, bad, or indifferent in nature. Continual, free, open and appropriate communication is a constant need in construction. Information, of course, need not be passed along to everyone imaginable, just for the sake of communicating. Rather, information must be sent to all those who are impacted by the content of the message. Assuming that someone knows (or worse, that everyone knows) a vital fact is a very damaging process.

More and more, communications are being made formal and secure. An array of standard forms is now being used to record messages. These are kept in secure files to protect and preserve them. Electronic systems provide security, but files must be protected in the event of data loss due to outages or malfunctions of machines, programs, or human action.

The other side of this coin is that the practice of sending messages to anyone who might remotely be involved or who "may" be interested is useless. Discretion in distribution is a sound management principle, and prevents the needless use of paper for no real benefit. Confusion can also be created where too much data is transmitted—even more so when it is not properly explained or transferred, or where it is of little or tangential use to the receiver. FYI (for your information) communications can be a good source of knowledge, mutual orientation, updating, and the like, if not carried to the extreme. Often the best communications policy is a carry-over from wartime, asking "Does the prospective receiver have a need to know?"

To facilitate communication, a good deal of construction data can be reduced to the use of standard forms. They eliminate the need for taking a long time to produce the message, and allow quicker, more positive, and accurate communication. Forms need not be invented anew for each project. Several construction organizations produce their versions of standard forms; none have a particular corner on the market, rather all offer what is thought to be a correct and expressive form. The groups include the AIA, NSPA, AGA, CSI, and other similar organizations that produce the forms as a convenience for their members.

The use of such forms also goes a long way toward ensuring that everything is contained in the forms' ancillary data, that proper signatures are affixed, and that the key message is sent via a vehicle that has some credence on its face (it's not just a scrap of paper to the receiver). Filing and retrieval is enhanced with sequential numbering or chronological methods. And lastly the form causes all pertinent information to be in the same format, the same location, and so forth for more rapid use.

The important issue to remember is that all of the documentation is really a part of the construction contract (agreement between owner and contractor). Some documents are of the first instance, in that they set forth basic and fundamental issues for the project. Other documents and forms are issued to support, reinforce, and elaborate on these basic issues.

CONTRACT FORMS

The Contract Documents

The owner, very early in the project, must decide what type of project delivery system will be used, and how the various contracts involved will be written. In the bustle of programming and designing the project, this need is often lost sight of, but it is vital to the success of the project and, indeed, to how the project will be completed.

The key to it all is the contract. A contract is a legal document, almost always in written form for construction projects, wherein the parties establish their relationship. This should be based on complete mutuality. Essential to the contract is a clear meeting of the minds of the parties as to what each will, and will not, do. This stipulation is absolutely necessary to ensure that the parties fully understand each other, are talking about the same issues in exactly the same way, and have complete agreement between them on every detail of the work, the relationships, and the contract obligations. The vast majority of lawsuits stem from the failure to have a meeting of minds prior to executing the contract. And where contracts are verbal (nothing written out) even more chances arise for discrepancies/problems as the parties remember issues in different ways. Once there is full agreement, the most prudent course is to reduce the contract provisions to written form. Every contract consists of several parts:

- A need (in construction, a description of what is to be built)

- An offer (the submittal of a bid or cost estimate from the contractor(s), which in essence says, "I will build what you wish, in accord with the contract documents, for "X" number of dollars)

- An acceptance of the offer, by the owner

- Compensation (payment of the proposed cost, from owner to contractor)

Often overlooked, or handled too informally, are modifications made to this contract *after* it is signed and executed in its original form. Things happen. Conditions change; minds change; the best of planning changes. All of these can cause changes in the project after the contract is signed. Each such incident *must* be carefully and fully documented, so the contract is changed or modified to reflect the new scenarios. This refers to added work and hence added cost; extensions of time because of the added work; deletions from the project and reduction of cost; exchanges without impact on time or cost (substitutions on an equal basis). Hence, the contract is really a dynamic document, which is active throughout the entire project construction cycle.

The initial contract, however, is established to meet the owner's needs and desires. Even before a formal declaration is made about the project delivery system, the owner must decide how the contracts will be drawn. Some are based on fully competitive bidding, on all or portions of the work. Some contracts are negotiated (mutually worked out or talked out) between owner and a selected contractor, or contractors. Others are given over on a "time and material" basis, usually on smaller projects, using of a contractor well-known to the owner or used pervasively. And still others evolve out of the nuances that come with the selected delivery system. Most owners, even families building new homes, use the services of an attorney in the contract work. Every contract *needs* to be *fair,* to all parties. The contract should not be conceived as a way to gain advantage over the other party. It should be a business agreement in which the needs of one party are met by the other, and a fair and agreed-upon compensation is paid. In being such, everyone receives in full measure that which is due them, in a fair and legally proper manner.

Whoever drafts the contract will almost automatically write it with some bias to their client. Attorneys acting for their clients will include provisions biased toward their client. Often contract writing by the attorneys becomes a legal tug-of-war, with the contract parties as bystanders. In addition, while all attorneys are well-versed in contract law, only a small portion of attorneys are as well-schooled in construction and the nuances of construction law. This is now a specialty within the legal profession; a very small number are dually trained as both architect/engineer and attorney. This lack of specific construction orientation is why a great many projects utilize standard contracts forms from such agencies as the AIA or the NSPE. These groups, fairly impartial entities, have worked long and hard to establish eminently fair and complete documents. Usually they are in standardized, printed form, with blanks that are to be filled in for the specific project. Often these need to be modified, slightly, to address certain specific or particular conditions of the project; in large measure, though, they suffice as written.

Many architects, engineers, and contractors try to utilize such forms, but this is rather ill-advised and quite risky. As projects become more complex, so too do the ancillary legal issues. Just as attorneys lack construction knowledge, the design professionals and contractors lack far more background in legal contract writing. They do need to be readily familiar with the way the contract works and how the provisions interface between parties. The design professional, by contract, is often set out as the impartial third-party who oversees (polices) the Owner-Contractor Agreement, to ensure correct exchanges of information, adherence to contract requirements, payment for work performed, and so forth, including many issues where controversy may erupt. Often the professional becomes the mediator to resolve disputes early on, before they become aggravated and threatening to the project.

It is easily seen that the contract is the primary project document, and must be used in tandem with its supporting documents—the drawings and specifications. As depicted in Figure 4–4, the project's major controlling documents are the Contract Documents. These are the Agreement, the Drawings, and the Specifications. In short, what is shown on the drawings and described in the specifications, comprises the work that is required by the contract to be performed on the project, and for which the contract amount will be paid.

The construction administrator serves as the vital link between performance by the contractor and acceptance by the owner. Effective administration of a construction contract requires a fundamental and in-depth understanding of all of the documents which make up the construction contract, how to interpret those documents in the event of ambiguity, and how to apply the construction contract to the events which occur during construction. The administrator needs to be expert with all of the other ancillary and contributive documents and forms that are issued during the period of construction. The documents, which collectively make up the construction contract, are typically referred to as the Contract Documents.

The construction contract is more than just the plans and technical specifications. The Owner-Contractor Agreement or the General Conditions usually define what is included in the Contract Documents. The Contract Documents include the Owner-Contractor Agreement, the General Conditions of the contract, the Supplementary Conditions of the contract, the drawings, the specifications, all Addenda issued prior to the execution of the contract, all modifications or written amendments to the contract signed by both parties, Change Orders, written interpretations issued by the design professional or owner, and written orders for minor change issued by the Design Professional or Owner. Generally the Contract Documents do not include the bidding documents such as the advertisement or invitation to bid, the instructions to the bidders, sample forms, or the contractor's bid, unless specifi-

cally attached to or incorporated by reference in the Owner-Contractor Agreement or in the General Conditions.

Perhaps a natural and potentially disastrous mistake of contract administrators (whose education and professional experience has ordinarily emphasized design and the preparation of plans and specifications) is to administer the construction project based upon the plans and specifications, without sufficient knowledge or deference to the General or Supplemental Conditions of the contract. This is to function within the technical aspects of the project, without regard for the intricate and quite important aspect of contractual obligations, individual responsibilities, legalities, interrelationships, and the other more administrative aspects of the project.

Form Contracts

Standard form construction contracts are frequently encountered. The most common form contracts for private projects are those which have been prepared by the AIA, EJCDC (of NSPE), and the AGC. Other organizations are also coming out with their versions of various documents, usually adapted to their specific perspective, for example, the Design/Build Institute and the Construction Management Association. While this allows the owner and other parties to have access to a number of documents, it also places an onus on the parties to select the most appropriate version for the particular project, with its overall conditions, circumstances, and scenarios involved. It doesn't necessarily make things easier. Most major utilities, as well as state and federal agencies also utilize their own standard form construction contracts.

The advantages of commonly used form contracts include:

1. They are proven in use and legally acceptable.

2. They are construed by court cases and therefore provide certainty as to legal ramifications and interpretations of their clauses.

3. They are updated regularly, on an 8–10 year cycle or less. This is done through extensive discussion and negotiations with other interested construction industry parties: engineering groups, construction and contractors association, legal counsels of the parties, industry legal scholars, etc. In this way, the new editions address and incorporate provisions that are acceptable to a wide range of parties. Some groups publish their own documents, as they see fit, to address certain issues in a form more to their liking.

4. They are standard and generally acceptable or known in the industry, which may lead to the reduction of contingencies in any bid.

5. They save contract preparation time and expense; for example, standard preprinted form contracts exist for everything from the bidding process through the construction project, including the Certificate of Substantial Completion.

6. Their use avoids typing mistakes.

7. They are generally fair.

On the other side of the coin, the use of standard preprinted forms carries certain disadvantages, which can be recognized and dealt with. These disadvantages include:

1. Parties using the forms must recognize that every job is different; hence some changes, be they minor or major, should be made to the form contracts.

2. The series of form contracts, such as the AIA contracts, have been prepared to be consistent with one another and include numerous interrelationships among them. Therefore, a change in one form contract may necessitate a change in others. Difficulties in administering the construction project will occur where there is an apparent ambiguity created by a change in one form contract that is deemed inconsistent with another provision remaining unchanged in the contract documents.

3. Form contracts are not always acceptable to both or all parties.

GENERAL RESPONSIBILITIES

The Contract Administrator

The authority of the Contract Administrator as the Owner's representative is usually defined in the Owner-Design Professional Contract and the General and Supplementary Conditions to the Owner-Contractor Contract Agreement. The responsibilities of an independent Contract Administrator are defined in the agreement between Owner and the CA. In such an instance, care should be taken to ensure that the responsibilities of the Contract Administrator defined in his or her contract with the Owner is consistent with the authority of the Owner and the Contract Administrator as defined in the Owner-Contractor Agreement.

Both the AIA and EJCDC standard contract forms provide that the Design Professional is *not* required to make exhaustive or continuous on-site inspections to check quality or quantity of work. The Design Professional is also *not* responsible for the means and methods, techniques, sequence, or procedures of the work selected by the Contractor or for safety procedures. Moreover, the Owner-Contractor Contract ordinarily provides that neither the Owner nor the Design Professional is responsible for the coordination of the work. Accordingly, the Design Professional should not undertake the responsibilities of the Contractor or issue directions as to the means or methods of construction.

The responsibilities of the Design Professional during construction are the focus of another portion of this agreement. Those responsibilities, among others, often include:

1. Review and approve Contractor submittals including shop drawings but only for conformance with design concepts.

2. With reasonable promptness issue Owner's instructions and issue necessary interpretations and clarifications of the Contract Documents.

3. Review application for payments.

4. Inspect for substantial and final completion.

5. Authorize minor variations which do not involve an adjustment in contract price or time and are consistent with the overall intent of the Contract Documents.

6. Require special inspection or testing and reject work believed to be defective. The cost and delay of uncovering the work is incurred by the Contractor if the work is defective, but by the Owner if the work is not defective.

7. Prepare Change Orders for Owner's approval and execution.

8. Make final decisions as to artistic effect if consistent with the intent of the Contract Documents.

The design professional is responsible for coordinating work or providing additional services only if it is expressly provided for in the contract with the owner.

The particular circumstances of the project or wishes of the owner may dictate that the design professional or owner's representative assume a greater role and on-site representation. The duties, responsibilities, and limitations of authority of such a project representative should be expressed in the Contract Documents. AIA Document B352 is often used in conjunction with the other AIA Contract Documents, including the Owner-Architect Agreement, where a Project Representative is employed to represent the Owner and to perform more than "basic" services on the site for the Owner.

The EJCDC has also produced and published a document titled "Suggested Listing of Duties, Responsibilities and Limitations of Authority of Resident Project Representative," Document No. 1910-1-a.

Subcontractors

Subcontractors do not have enforceable contracts with the owner, and therefore, they have no direct rights as to the owner. Their rights depend on their contract documents with the contractor or construction manager. Direct discussions with or instructions to the subcontractor from the owner's representative on the project should be discouraged to the extent possible. So long as the owner's representative maintains directions through contractual links with the prime contractor, the prime contractor will be responsible to the owner for any delay or defective work caused by the subcontractor.

The Role of Communications

While this may sound simple, in construction, particularly, communications is a very complex, wide-ranging, and detailed process that runs through many channels and throughout the entire project sequence. Any breakdown in this process will have an adverse impact on at least a portion of the construction activities. The communications "network" required by any project is so intricate and multifaceted that a book could be devoted solely to that topic.

This text will confine its examination of the communications system to the exchange of information during the actual construction work cycle. (Figure 4–1 shows again the entire sequence.) There are many other ancillary paths of communications working concurrently, but these are more restricted in the parties served, and in their breadth, as opposed to communication channels in the project as a whole.

An owner's initial verbal or written list of needs and wishes to be met by the project must be converted into other forms of information detailing relationships between personnel, locations, types of facilities and features, and so forth. These, in turn, must become both facts and concepts: preliminary designs and plans, and selection of materials or systems to name just a few. Actual content/documentation as expressed in the documents is a combination of lines, drawings or other graphic work, and words.

Some items, materials for example, are both shown graphically and described in written formats—i.e., they show up in drawings and specifications. While standard forms and formats prevail in this communications process,

some documents are used strictly to convey information, much of which is not directly related to how or what is erected or installed. All of this information—including more and more that is sent electronically—could be characterized as "media," or the physical items that allow transmission of the information.

Key Terms in Media

A number of the more prominent terms dealing with such media or documents used in the design and documentation phases (which incorporate technical construction terms defined in the Glossary) are briefly addressed in the text that follows. (See Figures 4–2 and 4–3 for overview.) This list is alphabetical; letters in parentheses indicate the phase of work, shown on the illustrations in which the document is used.

Addendum/Addenda (K)

Addenda are documents issued during the bidding period, to answer questions from bidders, or to correct, revise, add, or delete information. They can be issued in the form of written

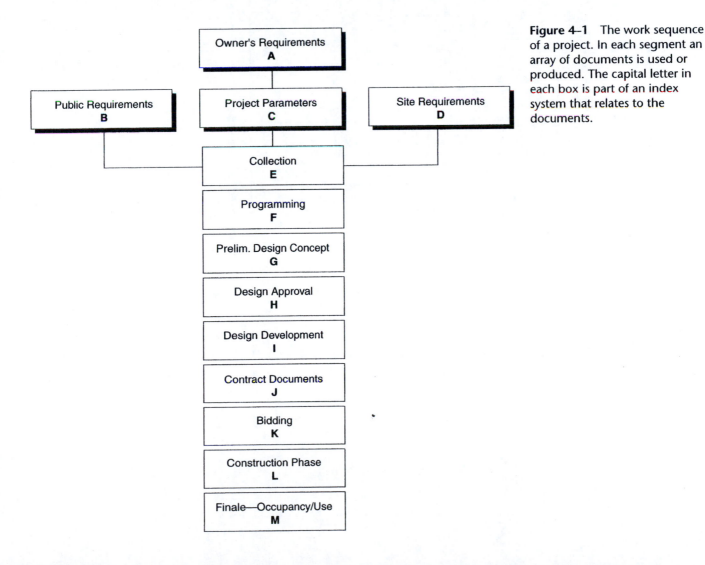

Figure 4–1 The work sequence of a project. In each segment an array of documents is used or produced. The capital letter in each box is part of an index system that relates to the documents.

A	B	C	D	E	F	G-H-I	J	K	L	M
Owner-Architect Contract	Building Code Other Regulations	Data gathering; use of resources, reference standards, etc.	Survey Deed Restrictions Easements Other Reserves or Restrictions	Feasibility Studies	Combine all elements from regulations, site, and owner; prepare program document for project	Work of creating and developing the design concept to meet the program; setting parameters for actual documentation of the project work	Contract Documents Drawings Specifications	Advertisement for Bids Bid Bond Bidding Documents Instruction to Bidders	Building Permit Change Orders Construction Documents Contract for Construction Field Instructions Inspection Records Notice to Proceed Shop Drawings Work Order	As-built drawings Certificate of Substantial Completion Certificate of Occupancy

Figure 4–2 A typical set of documents that can be produced for a project, and the phase of the sequence where each appears. Depending on the project, other documents may be required in addition to these basic items.

118

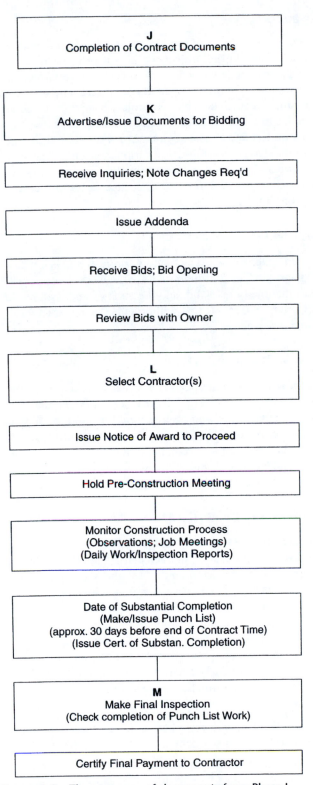

J Completion of Contract Documents
K Advertise/Issue Documents for Bidding
Receive Inquiries; Note Changes Req'd
Issue Addenda
Receive Bids; Bid Opening
Review Bids with Owner
L Select Contractor(s)
Issue Notice of Award to Proceed
Hold Pre-Construction Meeting
Monitor Construction Process (Observations; Job Meetings) (Daily Work/Inspection Reports)
Date of Substantial Completion (Make/Issue Punch List) (approx. 30 days before end of Contract Time) (Issue Cert. of Substan. Completion)
M Make Final Inspection (Check completion of Punch List Work)

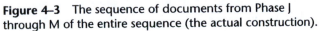

Certify Final Payment to Contractor

Figure 4–3   The sequence of documents from Phase J through M of the entire sequence (the actual construction).

or graphic (drawing) sheets. Information conveyed by addenda becomes part of the contract obligations.

Advertisement for Bids (K)

This "advertisement" is an explanation of the project (by building or work type) which is issued, or printed in the newspaper or other construction sources, basically seeking bids for the work. This announcement of the project must include all pertinent data—time of bidding, place to receive bids, place where documents are available, etc. This is a legal requirement for publicly funded projects so bidding is open to all qualified bidders on fully equal terms.

Allowances (L/K)

A procedure set out in the specifications whereby work is left undesigned, but still is a part of the project. For example, landscaping is installed very late in the project, so there is no need for an early final design. However, to provide a complete overall project cost, an "allowance" can be set up which requires each bidder to include a fixed amount of money for the landscape work. Later when the work is designed this amount can be adjusted, upward or downward, to meet the actual cost of the work.

Alternates (K)

Often portions of the project work are set out as alternates. This is done so separate prices can be submitted for these specific items. An alternate may be additional work, or work/items that can be evaluated separately, held for later purchase (so the project cost is kept within budget), or deleted entirely. Also, prices can be sought for different materials or systems—for example, two different ceiling systems—to see which is more reasonable. Basically, alternates allow the owner to be more flexible in how the project budget is spent, particularly where the budget is extremely restricted for the project envisioned. Further, it is much easier and less costly to add portions of work than to delete work.

American Institute of Architects (AIA)

The American Institute of Architects is a professional organization of registered architects which provides various membership services, publications, standard documents, lobbying efforts, government interface, information/education, and other professional services (see listing in Appendix F).

American Institute of Steel Construction (AISC)

The American Institute of Steel Construction is an organization that provides information, education, and publications regarding the use of structural steel in the construction of buildings and other projects (see listing in Appendix F).

Americans with Disabilities Act (ADA) (G)

This is a federal law (enforced through local building codes) that requires that an accessible route be established and designed into and throughout buildings for all persons. This is aimed particularly at allowing all persons, including those impaired in some way, to enter, move about, and use a building. This is done by designing in a manner that eliminates barriers against entering or using buildings. It provides that every person should be able to access any public area, facility, or service offered in a building; accessible entrances, ramps, door locations/sizes, restroom layouts, etc. are addressed. The law deals with impairments of sight, sound, physical ability, wheelchair confinement, and so on.

American Society for Testing of Materials (ASTM) (I)

The American Society for Testing of Materials is an organization dedicated solely to the independent testing and standardization of building materials, among other materials. Its reports and standards are reliable sources of information, that are used to set a specific basis or level to which a material must perform or be constructed (see listing in Appendix F).

Appraisal (D)

A review, or evaluation, of the work anticipated, or an inspection of a building (or piece of property) to establish a money value or to assess what amount and type of work is required. This is used prior to purchasing or renovating property/buildings, so a fair monetary value can be established.

Architect

Any person who is educated, trained, and active in the profession of architecture through a proper registration (licensing) process. Registration requires the successful completion of an extensive and comprehensive examination over all areas of practice. This verifies and establishes registrants' credentials as persons who are capable of designing any type of building or other facility through use of a combination of engineering and artistic considerations. In most cases, the architect is the prime design professional for the project, and leads the design/construction team. Many states require that a registered professional (architect or engineer) be retained for the design of the facility. This is aimed at providing quality construction design in the public interest. Such laws are known as "seal laws," since the professional who is responsible for the design must sign and apply her or his professional seal on the documents. Also, the professional is the direct agent of the owner, acting in the owner's behalf, but also monitoring the owner-contractor contract (for compliance by both). Architects are also active in code administration, teaching, environmental matters, field observation, and other tasks ancillary to the profession's comprehensive services.

As-builts (L/M)

A slang term for record drawings, which show all changes that are made in the project work as it progresses. These changes may be requested by the owner or made necessary by errors or by unforeseen field conditions. The drawings are turned over to the owner at project completion, and are intended to be an accurate record of the project as it was actually built (there almost always are deviations and changes from the design drawings, for various reasons). These aid the owner, later, in locating utility lines, bad soil conditions, and other features that influence future projects on the same site.

Bid Bond (K)

This document is issued by a surety company and is intended to "guarantee" the bid submitted for the work. In essence, it notes that the bid is valid, and the surety stands behind the cost submitted, as one that will provide the construction required (*see* Bond).

Bidding Documents (K)

One of several sets of documents which are used on a project. It is the combination of documents (see Figure 4–4) given to contractors who desire to bid for the right to build the project. Identical documents are given to all bidders to ensure fair and equitable competition with advantage to no single bidder. The Bidding Documents contain the Project Manual, the Construction Drawings, and all Addenda.

Bond; Surety Bond (K)

A legal instrument whereby one party (the surety) agrees to fulfill the obligations of another party (the contractor) for failure to perform as required by the third party (the owner). It is a financial guarantee, issued by a surety (usually a corporate insurance company) that work will be completed as described in the contract documents. The bond, paid for by the contractor, provides the owner with legal assurance that the obligations of the contractor will be fulfilled regardless of any misfortune occurring to the contractor. Bonds are normally issued as follows, if desired by the owner:

- *Bid bond*—guarantees that the bidder will enter into a contract, if bid is accepted
- *Performance* (Contract completion) *bond*—guarantees that the contract will be fulfilled regardless, if the contractor fails to perform
- *Lien* (Payment) *bond*—guarantees to owner (and all others) that the contractor will pay for all labor and materials furnished on the job
- *Roofing bond*—guarantees that installed roof system will perform as represented for a stated period of time

Bubble Diagrams (G)

A drafting/design device or system, where areas are roughly defined ("bubbles") and drawn, or areas are placed to define relationships, working arrangements, communications paths, work areas, locations of varying tasks, etc. which will be required in the finished building. These are not, at this point, given a definite size, but are used merely to show where different areas, rooms, or functions will be located.

Building Code (B/F)

A series of legal requirements specifying minimum design and construction requirements to ensure the health and safety of the people (the general public) using the building or structure. Such codes do not require that projects follow a fixed aesthetic design, but rather regulate the basic construction and protection systems to be built within the project. These codes become law upon their adoption (by states, counties, cities, or townships) and are enforced by local officials (Building Official, Inspector) having jurisdiction. In most states each political jurisdiction is permitted to adopt a building code. This leads to a situation that is confusing and often contradictory, where one area has many codes. In highly urbanized areas (Chicago, for example) there can be a large number of codes (Chicago area has some 250), each of which can vary from the others. However, compliance is mandatory; the builder simply must find out what the jurisdiction's code provides (see further explanation in Appendix B).

Building Permit (L)

Legal document or license issued by the local government authority, which oversees construction through enforcement of the building code. The issuance of the permit follows a review of the documents for code compliance by the government agency, and allows the start of construction. Also, it sets the project for a series of inspections, which review and ensure compliance as the construction work progresses. Also, this document is used to record the project, and to initiate the property tax program for the improvements. Other construction regulations (zoning, sewers, water, environmental) may be part of the permit requirements and system.

Building Sections (J)

A drawing which is cut by a vertical plane that is taken down through the entire building or structure, from roof to foundation. It can be used for just a major portion of the structure. Usually drawn at a small scale, it also shows the relationships of areas, structural features, and other building parts as they occur adjacent to or over each other, on the various floors or levels of the building.

Building Elevations (J)

These drawings show the exterior vertical surfaces of the building walls. Drawn to scale, they usually show the building over its full extent (height and width). The elevations show windows, doors, recesses, protruding wings, decorations, etc. which are built, installed, or mounted on the exterior of the building. Usually drawn at the same scale as the floor plans. There also are interior elevations, which function in the same manner, but show the inside of the building.

Calendar Day (J/M)

A time period (day) of twenty-four hours, measured from midnight to the next midnight, and including Saturdays, Sundays, and holidays (*see* Contract Completion Time).

Certificate of Occupancy (M)

Document issued by the local building regulations department noting that the building has been inspected, complies with all applicable regulations, and is suitable (ready) for use and occupancy. This is not a guarantee of the workmanship or completion, but is a statement regarding suitability and compliance with the regulations (not every facet of a building is regulated by the building permit).

Certificate of Substantial Completion (L/M)

This certificate is issued by the design professional when the project work has progressed and is completed to the point that all major work items are finished, and only small repair and touch-up work remains undone. The owner, with proper notice to others, could take full possession, and begin to occupy the building (while the minor unfinished work is done).

Change Order (L)

Sole means for authorizing a change in the work, an adjustment in the contract sum, and/or an adjustment in the contract completion time; entails a written order to the contractor signed by the owner and other parties and issued after the execution of the contract. An important document/form which describes some modification(s) of the work under contract, which is supposed to be done. The modification(s) can be adding work, changing work, or removing or deleting work. However, the Change Order also addresses any appropriate change in either the time to complete the entire project or the overall cost of the project or both. (Where project time and/or cost are not factors, the work is modified by using a field instruction form.)

Conditions and Restrictions (D)

The term used to designate any conditions(s) applicable to the use of land, where structures may not be placed, and the penalties for failure to comply. These can be either public provisions or private requirements set out in the deed for the property. An easement is an example of a condition/restriction placed on a piece of property.

Construction Documents (J/L)

As noted in Figure 4–4, this is another combination of documents compiled to address the project overall. This combination is different from the Bidding Documents and the Contract Documents (see Figure 4–4) by what is included and by the purpose for which they will be used. Construction Documents include all of the work included, depicted, described, covered, intended, necessary or required by the Agreement between Owner and Contractor. Also, includes the payment of a performance bond, the General, Supplemental, and Special Conditions, the drawings, the specifications, all Addenda, modifications, and Change Orders issued after execution of the contract. Construction Documents contain *all of the documents* above, *including* the bidding requirements.

Construction Drawings (J/L)

Drawings developed to show all of the construction information and details required to build the project; also called working drawings; referred to as contract drawings (after award of the construction contract) when they become part of the Contract Documents on which the contract is based. These are the graphic portion of the Construction Documents. They are similar to working or contract drawings, but share the purpose of the Construction Documents.

Contract for Construction (L)

In construction, an agreement between two or more parties for the pursuit of work on a building or construction project. One party is to perform the work, the other to pay for that work. This is called commonly the Owner-Contractor Agreement. Separate contracts are used for design work and the actual construction work. The construction contract includes the bid offer of the contractor, which should be totally responsive to all of the work, conditions, responsibilities, and obligations of the Contractor contained in the contract documents. All of this must be officially accepted by the Owner, evidenced by the Letter of Intended Acceptance, an executed Owner-Contractor Agreement or Contract, and other executed finance encumbrance documents. This is a formal, legal document, between the owner and the contractor for the construction of the project. Basically, it states what is to be built, who will be building it, how it is to be built, and how much the owner will pay the contractor for the construction work. (Normally in most delivery systems, there is no contract between owner and subcontractors.)

Contract Amount/Sum (K/L)

The total cost of the project as stated in the contract, including any authorized adjustments thereto. It is the total amount due the contractor for the performance of the work under the contract documents; payable by the owner.

Contract Completion Time (K/L)

Number of calendar days (usually) to complete the work as specified in the contract documents; compare to Substantial Completion. Using calendar days allows the contractor the option of working more than normal 8-hour work days and working on weekends and holidays. This gives the contractor flexibility in how the job is run and how the money can be spent.

Contract Documents (L)

This is the more common combination of documents; the purpose of these documents is strictly to build—and pay for—what is shown on the drawings and what is described in the specifications. Three elements comprise the Contract Documents; the Agreement (contract between Owner and Contractor), the Drawings, and the Specifications. Tied together they create the legal package which explains in detail the project and the various parties involved. Contract Documents compliment each other—whatever is required by one shall be as binding as if required by all.

Contract Documents contain the Bidding Documents (see above, but *excluding* the Bidding Requirements) and Contract Modifications (changes made after award of the contract for construction; may add, delete, or change work). The Contract Documents are the most crucial group, since the contract between Owner and Contractor is based on the proper execution of these documents.

The bulk of the technical information for a project is contained in the working drawings and their associated specifications. These two documents, along with the formal Agreement/Contract (for construction) comprise the Contract Documents. While they are one of several sets of drawings that can be formulated for a project (see Figure 4–4), it is these documents which most directly impact the actual construction work. This illustration notes the correct location for the various categories of information needed by the working contractors and their crews.

The contract contains all of the legal provisions for the project as a whole, and sets the responsibilities of the various parties, on an administrative level.

Contractor (L)

An individual or firm (whether privately held or corporation) which is party to the construction contract, and agrees to construct a building for a specified amount of money (*see also* Subcontractor).

Delivery Systems (J)

A modern term used to note how the various parties to the project will be combined, via contract(s), how they will function, and their individual responsibilities. The different

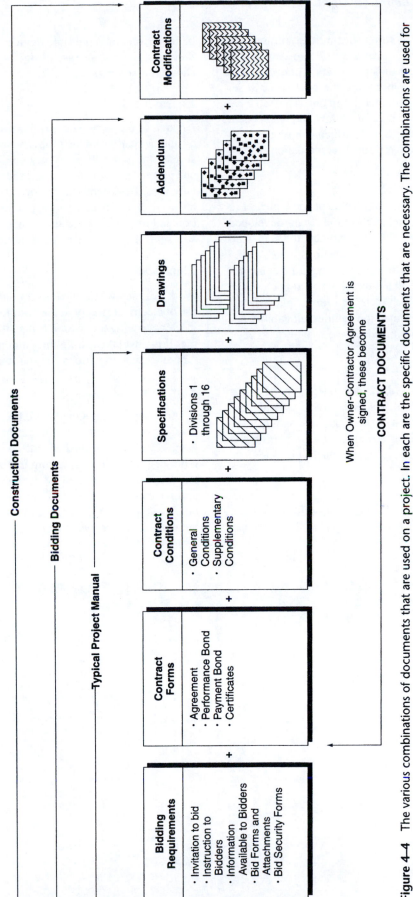

Figure 4–4 The various combinations of documents that are used on a project. In each are the specific documents that are necessary. The combinations are used for different submittals; not all parties to the contract are in need of every combination.

123

systems vary a good deal as to responsibilities, timing, and relationships. The array of systems is still growing and is driven by the needs and demands of owners. Time, cost, and overall responsibility and liability are the key issues in selecting a specific system, or in modifying one. They all have legal implications that need careful review and assessment before selection. The legalities will influence how the project is documented, and the sequence of construction.

Design (G)

The creation and development of a concept for a project to meet stated needs, desires, and goals of the client; developed in an overall, schematic form initially, showing the plan of all areas and their interrelationships and locations. Later elevations, sections, and other features necessary in the construction of a new building are added to support and enclose the plan layout. As used by architects, the term "plan" is restricted to the horizontal projection, while "elevation" applies to the vertical (or exterior) views.

Design Professional

A person educated, trained, skilled, and engaged in the actual planning, layout, and design of buildings, structures, and other facilities, including construction project systems or parts thereof. The term usually refers to the registered (licensed) architects and engineers (of various disciplines) engaged on the project.

Details (I/J)

Larger scale drawings which depict small portions or areas of the project work. Used to show exactly how the work is to be built, what materials and devices are to be used, and how they relate, work, or fasten together. Photos in Figure 4–5 show similar views.

Easement (D)

An area of property where rights are given over to or taken by another party (not the property owner) for specific and restricted purposes. This usually entails the placing of utility and power lines, drains, sewers, access drives, and other specific uses. Easements can be privately held, but usually are taken by government or utility functions for both construction and maintenance of their lines or facilities; building of structures usually is prohibited in these areas.

Electrical

Work or items which have to do with the supply, flow, and use of electrical energy in the building or project. Starts with the service entrance, which brings the power into the building. It is then taken to lighting and power panels, which, in turn, distribute to various fixtures and appliances.

Elevations (J)

In surveying measurements, the height of a point above sea level or some datum point. In drafting, the drawing or orthographic view of the vertical sides or walls of a building, interior or exterior. (*See* Building Elevations.) In addition, this term can refer to views of interior wall surfaces and, also, to grade elevations (reference points related to sea level, or other bench mark locations) for various spots on the site, the building, or other project features.

Figure 4–5 This series of photos shows small areas of construction. Note the relationships of different materials and how they are fitted together. These are "details," and are vital information for the constructors; they show exactly how the building is to be built. Photo of detail of concrete windowsill courtesy of Concrete Reinforcing Steel Institute.

Figure 4–5   (continued)

Figure 4–5   (continued)

Engineer

Person trained, skilled, and registered to practice (similar to architects; *see* Architect) in any of the many fields of engineering. Specifically in construction, these fields are civil, electrical, plumbing, fire suppression, HVAC, acoustics, etc. A project design scheme needs the services of various engineering disciplines in order to be completely functional, with all necessary utilities and services.

Factor of Safety

This is method of design whereby a material is not used to its maximum capacity; i.e., there is more strength in the material than is published in its design data. For example, a beam may be able to carry a total load of 50,000 pounds, but when it is listed in design information, this capacity will be shown as 20,000. All this is aimed at preventing overloading or other situations that may cause failure in the material. It is the ratio of ultimate strength of material to maximum permissible stress in use; unused capacity anywhere from two to five times that required.

Feasibility Studies (F/G)

Written and graphic presentations which show various schemes for the design of a project, or portions of same. Used to investigate all aspects of the situation, and to assess the implications of the many regulations and conditions that could interface with the project. This type of study can entail everything from cost analysis to environmental conditions. They are analytic devices to discover the best solutions when all conditions are considered.

Figure 4–5 (continued)

Figure 4–5 (continued)

Field Instruction (Directive) (L)

Written modification of work issued during construction that has no impact on project cost or time. It acknowledges revision of the project, but in such a way that there is no impact on time, cost, or the design concept (for contrast, *see* Change Order).

Floor Plan (G/J)

This is a sectional view (drawing) through the building, as if cut by a horizontal plane about 4 feet above the finished floor. Drawn as if the top of the building were lifted off, and one were looking down onto the remaining area. Shows layout and configuration of walls, features, doors, windows, equipment, etc. It must be drawn as one envisions the project when complete, to show what must be done to actually build the project. The floor plan is an important source of information, and a key drawing, as it provides a good deal of information to other drawings and documents.

Furnish

Means to "supply, and deliver to the job site, ready for unloading, unpacking, assembly, installation, and similar operations" (for contrast, *see* Install, and Provide).

General Contractor (GC) (L)

A contractor who has responsibility for the overall conduct of the construction project, and control of actual work and the various subcontractors doing work. Some of the project work may be performed by the GC's workforce, such as concrete work, carpentry, etc.; the subcontractors perform more specialized work. Also, the GC is responsible for overall superintendence, coordination, control, and safety on the site.

Improvements

Changes and additions to property which tend to increase its value; buildings, utilities, streets, etc.

Indicated

Term refers to graphic representations, notes, or schedules on the drawings, or to paragraphs and schedules in the specifications; used to help locate references and information in a manner similar to "shown," "noted," "scheduled," and "specified."

Inspection Record (L/M)

Similar documents written and retained by the building code field inspector (who views the work in progress for code compliance), and the project representative of the design professional, who also oversees the entirety of the work for compliance with all contract obligations. These records create a project history by showing what work was accomplished at what time and how well it was done; also used to record shortcomings and instructions given for remedial work.

Install (L)

Usually means on-site operations of "unloading, unpacking, temporary storage, assembly, erection, placing, anchoring, applying, working to dimension, connecting, testing, finishing, curing, protecting, cleaning, and similar activities for proper and complete use/operation of area, equipment, appliance, or item" (*see,* for contrast, Provide, and Furnish).

Installer (L)

Employee, subcontractor, or lower tier contractor hired to perform a specific, narrow-scope construction task or work

activity involving installation, erection, application, or making ready for use; trained to technician level, and experienced in such work as well as in troubleshooting problems to provide proper and complete installation.

Instructions to Bidders (K)

A listing of procedures, forms, and information that bidders must follow in order to create and submit a valid and proper bid for consideration. Standardizes the bidding process to eliminate any odd or advantageous elements whereby one bidder can be more successful than another, on some issue other than project cost. Also, meets legal issues by removing irregularities in the bid process on the part of owner, design professionals, and others. Simply, they tell the bidders exactly what to do, what form to put the information in, and where to submit the bid.

Isometric (I/J)

An axonometric drawing view which "tilts" an object (or isolated portion of a building) up onto one corner, thus showing three surfaces—top, left side, right side. This view is often helpful in that it aids in clarifying complex work, since it is more pictorial (three-dimensional and as the human eye sees normally). Not commonly used (most working drawings are two-dimensional, orthographic drawings), but is available where circumstances require a more inventive drawing for better explanation and clarity of the required work.

Legal Description (D)

A written indication of the location and boundaries of a parcel of land. It is usually part of the deed, and refers generally to the recorded plat or survey in official record files. It contains wording about the exact location of the parcel, the length and direction of property lines, markers at property corners, and usually will include restrictions (easements) taken by government regulations or utility companies, or imposed by private rights.

Lot (Property) Line (D)

Invisible line that can be established in the field with a transit, based on information (a length or distance and a direction) included in the legal description of the property. The lines form the legal boundary of a parcel, tract, or lot of property; also called *property line*.

Margin of Safety

Comparative value between actual capacity required and that which the member possesses—i.e., a beam which is capable of carrying 6,000 pounds is required to carry only 1,000 pounds; it has a 5,000 pound margin of safety (*see* Factor of Safety).

Master Plans (F)

Planning can be done on various levels: national, state, regional, local, etc., down to individual land holdings. Where a large tract of land is to be developed, a master plan usually will be developed. This will entail complete analysis of the property, the selection of best locations for the building or functions to be installed, and the features that must be avoided, or mitigated. They are an aid to the developer for long-term planning, for sequencing work, and ensuring the best use of the land and providing the best value to the tenants and users.

Mechanical

Everything having to do with the plumbing, heating, ventilating, air-conditioning, and fire protection systems in a building. This includes the utility service (incoming), as well as the distribution, modification, and proper use of the air or water involved. These can be very extensive and complex systems in buildings, so that there is adequate and proper service throughout. The systems involve piping, ductwork, pumps, air handling equipment, fans, diffusers, fixtures, exchangers, valves, etc. for completely functional systems.

Notice To Proceed (L)

Formal written notice from owner to contractor that acceptance and execution of a contract is imminant, and work may begin (*see also* Work Order). This allows the contractor to begin the process of writing subcontracts and preparing for field operations.

Owner-Architect Contract (L)

This is an agreement between the parties (Owner and Contractor) as to what each will do. The Contractor agrees to build the project according to the contract drawings and specifications, for a certain amount of money (listed in the agreement). The Owner agrees to pay that amount for the correct construction of the project as shown and described on the documents the owner provides to the Contractor. This is a legal contract, with deep implications, and often it stipulates a very large amount of money. The contract details the entire relationship and the rights and obligations of both parties, and how any disputes will be resolved. On most projects this is one of a series of standardized documents with varying provisions, which is selected to be specific to the project; it may be especially written if desired or necessary.

Owner-Furnished-Contractor-Install (OFCI) (L)

Equipment, material, or other components of a system or building which are purchased by the owner, directly, and furnished to the contractor, who receives, stores, protects, installs, connects, and tests each such item; this procedure can be modified as necessary.

Perspective (G)

A drawing technique which displays the building/project in visually correct terms (i.e., as the human eye would see it). This involves the setting of a horizon line and vanishing points (from one to three in number). This technique will produce drawings in a form "that look right" (for example, a long structure will appear to become shorter in height the farther away it is from the eye). Usually this is a presentation drawing, which aids the owner, etc. since it depicts the planned project in realistic terms (*see* Rendering).

Plans/Plan (G/J)

Short name for Floor Plan (*see* above); also used as a general term (mistakenly), when referring to all of the drawings for a project (not all drawings are "plans"). Besides the various floors of the building, there can be site plans (of the entire project location), utility plans (showing underground utility lines), landscape plans, exiting plans, drainage plans, etc. Plan, in general terms, is an overhead view, looking straight down on the work displayed, in two dimensions.

Presentation Models (G)

Often owners will want scale models of their project, for a better view and understanding of what the final result will be, or for displaying that intent to lenders, the public, etc. The models can be made very detailed and life-like, or can be simple cardboard to show massing, etc. Quite often the desire is to make a presentation that is realistic, including trees, autos, people, etc., much like a model railroad display. In some instances, industrial users/owners use the model to show process or production flow.

Prior Approval

A term that simply means to seek and have approval before performing some act or work. This could entail the start of work, a change in work, the use of a different material, device, or method, or the modification of the project in other ways.

Professional Association/Society

Organizations usually representing a given profession which combine single efforts (by members) into a larger and more extensive voice; present educational/informational efforts, information and document sales, and other combined services to individual members; somewhat of a lobbying group which acts on behalf of members (see listings in Appendix F).

Programs (C)

A program for a project is a document which lists the various problems, needs, and desires of the owner for the project. Also, it should include regulatory requirements and other information that is necessary to design a scheme which will serve the owner properly, but also meet other private and public mandated parameters. From this listing, the design professional can establish relationships and other aspects of the project as part of developing the overall design scheme for the project.

Project Manual (PM) (L)

The Project Manual, recently, has become a series of books which contain the technical and legal aspects of the actual construction. For example, many projects utilize separate volumes for administration, technical architectural specifications, and technical mechanical specifications. This is done since the amount of information is imposing and cannot be contained in just one book. (Usually this is a plastic spiral bound book.)

The Project Manual contains:

Bidding Requirements

- Invitation to bid
- Instruction to bidders
- Information available
- Bid forms and attachments
- Bid security forms

Contract Forms

- Contract (agreement)
- Performance bond
- Payment bond
- Certificates

Contract Conditions

- General Conditions
- Supplementary Conditions

Technical Specifications

- CSI Divisions 1–16

Proposal (L)

In construction, the proposal is a function of the Contractor(s) in that it is a document that lists the cost or price of work. Basically, it is the offer that the Contractor(s) makes to the Owner or General Contractor; i.e., the work noted will be performed for *X* number of dollars.

Provide

Means to furnish, pay for, and install in completely operational manner, ready for intended use (*see* Furnish, and Install for clarification).

Punch List (M)

At the time of Substantial Completion (approximately 30 days prior to the date of Contract Time) the Contractor is to request a final inspection. This is best done as a combined effort, between all Design Professionals for the project, the Owner, and the General or Prime Contractor(s). It involves a careful and complete inspection of the work for both completeness and for full compliance with the contract requirements. A listing is made (the punch list) of all discrepancies, even those as minute as missing screws in hinges, missing bumpers in door frames, up to and including major areas of required repair or replacement, improper installation, poor workmanship, etc. The fundamental issue is to compare the work in place with what was required on the drawings and in the specifications (the Contract Documents). Final project payment is not made until the punch list work is completed. Sometimes, unfortunately, contractors view this inspection as intrusive, unfair, bothersome, and unduly precise. It, however, is merely a verification that what the contract documents require (and what the Owner has paid for) is delivered, in the manner expected and described. It is verification that the elements of the contract have, indeed, been met, and the final payment for the work is due, in exchange for work promised and contracted.

Renderings (G)

Often clients want to see their project as it will look when completed. The best presentation for this is the rendering. This is a realistic perspective view, usually in color and including surroundings such as trees, autos, people, streets, walks, etc. Many clients use these drawings as announcements of their project or to gain public relations exposure (newspapers often call the renderings *artist's sketches*).

Schedule of Values (I)

This is a formal breakdown of the contract amount (sum), with each major portion and subcontract amount listed separately; allowances are included as separate items, also. It shows the allocation of the contract amount, and is valuable in analysis of the project cost, showing where certain work is above or below the average expected cost (based on other projects, or cost information).

Sections; Sectional Drawings (J)

Drawings created when an imaginary "cutting plane" is used to cut through a building or a portion of the building; both floor plans and details are section drawings, along with wall sections and building sections.

Shop Drawings (L)

Detailed plans prepared by a manufacturer or fabricator to guide the shop production of such building components as cut stonework, steel or precast concrete framing, curtain wall panels, and cabinetwork.

Site (D)

The area of land that is the location of a building project; may be all or a portion of any lot or tract of land.

Site (Plot) Plan (I/J)

This is a drawing of the entire job site area (and may include the entire property involved). It is developed from the survey, and shows all existing conditions, including topography and both natural and man-made features. To this is added the proposed improvements to the site through construction of the project work, including roads, utilities, buildings, reserved areas, project limits (outside which no work is to be done), and the overall arrangement of the project.

Specifications (J)

The written matter complementing and supplementing the building drawings; written by the design professionals and containing information that cannot be shown on the drawings. They also prescribe the materials that are to be used and indicate how these are to be handled and installed. In addition, they establish the level of quality required, the standards to which the work must conform, and legal and administrative procedures regarding the project.

Structural

Those matters which deal with the supporting framework of the building(s) are called structural. This includes the foundation system, the superstructure, and the roof framing. Much of this work is enclosed in the final project, but must be created and designed to fit and support the architectural design features.

Submittals (L)

In each (CSI) specification Section, there are requirements for various submittals, which deal with the materials/systems specified. Usually these entail shop drawings, samples of materials that are color ranged for selection by the architect, certificates, warranties, guarantees, etc. These all are for review and approval for use on the project, or for verification of use.

Substantial Completion (M)

The point at which the building project is complete, and ready for occupancy, except for a limited number of minor repairs or incomplete work items. Usually occurs about 30 days prior to the end of the Contract Time period. This allows time for completion of punch list work and final closeout of the project. It also is the point at which final payment can be made to contractor(s), and owner can move in.

Survey (D)

Someone owns every piece of land. Each landowner has a deed in which there is a detailed description of the limits of the portion of land. This description includes both magnetic directions and specific distances. A trained surveyor can use this information to create a mathematical calculation (called

a closure), which accounts for the exact size and placement of the land. In the field, the surveyor can establish the directions using a transit, and can measure the distance, thus laying out the land with a series of imaginary lines. Monuments (stakes, iron pins, or concrete markers) can be placed at the intersection of the lines as they are sighted by the surveyor. This provides a permanent set of markers from which the specific portion of land can be ascertained. From this information, depicted in a scaled drawing, the project designer can lay out the structures to be built, and can also ascertain the location of utilities, land formations, impediments to construction, and the like, all of which the surveyor can establish in the field, and place on the basic survey drawing.

Tract (D)

A specified area of land. Also, used in the larger designation of land areas other than lot, parcel, subdivision, etc.

Trade Association

Organizations with a common interest in construction materials, methods, operations, etc.; usually single-interest motivation in education, marketing, information, combined research and development, and representing numerous groups/manufacturers, etc. with a single combined effort; many also produce technical standards for their products (see listing in Appendix F).

Topography (D)

Usually refers to site characteristics such as contour of the land, trees, or other natural features.

Unit Prices

In contrast to allowances, unit prices indicate the cost of individual portions of work, e.g., excavation of 1 cubic yard of earth from deeper than 5 feet below grade. Most bidders are required to submit some unit prices, which are then used when more work is required than anticipated by the contract documents. Unit prices can be requested for any number or type of work items, but usually will reflect uncertain site conditions. Also, unit prices are actual costs retained by contractors which show accurate costs of portions of work, e.g., hanging a door, or installing a set of door hardware. The contractors use these prices as the basis for their bidding, since they know that the prices are correct for their workforce.

Wall Sections

Wall sections are drawings made to show the wall construction at various places around the building. Created by using the concept of a vertical cut down through the wall, and then viewing the end of the wall. They are two-dimensional views, which show all the materials in the wall, the floor-to-wall construction, and the roof-to-wall detail. They can include sections through doors and windows, if desired, and if the section is properly located in the building. This is a very important series of drawings, since they show how the wall is to be built.

Working Drawings

Drawings containing design details; plans, sections, details, and elevations according to which the actual construction is done; drawing portion of Contract Documents.

Work Order (L)

Written notice (also called Notice to Proceed) from the Owner to the Contractor authorizing the Contractor to commence work under the contract and establishing the beginning date from which the contract completion time shall be established.

Zoning (B/D)

Building regulations which control size, use, location, and type of structures to be built in specific areas.

EXERCISES

The following can be used to enhance the text material and provide wider exposure to and understanding of construction.

Some portions of these items may be assigned as individual projects, but overall they are group projects that every class member can benefit from. (*No activity that requires going onto a construction site should be undertaken by a single individual, nor without prior notice and permission from the site manager; ensure full and proper safety measures in any event.*)

1. Solicit contributions of sets of drawings and specifications from local professional offices (usually there are extra, unused sets available) for class review, use, and analysis. Often other related documents will be available, too. Most professionals and contractors will support this type of activity, and may prove to be resources for other related discussions and activities.

2. Have a professional relate and discuss with the class how the documents for a project are created, the work processes, the relationships, the drafting techniques, the information required, the legal implications, and so on.

3. Ask a professional to speak to the class about how the professional's field operations are conducted for a project, and how they interface with the office effort and with the client.

4. Secure copies of the various standard documents or forms used by local professional offices, assess their use, and set up problems requiring varying uses of the forms, or try to see which set of forms address one particular problem.

A Narrative of a Project Sequence

The following narrative is presented to expand the information provided in Chapter 3, The Sequence of a Project.

The actual construction work and activities are set forth in their proper sequence. Materials specified in various Sections of the Project Manual (specifications) are discussed as they are brought together to form other systems, or portions of the project.

It is hoped that this narrative will aid students in visualizing the sequential process of a project as related to the installation of the various materials, systems, devices, and equipment required to build the project. Also, the hope is to give an overall impression of exactly what is entailed by way of a co-ordinated effort so necessary to "putting a building together."

The very same type of process is required, though, to construct any type of project (not just buildings), and for projects of any size. It is only the amount of materials and so forth that changes.

There is a lesson for the student in the reading of a narrative of a project, based on the technical specifications and drawings.

Within the activities listed in Chapter 3, there are numerous small work items that must be completed in order to produce the finished project. These vary a good deal in size from project to project, but usually are similar. This work is the manifestation of the designs, drawings, information, and descriptions contained in the Contract Documents. In these work items things appear in their full size and in their proper location relative to other work. It is as if a huge model is being built based on the Contract Documents.

Using these documents crammed full of very diverse and disjointed information, alone, as a basis for understanding either the process or the actual construction is difficult. The student who is not familiar with construction materials, equipment, processes, language, and the like would be hard pressed to envision and formulate the process and sequence of the construction in her or his mind. A single work item may require information from several specification sections and from several drawing details. The student who is unfa-

miliar with the documents would have to research at random to find the exact condition to be addressed.

Although most specifications are now written in the 16-Division format of the Construction Specifications Institute (CSI), and are somewhat parallel to the normal work sequence, there are numerous things that are out of order. It is not the function of the specifications to assign the work to specific subcontractors or trades. One is often required to search through several sections to find exactly what is installed first, what second, and so forth; further, how those particular items are fitted together or finally constructed can be hard to find. The building, forming, or erection of building items such as roofs, walls, panels, systems, and devices are combinations of many parts and pieces often specified throughout the 16 CSI Divisions.

This paper gives some idea of the fundamental grasp of construction that is required of professionals, and how various items are combined into proper construction, and in what time sequence. The detailed descriptions of work, here, relate back to the Earthwork, Grading and Excavation listing, and those following, in Chapter 3 of this book.

However, it shows in more general terms the process of constructing a building project. Within each item of the sequence are the variables: foundation systems change, different envelope enclosure systems (exterior walls) are used, and roofs can be of differing types and shapes. In fact, each project carries its own unique set of materials, systems, details, construction, and other parameters; only repetitive construction, following a prototype design, will carry forth the parameters of another project.

The following narrative was written about a new elementary school which was built in a small town in Ohio. With bond issue money in hand and a firm determination to resolve their problems, the school board moved forward to plan the school project. First off, they commissioned an architectural firm from nearby Cincinnati to design the building and perform all normal architectural work. This firm had wide experience dealing with rural school construction projects, from one-room additions to complete new school buildings. The documents from this firm were used as the basis for much of the information in this narrative.

Although it was active in running the school district, the school board had very little experience with construction, and none with new buildings. The board relied on the architects for advice in the development of the entire project from the very outset of deciding what to build, how big a building to build, and selection of a suitable site (which could allow expansion), to the final selection of furnishings.

The major variant between this narrative and many projects is the overall extent or scope of the work involved. What is described here are activities of quite some duration—weeks, some of them months, in fact, a matter of years for the entire project. The mere fact that it can be described in a relatively few words should not be allowed to distract from or belie the size, complexity, or impact of the work.

THE NARRATIVE

First, of course, in the order of construction came the massive task of cutting and grading down the hill to provide a more usable site. The existing hill, which had a crest at elevation 116, had to be cut down to elevation 100, and regraded to meet the surrounding, undisturbed ground elevations. At this elevation a huge plateau was leveled off, and on this "pad" the building was to be set. A great number of cubic yards of earth had to be repositioned to make the site fully suitable for the planned construction, and the outdoor areas for the students' activities. The grading (cutting and filling) operations required large machines and a good period of time to accomplish, due to the vast site and extensive building.

In most cases the filled areas were over 3 feet deep and the tree stumps had to be cut low enough so they could remain under these areas. Since the building footings were carried to a depth of 3 feet beneath the finished grades, the trees were cut off well below the existing grade; they did not interfere with the new construction of the building and the foundations. However, in most cases even the stumps were removed to ensure satisfactory bearing for the foundation footings. Once the cutting and filling operations were finished, the General Contractor utilized a Civil Engineer/Surveyor, who worked with the property survey and the plot plan to lay out the building site, overall, and the various building lines and bench marks. Huge markers of two by fours set vertically in the ground and cross braced are set up at the building lines. Excavating for the footings and foundations begin at these lines.

Seven-foot-wide trenches are cut around the exterior lines of the building. They are the cuts into which the footings and foundation walls are placed, both for the exterior walls and the interior walls of the pipe trenches. The footings are boxed in to the required width. They vary from 16 to 22 inches wide depending upon the loads they carry and the condition of the

soil under them. Metal supports are used in the bottom of the footings to ensure accurate and permanent placement of the reinforcing. Usually two or three bars run the length of the footing and are crossed by shorter bars which run the width of the footing (see Figures A–1, A–2, and A–3). All of these bars are wired to each other and to the metal supports to guard against displacement of the rods when the concrete is poured. The rods are usually placed in the bottom third of the footing and in some places, especially in the exterior walls, reinforcing rods are run perpendicular to the footings. These rods are anchored in the footings and stick up out of the footings. They are the reinforcing for the foundation walls. These rods help to tie the walls to the footings as well as strengthen the walls themselves. The walls are also keyed into the footings at some places.

After the footings are poured and firm, the forms for the walls are set into place. These forms are made of T & G lumber. (Forms for exposed concrete walls are made up of plywood.) Two by four members are used for the framework of the forms. The sides of the forms are laterally braced and tied together, in a manner such as used generally in all formwork. The reinforcing for the walls is placed before the wall is poured. Some of the rods, as mentioned before, are anchored into the footings, but others of them, the horizontals, must be wired to the vertical rods before the pouring takes place. The walls are poured continuously and the work stops only when predetermined points are reached. Caution is taken to see that the concrete is mixed in a manner to prevent separation and that no voids or honeycombing takes place. Forms are removed after the 3000# concrete (concrete strength @ 28 days after placing = 3,000 pounds per square inch [psi]) is sufficiently set.

In some places both the footings and the foundation walls are widened to receive the structural steel columns, which, for instance, carry the trusses over the gym area.

The floor slabs either run over or into the foundation walls. The slabs need no formwork (except perhaps over the pipe trenches). A six-inch layer of bank run gravel is placed on the ground, which is properly leveled. Over the gravel is placed a layer of 30# (weight of a roll of felt) saturated felt paper vapor barrier, which in turn is covered with a layer of Perlite insulation. All slabs are to be four inches in depth except one in the boiler room which is to be some six inches in depth. All slabs are to be reinforced with 25# (weight of a roll of wire mesh—100 sq. ft.) wire mesh. The boiler room slab is the exception and, because of its greater depth and load, it is reinforced with 42# mesh.

Access openings are left in the various slabs so that workers can get to the pipe trenches left for the various pipes. The slabs that receive resilient tile are steel troweled and floated to a true plane to receive the tile. Slabs that run under a terrazzo topping are brought to the proper level and given a float finish, while exposed floors are treated with a concrete hardener. Four-inch drain tiles are placed under 12″ of washed gravel all around the perimeter of the footings.

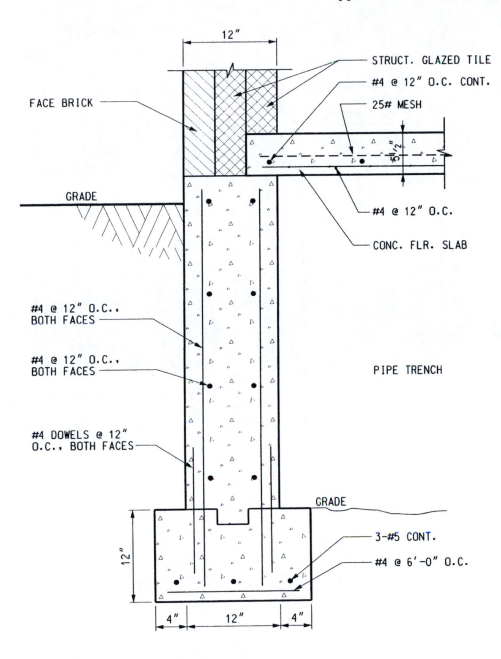

12"

FACE BRICK

STRUCT. GLAZED TILE

#4 @ 12" O.C. CONT.

25# MESH

GRADE

#4 @ 12" O.C.

CONC. FLR. SLAB

#4 @ 12" O.C.,
BOTH FACES

#4 @ 12" O.C.,
BOTH FACES

PIPE TRENCH

#4 DOWELS @ 12"
O.C., BOTH FACES

GRADE

3-#5 CONT.

#4 @ 6'-0" O.C.

12"

4"   12"   4"

After all of the concrete work is finished, the next task that is undertaken is the setting of the structural steel. This work at this time does not include the setting of the beams and lintels, etc. Rather the independent steel is to be set at this time. This includes the columns for the gym trusses, and the steel arches for the covered play area. All the steel is to be fabricated and predrilled according to the shop drawings, and the field connections are to be with rivets or high-strength bolts. All steel is to be set to true lines and planes and leveled. All members are shipped with a coat of rust inhibiting paint.

After the steel is set, the carpenters begin their job of laying out all of the exterior and interior lines for the block, tile, and brick partitions. This work determines the correct room and corridor sizes. All other trades are to work to the lines set up by the carpenters.

Lightweight aggregate concrete block is to be used for the backup of the face brick. The block is to be of the "Amlite" or Waylite type, free from any organic substances or other defects. All block must have passed the 1000# load bearing test. Block is also used for the interior partitions in connection with plaster and glazed structural tile. All external corners and jambs in block are to be bullnozed.

The face brick is to be an evenly burned brick measuring 2¼ by 8 by 3¾. The brick which is to be used in the long wall of the gym is to be a Norman brick which is some 12" long. All of the face brick work is to be laid up in Common bond with a header course every seventh course. These headers serve as the bond between the face brick and the backup block. The Norman brick of the gym wall is to be set up in stack bond.

Figure A-2 Interior pipe chase wall foundation built inside of the foundation wall to form a horizontal pipe chase, or trench, in which the various utility lines are run (installed).

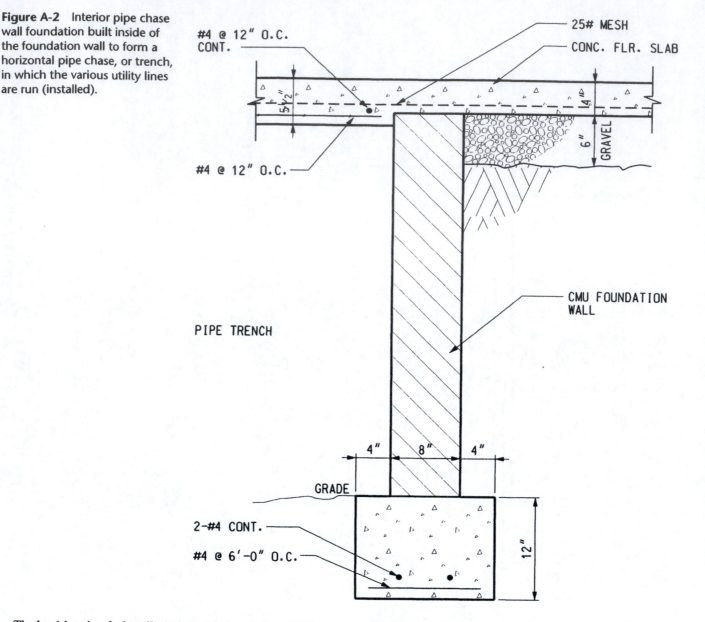

The load-bearing facing tile (structural glazed tile—SGT) which is used in the interior walls is to measure 5 by 12 nominally and is to be of grade "A" quality. Four-inch tiles and soaps are to be used in the double-faced walls. Many variations of the tile plaster and block are to be used in the several rooms and for different conditions.

The color of the tile changes from room to room and from area to area. Usually a field color is accented with a contrasting trim color.

A mortar of 1:2:6 ratio of portland cement, Mortarseal, and sand is to be used to join all brick, block, and tile work, in both facing and backup roles. The type S mortar is to have a 600# strength at 28 days and is to have a waterproof additive incorporated when it is used for exterior joining.

All joints are to be a uniform ⅜", and the face brick joints are to be tooled with a concave tool. Exposed interior walls are to have ⅜"-thick struck joints, while the tile work is to have a ¼"-thick tooled joint.

As the interior walls are laid up the carpenter sets the pressed steel (hollow metal) door frames. These frames are of 14 gauge metal and have a double rabbeted profile with a single stop. The corners are mitered and welded, and three wall anchors are spot welded to the jambs so that the frames are firmly anchored in place as the interior walls are laid up. All of the frames come with the necessary reinforcing and the necessary hardware cut-outs. The frames for the exterior classroom doors are to be set later as they are anchored into steel at the heads and into the windows at the one jamb.

Of course, the necessary lintels and beams were set as the interior walls were laid up, and now the remainder of the steel can be set in preparation for the roof joists.

The steel bar joists used at New Richmond vary in depth from 12 to 16 inches, and are composite sections of angles and rods. The composite joist is a much truer joist, free from the great warping so frequently found in the drawn type joists. All of the joists are held laterally by ½" rods which are

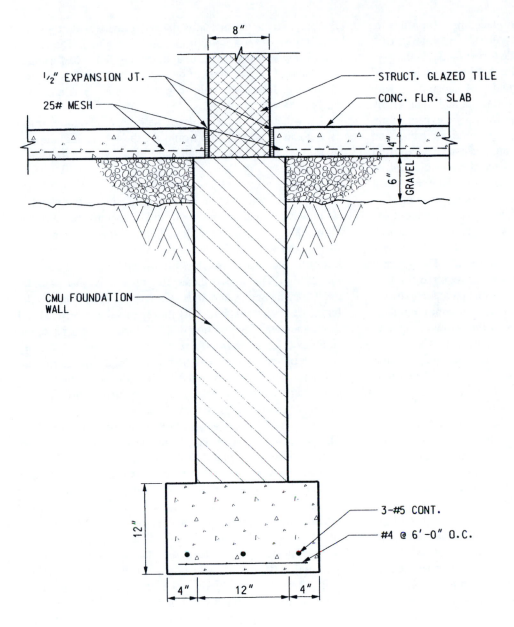

welded to each joist at the top and bottom chords. Anchors are provided so that the joist nearest a parallel wall can be anchored to that wall. The joists are set at 48″ centers and ensure a safe roof load of some 60#. In most instances these joists rest on masonry, where they are anchored and walled in, but in some spots they rest on steel, and here they are welded to the supporting members.

Bowstring trusses are incorporated over the gym area. This is done both for economy and for added load-bearing capacity. The trusses are placed at 20-foot centers and span from the north gym wall to the north wall of the boiler room and the kitchen area. In these walls are concealed 8″ H-columns which carry the various trusses. Under these columns are the spread foundation walls and the spread footings. The trusses have angles for the top chords and channels for the straight bottom chords. Strut angles weave their way from panel point to panel point. The trusses are braced laterally with angles between both the top and bottom chords.

One truss, the largest as far as depth is concerned, is placed at the junction of the gym and the cafeteria, and carries not only the gym roof but the roof of the cafeteria as well. This is accomplished by having the longspan joists used over the cafeteria rest on the bottom chord of the truss (and on the west cafeteria wall). Then, too, a series of 12-inch joists are placed between the top chords of the several trusses.

So, too, another series of joists are incorporated over the steel arches which roof the covered play area. These, too, span between the top chords. Here, just as in all of the areas using standard (not longspan) joists, the bar joists are set in such a manner that they fall on either side of the toplights of skylights. (These skylights will be discussed later.) Since nearly all of the joists used will carry more than the required 60#, they can be placed a little farther apart. This is done in connection with the skylights so that the joists rest at the width of the skylight plus the required clearances on center.

After the structural roof is set in place, the sub-purlins for the gypsum deck are welded directly to the joists at 32½"centers. To these purlins are attached the form boards for the gypsum and over this is laid the mesh of 12-gauge wires 4'-0" o.c., and in turn over this mesh is laid a 14-gauge mesh with the wires some 8" o.c. The second mesh is laid transversely across its predecessor. To this maze of wires the gypsum is applied. Actually it is poured to a depth of some two inches and when it is poured, it is of fine pouring consistency, free from lumps and other foreign objects. Since the gypsum will be poured sometime in summer the normal precautions against frost and snow can be foregone, but still the gypsum must be protected from the rain and also from too rapid drying if exposed to the hot sun. So, too, the workmen must work in a neat manner so that none of the white substance will slop over onto the side walls or onto other allied work. The gypsum contractor also must pour the cants and the required curbs.

The pre-fab skylights are the next things that are to be set into place. The units are made of standard aluminum insulated grid construction and use Owens-Illinois low-brightness, light-selecting glass. Each unit comes with a cap flashing attached to it, and the roofer's sheet metal flashings go on the outside of this flashing. The light well itself and the curb of the unit are bolted directly to the structural angles surrounding the opening. Wood blocking is screwed to the unit curb, and to the blocking is screwed the aluminum anchors which hold the top of the unit (containing the glass) to the unit's curb. The roof flashing is held in place under a flange on the unit by a cement mastic.

On the interior (at the ceiling line) an aluminum frame glazed with light-diffusing glass is mounted into the light well. This accounts for the large area affected by the top-lights. The smaller units, 3'-2" by 3'-2" with nine panels, are centered over the corridors in areas two and three, while the larger 15-panel units, 3'-2" by 6'-2", are centered 11'-6" in from the interior walls in all area two and three classrooms.

In the roof of the covered play area wood blocking is placed between the bar joists to receive a sort of skylight. Here extra heavy corrugated "Resolite" panels of a translucent nature are used to light the area under the steel arches.

Directly over the gypsum deck is installed one layer of 15# saturated felt vapor barrier, which is then mopped in hot asphalt. After the mopping, two layers of ¾" "Fiberglas" insulation is laid over the entire building.

The sheet metal work and the flashing follow the installation of the insulation. This is done before the final roofing layers are applied, and it includes all work where the roof is connected to any other work. The counter flashing method utilizing 16 gauge copper is to be used, and the flashing is to be used at the intersection of all vertical surfaces and the roof and at all openings in the roof proper. All flashing will extend down to within 3" of the roof surface, and the adjoining lengths shall be hook-seamed together.

After all of the sheet metal work has been installed (this includes gravel stops, gutters, downspouts, scuttles, and ven-

tilators) and the various units flashed or made watertight, the final layers of built-up roofing can be installed. The roof is built up with 4 plys of saturated 15# rag felt, 165# asphalt, and 300# of slag or 400# of pea gravel. The roof as a whole shall meet Johns-Manville specifications no. 3-A and shall carry a 20-year bond.

Now that the roof is in place, the work on the interior finishing can be started, and from here the job as a whole will go quite rapidly. First, though, the exterior walls will have to be erected.

In numerous places around this building a relatively common type of construction is to be used; this is the panel or window wall. In this building it is to be manufactured by the Wm. Bayley Co. of Springfield, Ohio. In most instances on this job the panel wall does not extend from floor line to roof, but rather it is set upon a low brick wall between 18 and 24 inches high. This allows the heating units to be placed under the wall. The enclosed details show panels at the top and the bottom, but on this school only the top panel will be used and the remainder of the section will be glazed. At the head, the small exterior angle is to be reversed, i.e., the horizontal leg will not be seen since it will be pointing to the interior of the building, thus hidden by the head section of the unit itself. The head section and angles are connected in all cases to some steel member (plate or wide flange).

First the 5S2 sill is set and bolted into place on the stone sill capping on the brick wall. Next one entire unit (one panel wide) is lifted into place so that it rests against the afore-applied exterior head angle. Of course, the angle is so placed that the unit will be set true and plumb. This first unit is then set up to give typical jamb conditions as shown. It is then held fast by the application of the interior head angle. This interior head angle is just as wide as the unit, since a continuous application would retard the installation of the several other units. (If the inside head angle were applied continuously, the units would have to be lifted up to the structural head so that the unit's sill section would clear the top of the sub-sill. This however is impossible in this installation since the exterior head angle is reversed. The leg of the angle would prevent the unit from being lifted to the structural head, thus the unit would not clear the sub-sill.)

The foregoing discussion was just to show the two types or possible types of installations. Actually the appearance of the head angle is neglected since it will be installed above the ceiling line, which is at the 5Z Rail.

Mastic is placed in the small receivers at the other jamb of the first unit. Into this mastic are slipped the closure plates of the 5V1 mullion. The bolt on the exterior is started into the holder bracket. The next unit, with mastic filled receivers, is lifted and slid into place and the interior head angle is secured. Then the holder brackets are drawn up tight and the installation of two units is complete. This procedure is repeated down the entire run until the last unit is ready to be set.

The last unit cannot be set as the interior (between end units) units were. The jamb plates are set in the second to last unit and the holder bracket screws are started. The last unit is lifted up so that it is almost flush with the masonry wall. (The masonry opening is large enough to allow about 3/8″ at each jamb. This is enough to allow the unit to clear the jamb plates.) When the unit is set up it is then slid into place so that it engages the jamb plates. So when typical jamb conditions are set, the holder brackets are drawn up tight and the interior angle is applied, as well as the jamb trim, and the installation is complete.

Standard projected sash, either in or out, can be used in this panel wall system. These projected sash by themselves are used around the upper part of the gym area. The sash and the window wall itself are glazed with ¼″ D.S. plate glass, but in some of the several openings a colored glass is utilized. This is done to add the color to the building that is lost when only the top panel is used in the panel wall. The panel that is used is of the porcelain enamel type and of a color to be chosen by the architects.

The exterior walls of all the classrooms are made up of brick, ventilating sash, and glass block. The brick wall is built up about 3½ feet above the interior floor line. The wall is capped with a stone sill, and on this sill are placed the special glass block units of ventilating sash. The sash units are 2′-9″ high and made to fit in groups of three between the structural steel mullions. The units are made of heavy aluminum sections, the jambs and sills of which are very similar to the sections of the panel wall system. The head section, of even heavier construction, is formed in the shape of a Z so that it can hold both the sash and the glass blocks and still act as the drip for the section. The unit is about 4½″ wide and has two muntins, thus making the unit some three lights high, the top two of which project outward.

Each door frame, with the transom, is set after the sash units are in place and before the glass blocks are laid up. The door frame must be made with a special section on the back of it to receive the glass block. It cannot be anchored to the block, so therefore it must be anchored at the one jamb, the head, and as far up the other jamb as possible (to the top of the brick wall). The elevation of the classrooms is capped with a porcelain enamel spandral panel, just under the bottom of the roof.

Now with the building thoroughly encased the interior work can be speeded up. First, of course, are the interior finishes, namely the lathing and the plastering.

A relatively small amount of plastering is to be done in this building. All of the exterior walls are to receive plaster, but the rest of the interior finishes are to be painted concrete block or glazed facing tile. The lathing is done with ¾″ channels which are attached to the walls at 16″ centers and to this system of channels a lath of cross wires equal to "Steeltex" plaster lath is applied. In all of the classrooms some furring must be done to create bulkheads over the lockers.

A series of three coats of a gypsum cement plaster is applied to the lath after the wall has been cleaned and dampened. The mix is to be of uniform color and consistency, and a mix that has hardened is not allowed to be retempered.

The scratch coat is applied in a fashion so as to ensure perfect keys at the joints. Before the scratch is thoroughly set it is to be scratched or raked so that there will be a bond between the first and second coats of plaster. The brown coat is applied after the first coat is set but is not yet thoroughly dried. The second coat is brought to a true and even surface at the grounds and thus makes the total plaster thickness ¾″ thick. The plaster is brought to either a float or stipple finish. The plastering can only be done in a fairly warm atmosphere, and caution must be taken against sagging, beads, blisters, pits, cracks and discoloration. Also the amount and the handling of the water for the mix must be watched so that it does not damage any other work of any trade.

Throughout the building, except for the music wing and other isolated spots, the ceiling is to be acoustical tile hung by the suspension system. The tile is of the incombustible variety, 12 by 12 by ³⁄₁₆ in size, and it will have a noise reduction coefficient of .70.

Metal tile of 26-gauge steel is to be used for the ceiling in the music wing. The perforated tiles here are to measure 12 by 24 and are to be scored to form 12 by 12 units. They are to have a baked enamel finish and are to have pads of fiber set inside them. These pads are held up from direct contact with the metal by a wire mesh. The tiles have an NRC of 85.

The suspension system members are to be zinc coated and of the type that have the transverse members interlocked with the supporting members. This is done every 24″ with a special cramping tool. The 1½″ channels are leveled and attached to the bar joists every four feet. A moulding is to be applied at the junction of the suspended ceiling and the walls.

The structural slabs that are to receive terrazo have been brought to level at a point about 2 inches below the finished floor line. After the necessary cleaning has been done, a layer of fine sand is spread evenly over the slab and in turn a layer of 15# saturated tar paper is laid over the sand. Over the tar paper is poured a layer of mortar, which is a mix of 1 part cement and 4 parts of sand. This mortar bed is brought to level at a point not less than ⅜″ below the finished floor line.

While the mortar bed is still in a workable or plastic state, the metal strippings will be put into place. These strips, measuring 1¼″ by ⅛″, are placed so that the major areas are divided into blocks about four feet square. The borders along the walls are to be about 18 inches wide. The architectural drawings show the different patterns that are to be used in the various areas. For instance, the floor in the cafeteria will have a block pattern of several colors, while the lobby floor near the office waiting room will have a strip that picks up and follows through with the serpentine line of the wall in the office.

Two parts of marble chips, matching approved samples, are then mixed with one part of cement and enough water to make a satisfactory mix. This mix is then poured into place and is tamped, rolled, and then trowelled to the required surface level. The newly poured mix is then covered with moist sand, paper, or mats and left to cure for some six days.

After a six-day curing period, the surface is machine ground smooth and lightly grouted with cement, which remains until the final cleaning. Finally the surface is machine rubbed and scrubbed leaving a thoroughly clean surface. One coat of sealer is applied to the final surface to make a less porous finished surface.

While the terrazo has been applied on the inside, the same contractor has had men installing the granite on the exterior. (The random ashlar stone at the gym lobby was set by the masonry contractor. The stone discussed here is at the office lobby.) First off, all of the granite dimensions have been checked in the field. The stone is then cut and drilled to fit the conditions exactly. This cutting and drilling is done at the quarry; there will be no field cuts. The stone is set in beds of mortar at a 1:3 ratio of cement and sand. These beds are not less than $\frac{3}{16}$" wide. The joints are pointed up with a mortar mix of 1 part of cement and screened sand. Bronze anchors are used to tie the granite to the backup material. The granite will have a Blue Pearl Polished finish and of course will be set true and even in line and plane. The granite is to be washed with water and a fiber brush as a final cleaning. Nothing is to be used on the stone that will in any way scratch or mar.

The remainder of the work lies in two sections of the specifications: carpentry and metal specialties. The carpenter has, of course, laid out the line for the various other trades to work to and has done numerous other small jobs. Now there is a large amount of cabinet work such as display case and flower box in the office, display cases in the classrooms, mail boxes, ticket counter, office counter, foot-light framing, all paneling on the specified walls, locker seats, built-in wood wardrobes, vanitories, shelving, risers in the music room, and the overhead doors. To go into the construction of all of these items would be lengthy, boring, and of little value to the overall picture of the construction of the school. Of course, all of the projects are made of the best quality material and are put together in a fine, skilled, workmanlike way.

The carpenter also is to install the plywood panels which will act as soffit boards on the under side of the roof extension. These boards are to be $\frac{3}{8}$" thick and are to be held fast by brass screws. In various places around the building, grills will be placed in the soffit boards to more or less "let the building breathe."

The carpenter is also responsible for the caulking of openings left as clearances for the window sections and the entrance doors and any other such work. The caulking is to be at least $\frac{1}{2}$" deep, and in some places the carpenter has to fill the joints to proper depth with backer rods.

The fences for the concrete play areas also fall under the carpentry contract. Here 4.2# standard, corrugated plastic sheets are applied to the round steel posts that were set by the structural steel contractor. The fences are to be two panels high, and the panels will be alternated, i.e., the top panel in one instance will be on one side of the post and the bottom panel will be on the other side. In the next section the panels

will be reversed. The panels will be held fast by galvanized screws and neoprene washers, and will be painted various bright colors.

The carpenter must also furnish and install all the miscellaneous equipment in the rest rooms, such as towel dispensers, mirrors, toilet partitions, hand dryers, etc. This has nothing to do with the installation or purchasing of the plumbing fixtures.

All interior wood and hollow metal doors are hung by the carpenter, but not the tin clad fire door, special doors, or the aluminum entrance doors. The carpenter also applies all of the finish hardware on the wood doors.

As the carpenter works, the last group of major projects is being finished by the metal specialities contractor. This man is responsible for the setting of the aluminum doors at the entrances. They appear in the three lobbies in groups of three or four pair per opening. The entire development includes transoms and side lights in addition to the doors and frames. Of course, they come equipped with the necessary hinges, closers, push and pull bars, and the required panic devices. All of the aluminum that comes in contact with or is set near masonry is to be painted with a zinc chromate paint to protect it. The carpenter, of course, will do all of the necessary caulking work at the jambs and heads.

Workers are also hanging the fire-rated doors in all of the classrooms. These are the exterior doors that lead from the classrooms to the various play areas. They will be hung in the unit steel frames that were set previously and which have special returns to receive the glass block units and the ventilating sash units.

In the boiler room, workers are hanging the sliding type tin clad door. The tin clad is installed here for added fire protection, and of course it will carry a three-hour underwriter's label. There is also a swinging fire-rated door in the same opening. This, of course, is both for appearance sake and because the tin clad will be open all of the time and will close only when its fuse link is melted by the heat of a fire. These are the only two labeled doors in the building, and this then is the only labeled opening. Fire and theft is also being foiled with simultaneous installation of the Mosler vault door in the office. There is also a rolling aluminum fire shutter between the dish-washing area and the cafeteria proper. This, of course, is for health reasons primarily and to some degree for fire protection.

Although it hasn't been mentioned in this report thus far, all of the plumbing pipes and the heating ductwork are installed in the pipe trenches which go all around the building. Much of the plumbing and heating work was done even before the floor slabs were poured. So with the pouring of the terrazo in the rest rooms the fixtures were set. Now as the interior is being finished, the toilet partitions and screens can be put into place. The partitions are to be of the ceiling-hung variety and are to be attached to a special ceiling channel that was set by the structural steel man. The screens are to be of the wall-hung type, so that neither the partitions nor the screens will touch the floor in any spot. This is done of course for simplicity of maintenance. Doors will be of one color and the pilasters and panels will be of another.

In the several classrooms workers are erecting the cork and chalk boards. Had these interior walls been plastered, the ground for the boards would have been set before plastering began, but here the boards will be surface-mounted. The chalkboard is to be dark green porcelain on a steel sheet and then placed on a plywood backing. The cork is to be a light gray to contrast with the dark chalkboard. The cork will be ¼" laminated to ¼" masonite, while the chalkboard will be ½" thick. Around and through the entire assembly will be an aluminum trim, which includes top, bottom, and side trim, chalktrough, and mullion trim (between cork and chalk). A strip of map rail will be set in just under the long strip of cork at the top, and this will provide a place to hang maps and charts, etc. Around the various designated rooms a picture mould will be placed at the ceiling line. This will provide a place to hang the pictures and still will protect the walls from being punctured haphazardly; thus the walls will look better longer.

In connection with the corkboards, the bulletin boards are also to be installed. These units are actually corkboards which have been installed in a heavy aluminum frame with glass in the doors. They will be installed in the lobbies and will be used to post schedules and announcements.

At various chosen places throughout the building, workers are installing the fire extinguisher cabinets. The majority of the cabinets will hold two extinguishers, but there are some single units. These cabinets are aluminum and are to be recessed into the wall with the trim lapping the rough opening.

On the exterior of the building workers are installing the porcelain enamel panels, facias, and spandrals. All of the work was checked for the correct dimension even before the back fill was pushed against the building. It was fabricated so that each panel or pan had its own place on the building. Now with backfill leveled off, the porcelain work is added as perhaps the last of the major work on the outside. All of the porcelain work was done on 16-gauge steel in accordance with all the usual specifications. This includes the panels to be used at the top of the panel wall. Noncorrosive fasteners are to be used, and none of the screw heads, etc. are to show. Caulking is to be used where necessary to give a watertight construction.

Since the terrazo floor is used only in the rest rooms, corridors, and lobbies, the floors in the classrooms still have to be finished. In all areas, except those mentioned and in the boiler room, vinyl tile is to be placed on the floor. The tile will be the standard 9″ by 9″ by ³⁄₁₆″ type, of varying colors to match the several color schemes. In the music wing, cork tile will be utilized for great sound reduction. This tile will be of the same size as the others, but will be some ⁵⁄₁₆″ thick.

In the kindergarten, the vinyl tile will act as a border for picture panels which will be installed in the floor. These pan-els will depict various nursery rhymes, and the border tile will be especially made with the alphabet and numerals.

A four-inch resilient cove base is to be installed around all of the walls and at the bottom of the built-in furniture. A six-inch base is to be utilized at the base of the risers in the music room. All of the necessary nosings and edgings will be installed with this work. All of the tile work and bases are then given a coat of protective wax.

At all of the entrances an area has been left and recessed in the slab to receive a door mat. The area is pitched to a drain in the center to carry off the water. The mats are ½" thick and are to be corrugated and perforated to carry off the water.

The slab in the gym area has been brought up to a point somewhat under the finished level of the cafeteria floor. A prime coat of asphalt is applied to the cleaned slab. Two by four sleepers are to be placed over this slab. The sleepers are to be shimmed up some ³⁄₁₆″ and are to be leveled. They will be held in place by the driven-pin method. After the sleepers are placed and held firm, the entire area is covered with a bed of hot asphalt to a depth so as to firmly embed the sleepers. Hard maple T & G flooring is to be applied directly to the sleepers. The underbed area will be ventilated with the drilling of holes near the walls. A one-inch expansion joint will be provided at the walls, and the joint at the doors will be packed with cork. The floor will be sanded and prepared for three coats of gym floor sealer. A two inch by two inch angle will be placed at the wall to serve as the base for the floor.

A threshold will be placed at the junction of the gym floor and the floor of the cafeteria. Above this an electrically operated folding partition will be installed. The partition will be held 1″ off the floor, and as the final operation of the closing cycle the door will be let down, compressing a sponge rubber moulding and thus cutting down noise transmission. The partition is carried on an I-beam track and rolls on four-wheel roller brackets.

There are also two basketball back stops that are to be installed in the gym. They are of the clear, rectangular, ceiling-hung variety. Once they are installed, the floor can be painted with the game lines and the sealer/finish applied.

At some point when the building is nearing completion, the blacktop for the drives and the parking areas is laid. After the areas are leveled, 8 to 10 inches of gravel are spread and packed firm (the 8″ of gravel go under the play areas and the 10″ goes under the drives and parking areas). The blacktop course is to be 2½" thick and is to vary just ⅜" in 10 feet according to a straightedge.

As shown on the plan, the flag pole is to be set in its own little area and is to have a seat around it. The pole itself is to be 40 feet high and descends down into a special ground socket some four feet. It will vary from a 5⁵⁄₁₆" diameter at the base to a 2⅞" diameter at the top. It will be capped by an aluminlited ball.

So with the setting of the flag pole the building is completed; it needs only to be furnished before it is ready for occupancy.

EXERCISES

The following activities can be used to enhance the text material and provide wider exposure to and understanding of construction.

Some portions of these items may be assigned as individual projects, but overall they are group projects which every class member can benefit from. (*No activity that requires going onto a construction site should be undertaken by a single individual, nor without prior notice and permission from the site manager; ensure full and proper safety measures in any event.*)

1. Review the narrative in this appendix. If this assignment is too imposing (analysis of a complete project), assign a single set of related specification sections to each student or small group and have them write a similar narrative. The task is to put into plain language the concepts and directions that appear out of order and in various places in the specifications. Make a comparison of specification language and the story-like narrative which combines the items that are put together there.

2. Invite a specification writer to class. Ask for an explanation of how one must dissect the project and place the necessary information in the correct place in the CSI format.

B

The Concept and Application of Building Codes and Other Construction Regulations

The planning, location, construction, and use of buildings are regulated by a variety of codes and other rules and regulations which are adopted based on the requirements enacted in various laws and ordinances. Usually these codes are adopted by local and state governments. The statutes, ordinances, and codes are specifically intended, formulated, and written to protect the health, safety, and welfare of the general public.

Over the last several decades federal lawmakers have enacted a tremendous number of new laws in the areas of energy conservation, occupational health and safety, environmental protection, accessibility/barrier removal, pollution controls, and consumer protection. These have either created federal agencies or have in turn caused enactment of new regulations and enforcement agencies at the state or local level. In addition, state and local governments have been active in legislative work also. This has produced added regulations and codes covering development, zoning, construction, and architectural review, as well as the more traditional area—building codes. All this combined legislation has made the building regulatory process ever more broadly based, imposing, and complex.

Generally, laws, ordinances, bills, or procedures are enacted that "enable" or allow the creation of regulations. The pattern of who enforces these regulations and who must comply with them is varied as appropriate. It is no wonder, then, that most project specifications include the broad, general (but legally inappropriate) statement that, "the Contractor(s) shall meet all applicable codes, rules and regulations governing the *performance* of the work." Courts, however, frown on this vague, all-inclusive language. This posture has come about since the specifications are, basically, documents of the Owner (of the project), and the Owner has the first-line responsibility for compliance of the project with "all law, rules, regulations, standards, etc." Even though all of the regulations are not known by the Owner, this responsibility is not delegable!

Two fundamental issues are critical, and require full understanding by all—owners, design professionals, and their staffs. First, a code becomes *law* when a jurisdiction adopts it by ordinance or resolution. In that respect, the jurisdiction has the right to formulate and direct its code as it deems necessary for the protection of its citizenry. Failure to meet the law is illegal action and negligence.

Secondly, while compliance of a new construction project is the basic responsibility of the owner, the design professional—as the agent of the owner—accrues the same responsibility via the professional services contract. Clients expect, and case law and professional codes of ethics require, that the professional establish the pattern and method(s) of compliance with all applicable codes, rules, and regulations. A project's Contract Documents must reflect the code search, decisions, selections, and resolution as required to meet the code provisions. Moreover, this jointly held responsibility is nondelegable; though most clients are not aware of this responsibility on their part.

There are some 19,000 jurisdictions in the United States which are currently controlled by building and other codes regulating construction and development. This is a valid "police power" granted states under the 10th Amendment of the U.S. Constitution. In the main, this reflects the attitude that the local government (at the state level at highest) is best prepared to protect its constituency. This occurs where the public cannot formulate collective action, and individual action is highly limited.

Included in the numerous local regulations are some 2,000 building codes. Although these are locally adopted, many are variations of, or based on, one of the three major "model" codes available in the United States, namely,

BOCA—Building Officials and Code Administrators, International, Inc.; BOCA National Codes, widely used in the North Central and North Eastern United States.
ICBO—International Conference of Building Officials, Inc.; Uniform Codes, used in most areas west of the Mississippi River.
SBCCI—Southern Building Code Congress International, Inc.; Standard Codes, used in most areas from mid-Texas across the South and including Florida.

These groups were formed at various junctures during the first half of the 20th century. Usually the codes were written and enacted as a reaction or response to a single major disaster, or a series of such events; fires and natural climatic situations spurred their creation, as well as increased development and greater density of buildings. The resulting codes from each of the groups reflect prudent regulation practices, as well as the unique conditions that exist within their area of influence. These include seismic related information and controls in the ICBO codes, more hurricane and shore development data than the Standard code does, as well as heavy emphasis on existing buildings, and close development seen in the highly developed northern section of the country, by BOCA. The lines around the areas of influence are surprisingly distinct, for the most part. Some states still write their own building codes, without using any model code text directly. All the codes were written and developed (within companion documents and codes) to provide controls over all types of buildings and building uses, while still allowing for new materials and methods of construction. In many aspects the three model codes are quite similar, controlling the same conditions in virtually the same manner, but with varying verbiage. Also, slight variations in the regulations have long been a source of irritation to regional and nationwide design and construction functions.

The Council of American Building Officials (CABO—an earlier grouping of the three model code agencies) published the fourth model code, for residential building: the CABO One- and Two-Family Dwelling Code. This was created by taking pertinent excerpts from the three major model codes. Using simplified construction methods and less stringent requirements, this code facilitates residential construction where adopted throughout the country.

Something over 80 percent of jurisdictions in the United States with populations of 10,000 or more utilize some form of a model code. However, only 25 percent of this number use a model code without modification. If this scenario could be changed, and model codes were not revised, it would go a long way toward more uniformity and less confusion and complexity in the code situation. Local self-interest groups, though, often are able to prevail and directly influence what the code provisions are. In addition, there are local codes written totally at the state, county, or township level. Each is individually developed as deemed necessary by the jurisdiction to protect the local constituency.

Over the last 10 years or so, the three model code groups have been under increased pressure to modernize their text, and make them more uniform in the level and type of regulation involved. In many cases, similar conditions were regulated in different manners, and often the regulations were stated in varying language, using nomenclature that meant the same thing, but was not the same. Both the resulting confusion and the need for more uniform regulation across the country brought the groups to form a single set of a building code and its companion codes (fire prevention, plumbing, mechanical, zoning, property maintenance, signs, etc.) Such a scenario will allow both design professionals' work and construction efforts to be more easily accomplished, since there will be no more minor (or major) nuances in the code.

In 2000, the International Building Code (and companions) will be published. CABO and the three individual groups are the sponsors and promulgators of this code. After this publication, the other groups will cease their code writing efforts, and will administer the International documents. There is an agenda to present and market this new code, worldwide, to further the cause of uniform regulation. This, of course, will have a major impact on organizations and companies that operate and build on a multinational basis; their designs can be simplified and even can be made repetitive where appropriate.

The CABO organization supports the International Code Council, which is the basic organization behind the new code program.

It is most important and prudent to seek out all information about the applicable code(s) early in the process of programming. Codes vary even in adjacent jurisdictions, so similar, closely located projects can be controlled in varying manners. This is particularly important when utilizing prototype projects, which are built on a repetitive basis. Highly urbanized metropolitan areas are prime examples; in the Chicago area, for instance, there is a building code department in each of the 250 jurisdictions in the metro area. Their codes vary.

After ascertaining all of the applicable codes and regulations, part of the programming process should be a "code search." This is best done as a formal process (printed checklists are available from various sources) of reviewing the codes, ascertaining and documenting all of the requirements applicable to the proposed project. Six basic determinations must be made, by the design professional, to access all of the code requirements. These are (1) occupancy group, (2) location of property, (3) type of construction, (4) floor area, (5) building height, and (6) occupant load. From these basic determinations other code provisions will evolve and present more detailed information. This all needs to be followed to a conclusive end. Any questions or problems which arise during this search should be fully resolved with the proper code official *prior to* any decision making or incorporation of the solutions to the requirement(s) into the design concept. In general, it is well to think of the code official as a "consultant," who is ready and able to discuss, explain, interpret, identify options, and offer guidance regarding code provisions. These officials do not, though, make decisions or offer design solutions for specific projects or portions thereof. The design professional is well advised to take advantage of this service as building codes, alone, cover such diverse yet intertwined areas as

- live/dead/snow/wind/seismic loading
- location of lot (fire separation)
- light and ventilation
- minimum room sizes/dimensions; relationships
- minimum ceiling heights
- sanitary facilities

- safe glazing
- area/unit/building fire separation
- fire-rated materials/assemblies/interior finishes
- egress/exits and exiting systems
- accessibility/ADA requirements
- door and corridor widths
- stair and ramp design/layout
- hand and guard rails
- fire detection/alarm systems
- fire suppression systems
- minimum foundation and footing criteria
- foundation drainage/damp- and waterproofing
- framing/structural systems
- site access
- noise abatement
- site earthwork/excavation/grading
- flood damage prevention
- HVAC/solar design criteria
- plumbing
- electrical service
- energy conservation
- administrative procedures for permit application/issuance/appeals/variances/material approvals

Many details and descriptions in such references as *Architectural Graphic Standards* contain notes which involve code issues—fire ratings, for example. Since such general code categories or designations apply to many different materials, systems, assemblies, and installations in varying ways, it is necessary to review the particular situation and then relate it back to the code requirement(s) and the decisions to be made. For instance, if the code calls for a "one-hour, fire-rated wall," several choices for the construction can be found in this book. It is, then, for the professional to decide what material, assembly, system, or detail is best suited for the project. In addition to the guidance of this book, other resources should be called into play as the professional deems necessary for his or her use and information.

Also important are the scheduled, periodic (often annual) changes made by the various code-writing groups. Although local adoptions will usually lag behind, the changes will eventually be incorporated into local law. Ensure that the code search includes the latest version of information, and code changes applicable to the project; verify this via the code official.

It is necessary to understand that the number of codes are compounded by their complexity and by variations in enforcement. In some states, all code activities are state-run functions; others use local control, after state review and permitting. Still others utilize a wholly local code administration and enforcement program. There is no pattern in these

variations; local determinations are required. With this, it is important for the design professional to acknowledge, and plan, a preconstruction period of time to allow for submittal of documents, permit application, plan review, resolution of problems/discrepancies, and the final issuance of the building permit. Often the final permit will depend on approval from several other regulatory agencies (a further complication of the entire process). However, the original law and local agency configurations often seat different regulations in different offices. These, hopefully, are linked in a logical manner, although dealing with several agencies is a complication that may entail even more time.

The current code/regulation situation requires qualified personnel to administer them. No matter how good a code may be, it must be administered/enforced by persons experienced, informed, and objective. The competent code official knows the job, and knows when the letter of the law/code should prevail, and when subjective and proper interpretation(s) should be made. These officials are constantly confronted with difficulties of judgment, and will seek to do their work, totally, "to check compliance." Obviously, this process can be greatly facilitated by design professionals who participate properly in code search, determinations, *and* discussions with the code official where prudent. This is not a "cat and mouse game" where one proceeds until "caught." Better to use an informed, cooperative approach than to proceed without due regard.

In truth, the design professionals should be full participants not only in the code administration process, but in the process of adopting and revising codes and other regulations over building projects. They should lend their expertise, advice, and concern to the process and the elected officials who will make the law(s). Ideally, this will further a proper and cooperative code program, one that reflects local conditions and serves every interest well.

Despite all of this, it must be remembered that the codes have been enacted as a method of preventing substandard, unsafe, hazardous, and unsanitary conditions in buildings. Every building is under attack, in many ways, after the professional has completed her or his work. Occupancy and use are the greatest threats to buildings, in a variety of ways. With the added, unregulated fire-loading (furnishings, decorations, paper goods, equipment, etc.) that the owner and occupants bring into buildings, it is incumbent on the design professions to provide a code-abiding structure that will perform well and mitigate unsafe conditions (particularly in fires) as much as possible. It is a valid and important function which requires participation by the design professional. By addressing the codes as part of the initial project programming, by properly addressing and resolving all the applicable code issues in the contract documents, and ensuring proper installation during construction, the professional will meet both the professional standard of care and the law.

The design professional, as agent of the Owner, has the charge by contract (and law), both to formulate the documents in a manner wherein the Owner is protected, and to ensure that all requirements of *applicable* (but *not all*) law and regulations are met. Here, too, the responsibility which lies with the design professional is nondelegable.

Since the initial programming of every construction project is a process which is designed specifically to seek out the requirements, parameters, and problems which will impact the project's design concept, the design professional should ensure that the building codes and other construction regulations are addressed.

Much of the programming information, of course, is client related, in that the client contributes the limits and requirements to be incorporated in the project. These are wide-ranging, but not all-inclusive. They are consistent, though, with the private aspects of the project since the client is developing the project to meet specific personal needs and desires.

In addition, however, there are public requirements (codes and regulations) which apply to every project, to some degree. These represent the interface between the general public and the various elements, uses, occupancies, hazards, and conditions which will be present in the finished project. These public requirements are usually contained in a combination of provisions from the applicable building, fire, zoning, and other pertinent regulations and codes.

In part, the current array of codes directly reflects the additional laws/regulations which have been enacted to control and administer the added (and increasing) complexity of the construction process itself. Also, the interface and complexity of the projects demand some control. In essence, codes are always enacted or revised in an attempt to match the current or anticipated conditions or hazards with adequate, suitable, or advisable protection. They are "preventative" measures, neither obtrusive, nor punitive. They reflect good practice, advisable procedure, or documented experience from previous, similar scenarios.

In large part, the adoption, creation, or formulation of a building code is seated with the local jurisdiction, its legislative body, and its code official. The matter to be reviewed and established is, what, exactly, does this jurisdiction *want* to regulate, and *why?*

Building codes establish minimum standards and requirements for the construction and occupancy of buildings in a manner that protects public health, safety, and welfare. They *do not* necessarily contain any criteria which assures efficient, convenient, or adequately equipped buildings. Nor do they direct, indicate, require, or restrict design concepts, features, schemes, or configurations. Many people complain that codes inhibit design, but this is not true. Most assuredly, it is far better to know the impact of the codes, up-front, prior to any "design commitment." They may necessitate some rethinking, or accommodation of required features/construction in the design concept, but they do not dictate any configurations, nor negate or prohibit any design concepts or principles.

Some distinction should be drawn between reference standards and regulations that are applicable to "the actual construction/work" as opposed to those applicable to "the methods, conditions, and performance of the physical labor involved." ("Work" can mean both the effort to construct,

and the items of construction themselves.) While codes and other regulations demand compliance (as standing law), "reference standards" are also often utilized. These documents, written by various sources other than the code-generating agency, provide a wealth of information, only part of which may be applicable to the "work." Since they are included in the adopted code(s), compliance with them is also required, *but only* as they apply to the work. To prevent gigantic volumes as codes, the reference standards used are incorporated by notation or "reference" and do not have their entire text replicated. Great care must be taken to address these standards, both in the professionals' offices and in the field. Even with these inclusions, codes do not attempt to address every issue involved in the construction process.

For example, a building code addresses none of the issues which are contained in the federal Occupational Safety and Health Administration (OSHA) regulations. The former regulates "how" or "what-with" the building will be built. The latter regulates the circumstances and conditions under which the work is to be performed, and controls nothing about the actual construction project (products, materials, devices, etc.) itself. This brings forth the additional scenario which the contractors face—a myriad of controls and regulations over their operation(s). These impact the way in which the construction work is pursued, not what the resultant project will be, nor how it will function.

Contractors are indeed faced with "a bucket of worms," as one author puts it, when they are under contract for a project. The following is a partial listing of regulations and standards that may be in place (depending on the jurisdiction), and applicable to the work and performance involved on any particular project:

job safety	licensing
labor employment	sanitation
insurance	zoning
building code(s)	air pollution
noise abatement	dust control
trash disposal	sanitary wastes
pile driving	blasting
riveting	demolition
fencing	open excavations
traffic control	housekeeping
fire protection/prevention	open burning
jurisdictional settlements	air rights
operation maintenance	public safety
barricades/trespassing	property maintenance

Even from this "short list" one can easily see the wide range and influence of the rules, regulations, and standards on both the project itself and the manner in which the work is performed. Perhaps a simplistic distinction can be drawn by saying that those regulations dealing with the project proper are oriented toward the actual "physical-being" work of the construction and the impact of the project on its surroundings and environment. Those that impact performance are more "people" oriented, in that they deal with mitigating the circumstances that are created by the construction process, and not the final resultant project.

Both efforts are basically oriented toward "people problems" which result from the project imposing, in various ways, upon the community. For the most part, rules and regulations do not necessarily prohibit new projects (although in some instances, they may), but rather control or direct the projects into a format which is acceptable and proper for its surrounding areas. At the same time, there are controls to protect even natural elements where they interface with the project (zoning, and hillside regulations are good examples).

In the usual specification process, the design professional will be able to address the "thing" items and provide a comprehensive list of the reference standards that apply. However, only the contractor(s) have access to all of the regulatory documents that regulate, control, or direct their working operations, personnel, vehicles, equipment, etc. It's part of their business operation to be fully aware of all current regulations applicable to their operations.

In addition, it must be established that some regulations do *not* belong in the building code. Some are required to be enforced by persons other than building code personnel. Further, adequate expertise is required in the permit/inspection cycle, to make it meaningful, and to properly enforce and properly protect the government interest and liability. Courts still differ over the premise that "bad inspections are better than none at all." This is highly debatable, in that very deceiving information and impressions can be meted out, leaving the jurisdiction with even greater liability vulnerability.

There is a basic, fundamental, and easily drawn distinction between building codes and other regulations. As mentioned before, one of the most obvious is the difference between building codes and OSHA regulations. The building codes *do not* refer to or in any way incorporate OSHA mandates into their documents. The primary reasons for this are

- The building code addresses the creation of "safe construction"; OSHA addresses the need for owners to provide their employees with a safe workplace. For example, the building codes may require a number of nails in a joint (to accomplish safe construction), whereas OSHA requires that the worker installing these nails be provided with a safe scaffolding and other safety devices while installing the nails.

- Regulations must be separated (as many courts determine) into those addressing what the construction (the *work*) must be, as opposed to others which address how the work is done (*performance* of the work).

In drawing this differentiation, there usually will *not* be an interconnecting of these regulations, nor enforcement by any single agency or operative, e.g., the design professional. Further, case law holds that the design professional is *not* the enforcer of OSHA requirements, *except* where employees of the professional are concerned.

In most jurisdictions, the building code is but one of numerous laws, rules, regulations and ordinances that impact construction, both new and renovative. In part these include control over

Land use/zoning
- location
- setbacks
- footprint
- district restrictions
- buffering
- barriers
- landscaping
- lighting

Drainage/related issues
- storm water drainage
- waste water drainage
- flood plain
- wetlands

Land formations
- earthwork/grading regulations
- erosion/sedimentation control
- environmental sensitivity

Other restrictions
- deed covenants
- reserves/protected areas
- air quality
- easements: public/private
- height for aviation

All of these regulations, and others, apply *in addition to* the building code. Their provisions, impact, and enforcement may or may not be part of or tied into the building code/permit process. Many jurisdictions tie several regulation programs together, for ease of use; some even provide "one-stop" agencies for both coordinated review and permitting, and for even easier use by the public and contractors.

In some instances, experienced design professionals will be able to indicate or make suggestions that other provisions *may* be applicable in addition to the building code. However, these will not be detailed, nor addressed by the professional, as they may be part of the work of other project participants. It is essential (and most prudent) though, that *all* regulatory impact be searched out, found, assessed, understood, coordinated, and resolved as early in the project as possible, so even the most basic and preliminary of designs can be adapted to meet or accommodate the various parameters from the outset.

Sample Specification (on Regulations)

The following is a sample specification section which has been included as an example of single-source section regulatory requirements. It is not intended to be used as a master or guide specification section. This section must be closely coordinated with the General Conditions (00700), Supplementary Conditions (00800), and other Division 1 sections, since it contains information that could conflict with these other sections and documents. Provisions included here should be limited to subjects unique to this section. Consider that Division 1 requirements do affect the cost of the work.

This Section is based on the use of Owner-Contractor Agreements, General Conditions, and associated documents published by the AIA and EJCDC that delineate contractual requirements for the work. Refer to CSI *Manual of Practice* (1996 edition); Part I, Chapter 8, "Division 1, General requirements."

CSI Monograph #01M060 offers a fuller explanation and the legal implications associated with the use of a specification section similar to this example.

SECTION 01060—REGULATORY REQUIREMENTS

Part 1—General

1.01 RELATED DOCUMENTS;
Drawings and general provisions of Contract, including General and Supplementary Conditions and other Division-1 Specifications sections, apply to work of this Section.

1.02 SUMMARY;
A. This section includes procedural and administrative requirements for compliance with governing codes, regulations, and standards applicable to the project. These requirements include obtaining permits, licenses, inspections, releases, and similar documentation; as well as payments, statements and similar requirements associated with the codes, regulations, and standards [see definitions in 1.04C below].
  1. Refer to General and Supplementary Conditions for requirements related to compliance with governing regulations.
B. Related work specified elsewhere:
  Document 00100—Instructions to Bidders
  Document 00500—Agreement Forms
  Document 00700—General Conditions
  Document 00800—Supplementary Conditions
  Section 01200—Project Meetings
  Section 01600—Material and Equipment
  Section 01630—Product Options and Substitutions
  Section 01700—Contract Closeout
  [*Vary Section numbers, above, as required*]

1.03 REFERENCES;
Standards cited, by reference, within the Contract Documents define minimum acceptable quality of workmanship and materials; reference to recognized standards, associations, or government standards, and manufacturers' names and catalog numbers.
A. Applicability: Except where more explicit or stringent requirements are written into the Contract documents, applicable construction industry standards have the same force and effect as if bound into, or copied directly into the contract documents. Such industry standards are made a part of the contract documents by reference. Individual specification sections indicate which code(s) and standard(s) the Contractor must keep available at the project site for reference.
B. Reference Standards: Standards referenced in applicable code/regulations take precedence over all other standards, and compliance is mandatory.

1. Other standards directly referenced in the contract documents take precedence over standards that are not referenced but generally recognized in the industry for applicability to the work.

C. Unreferenced Standards: Except as otherwise limited by the contract documents, standards not referenced but recognized in the construction industry as having direct applicability will be enforced for performance of the work. The decision as to whether an industry code or standard is applicable is the sole responsibility of the Architect/Engineer.

D. Publication Dates: Standards listed in governing codes and regulations, which carry publication dates, require compliance with those dated editions, even though more recent editions are available.

1. Except as otherwise indicated, where compliance with industry standards is required, comply with standard in effect as of date of contract documents.

2. Where standards are revised to new editions, or otherwise reissued with new requirements applicable to the project, and the Architect/Engineer desires (or is required) to incorporate the new requirements, submit suitable Modification (Change Order) proposals. Such proposals shall contain all changes in work, materials, or equipment required by the new requirements.

E. Conflicting Requirements: Where compliance with two or more different standards is specified, and where these standards establish different or conflicting requirements for minimum quantities or quality levels, the most stringent requirements will be enforced, unless the contract documents specifically indicate otherwise. Refer requirements that are different, but apparently equal, and uncertainties as to which quality level is more stringent, to Architect/Engineer for decision, before proceeding.

1. Minimum quantities and quality levels are shown or specified, and are intended to be the minimum to be provided or performed. Unless otherwise indicated, the actual work may either comply exactly, within specified tolerances, with the minimum quantity or quality level, or may exceed that minimum within reasonable limits. In complying with these requirements, the indicated numeric values are minimum or maximum, as noted, or as appropriate for the context of the requirements. Refer instances of uncertainty to Architect/Engineer for decision, before proceeding.

F. Copies of Standards: The contract documents require that each entity performing work be ex-perienced in that part of the work being performed. Each entity is also required to be fully familiar with industry standards applicable to that part of the work. Copies of applicable standards are not bound in the contract documents.

1. Where required for proper performance of the work, or enforcement of the requirements as requested by the Architect/Engineer, the Contractor is required to obtain such copies directly from the publication sources, and provide them to the project site personnel. Such copies may be required submittals, but Architect/Engineer reserves the right to request additional copies as may be necessary for enforcement of requirements.

1.04 DEFINITIONS;

A. General Explanation: Certain terms used in the contract documents are defined in this article. Definitions and explanations contained in this section are not necessarily complete but are general for the work to the extent that they are not stated more explicitly in another element of the contract documents.

B. General Requirements: Provisions and requirements of Division 1-sections apply to the entire work of the Contract and where so indicated to other elements which are included in the project.

C. Terms Defined: The following definitions are included to explain and clarify the terms, abbreviations and acronyms as used in the contract documents. Request explanation for unknown or unclear terms, etc. from Architect/Engineer;

1. Indicated: Phrases such as "indicated on Drawings", and "shown on Drawings" refer to graphic representations, notes, or schedules on Drawings. Terms such as "noted", "scheduled", and "specified" are used to help readers to locate referenced information, whether located in industry standards, Specifications, Drawings, or other Contract Documents, without limitation on location.

2. Code: A set of laws which govern procedure, conduct, work and performance requirements of construction projects.

3. Regulation: Laws, statutes, ordinances, and lawful orders issued by governing authorities; also, private rules, conventions, and agreements within the construction industry which effectively control performance of work.

4. (Construction) Industry Standard: A document, produced by a private or public source, which describes or sets a criteria for acceptable levels of performance or workmanship, based on testing and evaluation; applicable,

in whole or in part, to attributes, operation, and/or performance of materials, systems, equipment, work performed; may be narrow in scope, or broad, but is generally recognized, throughout the industry, as creditable.

5. Directed: Term which reflects action[s] of design professional or other authorized party; used in same manner as "requested", "authorized", "selected", "approved", "required", and "permitted".

6. Approved: Term used to indicate acceptance of condition, material, system, or other work or procedure; reflects action by design professional or other authorized party, but does not relieve basic responsibility of party seeking such approval, as written in other binding documents and provisions.

7. Furnish: Means to "supply, and deliver to the job site, ready for unloading, unpacking, assembly, installation, and similar operations." (see Install and Provide)

8. Install: Usually means on-site operations of "unloading, unpacking, temporary storage, assembly, erection, placing, anchoring, applying, working to dimension, connecting, testing, finishing, curing, protecting, cleaning, and similar activities for proper and complete use/operation of area, equipment, appliance, or item.

9. Installer: Employee, subcontractor, or lower tier contractor hired to perform specific construction task or activity involving installation, erection, application, or making ready for use; trained to technician level, and experienced in such work as well as in troubleshooting problems to provide proper and complete installation.

10. Provide: Means to furnish, pay for, and install in completely operational manner, ready for intended use; see Furnish, and Install for clarification.

11. Testing Agencies: Entity, separate from any of the contractual parties on a project, engaged to perform specific inspections, tests, and analysis either at the site, in a laboratory or elsewhere; reports results to proper project party, and interprets results if required; may function to meet specifications, or to investigate problems which arise; building codes list some such agencies which are approved and acceptable due to impartiality, reliability, and past performance.

   [Add other general definitions and any required for project]

D. Abbreviations and Names: Trade association names and titles of general standards are frequently abbreviated. The following acronyms or abbreviations are referenced in contract documents and are defined to mean associated names. Both names and addresses are subject to change, and are believed to be, but are not assured to be, accurate and up-to-date as of date of contract documents:

   [Appropriate list should be inserted here as required for the specified project: see Appendix F for reference list]

E. Federal Government Agencies: Names and titles of federal government standard or specification producing agencies are frequently abbreviated. The following acronyms or abbreviations are referenced in the contract documents, and indicate names of standard or specification producing agencies of the federal government. Names and addresses are subject to change, but are believed to, but are not assured to be, accurate and up-to-date as of date of contract documents:

   [Insert, list which applies to federal agencies and specified project: see Appendix F for reference list]

F. Drawing Symbols: Except as otherwise indicated, graphic symbols used on the drawings are those recognized in the construction industry for the purposes indicated. Where not otherwise noted or shown, symbols are defined by ARCHITECTURAL GRAPHIC STANDARDS, published by John Wiley and Sons, Inc., 9th edition.

1.05 SYSTEM DESCRIPTION:

A. Code and Regulatory Requirements: The design and construction of this project has been selected, developed, depicted and described, by the contract documents, in compliance with all applicable codes which govern the various work, materials, devices, equipment, systems and procedures. Construction must also be in full compliance with the following building, mechanical, and electrical codes, and other regulations applicable to the project/work;

   Building Code:
   Mechanical Code:
   Plumbing Code: *[List applicable editions*
   Electrical Code: *of all codes]*
   Energy Conservation Code:
   Fire Prevention Code:
   Zoning Code:

   [List all additional codes/regulations which govern work of this project]

B. General: The procedure followed by the Architect/Engineer has been to contact governing authorities as necessary to obtain information needed for preparation of contract documents; recognizing that such information may or may not be of significance in relation to the Contractor's responsibilities for performing the work. Contact governing authorities directly for necessary information and decisions having a bearing on the performance (not design) of the work.

1. If the Contractor observes, or is made aware, that a portion of the Contract Documents is at variance with applicable codes, or other regulations, that fact must be reported, immediately and in writing, to the Architect/Engineer.

C. Updating Code/Regulations: Where codes or other regulations are revised to new editions, or otherwise reissued with new requirements applicable to the project, and the Architect/Engineer desires (or is required) to incorporate the new requirements, submit suitable Modification (Change Order) proposals. Such proposals shall contain all changes in work, materials, or equipment required by the new requirements.

D. Methods of Specifying: Techniques or methods of specifying requirements vary throughout the text. The method used for specifying one element of the work has no bearing on requirements for another element of the work.

E. Assignment of Specialties: In certain circumstances, the specifications require or imply that specific elements of the work are to be assigned to specialists who must be engaged to perform that element of the work. Such assignments are special requirements over which the Contractor has no choice, or option. They are intended to establish which party or entity involved in a specific element of the work is considered as being sufficiently experienced in the indicated construction processes or operations to be recognized as "expert" in those processes or operations. Nevertheless, the ultimate responsibility for fulfilling all contract requirements remains with the Contractor.

1. These requirements should not be interpreted to conflict with the enforcement of building codes and similar regulations governing the work. They are also not intended to interfere with local trade union jurisdictional settlements, or similar conventions.

F. Trades: The use of certain titles such as "carpentry" in the specifications is not intended to imply that the work must be performed by accredited or unionized individuals of a corresponding generic name, such as "carpenter". It is not intended to imply that the requirements specified apply exclusively to tradespersons of that corresponding generic name.

G. Trade Union Jurisdictions: The Contractor shall maintain, and shall require prime subcontractors

to maintain complete, current information on jurisdictional matters, regulations, actions, and pending actions, as applicable to the work. Discuss new developments at appropriate project meetings at the earliest feasible time/dates. Record information of relevance along with the actions agreed upon.

1. The manner in which contract documents have been organized and subdivided is not intended to be an indication of trade or jurisdictional agreements. Assign and subcontract work and employ tradespersons and laborers in a manner which will not unduly risk jurisdictional disputes of a kind which could result in conflicts, delays, claims, and losses in the performance of the work.

1.06 SUBMITTALS:

Permits, Licenses, and Certificates: For the Owner's records, submit copies of all permits, licenses, certificates, inspection reports, releases, jurisdictional settlements, notices, receipts for fee payment, judgments, and similar documents, correspondence, and records established in conjunction with compliance with codes, standards, and other regulations, and otherwise pertinent to, or bearing on the performance of the work.

1.07 QUALITY ASSURANCE;

A. Qualifications: When required, submit statements of qualifications for contractor-employed design personnel, fabricators, installers, and applicators of products and completed work.

B. Certifications: Where required, provide statements from manufacturers that the systems, materials, manufactured units, equipment, components, and accessories being supplied comply with the specified requirements. Where specified, attach labels of testing authorities, or ensure the attachment by others, to materials, or assemblies involved.

C. Pre-Installation Conferences: When required, Contractor shall use this paragraph as authority to convene specified conferences for coordinating materials, techniques, and related work.

Part 2—Products

(Not Applicable)

Part 3—Execution

(Not Applicable)

End of Section 01060

A Project Checklist

This appendix is an example of the type of checklist that can be very helpful both in the documentation and in the actual construction of a project.

Although it is not necessarily complete, it is a good indicator of the information that is vital to the project architect and the staff. Many design firms have developed their own lists, but the following also are excellent resources for use as a project checklist:

Working Drawing Manual, by Fred A. Stitt
Published by McGraw-Hill Book Company, New York—
ISBN: 0-07-061554-3—1998

This is an extensive listing of items which need to be considered for inclusion in the working drawings.

DOCUMENT D200—Project Checklist
Published by the American Institute of Architects, Washington, D.C.

This is a comprehensive list of tasks and documentation in the format of a project progression; it is helpful in planning a logical sequence of activities and ensuring coverage and completion of necessary tasks.

The following checklist is of a type frequently used by on-site project representatives, as they oversee the actual construction work, in progress. It is an aid to ensuring that critical aspects of the project are reviewed and observed.

Although it appears that this list is a function of the latter part of a project, it is also a very good indication of what needs to be documented into the drawings and specifications, so they are proper, achievable, and enforceable during construction. The same aspects that need checking in the field are the ones that need proper depiction and description in the Contract Documents. Remember, the field observation is to check for compliance with the Contract Documents requirements. So they both (observation and documents) must use the same information; the documents apply it to the project, the observation ensures that the data is carried out as required. This list, then, is a coordination tool which is vital to project success. Also, in general, it is a good list for all staffers; their depth of knowledge may vary, but each item is important for project success.

Services and Procedures

I. *DUTIES AND RESPONSIBILITIES*
Know the specific duties and responsibilities for your particular position.
  A. Primary
    ☐ Important part of the team
    ☐ Not an adversary—an ally
    ☐ Not just a messenger—solve problems
    ☐ Prevent future problems
  B. Observe, report, and assist in what to do
    ☐ Documentation is critical
    ☐ What to do versus how to do
  C. Architect's Representative
    ☐ If position is Architect's Representative, duties are identified in AIA B352
    ☐ Site inspectors other than Architect's Representative have similar duties
  D. Be Firm, Fair, and Flexible.

II. *REVIEW*
Be familiar with all the contract related documents
  A. Contract Documents
    ☐ Drawings and Specifications
    ☐ General Conditions
    ☐ Supplementary Conditions
    ☐ Addenda
    ☐ Owner/Contractor Agreement
    ☐ Owner/Architect Agreement
  B. Codes

C. Responsibilities and Limitations
    1. If Architect's Representative
       ☐ Architect—AIA Handbook, Chapter 8
       ☐ AIA Document B352
    2. Non Architect's Representative
D. Special Project Conditions

III. START-UP
A. Preconstruction Conference
B. Set up work area
   ☐ Full set Drawings, Specs, Addenda
   ☐ Prepare Job Notebook
   ☐ Set up forms
   ☐ Files
      ☐ Correspondence
      ☐ Shop drawings
      ☐ RFI's
      ☐ Clarifications
      ☐ C.O.'s
   ☐ Schedule
   ☐ Directory
C. Basic tools

IV. SITE
A. Foundation drains & waterproofing
B. Final grade
C. Plantings
D. Consultants
E. Organization

V. STRUCTURE
A. Concrete—poured in place
   ☐ Pre-pour
   ☐ Slab flatness
   ☐ Slab inserts/openings
   ☐ Water seals/reglets
B. Concrete—Architectural
   ☐ Quality Control
   ☐ Columns
C. Steel
   ☐ Fireproofing
D. Consultants

VI. CURTAIN WALL SYSTEMS
A. Definitions
B. Shop Drawings, Samples
C. Mock-ups
D. Systems Tests
E. Metal
   ☐ Specific system?
   ☐ Finish
   ☐ Color vs. sample
   ☐ Joints
   ☐ Weep system
   ☐ Protection
   ☐ Quality control

F. Glass
   ☐ Specified material?
   ☐ Color vs. sample
   ☐ Seals
   ☐ Protection
   ☐ Quality control
G. Gaskets, Sealants
   ☐ Specified material?
   ☐ Color vs. sample
H. Installation
   ☐ Metal-to-metal joints
   ☐ Fasteners
   ☐ Flashings
   ☐ Glass setting techniques
   ☐ Gasket, sealants, temperature restrictions
   ☐ Safing
   ☐ Insulation
I. Store Front
   ☐ Hardware
   ☐ Safety glazing

VII. EXTERIOR FINISHES, SEALANTS
A. Brick
   ☐ Specified material?
   ☐ Sample
   ☐ Protection
      ☐ During installation
      ☐ After
B. Precast Concrete
   ☐ Finish and color vs. sample
   ☐ Handling
   ☐ Placement
   ☐ Joints
      ☐ Type
      ☐ Size
C. Sealants
   ☐ What and where?
   ☐ Approvals
      ☐ Type
      ☐ Color
   ☐ Application
      ☐ Weather restrictions
      ☐ Manufacturer's specs
      ☐ Backer rod
      ☐ Experienced mechanics

VIII. INTERIOR ENVIRONMENTS
A. Interfacing with Building Code
   ☐ Code analysis
   ☐ Fire ratings
   ☐ Special requirements
B. Walls
   1. Drywall construction
      ☐ Stud height limitations
      ☐ Gypsum board types

□ Shaft systems
□ Rated partitions
□ Acoustical
□ Installation
□ Tracks
□ Studs
□ Gypsum Board
□ Trim
□ Taping, Sanding
2. Other Inspection Considerations
   □ Cold water pipes in wall insulated
   □ Pipe flanges clear
   □ Finished wall flush with built
      in items
   □ Attachment supports
3. Masonry
   □ Joints vs. final finish
   □ Control joints

C. Floors
1. Concrete
   □ Finish
   □ Sealant
   □ Control joints
   □ Expansion joints

D. Floor Finishes
□ Resilient Flooring
   □ Material vs. sample
   □ Pattern
   □ Base
   □ Adhesive application
□ Ceramic, Quarry Tiles, Pavers
   □ Material vs. sample
   □ Layout
   □ Setting bed
   □ Grout color vs. sample
□ Wood
□ Marble/Slate
□ Carpet

E. Ceilings
□ Common types
□ Ceiling heights
   □ Per Contract Drawings
   □ Conflict
   □ Lighting clearance
□ Suspended ceilings
□ Rated assemblies
□ Hangers
□ Grid system
   □ Manufacturer
   □ Layout
   □ Tolerances
□ Ceiling tiles
   □ Material vs. sample
   □ Direction

□ Edge configuration
□ Concealed spline access
□ Drywall ceilings, soffits
   □ Access Panels
□ Plaster
   □ Skim coat on concrete, gypsum board
   □ Lath and plaster
□ Combinations

F. Finishes
□ Paints/coatings
   □ Type per location
   □ Application restrictions
   □ Lighting
   □ Substrate condition
□ Wallpaper/Vinyl wall coverings
   □ Application restrictions
   □ Lighting
   □ Priming, sizing
   □ Problems to watch for
□ Wood paneling
   □ Quality standards
   □ Details, shop drawings
   □ Special consideration
□ Ceramic Tile
   □ Material vs. sample
   □ Adhesive
   □ Substrate
   □ Special cuts
   □ Grouting
   □ Joints with dissimilar materials
□ Marble/Stone
   □ Material vs. sample
   □ Installation methods
   □ Protection
   □ Critical lighting

G. Lighting Systems
1. Inspection Considerations
   □ Support
   □ Protection
   □ Use
   □ Lamping
   □ Rated assemblies
2. Special Lighting
   □ Layouts
   □ Access

H. Coordinating with Mechanical Systems

IX. CABINETS
A. Shop Drawings, Samples, etc.
B. Inspection Checks
   □ Fit
   □ Laminate
   □ Tightness of joints
   □ Door and drawer fit

☐ Material flaws
☐ Hardware
    ☐ Type
    ☐ Operation
☐ Secured in place

X. *DOORS, FRAMES*
  A. Frames
    ☐ Materials
    ☐ Shop drawings, design details
    ☐ Masonry installation
    ☐ Drywall installation
    ☐ Fire ratings
    ☐ Inspection considerations
  B. Doors
    ☐ Materials
    ☐ Shop drawings, design details
    ☐ Fire ratings
    ☐ Inspection considerations
  C. Hardware
    ☐ Material vs. schedule
    ☐ Finish
    ☐ Specialty
    ☐ Inspection considerations
  D. Glazed Openings
    ☐ Metal frames
    ☐ Wire glass
  E. Specialty
    ☐ Revolving
    ☐ Institutional
    ☐ Rolling

XI. *SPECIAL FURNISHINGS*
  A. Elevators, Escalators
    ☐ Primary inspection responsibility
    ☐ Temporary use
    ☐ Protection
    ☐ Finishes
  B. Handrails
  C. Toilet Rooms
  D. Other Special Furnishings

XII. *PREPARING FOR PROJECT CLOSE-OUT*
  A. Punchlist Inspection
    ☐ Assess if ready
    ☐ Who
    ☐ How
    ☐ Tools, aids
    ☐ Typical problems to look for
    ☐ How to avoid long punch
  B. Coordination
    ☐ Operation and maintenance manuals
    ☐ Warranties
    ☐ Certificate of Occupancy
    ☐ County/city inspections
    ☐ Final payment
    ☐ Release of liens
    ☐ Certificate of Substantial Completion

E

Cost Estimating

Despite the size or complexity of a project, perhaps the most pervasive aspect of the project is the cost, and how the final, actual cost is ascertained.

The process of establishing cost starts early in the project. Several different types of estimates are produced at various points, set by contract terms, during the progress of the project; each differs from the others in the amount of detailed information involved and the accuracy that can be achieved. Examples of these are

- *Screening (order of magnitude) estimate;* produced before project is designed—must be based on comparative cost information, such as other similar buildings done previously, square foot costs for type of construction anticipated, etc.

- *Preliminary (conceptual) estimate;* based on the conceptual design of the project when most of the basic technologies are known—costs can begin to be assessed against known items and general quantities

- *Detailed (definitive) estimate;* done during detailed design when essential project features have been established and greater level of detailed information is available.

- *Engineered estimate;* produced by design professional when documents are complete and ready for bidding—utilizes finite detail of project and distinct quantities

- *Bid estimate;* produced by the contractor using detailed project information (from contract documents), known cost data (unit prices), and subcontractor pricing—developed to contractor's interest (as to method of estimate, discounting, use of chosen subs only, desire for work, level/type of competition, etc.)

The process of estimating is a construction specialty unto itself. Simply, it is based on a definite quantity of material or items and the best cost available to purchase and install them. Each item has its own "pattern" for estimating, such as

- *Concrete*—based on installed cost per cubic yard; may or may not include reinforcing, forms (installation/ removal), finishing/curing

- *Plywood*—based on installed cost per full (4′ × 8′) sheet

- *Floor tile*—based on number of boxes of tile (number of tiles per box known) to cover a given square foot area, including waste/cuts/breakage

- *Paint*—gallons of each type/color required based on number of coats applied over a given surface area (sq. ft.)

- *Wood trim*—priced by lineal foot based on size, type, profile

- *Nails*—expendables (needed, but exact quantity irrelevant) bought by boxes of several hundred/thousand items

- *Brick*—priced by thousands of units required based on number of units required per sq. ft. of wall area; add cost of special brick shapes, breakage, excess, installation cost, and cost of mortar, accessories, mobilization (moving crew/equipment in and out, and their scaffolding)

- *Equipment*—cost of each unit, provided by manufacturer, times the number of each type of unit; may or may not include cost of installation (units could be priced to be installed by contractor, owner, manufacturer, or separate subcontractor [see Glossary for definitions of "furnish," "install," and "provide"]).

The estimating process is both intensive and extensive. It cannot be done lightly, but requires a patient, methodical, thorough, and readily verifiable process. Usually an extensive checklist (see sample sheets following—Figures E-1 and E-2) is used to ensure that no physical item, nor any intangible cost is overlooked or forgotten. It is unforgivable, for example, to include the cost of concrete reinforcing, but forget to include a labor cost to install it.

ESTIMATING DIRECT AND INDIRECT COSTS

PROFIT FOR THE GENERAL CONTRACTOR, BOND COSTS, AND ESTIMATE SUMMARY

Determination of General Contractor Profit Margins is a management decision that varies based on competition, economic conditions, work backlog, and marketing considerations. After the Profit Margin is determined, the Estimate is completed by preparing a Project Estimate Summary Sheet. On the Project Estimate Summary Sheet list and Sub-Total all Direct Costs and Indirect Costs itemized on the Main Account Summary Sheets. *Add* General Contractor Profit and Bond Costs as required to arrive at the Total Estimated Project Cost.

ESTIMATE SUMMARY SHEET EXAMPLES

A Preliminary Construction Cost Estimate for a Three Story, 40,000 Square Foot Masonry/Concrete Industrial Office Building is illustrated in the following Main Account and Total Project Summaries. Summary Sheets would be compiled from Estimate Detail Sheets which are not shown. Each Main Account is Sub-Totaled and then Job Indirect Costs and a nominal 5% Sales Tax on Materials are added. Main Account Totals are carried forward to the Total Job Estimate Summary Sheet where General Contractor Profit and Bond Costs are calculated.

MAIN ACCOUNT SUMMARY
ACCOUNT 2-0 SITE WORK

DESCRIPTION	QUANTITY	MATERIALS UNIT PRICE	MATERIALS AMOUNT	LABOR UNIT MH	LABOR TOTAL MH	LABOR RATE	LABOR AMOUNT	SUBCONTRACT UNIT PRICE	SUBCONTRACT AMOUNT	TOTAL
2-1 Clear and Grub	270,000 SF	–	–	–	–	–	–	–	$ 3,177	$ 3,177
2-5 Site Grading	10,000 CY	–	–	–	–	–	–	–	30,100	30,100
2-15 Structural Excavation	600 CY	–	–	–	–	–	–	–	916	916
2-20 Load Excess Material	400 CY	–	–	–	–	–	–	–	240	240
2-21 Structural Backfill and Compaction	200 CY	–	–	–	–	–	–	–	2,190	2,190
2-23 Haul and Dump Excess	400 CY	–	–	–	–	–	–	–	3,140	3,140
2-30 PVC Sewer Pipe	390 LF	–	–	–	–	–	–	–	2,515	2,515
2-33 Concrete Drainage Pipe	1,025 LF	–	–	–	–	–	–	–	60,935	60,935
2-36 Concrete Drain Structure	13 EA	–	–	–	–	–	–	–	17,308	17,308
2-37 PVC Water Service	250 LF	–	–	–	–	–	–	–	4,723	4,723
2-40 Gate Valves & Boxes	2 EA	–	–	–	–	–	–	–	2,279	2,279
2-43 AC Paving & Striping	150,000 SF	–	–	–	–	–	–	–	160,094	160,094
2-45 Concrete Curbs & Gutters	12,500 SF	–	–	–	–	–	–	–	47,631	47,631
2-46 Concrete Walks & Drives	30,900 SF	–	–	–	–	–	–	–	69,384	69,384
Sub-Total, Direct Costs	1 LS	–	–	–	–	–	–	–	$404,632	$404,632
Job Indirect Costs:*										
Administrate Subcontracts	$404,632	–	–	–	–	–	–	10%	40,463	40,463
TOTAL ACCOUNT 2-0	1 LS	–	–	–	–	–	–	–	$445,095	$445,095

MAIN ACCOUNT SUMMARY
ACCOUNT 3-0 CONCRETE

DESCRIPTION	QUANTITY	MATERIALS UNIT PRICE	MATERIALS AMOUNT	LABOR UNIT MH	LABOR TOTAL MH	LABOR RATE	LABOR AMOUNT	SUBCONTRACT UNIT PRICE	SUBCONTRACT AMOUNT	TOTAL
3-1 Continuous Footing	297 CY	—	$ 16,853	—	(265)	—	$ 5,710	—	$ 6,820	$ 29,383
3-3 Square Footings	200 CY	—	11,197	—	(115)	—	2,354	—	4,886	18,437
3-5 4" Slab On Grade	167 CY	—	11,797	—	(284)	—	12,545	—	12,075	36,417
3-9 Square Columns	154 CY	—	16,480	—	(862)	—	26,785	—	23,876	67,141
3-15 One Way Slab and Beams	1,022 CY	—	97,147	—	(7,593)	—	186,306	—	117,208	400,661
3-22 Stairways	62 CY	—	9,468	—	(818)	—	23,646	—	7,687	40,801
5% Concrete Overpour (Allow)	95 CY	$58.50	5,558	—	—	—	—	—	—	5,558
Sub-Total, Direct Costs	1 LS	—	$168,500	—	(9,937)	—	$257,346	—	$172,552	$598,398
Job Indirect Costs:*										
3 Story Rate/Manhour	(9,937) MH	—	—	—	—	$14.98	$148,856	—	—	148,856
Administrate Subcontracts	$172,552	—	—	—	—	—	—	10%	17,255	17,255
Sales Tax on Materials	$168,500	5%	8,425	—	—	—	—	—	—	8,425
TOTAL ACCOUNT 3-0	1 LS	—	$176,925	—	(9,937)	—	$406,202	—	$189,807	$772,934

MAIN ACCOUNT SUMMARY
ACCOUNT 4-0 MASONRY

DESCRIPTION	QUANTITY	MATERIALS UNIT PRICE	MATERIALS AMOUNT	LABOR UNIT MH	LABOR TOTAL MH	LABOR RATE	LABOR AMOUNT	SUBCONTRACT UNIT PRICE	SUBCONTRACT AMOUNT	TOTAL
4-62 Reinforced Masonry Wall #10	23,000 SF	—	$153,870	—	(6,187)	—	$142,610	—	—	$296,480
Sub-Total, Direct Costs	23,000 SF	—	$153,870	—	(6,187)	—	$142,610	—	—	$296,480
Job Indirect Costs:*										
3 Story Rate/Manhour	(6,187) MH	—	—	—	—	$13.37	82,720	—	—	82,720
Sales Tax on Materials	$153,870	5%	7,694	—	—	—	—	—	—	7,694
TOTAL ACCOUNT 4-0	1 LS	—	$161,564	—	(6,187)	—	$225,330	—	—	$386,894

MAIN ACCOUNT SUMMARY
ACCOUNT 5-0 STRUCTURAL & MISCELLANEOUS STEEL

DESCRIPTION	QUANTITY	MATERIALS		LABOR				SUBCONTRACT		TOTAL
		UNIT PRICE	AMOUNT	UNIT MH	TOTAL MH	RATE	AMOUNT	UNIT PRICE	AMOUNT	
5-1 Ledger Angles	2,000 LF	—	$10,500	—	(100)	—	$2,680	—	—	$13,180
5-8 Stair Railings	300 LF	—	10,625	—	(30)	—	804	—	—	11,429
5-10 Miscellaneous Steel	8,000 LB	—	—	—	—	—	—	—	$32,800	32,800
Sub-Total, Direct Costs	1 LS	—	$21,125	—	(130)	—	3,484	—	$32,800	$57,409
Job Indirect Costs:*										
3 Story Rate/Manhour	(130) MH	—	—	—	—	$27.87	3,623	—	—	3,623
Administrate Subcontracts		—	—	—	—	—	—	10%	3,280	3,280
Sales Tax on Materials		5%	1,056	—	—	—	—	—	—	1,056
TOTAL ACCOUNT 5-0	1 LS	—	$22,181	—	(130)	—	$7,107	—	$36,080	$65,368

MAIN ACCOUNT SUMMARY
ACCOUNT 6-0 ROUGH AND FINISH CARPENTRY

DESCRIPTION	QUANTITY	MATERIALS		LABOR				SUBCONTRACT		TOTAL
		UNIT PRICE	AMOUNT	UNIT MH	TOTAL MH	RATE	AMOUNT	UNIT PRICE	AMOUNT	
6-1 Sills and Ledgers	2,000 LF	—	$1,820	—	(160)	—	$3,992	—	—	$5,812
6-2 Interior Partitions	10,800 SF	—	3,944	—	(238)	—	5,938	—	—	9,882
6-25 Wall Paneling	3,800 SF	—	8,550	—	(76)	—	1,896	—	—	10,446
Sub-Total, Direct Costs	1 LS	—	14,314	—	(474)	—	$11,826	—	—	$26,140
Job Indirect Costs:*										
3 Story Rate/Manhour	474 MH	—	—	—	—	$12.23	5,797	—	—	5,797
Sales Tax on Materials		5%	716	—	—	—	—	—	—	716
TOTAL ACCOUNT 6-0	1 LS	—	$15,030	—	(474)	—	$17,623	—	—	$32,653

MAIN ACCOUNT SUMMARY
ACCOUNT 7-0 MOISTURE PROTECTION

DESCRIPTION	QUANTITY		MATERIALS		LABOR				SUBCONTRACT		TOTAL
			UNIT PRICE	AMOUNT	UNIT MH	TOTAL MH	RATE	AMOUNT	UNIT PRICE	AMOUNT	
7-1 Underslab Vapor Barrier	13,500	SF	—	$ 965	—	(41)	—	$ 812	—	—	$ 1,777
7-3 Insulation & Partitions	10,800	SF	—	—	—	—	—	—	—	$ 3,024	3,024
7-4 Built Up Roofing	135	SQ	—	—	—	—	—	—	—	26,322	26,322
7-9 Flashing and Sheet Metal	1	LS	—	—	—	—	—	—	—	13,020	13,020
7-11 Roof Hatch	2	EA	—	924	—	(12)	—	293	—	—	1,217
7-13 Caulks and Sealants	5,000	LF	—	1,420	—	(175)	—	4,270	—	—	5,690
Sub-Total, Direct Costs	1	LS	—	$3,309	—	(228)	—	$5,375	—	$42,366	$51,050
Job Indirect Costs:*											
3 Story Rate/Manhour	(228)	MH	—	—	—	—	$11.73	2,674	—	—	2,674
Administrate Subcontracts	$42,366		—	—	—	—	—	—	10%	4,237	4,237
TOTAL ACCOUNT 7-0	1	LS	—	$3,474	—	(228)	—	$8,049	—	$46,603	$58,126

MAIN ACCOUNT SUMMARY
ACCOUNT 8-0 DOORS AND WINDOWS

DESCRIPTION	QUANTITY		MATERIALS		LABOR				SUBCONTRACT		TOTAL
			UNIT PRICE	AMOUNT	UNIT MH	TOTAL MH	RATE	AMOUNT	UNIT PRICE	AMOUNT	
8-1 Access Doors	20	EA	—	$ 1,480	—	(30)	—	$ 749	—	—	$ 2,229
8-4 Metal Doors w/Hdw.	90	EA	—	43,448	—	(405)	—	10,105	—	—	53,553
8-17 Roll-Up Metal Doors	4	EA	—	—	—	—	—	—	—	$ 9,651	9,651
8-31 AL Frame Entrance Doors	4	PR	—	—	—	—	—	—	—	5,255	5,255
8-32 Aluminum Curtain Wall	3,200	SF	—	—	—	—	—	—	—	64,500	64,500
Sub-Total, Direct Costs	1	LS	—	$44,928	—	(435)	—	$10,854	—	$79,406	$135,188
Job Indirect Costs:*											
3 Story Rate/Manhour	(435)	MH	—	—	—	—	$12.23	5,320	—	—	5,320
Administrate Subcontracts	$79,406		—	—	—	—	—	—	10%	7,941	7,941
Sales Tax on Materials	$44,928		5%	2,246	—	—	—	—	—	—	2,246
TOTAL ACCOUNT 8-0	1	LS	—	$47,174	—	(435)	—	$16,174	—	$87,347	$150,695

MAIN ACCOUNT SUMMARY
ACCOUNT 9-0 FINISHES

DESCRIPTION	QUANTITY	MATERIALS		LABOR				SUBCONTRACT		TOTAL
		UNIT PRICE	AMOUNT	UNIT MH	TOTAL MH	RATE	AMOUNT	UNIT PRICE	AMOUNT	
9-1 Suspended Channels	27,000 SF	—	—	—	—	—	—	—	$ 42,390	$ 42,390
9-3 Drywall	48,000 SF	—	—	—	—	—	—	—	50,064	50,064
9-10 Integrated Ceiling	13,500 SF	—	—	—	—	—	—	—	49,950	49,950
9-11 Ceramic Tile	4,000 SF	—	—	—	—	—	—	—	26,768	26,760
9-14 Resilient Floors & Base	23,000 SF	—	—	—	—	—	—	—	23,230	23,230
9-20 Painting	48,000 SF	—	—	—	—	—	—	—	24,336	24,336
Sub-Total, Direct Costs	1 LS	—	—	—	—	—	—	—	$216,730	$216,730
Job Indirect Costs:*										
Administrate Subcontracts	$216,730	—	—	—	—	—	—	10%	21,673	21,673
TOTAL ACCOUNT 9-0	1 LS	—	—	—	—	—	—	—	$238,403	$238,403

MAIN ACCOUNT SUMMARY
ACCOUNT 10-0 SPECIALTIES

DESCRIPTION	QUANTITY	MATERIALS		LABOR				SUBCONTRACT		TOTAL
		UNIT PRICE	AMOUNT	UNIT MH	TOTAL MH	RATE	AMOUNT	UNIT PRICE	AMOUNT	
10-1 Gypsum Partitions	600 LF	—	—	—	—	—	—	—	$ 30,000	$ 30,000
10-3 Partitions/Accessories	1 LS	—	—	—	—	—	—	—	23,700	23,700
10-4 Wire Mesh Partitions	198 LF	—	—	—	—	—	—	—	10,290	10,290
10-15 Metal Lockers	80 EA	—	—	—	—	—	—	—	4,560	4,560
10-18 Dock Equipment	1 LS	—	—	—	—	—	—	—	4,950	4,950
10-20 Elevators	2 EA	—	—	—	—	—	—	—	56,000	56,000
Sub-Total, Direct Costs	1 LS	—	—	—	—	—	—	—	$129,500	$129,500
Job Indirect Costs:*										
Administrate Subcontracts	$129,500	—	—	—	—	—	—	10%	12,950	12,950
TOTAL ACCOUNT 10-0	1 LS	—	—	—	—	—	—	—	$142,450	$142,450

MAIN ACCOUNT SUMMARY
ACCOUNT 15-0 MECHANICAL

DESCRIPTION	QUANTITY	MATERIALS		LABOR				SUBCONTRACT		TOTAL
		UNIT PRICE	AMOUNT	UNIT MH	TOTAL MH	RATE	AMOUNT	UNIT PRICE	AMOUNT	
15-14 Water Closets	1 LS	—	$ 13,703	—	(360)	—	$10,080	—	—	$ 23,783
15-15 Lavatories	1 LS	—	9,375	—	(192)	—	5,376	—	—	14,751
15-16 Urinal	1 LS	—	4,429	—	(98)	—	2,744	—	—	7,173
15-20 Service Sink	1 LS	—	3,751	—	(78)	—	2,184	—	—	5,935
15-22 Wash Fountain	1 LS	—	6,939	—	(59)	—	1,652	—	—	8,591
15-23 Emergency Shower	1 LS	—	3,806	—	(78)	—	2,184	—	—	5,990
15-24 Drinking Fountains	1 LS	—	3,562	—	(36)	—	1,008	—	—	4,570
15-25 Floor Drains	1 LS	—	6,518	—	(111)	—	3,108	—	—	9,626
15-28 Water Heater	1 LS	—	3,697	—	(24)	—	672	—	—	4,369
15-29 Vent Thru Roof & CO	1 LS	—	2,586	—	(80)	—	2,240	—	—	4,826
15-31 Roof Drains	1 LS	—	1,788	—	(52)	—	1,456	—	—	3,244
15-35 Copper Piping System	1 LS	—	29,775	—	(490)	—	13,720	—	—	43,495
15-37 CI Drain System	1 LS	—	3,171	—	(60)	—	1,680	—	—	4,851
15-79 Fire Extinguishers	1 LS	—	4,680	—	(36)	—	1,008	—	—	5,688
15-80 Piping Insulation	1 LS	—	—	—	—	—	—	—	$ 13,510	13,510
15-101 A/C Heat & Vent	1 LS	—	—	—	—	—	—	—	373,800	373,800
Sub-Total Direct Costs	—	—	$ 97,780	—	(1,754)	—	$49,112	—	$387,310	$534,202
Job Indirect Costs:*										
3 Story Rate/Manhour	(1,754) MH	—	—	—	—	$20.31	35,624	—	—	35,624
Administrate Subcontracts	$387,310	—	—	—	—	—	—	10%	38,731	38,731
Sales Tax on Materials	$97,780	5%	4,889	—	—	—	—	—	—	4,889
TOTAL ACCOUNT 15-0	1 LS	—	$102,669	—	(1,754)	—	$84,736	—	$426,041	$613,446

MAIN ACCOUNT SUMMARY
ACCOUNT 16-0 ELECTRICAL

DESCRIPTION	QUANTITY	MATERIALS			LABOR					SUBCONTRACT		TOTAL
		UNIT PRICE	AMOUNT	UNIT MH	TOTAL MH	RATE	AMOUNT			UNIT PRICE	AMOUNT	
16-1 Steel Conduit	1 LS	—	$ 8,165	—	(450)	—	$ 12,780			—	—	$ 20,945
16-20 Wire and Cable	1 LS	—	18,122	—	(150)	—	4,260			—	—	22,382
16-36 Plug-in Bus Duct	1 LS	—	31,411	—	(215)	—	6,106			—	—	37,517
16-60 Lighting Fixtures	1 LS	—	60,175	—	(132)	—	3,749			—	—	63,924
16-63 Exterior Lighting	1 LS	—	7,932	—	(54)	—	1,534			—	—	9,466
16-45 Lighting Panelboards	1 LS	—	5,153	—	(120)	—	3,408			—	—	8,561
16-52 Motor Control Center	1 LS	—	11,166	—	(40)	—	1,136			—	—	12,302
16-53 Control Stations	1 LS	—	2,563	—	(60)	—	1,704			—	—	4,267
16-40 Switchgear	1 LS	—	27,480	—	(44)	—	1,250			—	—	28,730
16-19 Conduit Hangers	1 LS	—	1,214	—	(40)	—	1,136			—	—	2,350
BRANCH CIRCUITS:												
16-91 Convenience Outlets	1 LS	—	6,631	—	(550)	—	15,620			—	—	22,251
16-92 Switches	1 LS	—	2,846	—	(215)	—	6,106			—	—	8,952
16-93 Lighting	1 LS	—	1,731	—	(180)	—	5,112			—	—	6,843
Sub-Total, Direct Costs	1 LS	—	$184,589	—	(2,250)	—	$ 63,901			—	—	$248,490
Job Indirect Costs:*												
3 Story Rate/Manhour	(2,250) MH	—	—	—	—	$21.02	47,295			—	—	47,295
Sales Tax on Materials	$184,589	5%	9,229	—	—	—	—			—	—	9,229
TOTAL ACCOUNT 16-0	1 LS	—	$193,818	—	(2,250)	—	$111,196			—	—	$305,014

164

MAIN ACCOUNT SUMMARY
ACCOUNT 100-0 PROCESS EQUIPMENT

DESCRIPTION	QUANTITY	MATERIALS		LABOR				SUBCONTRACT		TOTAL
		UNIT PRICE	AMOUNT	UNIT MH	TOTAL MH	RATE	AMOUNT	UNIT PRICE	AMOUNT	
100-1 Troughed Belt Conveyors	1 LS	—	$ 266,664	—	(696)	—	$ 18,583	—	—	$ 285,247
100-25 Roll Crushers	1 LS	—	438,880	—	(360)	—	9,612	—	—	448,492
100-50 Volumetric Feeders	1 LS	—	14,277	—	(64)	—	1,709	—	—	15,986
100-65 Vibrating Screens	1 LS	—	137,527	—	(258)	—	6,889	—	—	144,416
100-90 Vibrating Packers	1 LS	—	16,428	—	(72)	—	1,922	—	—	18,350
100-110 Industrial Fans	1 LS	—	282,351	—	(400)	—	10,680	—	—	293,031
100-120 Cyclone Collectors	1 LS	—	171,864	—	(400)	—	10,680	—	—	182,544
100-490 Hoists	1 LS	—	81,770	—	(120)	—	3,204	—	—	84,974
100-652 Motors	1 LS	—	153,789	—	(640)	—	17,088	—	—	170,877
100-656 Speed Reducers	1 LS	—	84,000	—	(270)	—	7,209	—	—	91,209
100-700 Freight	1 LS	—	40,846	—	—	—	—	—	—	40,846
Sub-Total, Direct Costs	1 LS	—	$1,688,396	—	(3,280)	—	$ 87,576	—	—	$1,775,972
Job Indirect Costs:*										
52' HT Rate Per Manhour	(3,280)	—	—	—	—	$25.37	83,214	—	—	83,214
Sales Tax on Materials	$1,688,396	5%	84,420	—	—	—	—	—	—	84,420
TOTAL ACCOUNT 100-0	1 LS	—	$1,772,816	—	(3,280)	—	$170,790	—	—	$1,943,606

*Job Indirect Costs added per Account 1-2.

To calculate the Estimated Total Construction Costs, summarize the Main Work Accounts, including the Job Indirect Costs and Sales Tax, on a Total Job Estimate Summary Sheet; *add* Profit to this total and then *add* Bond Costs if required. Profit is a management decision and varies depending on the marketplace and conditions. A 10% Profit Margin is shown as a nominal figure. Bond costs vary from 1% to 3%.

TOTAL JOB ESTIMATE SUMMARY

DESCRIPTION	QUANTITY	MATERIALS		LABOR				SUBCONTRACT		TOTAL
		UNIT PRICE	AMOUNT	UNIT MH	TOTAL MH	RATE	AMOUNT	UNIT PRICE	AMOUNT	
2-0 SITE WORK	1 LS	—	—	—	—	—	—	—	$ 445,095	$ 445,095
3-0 CONCRETE	1 LS	—	$ 176,925	—	(9,937)	—	$406,202	—	189,807	772,934
4-0 MASONRY	1 LS	—	161,564	—	(6,187)	—	225,330	—	—	386,894
5-0 STRUCTURAL & MISC STEEL	1 LS	—	22,181	—	(130)	—	7,107	—	36,080	65,368
6-0 CARPENTRY	1 LS	—	15,030	—	(474)	—	17,623	—	—	32,653
7-0 MOISTURE PROTECTION	1 LS	—	3,474	—	(228)	—	8,049	—	46,603	58,126
8-0 DOORS AND WINDOWS	1 LS	—	47,174	—	(435)	—	16,174	—	87,347	150,695
9-0 FINISHES	1 LS	—	—	—	—	—	—	—	238,403	238,403
10-0 SPECIALTIES	1 LS	—	—	—	—	—	—	—	142,450	142,450
15-0 MECHANICAL	1 LS	—	102,669	—	(1,754)	—	84,736	—	426,041	613,446
16-0 ELECTRICAL	1 LS	—	193,818	—	(2,250)	—	111,196	—	—	305,014
100-0 PROCESS EQUIPMENT	1 LS	—	1,772,816	—	(3,280)	—	170,790	—	—	1,943,606
All Accounts Include Job Indirect Costs and Sales Tax.										
SUB-TOTAL ALL ABOVE	1 LS	—	$2,495,651	—	(24,675)	—	$1,047,207	—	$1,611,826	$5,154,684

Add Profit @ 10%   515,468

Sub-Total $5,670,152

Add Bonds @ 1.5%   85,052

Preliminary Estimate, Total Construction Costs $5,755,204

RESIDENTIAL
COST ESTIMATE

OWNER'S NAME _____   APPRAISER: _____

RESIDENCE ADDRESS _____   PROJECT _____

CITY, STATE, ZIP CODE _____   DATE _____

CLASS OF CONSTRUCTION	RESIDENCE TYPE	CONFIGURATION	EXTERIOR WALL SYSTEM
☐ ECONOMY	☐ 1 STORY	☐ DETACHED	☐ WOOD SIDING—WOOD FRAME
☐ AVERAGE	☐ 1½ STORY	☐ TOWN/ROW HOUSE	☐ BRICK VENEER—WOOD FRAME
☐ CUSTOM	☐ 2 STORY	☐ SEMI-DETACHED	☐ STUCCO ON WOOD FRAME
☐ LUXURY	☐ 2½ STORY		☐ PAINTED CONCRETE BLOCK
	☐ 3 STORY	OCCUPANCY	☐ SOLID MASONRY (AVERAGE & CUSTOM)
	☐ BI-LEVEL	☐ ONE STORY	☐ STONE VENEER—WOOD FRAME
	☐ TRI-LEVEL	☐ TWO FAMILY	☐ SOLID BRICK (LUXURY)
		☐ THREE FAMILY	☐ SOLID STONE (LUXURY)
		☐ OTHER _____	

*LIVING AREA (Main Building)		*LIVING AREA (Wing or Ell) ( )		*LIVING AREA (Wing or Ell) ( )	
First Level	_____ S.F.	First Level	_____ S.F.	First Level	_____ S.F.
Second Level	_____ S.F.	Second Level	_____ S.F.	Second Level	_____ S.F.
Third Level	_____ S.F.	Third Level	_____ S.F.	Third Level	_____ S.F.
Total	_____ S.F.	Total	_____ S.F.	Total	_____ S.F.

*Basement Area is not part of living area

MAIN BUILDING	COSTS PER S.F. LIVING AREA
Cost per Square Foot of Living Area, from Page _____	$
Basement Addition: _____% Finished. _____ % Unfinished	*
Roof Cover Adjustment: _____ Type. Page _____ (Add or Deduct)	( )
Central Air Conditioning ☐ Separate Ducts ☐ Heating Ducts. Page _____	*
Heating System Adjustment: _____ Type. Page _____ (Add or Deduct)	( )
Main Building Adjusted Cost per S.F. of Living Area	$

MAIN BUILDING TOTAL COST	$ /S.F.	×	S.F.	×		=	$
	Cost per S.F. Living Area		Living Area		Town/Row House Multiplier Use 1 for Detached		TOTAL COST

WING OR ELL ( ) _____ STORY	COSTS PER S.F. LIVING AREA
Cost per Square Foot of Living Area, from Page _____	$
Basement Addition: _____% Finished. _____ % Unfinished	*
Roof Cover Adjustment: _____ Type. Page _____ (Add or Deduct)	( )
Central Air Conditioning ☐ Separate Ducts ☐ Heating Ducts. Page _____	*
Heating System Adjustment: _____ Type. Page _____ (Add or Deduct)	( )
Wing or Ell ( ): Adjusted Cost per S.F. of Living Area	$

WING OR ELL ( ) TOTAL COST	$ /S.F.	×	S.F.	=	$
	Cost per S.F. Living Area		Living Area		TOTAL COST

WING OR ELL ( ) _____ STORY	COSTS PER S.F. LIVING AREA
Cost per Square Foot of Living Area, from Page _____	$
Basement Addition: _____% Finished. _____ % Unfinished	*
Roof Cover Adjustment _____ Type. Page _____ (Add or Deduct)	( )
Central Air Conditioning ☐ Separate Ducts ☐ Heating Ducts. Page _____	*
Heating System Adjustment _____ Type. Page _____ (Add or Deduct)	( )
Wing or Ell ( ): Adjusted Cost per S.F. of Living Area	$

WING OR ELL ( ) TOTAL COST	$ /S.F.	×	S.F.	=	$
	Cost per S.F. Living Area		Living Area		TOTAL COST

TOTAL THIS PAGE [_____]

Total Page 1				$
		QUANTITY	UNIT COST	
Additional Bathrooms: _____ Full. _____ Half				
Finished Attic: _____ Ft. × _____ Ft.		S.F.		+
Breezeway: ☐ Open ☐ Enclosed _____ Ft. × _____ Ft.		S.F.		+
Covered Porch: ☐ Open ☐ Enclosed _____ Ft. × _____ Ft.		S.F.		+
Fireplace: ☐ Interior Chimney ☐ Exterior Chimney ☐ No. of Flues ☐ Additional Fireplaces				+
Appliances:				+
Kitchen Cabinets Adjustment:	(±)			
☐ Garage ☐ Carport: _____ Car(s) Description _____	(±)			
Miscellaneous:				+

ADJUSTED TOTAL BUILDING COST $ _____

REPLACEMENT COST	
ADJUSTED TOTAL BUILDING COST	$ _____
Site Improvements	
(A) Paving & Sidewalks	$ _____
(B) Landscaping	$ _____
(C) Fences	$ _____
(D) Swimming Pool	$ _____
(E) Miscellaneous	$ _____
TOTAL	$ _____
Location Factor	× _____
Location Replacement Cost	$ _____
Depreciation	−$ _____
LOCAL DEPRECIATED COST	$ _____

INSURANCE COST	
ADJUSTED TOTAL BUILDING COST	$ _____
Insurance Exclusions	
(A) Footings, Sitework, Underground Piping	−$ _____
(B) Architects Fees	−$ _____
Total Building Cost Less Exclusion	$ _____
Location Factor	× _____
LOCAL INSURABLE REPLACEMENT COST	$ _____

SQUARE FOOT AREA (*EXCLUDING BASEMENT*) FROM ITEM 11 _____ SQ. FT. _____

PERIMETER FROM ITEM 14 _____ LIN. FT _____

ITEM 17—MODEL SQUARE FOOT COST (*FROM MODEL SUB-TOTAL*) $ _____

Field Description & Calculation Section

NO.	SYSTEM/COMPONENT	DESCRIPTION	UNIT	UNIT COST	NEW SF COST	MODEL SF COST	+/− CHANGE
1.0	**Foundation**						
.1	Bldg. Excavation	Depth					
		Area	S.F.				
	Trench Excavation	Depth Width Length	L.F.				
.2	Footings: Strip Width	L.F. Length	L.F.				
	Footings: Spread	Bay Size	S.F. Gnd.				
		Other					
.3	Foundation Wall	Material					
		Height Thickness	L.F. Wall				
.4	Slab on Grade	Material Thickness	S.F. Gnd.				
3.0	**Superstructure**						
.1	Elevated Floors	Bay Size Material					
		Member Size	S.F. Floor				
.2	Roof Structure	Material					
		Bay Size					
		Member Size	S.F. Roof				
.3	Column/Bearing Wall						
	Column	Size	L.F. Col.				
		Bay Size					
	Bearing Wall	Material					
		Thickness	L.F. Wall				
.4	Fireproofing	Material	S.F. Surf.				
4.0	**Exterior Walls**	Building Ht. _____ Ft.					
.1	Outer Wall	Material					
		Thickness	S.F. Wall				
.2	Interior Finish		S.F. Wall				
.3	Windows	Type					
		% of Wall	S.F. Wind.				
.4	Doors	Type					
		Density	S.F. Door				
5.0	**Roofing**						
.1	Roof Covering	Material	S.F. Roof				

BID ANALYSIS EXERCISE

The chart that follows lists all the bidders for a portion of a large project. There was a Base Bid project, and then separate prices were taken (Add Alternates) for other smaller portions of the work that could be added to the Base Bid (to form the total Bid Package project).

Look through the chart and ascertain:

1. Who is the low bidder if all Add Alternates are accepted?

2. Who are the low bidders if each one of the Alternates is taken separately (e.g., Base + Alt. 1 only; Base + Alt. 2 only)

3. Where do you think estimating errors were made? Why?

4. Where, more than likely, were the same sub-bids used?

5. Who submitted the "courtesy bid" and really was not that interested in getting the work?

6. Using the European method, who should be awarded the project for the Base Bid work alone?

7. What fair conclusion can you come to based on the Alt. 4 bids?

ANALYSIS OF BIDS: Package #2—Cast-in-place (C.I.P.) & Architectural Pre-cast Concrete				February 11, 19___	
Bidder's Name	**Base Bid**	**N. Concourse Security Checkpoint & Util. Tunnel**	**S. Concourse Security Checkpoint & Util. Tunnel**	**Terminal C.I.P. Conc. & Struct. Masonry**	**Terminal Precast Concrete**
"ADD" Alternates	—	**1**	**2**	**3**	**4**
Universal Contracting	$2,099,000	$96,844	$51,229	$1,422,959	$447,968
Charter Construction Co.	$2,143,000	$120,000	$60,000	$1,143,000	$420,000
Hardaway Construction, Inc.	$2,160,900	$123,000	$75,000	$1,061,900	$411,000
Powell Concrete Construction	$2,165,000	$30,000	$30,000	$1,742,000	$450,000
Ray Belle Construction	$2,373,000	$116,000	$69,000	$1,760,000	$428,000
J.H. Shanklin Building Co.	$2,439,190	$170,696	$97,541	$1,703,582	$467,376
Lacona, Inc.	$2,456,878	$72,708	$111,613	$1,814,087	$458,970
W.F. Holt Contracting, Inc.	$3,108,000	$165,000	$140,000	$2,328,000	$475,000
TCC Estimate	$3,136,800	$220,000	$141,000	$2,136,000	$639,000

Trade Associations Standards-Generating Organizations Governing Authorities

Because of the massive amount of information required for any project, design professionals often utilize technical information and reference standards contained in publications produced by various organizations. Trade associations, standards-generating organizations, and governing authorities are invaluable sources of technical information, literature, and audio/visual aids. This information is specific, complete, and in-depth. It includes design, fabrication, processing, production, and installation data, with pertinent details. Usually, there is far more information than required, in that the testing and manufacturing procedures may be noted. Many items are provided gratis, but ask for catalog and applicable price list for available items and complete ordering information.

These documents are generally categorized as "reference standards." The data are promotional in nature, not directed toward sales, but toward understanding and the correct use and implementation of the products involved.

In lieu of repeating all of the necessary information on the drawings or in the specifications, professionals usually use a system of referring to the required materials, often using acronyms or abbreviations to represent the full names of the organizations involved. Following is a partial list of many such organizations; numerous other organizations exist that are not listed. Names and addresses are subject to change, but are believed to be accurate as of the date of production of this book. To verify or update information readers are advised to consult one of the following:

Encyclopedia of Associations,
Published by Gale Research Company.

National Trade and Professional Associations of the United States and Canada and Labor Unions,
Published by Columbia Books, Washington, DC.

ARCAT,
Published by The Architect's Catalog, Inc., Fairfield, CT.

Sources of Information section of *The Directory,*
Published by the Sweet's Group of McGraw-Hill Construction Information Group

Architectural Graphics Standards, 9th ed.,
Manual published by John Wiley and Sons, Inc., New York, NY

Also, most larger public libraries have a (free) directory service, which will locate addresses and telephone numbers in various cities.

AA	Aluminum Association 900 Nineteenth St. NW, Suite 300 Washington, DC 20006 (202) 862-5100 *www.aluminum.org*
AAA	American Arbitration Association 140 West 51st St. New York, NY 10020 (212) 484-4000 *www.adr.org*
AABC	Associated Air Balance Council 1518 K St. NW, Suite 503 Washington, DC 20005 (202) 737-0202 *www.aabchq.com*
AAMA	American Architectural Manufacturers Association 1827 Walden Office Square, Suite 104 Schaumberg, IL 60173 (847) 303-5664 *www.aamanet.com*
AAMA	Architectural Aluminum Manufacturers Association 2700 River Rd., Suite 118 Des Plaines, IL 60018 (312) 699-7310

AAN   (*See* ANLA)

AASHTO   American Association of State Highway and Transportation Officials
444 North Capitol St., Suite 249
Washington, DC 20001
(202) 624-5800
www.aashto.org

AATCC   American Association of Textile Chemists and Colorists
P.O. Box 12215, 1 Davis Drive
Research Triangle Park, NC 27709
(919) 549-8141
www.aatcc.org

ACI   American Concrete Institute
38800 Country Club Dr., P.O. Box 9094
Farmington Hills, MI 48331
(248) 848-3700
www.aci-int.org

ACIL   American Council of Independent Laboratories
1629 K St. NW
Washington, DC 20006   (202) 887-5872
www.acil.org

ACPA   American Concrete Pipe Association
222 West Las Colinas Blvd., Suite 641
Irving, TX 75039   (214) 506-7216
www.concrete-pipe.org

ADC   Air Diffusion Council
11 South LaSalle St., Suite 1400
Chicago, IL 60603   (312) 210-0101

AFPA   American Forest & Paper Council/American Wood Council (formerly National Forest Products Association—NFoPA)
1111 19th St. NW, Suite 800
Washington, DC 20036   (202) 463-2700
www.afandpa.org

AGA   American Gas Association
1515 Wilson Blvd.
Arlington, VA 22209   (703) 841-8648
www.aga.com

AGA   American Galvanizers Association
1200 E. Iliff Ave., Suite 204
Aurora, CO 80014   (303) 750-2900

AGC   Associated General Contractors of America
333 John Carlyle Street, Suite 200
Alexandria, VA 22314   (703) 548-3118
www.agc.org

AHA   American Hardboard Association
1210 W. Northwest Highway
Palatine, IL 60067   (847) 934-8800

AHAM   Association of Home Appliance Manufacturers
20 N. Wacker Dr., Suite 1500
Chicago, IL 60606   (312) 984-5800
www.aham.org

AHMI   Appalachian Hardwood Manufacturers, Inc.
P.O. Box 427
High Point, NC 27261   (910) 885-8315
www.appalachianwood.org

AI   Asphalt Institute
Research Park Drive, P.O. Box 14052
Lexington, KY 40512   (606) 288-4960
www.asphaltinstitute.org

AIA   American Institute of Architects
1735 New York Ave. NW
Washington, DC 20006   (202) 626-7359
www.aia.org

A.I.A.   American Insurance Association
1130 Connecticut Ave., NW, Suite 1000
Washington, D.C. 20036   (202) 828-7100

AIHA   American Industrial Hygiene Association
2700 Prosperity Avenue, Suite 250
Fairfax, VA 22031   (703) 849-8888
www.aiha.org

AISC   American Institute of Steel Construction
One E. Wacker Dr., Suite 3100
Chicago, IL 60601   (312) 670-2400
www.aisc.web.com

AISI   American Iron and Steel Institute
1101 Seventeenth St. NW, Suite 1300
Washington, DC 20036   (202) 452-7100
www.steel.org

AITC   American Institute of Timber Construction
7012 S. Revere Parkway, Suite 140
Englewood, CO 80112   (303) 792-9559
www.aitc-glulam/org

ALI   American Lighting Institute
435 N. Michigan Ave.
Chicago, IL 60611   (312) 644-0828

ALI   Associated Laboratories, Inc.
1323 Wall St., P.O. Box 152837
Dallas, TX 75315   (214) 565-0593
www.assoc-labs.com

ALSC   American Lumber Standards Committee
P.O. Box 210
Germantown, MD 20874   (301) 972-1700

AMCA   Air Movement and Control Association
30 W. University Dr.
Arlington Heights, IL 60004
(312) 394-0150
www.amca.org

ANLA   American Nursery and Landscape Association (formerly Amer. Association of Nurserymen)
1250 Eye St. NW, Suite 500
Washington, DC 20005   (202) 789-2900
www.anla.org

ANSI   American National Standards Institute
11 W. 42nd St.
New York, NY 10036   (212) 642-4900
www.ansi.org

APA   (*See* EWA)

APFA   American Pipe Fittings Association
              7297 Lee Highway, Suite N
              Falls Church, VA 22042   (703) 533-1321

API   American Petroleum Institute
              1220 L St., NW
              Washington, DC 20005   (202) 682-8000
              www.api.org

ARI   Air-Conditioning and Refrigeration Institute
              4301 N. Fairfax Dr., Suite 425
              Arlington, VA 22203   (703) 524-8800
              www.ari.org

ARMA   Asphalt Roofing Manufacturers Association
              Center Park—Suite 404
              4041 Powder Mill Road
              Calverton, MD 20705   (301) 231-9050
              www.asphaltroofing.org

ASA   Acoustical Society of America
              500 Sunnyside Blvd.
              Woodbury, NY 11797   (516) 576-2360
              www.asa.aip.org

ASC   Adhesive and Sealant Council
              1627 K St., NW, Suite 1000
              Washington, D.C. 20006   (202) 452-1500
              www.ascouncil.org

ASCE   American Society of Civil Engineers
              World Headquarters
              1801 Alexander Bell Drive
              Reston, VA 20191   (703) 295-6196
              www.asce.org

ASHRAE   American Society of Heating, Refrigerating
              and Air-Conditioning Engineers
              1791 Tullie Circle NE
              Atlanta, GA 30329   (404) 636-8400
              www.ashrae.org

ASME   American Society of Mechanical Engineers
              United Engineering Center, 345 E. 47th St.
              New York, NY 10017   (212) 705-8500
              www.asme.org

ASSE   American Society of Sanitary Engineering
              28901 Clemens Road
              Westlake, OH 44145   (440) 835-3040
              www.asse-plumbing.org

ASSE   American Society of Safety Engineers, Inc.
              1800 East Oakton St.
              Des Plaines, IL 60016   (708) 692-4121
              www.asse.org

ASTM   American Society for Testing and Materials
              100 Barr Harbor Dr.
              West Conshohocken, PA 19428
              (610) 832-9585
              www.astm.org

AWA   Fine Hardwoods—American Walnut Association
              5603 W. Raymond St., Suite O
              Indianapolis, IN 46421   (317) 244-3312

AWI   Architectural Woodwork Institute
              1952 Isaac Newton Square West
              Reston, VA 20190   (703) 733-0600
              www.awinet.org

AWPA   American Wood Preservers Association
              P.O. Box 5690
              Granbury, TX 76049   (817) 326-6300
              www.awpa.com

AWPB   American Wood Preservers' Bureau
              (organization defunct)

AWS   American Welding Society
              550 NW Le Jeune Rd.
              Miami, FL 33126   (305) 443-9353
              www.amweld.org

AWWA   American Water Works Association
              6666 W. Quincy Ave.
              Denver, CO 80235   (303) 794-7711
              www.awwa.org

BANC   Brick Association of the Carolinas
              (formerly Brick Assoc. of North Carolina)
              P.O. Box 13290
              Greensboro, NC 27415   (919) 273-5566
              www.gobrick.com

BHMA   Builders Hardware Manufacturers Association
              355 Lexington Ave., 17th Floor
              New York, NY 10017   (212) 661-4261

BIA   Brick Industry Association
              (formerly Brick Institute of America)
              11490 Commerce Park Dr., Suite 300
              Reston, VA 20191   (703) 620-0010
              www.bia.org

BIFMA   Business and Institutional Furniture
              Manufacturers Association
              2680 Horizon Drive, SE, Suite A1
              Grand Rapids, MI 49546   (616) 285-3963
              www.bifma.com

BSI   Building Stone Institute
              P.O. Box 507
              Purdys, NY 10578   (914) 232-5725

CAGI   Compressed Air and Gas Institute
              c/o Thomas Associates, Inc.
              1300 Sumner Road
              Cleveland, OH 44115   (216) 241-7333
              www.taol.com/cagi

CAUS   Color Association of the United States
              409 W. 44th Street
              New York, NY 10036   (212) 582-6884

CBMA   Certified Ballast Manufacturers Association
              355 Lexington Ave., 17th Floor
              New York, NY 10036   (212) 661-4261
              www.certbal.org

CDA   Copper Development Association
              600 Rocky Drive
              Boiling Springs, PA 17007   (717) 258-3904
              www.copper.org

CGA   Compressed Gas Association
           1725 Jefferson Davis Highway
           Arlington, VA 22202   (412) 979-0900
           www.cgnet.com

CISCA   Ceilings and Interior Systems Construction
           Association
           1500 Lincoln Highway—Suite 202
           St. Charles, IL 60174   (630) 584-1919
           www.cisca.org

CISPI   Cast Iron Soil Pipe Institute
           5959 Shallowford Rd., Suite 419
           Chattanooga, TN 37421   (423) 892-0137
           www.cispi.org

CLFMI   Chain Link Fence Manufacturers Institute
           9891 Broken Land Parkway, Suite 300
           Columbia, MD 21046   (301) 596-2584
           www.baileadership.com

CLPA   California Lathing and Plastering Association
           25332 Narbonne, Suite 170
           Lomita, CA 90717   (213) 539-6080

CMAA   Construction Management Association of
           America
           7918 Jones Branch, #540
           McLean, VA 22102   (703) 356-2622
           www.access.digex.net/~cmaa/

CPA   Composite Panel Association
           18928 Premiere Court
           Gaithersburg, MD 20879   (301) 670-0604

CRA   California Redwood Association
           405 Enfrente Dr., Suite 200
           Novato, CA 94949   (415) 382-0662
           www.calredwood.org

CRI   Carpet and Rug Institute
           310 S. Holiday Avenue
           Dalton, GA 30722   (706) 278-3176
           www.carpet-rug.com

CRSI   Concrete Reinforcing Steel Institute
           933 N. Plum Grove Rd.
           Schaumburg, IL 60173   (847) 517-1200
           www.crsi.org

CTI   Ceramic Tile Institute of America
           12061 West Jefferson Blvd.
           Culver City, CA 90230   (310) 574-7800

C.T.I.   Cooling Tower Institute
           Box 73383
           Houston, TX 77273   (713) 583-4087
           www.cti.org

DASMA   Door and Access Systems Manufacturers
           Association, International
           (formerly National Association of Garage
           Door Manufacturers)
           c/o Thomas Associates, Inc.
           1300 Sumner Avenue
           Cleveland, OH 44115   (216) 241-7333
           www.taol.com/dasma

DBIA   Design-Build Institute of America
           1010 Massachusetts Ave., NW, Suite 350
           Washington, D.C. 20001   (202) 682-0110
           e-mail: *dbia@dbia.org*

DHI   Door and Hardware Institute
           (formerly National Bldrs. Hardware Assoc.)
           14170 Newbrook Dr.
           Chantilly, VA 20151   (703) 222-2010
           www.dhi.org

DIPRA   Ductile Iron Pipe Research Association
           245 Riverchase Parkway-E, Suite O
           Birmingham, AL 35244   (205) 988-9870
           www.dipra.org

DLPA   Decorative Laminate Products Association
           (now part of KCMA)

DORCMA   Door Operator and Remote Controls
           Manufacturers Association
           1200 Sumner Ave.
           Cleveland, OH 44115   (216) 214-9333

EIA   Electronics Industries Association
           2500 Wilson Blvd., 4th Floor
           Arlington, VA 22201   (703) 907-7500
           www.eia.org

EIMA   EIFS Industry Members Association
           402 N. Fourth St., Suite 102
           Yakima, WA 98901   (509) 457-3500
           www.eifsfacts.com

ETL   ETL Testing Laboratories, Inc.
           [now part of ITS]

EWA   Engineered Wood Association
           (formerly American Plywood Association)
           P.O. Box 11700
           Tacoma, WA 98411   (253) 565-6600
           www.apawood.org

FCI   Fluid Controls Institute
           % Thomas Associates, Inc.
           1300 Sumner Road
           Cleveland, OH 44115   (216) 241-7333
           www.taol.com/fci

FGMA   (*See* GANA)

FM   Factory Mutual Engineering and Research
           1151 Boston-Providence Turnpike
           Norwood, MA 02062   (781) 762-4300
           www.factorymutual.com

FPRS   Forest Products Research Society
           2801 Marshall Court
           Madison, WI 53705   (608) 231-1361

FTI   Facing Tile Institute
           c/o Box 8880
           Canton, OH 44711   (216) 488-1211

GA   Gypsum Association
           810 First St. NE, Suite 510
           Washington, DC 20002   (202) 289-5440

GAMA	Gas Appliance Manufacturers Association, Inc. 1901 North Moore St., Suite 1100 Arlington, VA 22209 (703) 525-9565
GANA	Glass Association of North America (formerly Flat Glass Marketing Association) 3310 S.W. Harrison St. Topeka, KS 66611 (785) 271-0166 *www.glasswebsite.com/gana*
HEI	Heat Exchange Institute c/o Thomas Associates, Inc. 1300 Sumner Ave. Cleveland, OH 44115 (216) 241-7333 *www.taol.com/hei*
HI	Hydronics Institute P.O. Box 218 35 Russo Place Berkeley Heights, NJ 07922 (201) 464-8200 *www.gamanet.org*
HMA	Hardwood Manufacturers Association (formerly Southern Hardwood Lumber Manuf. Assoc.) 400 Penn Center Blvd., Suite 530 Pittsburgh, PA 15235 (412) 829-0770 *www.hardwood.org*
HPVA	Hardwood Plywood & Veneer Association 1825 Michael Farraday Drive, P.O. Box 2789 Reston, VA 20190 (703) 435-2900 *www.hpva.org*
HVI	Home Ventilating Institute 30 West University Drive Arlington Heights, IL 60004 (708) 394-0150
ICC	International Code Council 5203 Leesburg Pike-#708 Falls Church, VA 22041 (703) 931-4533 *www.intlcode.org*
ICEA	Insulated Cable Engineers Association, Inc. P.O. Box 440 South Yarmouth, MA 02664 (617) 394-4424 *www.icea.net*
IEC	International Electrotechnical Commission (available from ANSI)
IEEE	Institute of Electrical and Electronic Engineers 345 E. 47th St. New York, NY 10017 (212) 705-7900 *www.ieee.org*
IESNA	Illuminating Engineering Society of North America 120 Wall St.—17th Floor New York, NY 10005 (212) 248-5000 *www.iesna.org*
IGCC	Insulating Glass Certification Council P.O. Box 9 Henderson Harbor, NY 13651 (315) 938-7444 *www.igcc.org*
ILI	Indiana Limestone Institute of America Stone City Bank Building, Suite 400 Bedford, IN 47421 (812) 275-4426 *www.iliai.com*
IMSA	International Municipal Signal Association P.O. Box 539, 165 E. Union St. Newark, NJ 14513 (315) 331-2182 *www.imsafety.org*
IRI	Industrial Risk Insurers 85 Woodland St., P.O. Box 5010 Hartford, CT 06102 (203) 520-7300 *www.industrialrisk.com*
ISA	International Society for Measurement and Control P.O. Box 12277 67 Alexander Dr. Research Triangle Park, NC 27709 (919) 549-8411 *www.isa.org*
ITS	Intertek Testing Services (formerly Inchcape Testing Services) P.O. Box 2040 3933 US Route 11 Cortland, NY 13045 (607) 753-6711 *www.itsglobal.com*
KCMA	Kitchen Cabinet Manufacturers Association 1899 Preston White Drive Reston, VA 22091 (703) 264-1690 *www.kema.org*
LGSI	Light Gauge Structural Institute c/o Loseke Technologies, Inc. P.O. Box 560746 The Colony, TX 75056 (972) 625-4560
LIA	Lead Industries Association, Inc. 292 Madison Avenue New York, NY 10017 (212) 578-4750 *www.leadinfo.com*
LPI	Lightning Protection Institute 3365 N. Arlington Heights Rd., Suite E Arlington Heights, IL 60004 (847) 577-7200 *www.lightning.org*
LRI	Lighting Research Institute 120 Wall St. New York, NY 10005 (212) 248-5014
MBMA	Metal Building Manufacturers Association c/o Thomas Associates, Inc. 1300 Sumner Ave. Cleveland, OH 44115 (216) 241-7333 *www.taol.com/mbma*

MCAA   Mechanical Contractors Association of
America
1385 Piccard Drive
Rockville, MD 20850   (301) 869-5800
www.mcaa.org

MFMA   Maple Flooring Manufacturers Association
60 Revere Dr.-Suite 500
Northbrook, IL 60062   (708) 480-9138
www.maplefloor.com

MHI   Material Handling Industry Association
8720 Red Oak Blvd., Suite 201
Charlotte, NC 28217   (704) 522-8644
www.mhia.org

MIA   Marble Institute of America
30 Eden Alley, Suite 201
Columbus, OH 43215   (614) 228-6194
www.marble-institute.com

M.I.A. Masonry Institute of America
2550 Beverly Blvd.
Los Angeles, CA 90057   (213) 388-0472
www.masonryinstitute.org

ML/SFA Metal Lath/Steel Framing Association
(Division of NAAMM)
8 South Michigan Avenue, Suite 1000
Chicago, IL 60603   (312) 456-5590

MSS   Manufacturers Standardization Society of the
Valve and Fittings Industry
127 Park St. NE
Vienna, VA 22180   (703) 281-6613
www.mss-hq.com

NAA   National Aggregate Association
900 Spring St.
Silver Spring, MD 20910   (301) 587-1400

NAAMM   National Association of Architectural Metal
Manufacturers
8 South Michigan Avenue, Suite 100
Chicago, IL 60603   (312) 332-0405
www.gss.net/naamm

NAIMA   North American Insulation Manufacturers
Association
(formerly Thermal Insulation Manufacturers
Association)
44 Canal Center Plaza, Suite 310
Alexandria, VA 22314   (703) 684-0084
www.naima.org

NAMM   National Association of Mirror Manufacturers
(*See* GANA)

NAPA   National Asphalt Pavement Association
NAPA Building
5100 Forbes Blvd.
Lanham, MD 20706   (301) 731-4748
www.hotmix.org

NAPF   National Association of Plastic Fabricators
(now DLPA)

NAWIC   National Association of Women in
Construction
327 S. Adams St.
Fort Worth, TX 76104   (800) 552-3506

NBGQA   National Building Granite Quarries
Association
1220 L St., NW—Suite 100-167
Washington, DC 20005   (800) 557-2848

NBHA   National Building Hardware Association (see
DHI)

NCMA   National Concrete Masonry Association
2302 Horse Pen Rd.
Herndon, VA 20171   (703) 713-1900
www.ncma.org

NCRPM   National Council on Radiation Protection and
Measurement
7910 Woodmont Ave., Suite 800
Bethesda, MD 20814   (301) 657-2652
www.ncrp.com

NDMA   National Dimension Manufacturers
Association
1000 Johnson Ferry Rd.
Marietta, GA 30068   (404) 565-6660

NDPA   National Decorating Products Association
1050 North Lindbergh Blvd.
St. Louis, MO 63132   (314) 991-3470

NEC   National Electric Code (document available
through NFiPA)

NECA   National Electrical Contractors Association
3 Bethesda Metro Center, Suite 1100
Bethesda, MD 20814   (301) 657-3110
www.necanet.org

NEI   National Elevator Industry, Inc.
185 Bridge Plaza North, Suite 310
Fort Lee, NJ 07024   (201) 944-3211

NEMA   National Electrical Manufacturers
Association
2101 L St. NW, Suite 300
Washington, DC 20037   (202) 457-8400
www.nema.org

NFPA   National Fire Protection Association
Batterymarch Park, P.O. Box 9101
Quincy, MA 02269   (617) 770-3000
www.nfpa.org

NFoPA   National Forest Products Association
(name change; *see* AFPA listing)

NHLA   National Hardwood Lumber Association
P.O. Box 34518
Memphis, TN 38184   (901) 377-1818
www.natlhardwood.org

NKCA   National Kitchen Cabinet Association
(now KCMA)

NOFMA	National Oak Flooring Manufacturers Association P.O. Box 3009 Memphis, TN 38173 (901) 526-5016 *www.nofma.org*
NPCA	National Paint and Coatings Association 1500 Rhode Island Ave. NW Washington, DC 20005 (202) 462-6272 *www.paint.org*
NRCA	National Roofing Contractors Association 10255 W. Higgins Rd., Suite 600 Rosemont, IL 60018 (847) 299-9070 *www.roofonline.org*
NRDCA	National Roof Deck Contractors Association 600 S. Federal St. Chicago, IL 60605 (312) 922-6222
NRMCA	National Ready Mixed Concrete Association 900 Spring St. Silver Spring, MD 20910 (301) 587-1400 *www.nrmca.org*
NSF	NSF International (formerly National Sanitation Foundation) P.O. Box 130140 3475 Plymouth Rd. Ann Arbor, MI 48105 (313) 769-8010 *www.nsf.org*
NSPE	National Society of Professional Engineers 1420 King St. Alexandria, VA 22314 (703) 684-2800 *www.nspe.org*
NSSEA	National School Supply and Equipment Association 8300 Colesville Road, No. 250 Silver Spring, MD 20910 (301) 495-0240 *www.nssea.org*
NSPI	National Spa and Pool Institute 2111 Eisenhower Ave. Alexandria, VA 22314 (703) 838-0083
NSWMA	National Solid Wastes Management Association 1730 Rhode Island Ave. NW Washington, DC 20036 (202) 659-4613 *www.envanns.org*
NTMA	National Terrazzo and Mosaic Association 3166 Des Plaines Ave., Suite 121 Des Plaines, Il 60018 (312) 635-7744 *www.ntma.com*
NWMA	National Woodwork Manufacturers Association (now NWWDA)
NWWDA	National Wood Window and Door Association (formerly NWMA) 1400 E. Touhy Ave., Suite 470 Des Plaines, IL 60018 (847) 299-5200 *www.nwwda.org*
PCA	Portland Cement Association 5420 Old Orchard Road Skokie, IL 60077 (847) 966-6200 *www.portcement.org*
PCI	Precast/Prestressed Concrete Institute 175 W. Jackson Blvd. Chicago, IL 60604 (312) 786-0300 *www.pci.org*
PDCA	Painting and Decoration Contractors of America 3913 Old Lee Highway Fairfax, VA 22030 (703) 359-0826 *www.pdca.com*
PDI	Plumbing and Drainage Institute 45 Bristol Dr., Suite 101 South Easton, MA 02375 (508) 230-3516 *www.pdionline.org*
PEI	Porcelain Enamel Institute 4004 Hillsboro Pike, Suite 224-B Nashville, TN 37215 (615) 385-5357 *www.porcelainenamel.com*
PI	Perlite Institute 88 New Dorp Plaza Staten Island, NY 10306 (718) 351-5723
PPFA	Plastic Pipe and Fittings Association 800 Roosevelt Road—Bldg. C, Suite 20 Glen Ellyn, IL 60137 (630) 858-6540
PPI	Plastic Pipe Institute (formerly The Society of the Plastics Industry, Inc.) 1801 K Street, NW—Suite 600K Washington, DC 20006 (202) 974-5318 *www.plasticpipe.org*
PWC	Professional Women in Construction 342 Madison Ave. New York, NY 10173 (212) 687-0610
RCSHSB	Red Cedar Shingle and Handsplit Shake Bureau 515 116th Ave. NE, Suite 275 Bellevue, WA 98004 (206) 453-1323
RFCI	Resilient Floor Covering Institute 966 Hungerford Dr., Suite 12-B Rockville, MD 20805 (301) 340-8580
RIS	Redwood Inspection Service c/o California Redwood Association 405 Enfrente Drive, Suite 200 Novato, CA 94949 (415) 382-0662
RMA	Rubber Manufacturers Association 1400 K St. NW, Suite 900 Washington, DC 20005 (202) 682-4800 *www.rma.org*
SAMA	Scientific Apparatus Makers Association 1101 Sixteenth St. NW Washington, DC 20036 (202) 223-1360

SDI Steel Deck Institute
P.O. Box 25
Fox River Grove, IL 60021
(847) 462-1930
www.sdi.org

S.D.I. Steel Door Institute
30200 Detroit Rd.
Cleveland, OH 44145 (440) 899-0010
www.steeldoor.org

SFPA Southern Forest Products Association
P.O. Box 64170
Kenner, LA 70064 (504) 443-4464
www/southernpine.com

SGAA Stained Glass Association of America
Box 22642
Kansas City, MO 64113 (816) 333-6690

SGCC Safety Glazing Certification Council
(*See* ETL listing; co-located)

SHLMA Southern Hardwood Lumber Manufacturers
Association
(now HMA)

SIGMA Sealed Insulating Glass Manufacturers
Association
401 N. Michigan Avenue
Chicago, IL 60611 (312) 644-6610
www.sigmaonline.org/sigma

SJI Steel Joist Institute
3127 10th Avenue North
Myrtle Beach, SC 29577 (843) 626-1995

SMACNA Sheet Metal and Air Conditioning Contractors
National Association
4201 LaFayette Center Dr.
Chantilly, VA 20151 (703) 803-2989
www.smacna.org

SPIB Southern Pine Inspection Bureau
4709 Scenic Highway
Pensacola, FL 32504 (904) 434-2611
www.spib.org

SPRI SPRI
(formerly Single-Ply Roofing Institute)
200 Reservoir Street, Suite 309A
Needham, MA 02194 (718) 444-0242
www.spri.org

SSPC Society for Protective Coatings
(formerly Steel Structures Painting Council)
40 24th Street, 6th floor
Pittsburgh, PA 15222 (412) 281-2331
www.sspc.org

SWI Steel Window Institute
c/o Thomas Associates, Inc.
1230 Keith Bldg.
Cleveland, OH 44115 (216) 241-7333
www.taol.com/swi

TCA Tile Council of America
100 Clemson Research Blvd.
Anderson, SC 29625 (864) 646-8453
www.tileuse.com

TIMA Thermal Insulation Manufacturers Association
(now NAIMA)

TPI Truss Plate Institute
583 D'Onofrio Dr., Suite 200
Madison, WI 53719 (608) 833-5900

UL Underwriters Laboratories
333 Pfingsten Rd.
Northbrook, IL 60062 (847) 272-8800
www.ul.com

VA Vermiculite Association, Inc.
600 S. Federal St., Suite 400
Chicago, IL 60605 (312) 922-6222

WA Wallcoverings Association
401 N. Michigan Avenue
Chicago, IL 60611 (312) 644-6610

WCLIB West Coast Lumber Inspection Bureau
P.O. Box 23145
Portland, OR 97281 (503) 639-0651

WCMA Wall Covering Manufacturers Association
66 Morris Ave.
Springfield, NJ 07081 (201) 379-1100

WIC Woodwork Institute of California
P.O. Box 980247
Sacramento, CA 95798 (916) 372-9943
www.wicnet.org

WRCA Western Red Cedar Association
Box 120786
New Brighton, MN 55112 (612) 633-4334

WRCLA Western Red Cedar Lumber Association
1200-555 Burrand St.
Vancouver, BC, Canada (604) 684-0266
www.cofi.org

WRI Wire Reinforcement Institute
301 E. Sandusky St.
Findlay, OH 45840 (419) 425-9473
www.bright,net/~rreiter

WSC Water Systems Council
Building C, Suite 20
800 Roosevelt Road
Glen Ellyn, Il 60137 (603) 545-1762
www.wschome.org

WSFI Wood and Synthetic Flooring Institute
(now MFMA)

WWPA Western Wood Products Association
1500 Yeon Building
522 SW 5th Avenue
Portland, OR 97204 (503) 224-3930
www.wwpa.org

W.W.P.A. Woven Wire Products Association
2515 N. Nordica Ave.
Chicago, IL 60635 (312) 637-1359

Federal Government Agencies

Names and titles of federal government standards or specification-producing agencies are frequently abbreviated. The following acronyms or abbreviations as referenced in the contract documents indicate names of standards or specification-producing agencies of the federal government. Names and addresses are subject to change but are believed to be accurate.

CE Corps of Engineers
   (U.S. Department of the Army)
   20 Massachusetts Avenue, NW
   Washington, DC 20314 (202) 761-0660
   www.usace.army.mil

CFR Code of Federal Regulations
   (available from Government Printing Office)
   Washington, DC 20401
   (material is usually first published in the *Federal Register*) (202) 512-0000
   www.access.gpo.gov

CPSC Consumer Product Safety Commission
   East West Towers
   4330 East-West Highway
   Bethesda, MD 29814 (800) 638-2772
   www.cpcs.gov

CS Commercial Standard
   (U.S. Department of Commerce)
   Government Printing Office
   Washington, DC 20402 (202) 512-1800
   www.nist.gov

DOC Department of Commerce
   14th Street and Constitution Avenue
   Washington, D.C. 20230 (202) 482-2000
   www.doc.gov

DOT Department of Transportation
   400 Seventh St. SW
   Washington, DC 20590 (202) 366-4000
   www.dot.gov

EPA Environmental Protection Agency
   401 M St. SW
   Washington, DC 20460 (202) 260-2090
   www.epa.gov

FAA Federal Aviation Administration
   (U.S. Department of Transportation)
   800 Independence Ave. SW
   Washington, DC 20591 (202) 366-4000
   www.faa.gov

FCC Federal Communications Commission
   1919 M St. NW
   Washington, DC 20554 (202) 418-0126
   www.fcc.gov

FHA Federal Housing Administration
   (U.S. Department of Housing and Urban Development)
   451 Seventh St. SW
   Washington, DC 20401 (202) 401-0388
   www.hud.gov

FS Federal Specifications Unit
   (available from General Services Administration)
   470 East L'Enfant Plaza, SW, Suite 8100
   Washington, DC 20407 (202) 619-8925
   www.gsa.gov

GSA General Services Administration
   F St. and 18th St. NW
   Washington, DC 20405 (202) 708-5082
   www.gsa.gov

MIL Military Standardization Documents
   (U.S. Department of Defense)
   Defense Printing Service
   700 Robbins Avenue, Bldg. 4D
   Philadelphia, PA 19111 (215) 697-2179
   www.dodssp.das.mil

NIST National Institute of Standards and Technology
   (U.S. Department of Commerce)
   Building 101, #A1134
   Route I-270 and Quince Orchard Road
   Gaithersburg, MD 20899 (301) 975-2000
   www.nist.gov

OSHA Occupational Safety and Health Administration
   U.S. Department of Labor/OSHA
   200 Constitution Ave. NW
   Washington, DC 20210 (202) 219-7725
   www.osha.gov

PS Product Standards (National Bureau of Standards)
   (U.S. Department of Labor)
   Government Printing Office
   Washington, DC 20402 (202) 512-1800
   www.nist.gov

RUS Rural Utilities Service
   (formerly Rural Electrification Administration—REA)
   (U.S. Department of Agriculture)
   14th St. and Independence Ave. SW
   Washington, DC 20250 (202) 720-9560

TRB Transportation Research Board
   2101 Constitution Ave. NW
   Washington, DC 20418 (202) 334-2934
   www.nas.edu/trb

USDA U.S. Department of Agriculture
   14th St., and Independence Ave., SW
   Washington, DC 20205 (202) 720-8732
   www.usda.gov

USPS U.S. Postal Service
   475 L'Enfant Plaza SW
   Washington, DC 20260 (202) 268-2000
   www.usps.gov

Other Sources

Names and titles of other standards, code, or specification-producing agencies are also frequently abbreviated. The following are subject to change but are believed to be accurate.

ACEC   American Consulting Engineers Council
            1015 E. 47th St.
            New York, NY 10017

BOCA   Building Officials and Code
            Administrators International, Inc.
            National Building Code and others
            4051 West Flossmoor Rd.
            Country Club Hills, Il 60477

CABO   (*See also* ICC)
            Council of American Building Officials
            One and Two Family Dwelling Code
            5203 Leesburg Pike
            Falls Church, VA 22041

CSI   Construction Specifications Institute
            601 Madison St.
            Alexandria, VA 22314

EJCDC/NSPE Engineers Joint Contract Documents
            Committee
            c/o National Society of Professional
            Engineers
            1420 King St.
            Alexandria, VA 22314

ICBO   International Conference of Building
            Officials
            Uniform Building Code and others
            5360 S. Workman Mill Rd.
            Whittier, CA 90601

ICC   International Code Council
            International Building and other Codes
            5203 Leesburg Pike, Suite 908
            Falls Church, VA 22041

NFiPA   National Fire Protection Association
            Life Safety Code, National Electric Code
            and other standards
            (address in main listing)

SBCCI   Southern Building Code Congress
            International
            Standard Building Code and others
            900 Montclair Road
            Birmingham, AL 35213

Magazine, Digest, and Research Sources

AIA   American Institute of Architects
            Architectural Record magazine
            Box 2063
            Marion, OH 43305

CSI   Construction Specifications Institute, Inc.
            Construction Specifier
            601 Madison St.
            Alexandria, VA 22314

FPL   Forest Products Laboratory
            Wood Handbook, USDA Handbook 72
            U.S. Government Printing Office
            Washington, DC 20402   (202) 783-3328

HHFA   Housing and Home Finance Agency
            Housing Research Papers
            Washington, DC 20402

NIBS   National Institute of Building Sciences
            Building Science Newsletter
            1015 15th Street, N.W.
            Washington, DC 20005

NIST   National Institute of Standards and Technology
            Building Science Series
            U.S. Superintendent of Documents
            Washington, DC 20402

NRC   National Research Council
            Canadian Building Digest
            Ottawa, Canada KIA OR6

Private   *Architecture* magazine
            1515 Broadway
            New York, NY 10036

SHC   Small Homes Council
            School of Architecture—Building Research
            Council
            Reports (misc. topics; send for listing)
            University of Illinois
            1 E. St. Mary's Road
            Champaign, IL 61820
            www.arch.uiuc.edu/brc

Other Web Sites

The following is an assortment of other web sites that lead to construction organizations and their products, literature, and information. This listing, though, is only a small portion of the sites that exist (citing of which would prove to be too numerous and overwhelming for this text). In searching for construction information, it is necessary to search every conceivable combination of words, phrases, jargon, colloquialisms, names, and so forth. It goes without saying that this type of access will greatly increase in future.

AFL-CIO	*http://www.aflcio.org/*
Air Transport Association	*http://www.air-transport.org*
Air & Waste Management Association	*http://www.awma.org*
American Association of Airport Executives	*http://www.airpornet.org/*
American Bar Association Forum on the Construction Industry	*http://www.abanet.org/forums/construction.html*
American Consulting Engineers Council (ACEC)	*http://www.acec.org*
American Road & Transportation Builders Association	*http://www.artba.org*
American Society of Mechanical Engineers (ASME)	*http://www.asme.org*
American Society for Photogrammetry and Remote Sensing (ASPRS)	*http://www.us.net/asprs*
American Society of Professional Estimators (ASPE)	*http://www.cmpi.com/aspe*
American Subcontractors Association	*http://www.asaonline.com*
Asian Development Bank	*http://www.asiandevbank.org*
Associated Builders & Contractors	*http://www.abc.org*
Associated Equipment Distributors	*http://www.aednet.org*
Associated General Contractors	*http://www.agc.org*
Associated Owners & Developers	*http://www.constructionsite.net/aod*
Association of Higher Education Facilities Officers (APPA)	*http://www.appa.org/*
Association of Iron and Steel Engineers	*http://www.aise.org/*
Associated Schools of Construction	*http://www.it.ilstu.edu/asc/asc.html*
The Association of the Wall and Ceiling Industries International	*http://www.awci.org*
Australian Commonwealth Scientific and Industrial Research Organisation (CSIRO), Structural Engineering WWW Server	*http://philpc.mel.dbce.csiro.au*
Blow in Blanket Contractors Association (BIBCA)	*http://www.cms.net/bibca*
Building Owners & Managers Association International	*http://www.boma.org*
Case Foundation	*http://www.casefoundation.com/*
Civil Engineering Research Foundation (CERF)	*http://www.cerf.org*
Construction Information Systems	*http://www.ozemail.com.au/NATSPEC*
Canadian Institute of Steel Construction	*http://www.buildingweb.com/cisc/index.html*
Construction Industry Manufacturers Association	*http://www.cimanet.com*
Construction Industry Research and Information Association (UK)	*http://www.ciria.org.uk/ciria* or *http://www.gold.net/ciria*
Construction Innovation Forum	*http://www.cif.org/*
Construction Metrication Council	*http://www.nibs.org/cmcl.htm*
Construction Specifications Institute (CSI)	*http://www.csinet.org*
Copper Development Association	*http://www.copper.org*
Design-Build Institute of America	*http://www.dbia.org/*
Dispute Review Board Foundation	*http://www.drb.org/home*
Ductile Iron Pipe Research Association	*http://www.dipra.org/home*
Edison Electric Institute	*http://www.eei.org/*
The Equipment Managers Council of America	*http://www.emca.org/*
Global Environmental Management Initiative	*http://www.gemi.org*
Golden Gate Bridge, Highway and Transportation District, San Francisco	*http://www.thermatrix.com*
Health Facility Institute	*http://www.hfi.org*
Industry Alliance for Interoperability	*http://www.interoperability.com*
Institution of Civil Engineers (UK)	*http://www.ice.org.uk*
Institute for Research in Construction (Canada)	*http://www.cisti.nrc.ca/irc*
Institution of Electrical Engineers	*http://www.iee.org.uk*
Inter-American Development Bank	*http://www.iadb.org*
International Cost Engineering Council (ICEC)	*http://www.ICostE.org*
International Council for Building Research Studies and Documentation (CIB)	*http://delphi.kstr.lth.se/w78*

International Road Federation	http://www.irfnet.org/irfnet
National Academy of Engineering's list of engineering societies	http://www4.nationalacademies.org/nae/nae.nsf/links/ Professional+Engineering+Associations+and+Societies? OpenDocument#engineering
National Asphalt Pavement Association (NAPA)	http://www.hotmix.org
National Association of Demolition Contractors	http://www.demolitionassn.com
National Association of Environmental Professionals (NAEP)	http://www.enfo.com
National Association of Home Builders	http://www.nahb.com
National Association of Women in Construction	http://www.nawic.org
National Board of Boiler and Pressure Vessel Inspectors	http://www.nationalboard.org
National Council on Structural Engineers Associations (NCSEA)	http://www.Libertynet.org/~NCSEA
National Railroad Construction and Maintenance Association (NRC)	http://www.nrcma.org/
National Research Council	http://www.nas.edu/nrc/
National Society of Professional Engineers (NSPE)	http://www.nspe.org/
North American Society for Trenchless Technology	http://www.bc.irap.nrc.ca/nodig
Office of Management and Budget	http://www.whitehouse.gov/WH/EOP/omb
Project Management Institute	http://www.pmi.org/enr.html
Public Works, Online Edition: Associations	http://www.pwmag.com/associations.htm
PVC Geomembrane Institute (PGI)	http://members.aol.com/forpvcl
Rebuild America Coalition	http://www.rebuildamerica.org
Salt Institute	http://www.saltinstitute.org
Society for Marketing Professional Services (SMPS)	http://www.smps.org
Swedish Institute of Steel Construction (SBI)	http://www.algonet.se/~sbi
Tilt-Up Concrete Association, Mount Vernon, Iowa	http://www.tilt-up.org
Washington Building Congress	http://www.wbcnet.org
Water Environment Federation	http://www.wef.org
Women Contractors Association (WCA)	http://www.womencontractors.org

G

Leading Firms in the Industry

The following is a short listing of the various construction-related firms, companies, and organizations at the top of the list due to their worldwide effort, high staffing rates, and the number, type and cost of the projects they execute.

Primarily, this listing is included so the reader can ascertain the number of firms which are active in various delivery systems, so heavily active that they rank very high in each category. This is really part of the balance the firms seek; the ability to market their services in any format is a formidable advantage.

In addition, the list gives readers some names that will become more familiar as their studies in construction continue. These firms are the cutting edge of the industry in innovation, management, and expertise, able to execute almost any type of project, anywhere in the world. They are, in general, massive in influence, astute in their approach, and businesslike in execution. They deal in overwhelming amounts of money, turning acceptable profits from their operations.

Figure G–1   Top 50 design firms for 1998 as listed by *Engineering News Record* magazine (ENR), from list of top 500 firms published annually.

Companies are ranked according to revenue for design services performed in 1998 in $ millions (*). Those with subsidiaries included (†) are listed by company rank on pp. 92, 93 and 94 of the April 19, 1999 issue [of *ENR*].

Key to type of firm:
A = architect; E = engineer; EC = engineer-contractor; AE = architect-engineer; EA = engineer-architect; ENV = enviromental; GE = soils or geotechnical engineer; P = planner. Other combinations possible. Firms classified themselves.

1999 Rank	Firm	Type
1	Fluor Daniel Inc., Irvine, Calif.†	EC
2	Bechtel Group Inc., San Francisco, Calif.†	EC
3	Jacobs Sverdrup, Pasadena, Calif.†	EAC
4	Kellogg Brown & Root, Houston, Texas†	EC
5	Parsons Corp., Pasadena, Calif.†	EC
6	URS Greiner Woodward-Clyde, San Francisco, Calif.†	EA
7	Foster Wheeler Corp., Clinton, N.J.†	EC
8	CH2M Hill Cos. Ltd., Denver, Colo.†	EA
9	Parsons Brinckerhoff Inc., New York, N.Y.†	EA
10	ABB Lummus Global Inc., Bloomfield, N.J.†	EC
11	Raytheon Engineers & Constructors Int'l, Cambridge, Mass.†	EC
12	Dames & Moore Group, Los Angeles, Calif.†	E
13	Earth Tech, Long Beach, Calif.	E
14	ICF Kaiser International Inc., Fairfax, Va.†	EC
15	Black & Veatch, Kansas City, Mo.†	EC
16	Duke Engineering & Services, Charlotte, N.C.	E
17	Stone & Webster, Boston, Mass.†	EC
18	Montgomery Watson Inc., Pasadena, Calif.†	EC
19	Tetra Tech Inc., Pasadena, Calif.†	E
20	Camp Dresser & McKee Inc., Cambridge, Mass.†	EC
21	The IT Group, Monroeville, Pa.†	E
22	The Louis Berger Group, East Orange, N.J.†	EA
23	HNTB Corp., Kansas City, Mo.†	EA
24	Law Engineering & Environmental Svcs. Inc., Alpharetta, Ga.†	E
25	Hellmuth, Obata + Kassabaum (HOK), St. Louis, Mo.†	AE
26	Sargent & Lundy LLC, Chicago, Ill.†	EA
27	Lockwood Greene Engineers Inc., Spartanburg, S.C.†	EC
28	ERM Group, Exton, Pa.†	ENV
29	Daniel, Mann, Johnson, & Mendenhall, Los Angeles, Calif.	AE
30	HDR Inc., Omaha, Neb.†	EA
31	Morrison Knudsen Corp., Boise, Idaho†	EC
32	Gensler, San Francisco, Calif.	A
33	The PBSJ Corp., Miami, Fla.†	EAP
34	AGRA Infrastructure, Mesa, Ariz.†	E
35	BE&K Inc., Birmingham, Ala.†	EC
36	CDI Engineering Group Inc., Philadelphia, Pa.†	EA
37	Burns and Roe Enterprises Inc., Oradell, N.J.†	EC
38	Professional Service Industries Inc., Lombard, Ill.	E
39	General Physics Corp., Columbia, Md.†	E
40	Frederic R. Harris Inc., New York, N.Y.†	E
41	Aqua Alliance Inc./Metcalf & Eddy, Wakefield, Mass.	E
42	Michael Baker Corp., Pittsburgh, Pa.†	EA
43	Roy F. Weston Inc., West Chester, Pa.†	ENV
44	McDermott International Inc., New Orleans, La.	EC
45	ENSR, Acton, Mass.†	ENV
46	Fugro Inc., Houston, Texas†	E
47	Malcolm Pirnie Inc., White Plains, N.Y.	E
48	ARCADIS Geraghty & Miller Inc., Denver, Colo.†	E
49	Day & Zimmermann International Inc., Philadelphia, Pa.†	EC
50	Holmes & Narver, Orange, Calif.†	EA

1	Bechtel Group Inc., San Francisco, Calif.
2	Fluor Daniel Inc., Irvine, Calif.
3	Kellogg Brown & Root, Houston, Texas
4	CENTEX Construction Group, Dallas, Texas
5	The Turner Corp., New York, N.Y.
6	Foster Wheeler Corp., Clinton, N.J.
7	Skanska (USA) Inc., Greenwich, Conn.
8	Peter Kiewit Sons Inc., Omaha, Neb.
9	Gibane Building Co., Providence, R.I.
10	Bovis Construction Corp., New York, N.Y.
11	McDermott International Inc., New Orleans, La.
12	Raytheon Engineers & Constructors, Cambridge, Mass.
13	J.A. Jones Inc., Charlotte, N.C.
14	Jacobs Sverdrup, Pasadena, Calif.
15	Morrison Knudsen Corp., Boise, Idaho
16	Black & Veatch, Kansas City, Mo.
17	PCL Enterprises Inc., Denver, Colo.
18	Structure Tone Inc., New York, N.Y.
19	The Clark Construction Group Inc., Bethesda, Md.
20	The Whiting-Turner Contracting Co., Baltimore, Md.
21	Granite Construction Inc., Watsonville, Calif.
22	Dillingham Construction Holdings Inc., Pleasanton, Calif.
23	Parsons Corp., Pasadena, Calif.
24	DPR Construction Inc., Redwood City, Calif.
25	ABB Lummus Global Inc., Bloomfield, N.J.
26	Hensel Phelps Construction Co., Greeley, Colo.
27	Huber, Hunt and Nichols Inc., Indianapolis, Ind.
28	Perini Corp., Framingham, Mass.
29	Morse Diesel International Inc., New York, N.Y.
30	The IT Group, Monroeville, Pa.
31	M. A. Mortenson Co., Minneapolis, Minn.
32	Swinerton Inc., San Francisco, Calif.
33	McCarthy, St. Louis, Mo.
34	Dunn Construction Group, Kansas City, Mo.
35	The Walsh Group, Chicago, Ill.
36	Stone & Webster, Boston, Mass.
37	Opus Group of Companies, Minnetonka, Minn.
38	Austin Industries, Dallas, Texas
39	BE&K Inc., Birmingham, Ala.
40	Barton Malow Co., Southfield, Mich.
41	Chicago Bridge & Iron Co., Plainfield, Ill.
42	Marnell Corrao Associates Inc., Las Vegas, Nev.
43	Devcon Construction Inc., Mulpitas, Calif.
44	Walbridge Aldinger, Detroit, Mich.
45	H.B. Zachry Co., San Antonio, Texas
46	Tutor-Saliba Corp., Sylmar, Calif.
47	Kraus-Anderson Construction Co., Minneapolis, Minn.
48	The Pepper Cos., Chicago, Ill.
49	Turner Industries, Baton Rouge, La.
50	The Weitz Company Inc., Des Moines, Iowa

Figure G–2 1999 ENR Top 400 Contractors (1–50).
 Companies are ranked according to construction revenue in 1998 in $ millions.

Figure G–3   1999 ENR Top 100 Design Build Firms (1–50).

Companies are ranked in $ million based on 1998 revenue from design-build contracts where the project is designed by employees of the firm or joint venture partner and built by its own force or subcontractors under its supervision.

1	Bechtel Group Inc., San Francisco, Calif.
2	Fluor Daniel Inc., Irvine, Calif.
3	McDermott International Inc., New Orleans, La.
4	Kellogg Brown & Root, Houston, Texas
5	Jacobs Sverdrup, Pasadena, Calif.
6	Raytheon Engineers & Constructors, Cambridge, Mass.
7	Black & Veatch, Kansas City, Mo.
8	ABB Lummus Global Inc., Bloomfield, N.J.
9	Opus Group of Companies, Minnetonka, Minn.
10	Foster Wheeler Corp., Clinton, N.J.
11	Chicago Bridge & Iron Co., Plainfield, Ill.
12	Stone & Webster, Boston, Mass.
13	Peter Kiewit Sons Inc., Omaha, Neb.
14	The IT Group, Monroeville, Pa.
15	Marnell Corrao Associates Inc., Las Vegas, Nev.
16	Morrison Knudsen Corp., Boise, Idaho
17	Parsons Corp., Pasadena, Calif.
18	The Haskell Co., Jacksonville, Fla.
19	Ryan Cos. US Inc., Minneapolis, Minn.
20	The Austin Co., Cleveland, Ohio
21	Duke Construction LP, Indianapolis, Ind.
22	Huber, Hunt and Nichols Inc., Indianapolis, Ind.
23	H&N/McClier, Chicago, Ill.
24	Angelo Iafrate Construction Co., Warren, Mich.
25	The Stellar Group, Jacksonville, Fla.
26	HBE Corp., St. Louis, Mo.
27	BE&K Inc., Birmingham, Ala.
28	Clayco Construction Co., St. Louis, Mo.
29	James N. Gray Co., Lexington, Ky.
30	Pitt-Des Moines Inc., The Woodlands, Texas
31	H and M Construction Co., Jackson, Tenn.
32	The Turner Corp., New York, N.Y.
33	Dick Corp., Pittsburgh, Pa.
34	Marshall Erdman & Associates Inc., Madison, Wis.
35	Kajima Construction Services Inc., Englewood Cliffs, N.J.
36	The Facility Group Inc., Smyrna, Ga.
37	ICF Kaiser International Inc., Fairfax, Va.
38	NEPCO, Redmond, Wash.
39	Barton Malow Co., Southfield, Mich.
40	AJ Contracting Co. Inc., New York, N.Y.
41	Devcon Construction Inc., Mulpitas, Calif.
42	Hoffman Corp., Portland, Ore.
43	The McShane Cos., Rosemont, Ill.
44	Earth Tech Inc., Long Beach, Calif.
45	Herzog Contracting Corp., St. Joseph, Mo.
46	Roy Anderson Corp., Gulfport, Miss.
47	OC America Construction Inc., Los Angeles, Calif.
48	Holder Construction Co., Atlanta, Ga.
49	CENTEX Construction Group, Dallas, Texas
50	John S. Clark Co., Inc., Mount Airy, N.C.

1	Parsons Corp., Pasadena, Calif.	EC
2	Bechtel Group Inc., San Francisco, Calif.	EC
3	Kellogg Brown & Root, Houston, Texas	EC
4	Foster Wheeler Corp., Clinton, N.J.	EC
5	Jacobs Sverdrup, Pasadena, Calif.	EC
6	Fluor Daniel Inc., Irvine, Calif.	EC
7	CH2M Hill Inc., Denver, Colo.	EC
8	Morrison Knudsen Corp., Boise, Idaho	EC
9	The Turner Corp., New York, N.Y.	C
10	O'Brien-Kreitzberg Inc., San Francisco, Calif.	CM
11	Raytheon Engrs. & Constrs., Cambridge, Mass.	EC
12	ICF Kaiser International Inc., Fairfax, Va.	EC
13	Parsons Brinckerhoff Inc., New York, N.Y.	D
14	Earth Tech Inc., Long Beach, Calif.	EC
15	Tishman Construction Corp., New York, N.Y.	CM
16	Bovis Construction Corp., New York, N.Y.	C
17	Structure Tone Inc., New York, N.Y.	C
18	Dillingham Construction, Pleasanton, Calif.	EC
19	Daniel, Mann, Johnson, & Mendenhall, Los Angeles, Calif.	EC
20	Heery International Inc., Atlanta, Ga.	D
21	Morse Diesel International Inc., New York, N.Y.	C
22	CENTEX Construction Group, Dallas, Texas	EC
23	Day & Zimmermann Int'l Inc., Philadelphia, Pa.	EC
24	URS Greiner Woodward-Clyde, Paramus, N.J.	D
25	Hensel Phelps Construction Co., Greeley, Colo.	D
26	Kajima Construction Services, Englewood Cliffs, N.J.	EC
27	Hill International Inc., Willingboro, N.J.	CM
28	Capitol Construction Group Inc., Wheeling, Ill.	C
29	Frederic R. Harris Inc., New York, N.Y.	EC
30	Vratsinas Construction Co., Little Rock, Ark.	C
31	Hanscomb Inc., Atlanta, Ga.	CM
32	The Whiting-Turner Contracting Co., Baltimore, Md.	C
33	Lockwood Greene Engineers Inc., Spartanburg, S.C.	D
34	Gilbane Building Co., Providence, R.I.	C
35	Harza Engineering Co., Chicago, Ill.	D
36	Brinderson Corp., Newport Beach, Calif.	C
37	The PBSJ Corp., Miami, Fla.	D
38	Eichleay Holdings Inc., Pittsburgh, Pa.	EC
39	Tetra Tech Inc., Pasadena, Calif.	D
40	Vanir Construction Mgmt., Sacramento, Calif.	CM
41	Beaver Builders Ltd., Newton, Mass.	C
42	3D/International Inc., Houston, Texas	D
43	EMCON, San Mateo, Calif.	EC
44	Ecology and Environment, Inc., Lancaster, N.Y.	EC
45	H&N/McClier, Chicago, Ill.	C
46	Harris & Associates Inc., Concord, Calif.	D
47	The IT Group, Monroeville, Pa.	EC
48	BE&K Inc., Birmingham, Ala.	EC
49	The Liro Group, Syosset, N.Y.	D
50	Brown and Caldwell, Pleasant Hill, Calif.	EC

Figure G–4   1999 ENR Top 100 CM Firms (1–50).

Companies are ranked based on total 1998 billings in $ millions for construction management or project/program management services performed as a professional service for a fee. Key to type of firm: D = design firm; C = contractor; EC = engineer-contractor; CM = construction manager; ENV = environmental

Glossary

This glossary has been compiled to be as comprehensive as possible for students in Architectural, Engineering, and Construction Technology programs. It is *not* complete in that each construction phase, system, trade, and material has its own "jargon" and nomenclature, and in many cases its own definitions, too. These number in the tens of thousands. Therefore, it is impossible to know them all; it is well to become familiar with them as the need arises. Also, there is a need to caution that often things are called by familiar names which are not accurate—for example, it is plastic laminate, not Formica; it is concrete, not cement; it is steel, not iron.

The following is a short list of resources and references that may provide the definition of terms being sought by the student. Be advised that the latest editions should be verified with the publishers.

Construction Dictionary, 9th ed.
Greater Phoenix Chapter
National Association of Women in Construction
P.O. Box 6142
Phoenix, AZ 85005
(602) 263-7680

Dictionary of Architecture and Construction, 2d ed.
by Cyril M. Harris
ISBN 0-07-026756-1
Published by McGraw-Hill Book Company

Building News Construction
Dictionary Illustrated
Published by ENR/BNI Books
1221 Avenue of the Americas
New York, NY 10020

Construction Glossary, 2d ed.
by J.S. Stein
ISBN 0-471-56933-X
Published by John Wiley and Sons, Inc.

Means Illustrated Construction Dictionary
ISBN 0-87629-218-X
Published by R.S. Means Co., Inc.
100 Construction Plaza
P.O. Box 800
Kingston, MA 02364

More definitions are listed in Chapter 4. Also, many publications of the trade and professional organizations listed in Appendix F provide definitions and descriptions which are specific to their products or services.

A

Acoustic materials   Composition board installed on ceilings or walls for the purpose of reducing sound reflection (or echo); board is generally the same as that used for ordinary insulating purposes, or can be specially manufactured material for added acoustic capabilities; acoustical tile for ceilings is often perforated or fissured to increase the area of sound-absorbing surface; may be boards, batts, blocks, foam, spray-on, panel, sheets, pads, or tile materials.

Adhesive   A natural or synthetic material, generally in paste or liquid form, used to fasten or glue material together, install floor tile, fabricate plastic laminate-covered work, or otherwise attach work items together.

Admixture   A substance other than portland cement, water, and aggregates included in a concrete mixture, for the purpose of altering one or more properties of the concrete; aids setting, finishing, or wearing of the concrete.

Aggregate   Hard, inert material, such as sand, gravel, and crushed stone, which is combined with portland cement and water to produce concrete; must be properly cleaned and well graded as required.

Angle (steel)   A piece of rolled structural steel bent to form a 90 degree angle; may have equal or unequal legs; identified by the symbol "L".

Approved   Term used to indicate acceptance of condition, material, system, or other work or procedure; reflects action by design professional or other authorized party, but does not relieve basic responsibility of party seeking such approval, as written in other binding documents and provisions.

Arch   A curved structure that will support itself and the weight of wall above the opening, by mutual pressure.

Asphalt   A mineral pitch insoluble in water and used extensively in building materials for waterproofing, roof coverings, shingles, floor tile, paints, and paving.

Asphalt expansion joint material   A composition strip of felt and asphalt material made to specified thickness and used to take up the expansion in concrete floor and sidewalks.

Asphalt roofing   On a flat surface the roofing is composed of alternate layers of roofing felt and hot-applied asphalt (called built-up roof). Asphalt is the most widely used material for covering roofs because it possesses the characteristics needed for protection against weather and is easily applied, at a relatively inexpensive cost.

Asphalt shingles   Composition roof shingles made from asphalt-impregnated felt covered with mineral granules, reinforced with strands of fiberglass; available in several weights.

Assemblies   Portion of a building in combination; for example, a roof/ceiling assembly, or a ceiling/floor assembly, where different materials are combined, installed, and interfaced to form protectives and other aspects of construction for an entire building.

Attic   The space/area between the roof and top ceiling of a building.

B

Backfill   Coarse earth or granular material used to fill in and build up the ground level around the foundation wall to provide a slope for drainage away from the foundation wall.

Backup   A material, usually not in view, which acts as a support, filler, or rigidity reinforcement for another material (example—concrete masonry units act as "backup" to face brick).

Balcony   A deck projecting from the wall of a building above ground or at floor level.

Ballast   A heavy material (usually gravel or stone) installed over a roof membrane to prevent wind uplift and to shield the membrane from sunlight and aid water evaporation.

Balloon framing   Name of a system of light-wood or house framing characterized by the studs extending in one piece from the foundation sill to the roof plate; not widely used because it requires applied fire blocking and a let-in ribbon for the second floor framing; utilizes long pieces of lumber, not readily available; also called Eastern framing.

Baluster(s)   Small vertical posts supporting a handrail; more commonly known as bannister spindles.

Bar   Small rolled or drawn steel shape, round, square or rectangular in cross section; a deformed steel shape used for reinforcing concrete.

Bar joists   Structural framing units made from bar- and rod-shaped steel and other lightweight members, for supporting moderate roof and floor loads; also known as open-web steel joists, or steel lumber.

Barrier-free design   Providing layout and design that affords accessible routes for all persons; meets requirements of ADA regulations and local codes.

Base   The bottom part of any unit on which the entire thing rests; can be a separate concrete pad under equipment; slang for "baseboard."

Baseboard   Interior wall trim at the floor line to cover the joint between wall and floor materials; strip of wood placed along the base of a wall or column to protect the finish from damage by shoe.

Base cabinet(s)   The lower, floor mounted cabinets that support the work- or countertop, in offices, laboratories, kitchens, or other work areas.

Base plate   A steel plate forming the bottom or base of a steel column; usually larger than the column to disperse the imposed load, to allow proper anchorage to the bearing surface.

Batt insulation   Flexible blanket-like or roll of insulating material (usually faced or unfaced fiberglass) used for thermal or sound insulation by being installed between framing members in walls, floors, or ceilings.

Batten   Narrow strip of wood or other material used to cover joints in sheets of decorative materials, plywood, or wide boards.

Bay window   Any fixed window space projecting outward from the walls of a building, either square or polygonal in plan.

Beam   A structural member that is normally subject to bending loads, and is usually a horizontal member carrying vertical loads (an exception to this is a purlin); three types are
1. Continuous beam—has more than two points of support.
2. Cantilevered beam—supported at only one end, and restrained against rotation and deflection by design and connection.
3. Simple beam—freely supported at both ends.

Bearing plate   Steel plate set on grout bed (nonshrinking) under the end of a beam or other structural member; distributes the load carried on the member over a greater area of the wall; may also be a "pad" made of a block of plastic or synthetic rubber which cushions point at which members meet.

Bearing wall or partition   Wall that supports all or part of the floors, roofs, or ceilings in a building; partition that carries the floor joists and other partitions above it.

Bed rock   Unweathered (never exposed to light), solid stratum of rock; excellent bearing surface for foundation systems.

Bench mark (B.M.)   A fixed point used as the basis for computing elevation grades; identified by marks or symbols on stone, metal or other durable surveying items/matter, permanently affixed in the ground and from which differences of elevation are measured; also referred to as a "datum" or "datum point."

Blacktop   An asphaltic compound with small aggregate placed in a thick liquid which hardens into a paving surface; also, called "bituminous concrete."

Blocking   Method of bonding two adjoining or intersecting walls not built at the same time; also, various wood members sized and shaped and used as fillers.

Board measure   A system for specifying a quantity of lumber; one unit is one board foot, which is the amount of wood in a piece $1'' \times 12'' \times 12''$.

Braced framing   Supported framework of a house, especially at the corners; diagonal or let-in braces (wood or metal) form a triangular shape to make the frame rigid and solid; plywood sheets at corners provide the same function.

Bracing   Support members in framing that are used to make the major structural members more rigid.

Brick Masonry unit(s) composed of clay or shale; formed into a rectangular prism while soft, then burned or fired in a kiln; can have voids or recessed panel to reduce weight and increase bond to mortar; many types of brick, face brick being most familiar (can be exposed—many colors, textures and sizes).

Brick veneer Single wythe (thickness) of brick facing applied over wood frame construction, or masonry other than brick; this facing is nonstructural.

Bridging (1) Method of bracing floor joists to distribute the weight over more than one joist; joins joists to act as a diaphragm unit and not individually; prevents displacement and wracking; usually two wood (1″ thick) or light metal pieces crisscrossed between joists; also can be wood stock same size as joists and is called "solid bridging"; must be installed continuously from end wall to end wall. (2) Also, a newer method of project delivery which involves an owner's separately contracted design professional, and a design/build contract.

Btu (British thermal unit) The amount of heat required to raise the temperature of one pound of water one degree Fahrenheit (F).

Building line Lines established and marked off by a surveyor which denote the exterior faces of a proposed building; used by tradespersons as guidelines; surveyors get their information from the plans, specifications, and official records; building line is generally extended and marked on batter boards placed about 6 feet outside the corners/lines of the building excavation.

Building paper Heavy sheet material used between sheathing and siding/facing for insulation and windbreaking purposes; four types: (1) red rosin paper, (2) sisal paper, (3) plain asphalt felt paper (tar paper), and (4) plastic sheeting.

Built-up roof A roof covering made of alternate layers of building (roofing) felt and hot liquid asphalt, with a final surfacing of gravel; laid on a low-slope or comparatively level roof.

Butt Type of door hinge that allows the edge of a door to butt into the jamb of the frame.

Butt joint The junction of two members in a square-cut joint, end-to-end, or side-to-side (edge-to-edge).

C

Caisson A deep shaft drilled into ground down to adequate bearing soil, then filled with concrete; used to support a column or to provide other structural foundation.

Callout A note on a drawing with a leader line to the feature, location, material, or work item involved.

Cant strip An angular board installed at the intersection of the roof deck and a wall, curb, or other penetrating item; used to avoid sharp right angles when the roof covering is installed.

Cantilever Projecting beam or slab supported at one end only.

Casement window A side-hinged window that opens outward by a crank device or push-bar.

Casework Manufactured or custom built cabinetry, including shelves, cabinets (base or wall), countertops, and ancillary equipment; can be metal, wood, laminate covered, etc.

Cast-in-place (concrete) Current and proper term for the placing of concrete into its forms on the job site; also called "site-cast," which replaces the word "poured," which has negative connotations relating to a watery mix inappropriate for construction use.

Caulk(ing) A waterproof material used to seal cracks and various types of joints between materials or building parts; *see also* Sealants.

Cavity wall A masonry wall made of two or more wythes of masonry units joined with ties, but having an air space between them.

Cement, portland A gray, powdery material which when mixed with water will harden; used with aggregate of various sizes in concrete and mortar.

Centerline Actual or imaginary line through the exact center of an object.

Center-to-center Measuring distance from centerline to centerline of adjacent units; term meaning "on center," as in the spacing of joists, studding, or other structural parts.

Channel Structural section, steel or aluminum, shaped like a rectangle, but with one long side missing; "C"-shaped.

Chase In masonry a channel cut or built in the face of a wall to allow space for receiving pipes, conduits, etc.; also a recess in any wall to provide space for pipes and ducts.

Chimney A vertical shaft for drawing smoke from a heating unit, fireplace, or incinerator, and venting it to the outside.

Clear dimension; Clear opening Designation used to indicate the distance between opposing inside faces of an opening, frame, room, etc.

Column A vertical structural member supporting horizontal or sloped members; can also be purely decorative.

Common bond Brick laid in a pattern consisting of five courses of stretchers, followed by one "bonding" course of headers.

Common rafter Rafter extending from the top of the wall to the roof ridge.

Composite wall A masonry wall that incorporates two or more different types of masonry units, such as clay brick and concrete masonry units (CMUs).

Concave joint A mortar joint tooled into a curved, indented profile.

Concrete A thick, pasty (but plastic/formable) mixture of portland cement, sand, gravel, and water; can be formed into any shape which it retains when hardened and cured; mixes may be varied in proportioning, strength, and other attributes.

Concrete block See concrete masonry unit (CMU).

Concrete brick A solid concrete masonry unit the same size and proportions as a modular clay brick.

Concrete masonry unit (CMU) Units of hardened concrete formed to varying profiles, sizes, and strengths, some solid, others with hollow cores (voids); designed to be laid in same manner as brick or stone to form walls, partitions, etc.

Concrete slump test A test to determine the plasticity of concrete. A sample of fresh concrete is placed in a cone-shaped container 12″ high. Concrete is compacted with 25 rod strokes at ⅓, ⅔, and completely full. The container is then slowly lifted; the concrete will "slump" as the form is removed. The flattened concrete is then measured to ascertain how much lower than the 12″ original height remains, i.e., how much the concrete has "slumped" down from the 12″ cylinder height. This "slump" will be specified and the actual test results note the acceptability of the concrete (for use in the project). This test is completely site-accomplished. Usually a slump of 3–5 inches is required or acceptable; it varies as required to meet the various job conditions.

Conduit, electrical A pipe, usually metal or plastic, in which wire is installed for electrical service.

Contour line(s) Lines on a survey plat, site plan, or topographic map which connect points of like (same) grade elevation above/below sea level or other datum point(s).

Control joint   An intentional, linear discontinuity in a structure or component, designed to form a plane of weakness where cracking can occur in response to various forces so as to minimize or eliminate cracking elsewhere in the structure.

Crawl space   A space beneath a house or structure that lacks a basement, but which allows access to utilities; may also refer to the space in an attic that is too low to walk in, but high enough to crawl through or store in.

Cubic foot   Measure of volume that has three 12″ dimensions—width, height and depth; contains 1,728 cubic inches (12″ × 12″ × 12″).

Cubic yard   Measure of volume that is 3 feet on each side—width, depth, and height; contains 27 cubic feet (3′-0″ × 3′-0″ × 3′-0″).

Cul-de-sac   A street or court with no outlet, but providing a circular turn-around for vehicles.

Cupola   Small, decorative structure built on a roof of a house; often placed over an attached garage; may be utilized for outside air intake for ventilation purposes.

Curb   Linear edging, raised or partially concealed around pave areas, at walks, around other areas; also, a raised box installed around roof openings for passage of equipment, piping, devices, and the watertight mounting of same.

Curing   The slow chemical process that takes place in concrete after it is placed, and as it attains its load-bearing strength over a period of time.

Curtain wall   Non-loadbearing wall placed over the structural skeletal frame construction of a building; an exterior "skin" (a relatively thin wall).

Cut stone   Decorative, natural stone of various types, cut to given sizes and shapes (veneers, sills and copings, for example).

D

Damper   Movable plate that regulates the draft of air in a stove, fireplace, or furnace.

Dampproofing   Layer of impervious material, spread or sprayed on walls usually, to prevent moisture from passing through.

Datum (point)   *See* Bench mark.

Dead load   Load on a structure imposed by its own weight, i.e., the weight of the materials of which it is built, and other fixed loads.

Decibel   Unit used to measure the relative intensity or loudness of sound; higher numbers indicate greater sound.

Deck   Exterior floor, similar to a concrete slab, patio, or porch; usually wood and extending out from building wall; usually slightly elevated above ground surface.

Deed   Legal document indicating that ownership of a parcel of land has been transferred from one party to another; gives legal description of the land, and may contain applicable restrictions as to the use of the land (easements, for example).

Deflection   Amount of sag at the center of a horizontal structural member (between supports) when subjected to a load.

Dimension lumber   Framing lumber that is 2 inches thick and from 4 to 12 inches wide (nominal sizes).

Directed   Term which reflects action(s) of design professional or other authorized party; used in same manner as "requested," "authorized," "selected," "approved," "required," and "permitted."

Door jamb   Two vertical pieces of the door frame (wood or metal) held together by the head (top, horizontal piece), forming the inside lining of a door opening, into which the door itself is set.

Dormer   A rooftop projection built out from and above a sloping roof to provide greater headroom inside.

Double glazing   Making a sealed glass unit of two or more panes of glass, with air space between panes, to provide added insulating value; also called "insulated glass."

Double header   Two or more structural members joined together for added strength; also, the shorter framing, of two members, to create an opening in structural framing.

Double-hung window   A window unit having a top and bottom sash, each capable of moving up and down, independently, by-passing each other.

Double-strength glass   Glass that is approximately ⅛ inch (3 mm) in thickness.

Downspout   A tube or pipe of plastic or sheet metal, for carrying rainwater from the roof gutter to the ground, or to a sewer connection; also called a "leader," or "conductor."

Drainage   Flow or removal of water.

Drip   A projecting construction member or groove in the underside of a member, to throw-off rainwater.

Drywall construction   Interior wall construction other than plaster; usually referred to as "gypsum board," "wall board," or "plasterboard"; sheets of material are applied to a stud framework.

Duct   In a building, usually round or rectangular metal pipes for distributing warm or conditioned air from the air handling units to the various rooms; also may be made of composition materials.

E

Earth-sheltered dwelling (building)   A structure which is totally or partially underground; uses soil coverings to reduce heat loss (or gain).

Eaves   The projecting lower edges of a roof overhanging the walls of the building.

EIFS (Exterior Insulation Finish System)   A material, usually a polymer, used as an exterior finishing material applied over insulation foam; stucco-like coating in several colors which conforms to any profile cut and constructed in the foam backing; adds thermal performance and decreases air infiltration.

Engineered fill   Earth compacted in such a way that it has predictable physical properties, based on field and laboratory tests; produced using specified, supervised installation procedures.

Erect   To raise or construct a building frame; generally applied to prefabricated materials, such as structural steel, as they are installed on the job site.

Erector   The subcontractor who raises, connects, and accurately sets (plumb and level) a building frame from fabricated steel or precast concrete members.

Erosion control   Temporary or permanent facilities installed to prevent/minimize erosion during construction; silt fences, straw bale lines, sheet plastic barriers used temporarily; permanent area for temporary storage of water (retention and detention ponds); rip-rap, swales, drainage ways, culvert pipes, etc.

Excavation   A cavity or pit produced by digging and removing the earth in preparation for construction.

Expansion bolt   A combination of a bolt and a sleeve used when an ordinary bolt is unsuitable; sleeve is inserted in predrilled hole, bolt is then inserted and turned to expand a "V" shaped piece into the sleeve and forces sleeve to become wider at bottom; tightened until assembly is firmly anchored in material.

Expansion joint   Joint in walls, floors, or other materials to permit and take up expansion caused by temperature changes without damage to surrounding surfaces; all materials expand in warm/hot weather and contract in cold; joint provided for resultant cracking at the joint where it is not noticeable and with least damage.

Exposed aggregate finish   Concrete surface in which the top of the aggregate (usually "pea gravel") is exposed; can be used in walks or wall panels.

F

Fabricator   Company that prepares materials or members (such as structural steel) for erection and installation to specific project conditions by cutting, fitting, punching, coping, and otherwise making ready for specific installations.

Face brick   Brick of higher quality, and made specifically for exposure to weather; usually hard-burned and frostproof; available in large array of colors, textures, sizes, and combinations.

Facing   Any material attached to the outer portion of a wall and used as a finished surface.

Fascia   Vertical member that runs horizontally on the edge of a roof or overhang; closes off ends of rafters/trusses and is backing for gutter.

Fasteners   General term for metal devices, such as nails, bolts, screws, etc., used to secure materials and members within a building.

Fiberglass   Glass spun into fine threads, and made into batting which is used as an insulation material; can also be pressed into rigid board insulation; and can be fashioned into intricate shapes.

Fill   Clean sand, gravel, or loose earth used to bring a subgrade up to desired level around a building, in a trench, etc.

Finish carpentry   Carpentry work which will be exposed to view in the final project; casing of openings, running trim (base, chair rail, crown molds, etc.), bookshelves, panelling, and so forth (*see* Rough carpentry for contrast).

Finish floor (covering)   The floor material exposed to view as differentiated from the subfloor, which is the load-bearing floor material beneath.

Finish hardware   Devices and features of door hardware; in particular, knobs, rosettes, escutcheons, push/pull plates, closers, hinges, etc., which are exposed and which have decorative finishes (*see* Rough hardware for contrast).

Finish lumber   Good quality lumber used to form surfaces that will be finished (often in natural finish) and exposed to view.

Firebrick   A refractory brick that is especially hard and heat resistant; for use in fireplace fire boxes, and as smokestack linings.

Fireproofing   Material to protect portions of buildings, primarily structural members, against fire; can be stiff material (brick, concrete, tile, gypsum) or flexible (spray-on, wraps, paints).

Fire protection system   An interconnected system of devices and equipment installed throughout a structure (or in specific hazardous areas) to detect a fire, activate an alarm, suppress or control a fire, or any combination thereof; fire alarm systems, sprinkler systems, and smoke detectors are examples.

Fire-rated doors   Doors designed to resist the passage of fire from one side to the other; constructed to match those tested in standard fire tests, and subsequently awarded an hourly rating and label.

Fire-rating   The comparative resistance of a material to failure, as stated in hours, when subjected to fire testing; ratings are standardized by fire underwriters (the Underwriters' Laboratories/UL for example), who publish full data on tests, results, and material performance.

Fire-resistant   Incombustible; slow to be damaged by fire; forming a barrier to the passage of fire.

Fire-separation wall/partition   Wall required by building codes to separate two areas of a building as a deterrent to the spread of fire.

Fire-stop   Any material, even wood, placed to prevent the rapid spread of fire; used to block the passage of flames or air currents upward or across and in concealed building parts; includes draft-stops.

Fire-stopping system   Installation of a combination of fire-resistant wraps, packing, and sealants in holes around piping, etc. in walls and floors, to preclude the passage of fire and smoke.

Fire wall   Walls designed and constructed to remain in place, despite collapse of structure on either or both sides of the wall, to resist the spread and passage of fire from one portion of a building to another for extended period of time (up to 4 hours).

Fixed window   Unit of glass mounted in an inoperable frame, mounted in a wall opening.

Flange   Horizontal bottom and top portions of an I-beam, wide-flange beam, or channel member.

Flashing   Sheet metal or rubberized plastic material used for making joints, openings, and connections in roofs and walls watertight; used in roof valleys, at dormers, chimneys, and other vertical penetrations through roofs; also at window and door openings; usually covered, at least in part, by finished material such as siding or roofing so water is directed away from the areas in which leaks could occur.

Flat-slab construction   Type of reinforced concrete floor/roof construction having no beams, girders, or joists below the underside; requires thick slabs, moderate spans, and special reinforcement at columns.

Flue   Space or passage in a chimney through which smoke, gasses, and fumes ascend; each fuel-burning appliance requires its own flue.

Flue lining   Special, high-temperature fire clay or terra-cotta pipe, round or square, usually made in all ordinary flue sizes and in 3-foot lengths; used for inner lining of chimneys with brick or masonry work surrounding; runs from above the smoke chamber to several inches above the top of the chimney.

Flush door   A door with two flat faces (no panels), resembling a "slab"; can have a hollow or solid core; can have glass or louvered openings; can be fire-rated.

Footing   Lowest part of a structure, generally of reinforced concrete; spread out flat to distribute the imposed load of the wall, column, grade beam, chimney, foundation wall, or other feature it supports, over sufficient area of earth to provide stability.

Form (work)   Temporary framing, basically a "mold," into which concrete is placed; serves to give shape to cast-in-place concrete, and to support it and keep it moist as it cures; built of wood, plywood, or metal for holding and shaping concrete.

Form tie   Mesh, strap or heavy wire/rod used to hold wall forms in place, but of proper length to provide specified width; spaced at intervals over the entire area of forms, as necessary.

Foundation   Lowest portion of structure, fully or partially below grade; substructure of building, consisting of foundation system (walls, grade beams, etc.) and supports (caissons, footings, etc.).

Framing   Process of putting the skeletal part (beams, columns, studs, etc.) of a building together; rough lumber, steel, or concrete frame including floors, roofs, and partitions; in light wood framing there are "Platform" and "Balloon" systems.

Furring   Narrow strips of wood or other material (metal channels) attached to a surface to provide a level, true-to-line, and plumb plane for attachment of finish wall or ceiling materials; provides some added insulation space.

G

Gable   End wall of a building where the roof slopes on only two sides; gable is that triangular shaped part of the wall between the eaves and ridge.

Galvanized iron   Sheet iron (steel) which has been dipped into, and coated with, molten zinc to protect it against rust.

Gauge   A uniform standard of measure for wire diameters and thicknesses of sheet metal, plates, etc.; also a measure of other materials in regard to spacing or thickness.

Girder   Larger of principle structural members of wood, steel, or concrete used to support concentrated loads at isolated points along its length, e.g., at the bearing points of a series of supported beams.

Glass block   Hollow masonry units made of glass; usually square, and made of diffused or molded glass; translucent.

Glass fiber batt   Thick, fluffy, nonwoven insulating blanket of filaments spun from glass.

Glazing   Placing glass or other similar materials (acrylic plastic, for example) into windows and doors, or tubular grid curtain wall systems.

Glue-laminated (Glu-Lam) timber   Timbers and rigid frames (arches) built-up from a large number of small strips (laminations) of wood, glued together; used where solid wood timbers are not available for the loads and spans involved.

Grade   (1) Construction/building trade term used in referring to the ground level around the building; (2) lumber term to denote the quality and classification of the pieces related to their adaptability for different uses; (3) the slope or gradient of a roof, piece of land, ramp, etc.

Grade beam   Concrete foundation (wall) formed into a beam configuration (by pattern of reinforcement), which spans across isolated footings, piles, or caissons spaced at intervals; used where soil bearing pressure is inadequate for continuous support.

Grade, wood   Designation given to indicate quality of manufactured lumber.

Gradient   Inclination or slope of a road, piping, ramp, ground level, etc.

Grain   In wood, the direction of the longitudinal axes of wood fibers, or the figure formed by the fibers.

Granite   Igneous rock with visible crystals of quartz and feldspar.

Gravel stop   Metal (usually) strip or piece formed with a vertical lip used to retain the gravel on the roof surface around the edge of a built-up roof; can be enlarged to act as the fascia also.

Grout   A thin cement mortar used for leveling bearing plates and filling masonry cavities; usually a nonshrinking type is preferred.

Gunnable sealant   A sealant material of any formulation that is extruded in thickened liquid or mastic form under pressure from a caulking gun.

Gusset plate   Plywood or metal plate used to overlay adjacent/intersecting members in a truss joint to connect and strengthen the joint; plate is nailed in place.

Gutter   A U-shaped trough, along roof line of buildings, of metal or plastic to receive and carry off various types of drainage, usually nonsanitary; flat areas out from street curb for drainage.

Gypsum (wall) board   Sheet material having a gypsum core laminated between layers of heavy paper (exposed face is manilla in color—the back [concealed] face is gray); also called "drywall" and "plasterboard"; available in varying thicknesses, edge treatments, finishes (some prefinished), and fire-ratings; overall usually 4′ × 8′, 10′, or 12′.

H

Hanger   Wire, rod, or bar (or other shape required for loading) suspended from roof or other structural members used to support and carry piping, balconies, runways, etc.; stirrup-like drop support attached to wall to carry ends of beam.

Hardware   A wide variety of items, in both rough and finished form, which provide various functions such as attachment, operation, etc.; *see* Rough hardware, and Finish hardware for further distinction.

Hardwood   Wood cut from broad-leaved trees or trees that lose their leaves annually; examples include oak, maple, walnut, and birch; utilized in a number of construction and architectural items, primarily as finish carpentry.

H-beam   Another name or designation for steel beam shapes; most often refers to an I-beam used as a column—"H-column"; *see* I-beam, and Wide-flange.

Head   The top of a frame at a door, window, or other opening; also, a standing depth of water which exerts downward pressure.

Header   (1) Doubled members installed perpendicular to trimmer joists on each end of openings for stairs, chimneys, or other features for attachment of joists cut short to allow the opening; also wood lintels; (2) in masonry, units laid on the large flat face with small end exposed.

Head room   Vertical clear space in a doorway, or in the height between a stair tread and the ceiling overhead.

Hearth   The incombustible floor or covering extension in front of and in a fireplace (actual floor of firebox); can be brick, stone, or tile.

High-tension bolts   Steel bolts designed to be tightened with calibrated wrenches to high tensile strength; used as a substitute for conventional rivets in steel frame construction.

Hip roof   Roof that rises by inclined planes from all four sides of a building.

Hollow core door   Door consisting of two wood veneer panels separated by a lightweight core (grid, eggcrate, strips) installed to reinforce and stabilize the faces; solid wood members for stiles and rails.

Hopper window   Window with sash pivoted along the sill; opens by tilting the top inward.

Hose bibb   A water faucet made for the threaded attachment of a hose; exterior bibbs should be frostproof.

I

I-beam   Rolled structural steel section with a cross section resembling the letter "I"; often called "H-column" when used vertically; usually higher than it is wide; can be made of wood in similar profile; used for larger spans across openings, etc.

Indicated Term refers to graphic representations, notes, or schedules on the drawings, or to paragraphs and schedules in the specifications; used to help locate references and information in manner similar to "shown," "noted," "scheduled," and "specified."

Insulating board Material in rigid board form of various sizes and thicknesses for insulating purposes; usually manufactured from vegetable fibers or synthetic chemicals, and pressed or caused to "foam" into finished profile.

Insulating concrete Concrete with vermiculite added to produce lightweight concrete, with insulating properties, used for subfloor and roof fills.

Insulating glass Multiple panes of glass, separated by air spaces (for insulation purposes), and sealed in a single frame/unit.

Insulation A variety of materials designed and manufactured for protection from heat or cold, protection against fire, or reduction of sound transmission; usually paper, composition board, fiberglass, wools, foam products are good insulators (poor conductors).

Interior finish Term applied to the total effect produced by the inside finishing of a building; includes not only the material used, but the fashion of their installation and decoration.

Interior trim General term for all finish moldings, casings, baseboards, cornices, and other applied running and isolated trim pieces inside a building; installed by finish carpenters for fine fitting, finishing, and decorative expression.

Intumescent coating Paint or mastic that expands to form a stable, foam-like, insulating char when exposed to fire, that acts as an insulating agent (against the fire) for surfaces to which applied.

J

Jalousie Type of window with a number of long, narrow, hinged glass panels, which operate in unison—outswinging; can be used in doors, or as isolated window units.

Jamb Lining or frame mounted in a rough opening for installation of a door or window; side of an opening.

Joint Line, point, or position where two items meet or adjoin each other; in masonry, the layer of mortar between the horizontal courses of units (tooled to raked, flush, weeping, concave, tooled, or V-shape).

Joist Horizontal member used with others as a support for floor, ceiling, or roof; identified by location/placement; usually smaller than a beam, and rests on same; can be wood, steel or concrete.

Junior beam Smaller, lightweight rolled structural steel sections similar to an I-beam; used for short spans and light loads, bracing, etc.

K

Keene's cement White finish plaster which produces a very durable and moisture-resistant surface; used in bathrooms around bath tubs and showers, and in areas of high pedestrian traffic wear or abuse.

L

Lag screw Large wood screw with hexagonal or square head for turning/tightening with a wrench.

Lally column A steel pipe column, with or without concrete/sand fill; used for loads up to moderate sizes, including residential floor loads.

Laminated beam Beams, arches, and other members formed by pressure-gluing multiple layers or strips (laminations) together to form the shapes and size desired; substitute for solid wood members due to limited availability of same (*see* Glue-laminated timber).

Landing Platform between two flights of stairs where they end or change direction as they run between floors of a building.

Lath Material secured to framing on which plaster is applied; can be gypsum lath (solid or perforated) or metal lath, each providing a mechanical or chemical bond for the plaster.

Lattice Framework of crossed wood or metal slats; lightweight, usually, but can be heavy where used as bracing in structures.

Leader Vertical pipe—downspout—that carriers rain water drainage from roof gutter to ground or storm sewer.

Level (1) On a perfectly flat, horizontal line or plane; (2) tool used by workers to determine such level plane or line; (3) surveyor's instrument, similar to or a function of a transit, for establishing grade elevations.

Lift slab System of construction where the various floor slabs are poured at ground level, and then subsequently lifted into proper position by hydraulic jacks, working simultaneously at each column; cast-in, steel collars are welded to steel columns to hold slabs in place.

Light A pane of glass.

Light steel framing (LSF) Construction method utilizing light gauge steel members for the structure; also called cold-formed metal (steel) framing.

Lintel Structural member (wood, steel, concrete, stone, etc.) placed horizontally across the top of an opening, to support the wall above.

Live load All furniture, persons, and other movable loads not included as a permanent part of the structure.

Load-bearing wall Wall designed to support the weight (load) imposed on it from walls and structural members.

Louver Opening or slatted grille that allows ventilation while providing protection from rain, sight, sound, or light.

M

Masonry General term applied to construction made of brick, stone, concrete masonry units, and similar materials; sometimes called "unit masonry."

Masonry cement Factory-made mixture of portland cement and admixtures specially designed to increase the workability of mortar; usually better than site mixing, due to control available at plant.

Masonry unit A brick, stone, concrete masonry unit, glass block, or hollow clay tile intended to be laid in courses and embedded in mortar.

Masonry veneer A single-wythe, non–load-bearing facing installed over a structural frame, e.g., brick veneer applied to a wood frame house.

Mastic A thick, paste-like adhesive or other coating material used for attachment, dampproofing, etc.

Member Individual element of structure such as a beam, girder, column, joist, piece of decking, stud, truss chord, brace, etc.

Membrane Sheet or mastic material which is impervious to water or water vapor.

Metal lath Steel mesh created by slitting sheet steel and pulling it out until it forms a grid or mesh; used primarily as an excellent plaster base due to mechanical "keying" of plaster around mesh wires.

Metal wall ties Strips of corrugated sheet metal (galvanized) used to anchor (tie) brick veneer construction to the structural frame behind.

Mil Unit of measure (thickness) for very thin sheets; one thousandth part of an inch (.001″).

Millwork General term for interior woodwork and trim which is machined to profile, size, and finish; usually does not include flooring, ceiling and siding materials; finished carpentry work, as opposed to rough carpentry (framing).

Mineral wool Type of batt insulation consisting of many fine threads of a wood by-product; also used for fireproofing and acoustical treatment.

Modular housing Buildings (usually small in size or made of several units) fully constructed, built, and assembled in a factory and then transported to the site for final attachment and connections.

Moisture barrier Material—plastic or specially treated paper—that retards the passage of moisture or vapor into walls, and prevents condensation; *see* Vapor barrier.

Molding Single strip/piece or series of pieces of material cut, shaped, and finished to serve as an ornament; can be made of various material—wood, stone, fiberglass, plaster, etc.

Monolithic Term used for concrete and other materials placed or installed without joints; as one-piece, or a unit.

Mortar A mixture of masonry cement, sand and water, used by masons as the bonding agent between masonry units; the "joint material" in masonry.

Mosaic Small colored tile, glass, stone, or similar material, regular or irregular in shape but arranged to produce a decorative surface; used on walls or floors.

N

Nail-base sheathing Sheathing material, such as wood boards, panels, or plywood to which siding can be attached by nailing; such nailing is not provided by fiber board or plastic foam materials used as sheathing (primarily for better insulation).

Nailer Wood member, shaped to fit, in any of several places used to provide a nailing base for other members or materials; called "blocking" in some locations.

Needling Series of steel or wood beams (called "needle beams") threaded through a bearing wall to support it while its foundation is underpinned.

Nominal size Size of material before final working and dressing; not the actual size; as a 2 × 4 (nominal) is 1½″ × 3½″ (actual).

Nonbearing partition wall Term used for space dividing partitions or other walls which carry no imposed floor or roof load.

Nosing Portion/edge of stair tread which projects beyond the riser below it; any other similar projections.

Notch A three-sided slot, groove, or opening cut into a piece of material, usually along an edge.

O

On-center (o.c.) Method of indicating spacing of framing members or other items; measurement is from center of one object to the center of each of those adjacent.

Open web (steel) joist Prefabricated, light steel truss-like member with a welded lattice-like web; closely spaced for moderate spans; also called "bar joist" or "steel lumber."

Ordinary construction Building type with exterior masonry-bearing walls, and an interior structure of wood framing.

Orientation (1) Direction in which a building or structure faces; (2) relationship to a direction or bench mark/line; (3) relating contract drawings to the actual structure.

Oriented-strand board (OSB) Building panel composed of long shreds of wood fiber oriented in specific directions and bonded together with an adhesive matrix under pressure.

Overhang Area or portion of upper story, building part, or roof at the eave, which projects beyond the wall below.

P

Pad Extra concrete slab installed on top of a floor slab, as the mounting surface for mechanical or other equipment; adds some strength, but mainly provides a better, slightly elevated surface for mounting the unit(s).

Panel (1) A fabricated section of a wall, ceiling framing; (2) a sheet of material; (3) an electrical box device for current distribution, etc.

Panel door Door constructed with thin panels installed between solid rails and stiles (perimeter frame).

Panelling Thin sheet material of composite, synthetic, or wood composition which is used as a lining or interior wall finish; can be nailed or glued into place over various subsurfaces.

Parapet The portion of a wall that extends above the top of the roof; usually in exterior walls, or interior fire walls.

Particle board Composition board made from wood chips or particles bonded together in an adhesive matrix under pressure.

Partition Interior wall, full or part-high for dividing, separating, or screening spaces one from another, or for directing traffic.

Party wall Single wall between and common to two adjoining buildings owned by different owners; also common walls between row houses.

Patio Paved, open area outside a house; also called a terrace, and can be a structure such as a deck.

Paver Clay masonry (brick) made specifically for finish floor surfaces, walks, drives, and terraces, etc.; must be frostproof and serviceable for heavy traffic.

Paving Concrete or asphaltic material (or composites) used as installed ground cover as a hard-stand for vehicle access or parking; usually asphaltic concrete (blacktop) or cast-in-place concrete over a compacted gravel fill; can be light duty or heavy duty depending on traffic requirements and construction.

Penthouse A relatively small structure/enclosure, usually roof mounted, usually to enclose mechanical and/or elevator equipment without taking up valuable interior floor space.

Pier Vertical structural member, usually of concrete or masonry; also, short foundation columns, between window/door openings; also mass masonry supports such as for bridges, gates, and girders.

Pilaster Rectangular pier engaged in a wall, for the purpose of strengthening it; also can be decorative, or act as a beam support (expanded bearing area at the wall).

Pile (Piling) Concrete, wood, or steel member driven into the ground to act as an undergrade column to support the building; used to carry building load to sufficient bearing soil.

Pitch Slope of roof or other inclined/sloped surface(s).

Plank Long, flat wood members 2–4″ thick and 6+ inches wide.

Plaster A cementitious material usually applied to gypsum or metal lath or masonry surfaces; formed of a gypsum or portland cement mixture; applied in paste form, which hardens into a hard smooth surface (or other finish desired).

Plastic laminate   Composite material made from compressing kraft paper into phenolic resin layers to form a decorative material; usually has a melamine exposed (decorated) surface; used for covering doors, countertops, wall panelling, cabinets, etc.

Plat   Drawing of a parcel or parcels of land based on and giving its legal description, and perhaps other survey data; may be filed as an official record of the land.

Plate   Horizontal members at top (doubled) and bottom of stud walls (sole plate); also, refers to bearing, top, and base plates for structural steel members.

Plate glass   Glass of high optical quality produced by grinding and polishing both faces of the glass sheet; glass with parallel faces and minimal distortion.

Platform framing   System of light-wood framing for housing where each story is built on top of the one below, but framed independently (upper story rests on flooring decking applied to top of first floor ceiling joists); also, called "Western framing"; *see* and contrast with Balloon framing.

Plot   Lot, parcel, or other piece of land (real estate) with specific dimensions; potential building/construction site.

Plumb   Absolutely vertical; straight up and down; a plumb line is created when a weight (plumb bob) is tied on a cord and held vertically.

Plywood   Wood panel, of many varieties and types, composed of a number of thin veneers bonded together, glued under pressure; normally 4 feet wide by 8 feet, although longer lengths are available; has various face finishes and can be used as a finish or rough material.

Portland cement   Very fine, powder-like, gray-colored limestone material (crushed and pulverized) made from burning compounds of lime, silica, and alumina together; is the bonding agent in concrete, grouts, etc.

Post-and-beam construction   Wall and roof construction system using widely spaced posts and beams as the frame; plank decking applied transversely across the beams for stability and roof structure; a wood version of a rigid frame, in concept.

Pour   Outdated term, meaning to place concrete, casting concrete in place without interruption; not used today, because of negative impression of a thin, watery, inadequate substance.

Precast   The shaping of structural members in a factory, which are then transported and installed in a building; includes concrete joists, beams, tee-slabs, as well as nonstructural terrazzo, stair treads and risers, and miscellaneous trim, such as copings, sills, etc.

Precut   Cutting wood stock to exact dimensions at a mill, yard, or job site, before using/installation; for standardizing building components and minimizing errors.

Prefabricated   Sections or component parts of a building built in a factory and installed/assembled as a whole on the job site; *see* Modular housing.

Pressure-treated lumber   Lumber that has been impregnated with chemicals under pressure, for the purpose of retarding rot, decay, vermin, or fire.

Professional association/society   Organization usually representing a given profession which combines single efforts (by members) into a larger and more extensive voice; presents educational, informational efforts, information and document sales, and other combined services to individual members; somewhat of a lobbying group which acts on behalf of members. (see listing in Appendix F)

Q

Quarry tile   Unglazed, machine-made tile used for floors with sanitary requirements and open to wet conditions; usually red or tan color, and 6″ × 6″.

Quarter round   Small molding whose profile is a quarter circle.

Quarter sawn   Lumber, usually flooring or veneer, that has been sawn so that the medullary rays showing on end grain are nearly perpendicular to the face.

Quoins   Large squared stone pieces, or slightly projected panels of brick, set in the corners of masonry walls for decorative purposes.

R

Rafter   A sloped/inclined structural roof member running from the wall to the ridge or top of the roof; designed to support the roof deck, roofing, and other loading; such rafters for a flat roof are called "joists."

Rake   An incline or slope, as in a pitched roof.

Ramp   A sloped surface for walking, or rolling equipment for easier access than stairs; required as access under the ADA regulations for disabled persons; can be utilized with stairs.

Raze   To demolish or wreck work, usually to provide place for new construction.

Re-bars   Contracted term indicating "reinforcing bars" (rods/steel); *see* Reinforcing steel.

Reinforced concrete   A composite material in which steel bars are placed in the concrete to reinforce its tensile strength; material bonded together to act in unison with a combined capacity that exceeds that of either material alone; various design principles utilize varying amounts of reinforcing.

Reinforcing steel   Steel bars (rods) deformed with projecting ridges to ensure bonding, placed in concrete to add tensile strength; bars are bent or straight as required, and tied in shapes, grids or other configurations as required for concrete member; come in various diameters; most are round, but some are square in cross section.

Resilient flooring   Manufactured sheet or tile flooring material of asphalt, vinyl, vinyl composition, polyvinyl chloride, rubber, cork, or other similar resilient materials; installed with adhesive.

Retaining wall   Wall that holds back an earth embankment; usually concrete, but can be wood, stone, or masonry.

Return   Change in direction of a molding, cornice, or other design feature, without breaking the continuity of the profile.

Reveal   Side of an opening for a window or door in a masonry or wood structure; margin to which the casing is set on the jamb for appearance, and to accommodate the door hinges.

Ridge/Ridge board   The top edge of a roof where two slopes meet; also, the vertical board running horizontally between, and to which opposing rafters are attached, running the length of the roof structure.

Rise   In stairs, the vertical height of a step, or a flight of stairs; also, distance from one floor to the next for stair design is called "total rise"; also, vertical height of a roof above the surrounding walls.

Riser   In general, the vertical part of a stair step; in plumbing, a vertical water supply line.

Roof sheathing   Boards or sheet material fastened to the roof framing (rafters/trusses, etc.) and to which the shingles or other roof covering is attached; also called "roof deck or decking."

Rough carpentry That work of the carpenter trade which is for the most part concealed, such as framing, blocking, etc.; usually involves dimensioned lumber, and rough hardware.

Rough hardware All devices such as nails, screws, bolts, hangers, etc., which aid in the construction of the framing and rough construction of the project; also called "builders' hardware"; *see* Finish hardware.

Rough opening Framing around a window or door opening that has been sized to accept the finished units with allowances for fitting, shimming, and leveling.

Roughing-in The erection of the framing of the structure; in plumbing the installation of the underground lines and all associated plumbing piping, but not the fixtures themselves.

Rowlock Method of laying brick on the side, so the vertical ends appear in the face of the wall; a vertical header.

Run Horizontal distance of a flight of stairs; also, the horizontal distance from the top of the sidewall to the ridge of a roof.

Running bond Brick bonding pattern consisting entirely of stretchers overlapping by half a brick; i.e., vertical joints centered over brick below.

S

Safing insulation Fire-resistant material inserted into space between piping, ducts, curtain wall, conduit, beam, column, wall, floor, etc. where fire might pass through; packing behind fire penetration sealant used to close top of such openings and retard passage of fire and smoke.

Sandwich panel Panel consisting of two outer faces of wood, metal, or concrete bonded to a core of insulating material.

Sash Individual frames around glass in windows; movable part of window.

Scale Use of proportional measurements, i.e., using a small increment of measure to represent one foot (usually); also a drafting tool with markings at different intervals to permit measuring using different increments.

Scupper Opening through a wall for drainage of water from floor or roof into a downspout; requires careful and extensive flashing for watertight installation.

Scuttle Opening in a ceiling or roof that provides access to an attic or roof.

Sealant Thickened liquid or paste substance used to seal cracks, joints, and porous surfaces; must adhere to surrounding material and permit expansion and contraction without rupture; many varieties, chemical compounds, types, colors, and uses involved; may also be in tape or gasket form.

Seismic load Load on a structure caused by movement of the earth relative to that structure during an earthquake; varies by locale, and history of earthquake incidents.

Select lumber Lumber without knots or other deformities. It is the best lumber. In hardwood it refers to a specific grade.

Set The change in concrete and mortar from a plastic (semi-liquid) to a solid (hardened) state.

Setback A required minimum distance from the property line to the face of a building.

Shakes Handcut wood shingles.

Sheathing The rough covering over the framing of a house; not exposed in complete building.

Sheet metal Flat rolled metal less than ¼ inch (6.35 mm) in thickness.

Shoring The placing of a series of supports under formwork; also refers to the bracing or sheeting used to hold back an earth bank.

Sidelight A tall, narrow glass panel on either or both sides of a door.

Siding Boards placed over the outside wall of a frame building and nailed to the sheathing. Although wood or plywood is generally used, composition board is also popular. Wood siding is made in several different patterns, as are vinyl and aluminum.

Signage The entire coordinated system or pattern of signs used on, around, and throughout a building, interrelated and color coded or coordinated.

Silicone A polymer used for high range sealants, roof membranes, and masonry water repellant.

Sill General: the lowest part of an opening in a wall such as a door or window sill. Frame construction: the bottom rough structural member that rests on the foundation.

Sisal kraft paper A paper reinforced with strands of sisal fibers. The strands of sisal are placed between two layers of paper stuck together with a coat of pitch. This paper has many uses around construction because of its toughness and durability.

Site-cast (Cast-in-place) concrete Concrete placed and cured in its final position in a building.

Skylight A window built into a roof or ceiling.

Slab A thick slice of stone or other masonry material; word generally used when referring to a concrete floor; concrete pavements and sidewalks are also concrete slabs.

Slab-on-grade A concrete surface lying upon, and supported directly by, the ground beneath.

Slope Ratio between rise and run of a roof; amount of incline on any nonlevel surface.

Smoke chamber The portion of a chimney flue located directly over the fireplace.

Softwood Wood produced from coniferous trees, or trees that bear cones. Most commonly used are the pines, but also included are such trees as fir, spruce, redwood, and cedar. The term has no reference to the actual hardness or softness of the wood.

Soil boring Holes drilled into subsurface soil for the purpose of investigating the load-bearing and stability characteristics of the earth under a building.

Solid core door A flush door with no internal cavities.

Span The horizontal distance between supports for joists, beams, trusses, and other structural members.

Spandral The wall area above a window.

Splash block A small precast block of concrete or plastic at the bottom of a downspout used to divert water away from the foundation.

Splice The joining of two members to form one piece.

Spread footing A concrete footing larger than the structural member it supports, constructed for the purpose of spreading the load over the bearing soil; used under piers, columns, and foundation walls.

Sprinklers *See* Fire protection systems

Square A unit of measurement used by roofers that designates 100 square feet. Generally roof area estimates are expressed in the number of squares of material required for application. Also indicates perpendicular.

Stair well A compartment extending vertically through a building, into which stairs are placed.

Steel joist A light, steel truss made from bars, rods, or angles welded into rigid units.

Storefront construction System of light aluminum tubular sections interconnected to form a network of glass frames, utilizing large glass panels; usually includes the entrance complex, and acts as both wall and fenestration.

Storm sewer (drain)   A sewer, pipe, or other features (natural or man-made) used to carry away surface water but not sewage.

Story   Space between two floors of a building; top of floor to top of floor.

Straightedge   Used to strike off the surface of a concrete slab using screeds and a straight piece of lumber or metal.

Stringer   General construction: the member of each side of a stair that supports the treads and risers. Reinforced concrete construction: horizontal structural member supports.

Strip flooring   Wood finish flooring in the form of long, narrow tongue and groove boards.

Structural glazed (clay) tile   Hollow clay tile with glazed faces; used for constructing interior partitions where sanitation or cleanliness are concerns.

Structural shapes   "H", "I", "T" beams, angles, channels, and plates.

Structural tubes   Usually welded-seam, hollow tubular sections, of various sizes used as light columns, struts, and bracing; also, other structural and sometimes decorative installations; can be square or rectangular.

Stucco   Most commonly refers to an outside plaster made with portland cement as its base.

Stud   In building and upright member, usually a piece of dimension lumber, 2×4 or 2×6, used in the framework of a partition or wall.

Subcontractor   A company (or individual) who enters into an agreement with a general contractor. The subcontractor usually agrees to do certain specific skilled work on a building. Plumbing, heating, electrical work, and other portions of construction work are sublet to contractors who specialize in that one kind of work.

Subfloor   Carpentry: a term applied to flooring laid directly on the joists and serving that purpose during construction. When all rough construction work is completed, the finish floor is laid over the subfloor.

Subgrade   A fill or earth surface upon which concrete is placed.

Substructure   Foundation system, and portion of structure/building below grade line; lowest support for superstructure.

Superstructure   The above ground portion of a building.

Suspended ceiling   A ceiling hung below the underside of the building structure. Wire and channel section are commonly used to support the ceiling material.

T

Tee   A metal or precast concrete member with a cross section resembling the letter T.

Tempered glass   Glass that has been heat treated to increase its toughness and its resistance to breakage.

Tension   A stretching force; to stretch.

Testing agency   Entity, separate from any of the contractual parties on a project, engaged to perform specific inspections, tests, and analysis either at the site, in a laboratory, or elsewhere; reports results to proper project party, and interprets results if required; may function to meet specifications or to investigate problems which arise; building codes list some such agencies which are approved and acceptable because of their impartiality, reliability, and past performance.

Threshold   A strip of wood or metal with beveled edges used over the joint between finish floor and the sill of exterior doors.

Tile   A fired clay product that is thin in cross section as compared to a brick; either a thin, flat element (ceramic tile or quarry tile), a thin, curved element (roofing tile), or a hollow element with thin walls (flue tile, tile pipe, structural clay tile); also a thin, flat element of another material, such as an acoustical ceiling unit or a resilient floor unit.

Tilt-up construction   A method of constructing walls, and sometimes floors, by pouring concrete or putting wooden walls together in flat panels. When complete, they are moved to the building site where they are tilted into permanent place.

Timber   Construction lumber larger than $4'' \times 6''$ (102×152 mm) in cross section.

Tinted glass   Glass that is colored with pigments, dyes, or other admixtures.

Toilet room accessories   Various items of equipment such as towel dispensers, soap dispensers, waste receptacles, napkin and seat dispensers, robe hooks, tissue holders, etc. for installation in restrooms.

Tongue and groove   A continuous projection on the edge of a board that fits into a groove formed on another board.

Transom   A window placed above a door or permanent window which is hinged for ventilation purpose.

Tread   The horizontal board in a stairway on which the foot is placed.

Trim   The finished woodwork of a structure. The term is also used in reference to painting and decorating.

Truss   Structural steel or wood members fastened together to make a framework that will span long distances; utilizes principle of rigid triangular panels.

Two-way ribbed slab   Structural concrete slab with ribs (joists) running in two directions between supports; also called "waffle slab"; can be left exposed and unfinished as a decorative texture/pattern for the ceiling of space below; light fixtures can be mounted in the voids, if desired.

Two-way slab   A concrete slab in which the reinforcing steel is placed in perpendicular directions; usually a structural floor or roof slab.

Type-X gypsum board   A fiber-reinforced gypsum board used where greater fire resistance is required; fire-rated board.

U

Underlayment   Floor covering of plywood or fiberboard used to provide a smooth, level surface for carpet or other resilient flooring.

Underpinning   The process of placing new foundations beneath an existing structure.

V

Valley   A depression in a roof where two parts of a roof at different slopes come together.

Vapor barrier (retarder)   A watertight material used to prevent the passage of moisture or water vapor into and through walls and slabs.

Veneer   (1) A thin sheet of wood or other material. The outside sheet is generally of superior quality, chosen for its beauty. Plywood is made by gluing sheets of wood veneer together. (2) Brick veneer consists of one row of brick placed around a framework. Most brick houses have wood frames covered by veneer.

Vestibule   An open area at an entrance to a building.

V-joint   A joint between two pieces of a material. The corners are beveled to form a joint profile resembling the letter "V."

Void   Air space between material or between substance in material.

W

Waferboard   A building panel made by bonding together large, flat flakes of wood.

Waffle slab   A two-way concrete joist system (ribbed slab), formed with square pan forms; *see* Two-way ribbed slab.

Wainscot   The lower section of a wall made of different material from the upper part; usually composed of wood, tile, or wall covering.

Wall board   A general term used to refer to large rigid sheets used to cover interior walls. It can be made of wood fibers, gypsum, or other material.

Wall tie   A small metal strip or steel wire used to bind wythes of masonry in cavity-wall construction or to bind brick veneer to the wood-frame wall in veneer construction.

Warp   To bend or twist out of shape.

Waterproof   To render a material or surface impervious to water. This is generally done by coating it with another material that will not let water pass through it. Tar, asphalt, mortar parging, and heavy-body cementitious paints are common waterproofing agents.

Weatherstripping   A strip of fabric or metal fastened around the edge of windows and doors to prevent air infiltration; can be interlocking or spring fit.

Weep hole   Holes or slots (usually in vertical joints) near the bottoms of masonry walls to allow the release of accumulated moisture; important in brick veneer work.

Weld   A joint between two pieces of metal formed by fusing the piece together, usually with the aid of additional metal melted from a rod or electrode.

Weld-wire-fabric (WWF)   Steel wires welded together to form a grid for concrete slab reinforcing; commonly called "mesh."

Wide-flange section   Any of a wide range of steel sections rolled in the shape of a letter I or H, with different dimensions than I-beams.

Wind brace   A diagonal structural member whose function is to stabilize a frame against lateral (wind) forces.

Wind load   Lateral forces acting against a building that, in particular, must be considered in the design of high-rise buildings.

Wired glass   Glass in which a large-gauge wire mesh has been embedded during manufacture.

Wood shakes (shingles)   Individual wood roofing pieces, made of cedar (usually) which are hand split, or machined to useable size; can be fire-rated for added protection.

Work   The tasks, construction, installation, etc., that must occur to build, finish, and produce the project anticipated and under contract; comprises the complete scheme of construction required by the contract documents including all labor, material, systems, tests, ratings, devices, apparati, equipment, supplies, tools, adjustments, repairs, expendables, aids, temporary work or equipment, superintendency, inspection/approvals, plant, release, and permissions required to perform and complete the contract in an expeditious, orderly, and workmanlike manner.

Wythe   A section of a masonry wall (in plan) which is 4 inches wide; pertains to the number of 4-inch sections in the full width of a masonry wall.

Y

Yard   Usually that area of a lot from the building to the property lines; in zoning, that minimum prescribed distance back from the property lines where building cannot occur (also called setbacks.)

Z

Zoning   Government regulations which control the use of land, so adjacent uses are compatible and not intrusive; also regulate access, open areas, setbacks; create a positive, general atmosphere or environment in neighborhoods.

Index